IN THE SHADOW OF SLAVERY

HISTORICAL STUDIES OF URBAN AMERICA

Edited by Kathleen Conzen, Timothy Gilfoyle, and James Grossman

ALSO IN THE SERIES:

IN THE SHADOW OF SLAVERY

AFRICAN AMERICANS IN NEW YORK CITY, 1626–1863

LESLIE M. HARRIS

The University of Chicago Press
Chicago and London

The University of Chicago Press, Chicago 60637
The University of Chicago Press, Ltd., London
© 2003 by The University of Chicago
All rights reserved. Published 2003
Paperback edition 2004
Printed in the United States of America

12 11 10 09 08 07   4 5
ISBN: 0-226-31774-9 (cloth)
ISBN: 0-226-31773-0 (paperback)

Library of Congress Cataloging-in-Publication Data

Harris, Leslie M.
    In the shadow of slavery : African Americans in New York City, 1626–1863 /
Leslie M. Harris.
        p.   cm.—(Historical studies of urban America)
    Includes bibliographical references and index.
    ISBN 0-226-31774-9 (cloth : alk. paper)
    1. African Americans—New York (State)—New York—History. 2. New York
(N.Y.)—History—Colonial period, ca. 1600–1775. 3. New York (N.Y.)—History—
1775–1865. 4. New York (N.Y.)—Race relations—History. I. Title. II. Series.

F128.9.N4H37 2003
305.896'07307471'09—dc21

                                                                2002027144

CONTENTS

ACKNOWLEDGMENTS

It takes at least a community to produce a book, and I relied on many over-lapping communities in the research and writing of this one. My few re-marks here only dimly reflect the debts I owe to institutions, colleagues, friends, and family.

I am fortunate to have had numerous worthy mentors who were excellent examples of the best in academic life. During my undergraduate years at Columbia, James Shenton provided a vibrant example of dedication to teaching. Often during the writing of this book I have thought of his passion for teaching about the history of race and ethnicity in this country and his love of New York City. Doron Ben-Atar, Randy Bergstrom, Rebecca Berlow, Steve Forrey, and Eric Foner all believed that I had a contribution to make as a historian and encouraged me to consider an academic career.

At Stanford, Carl Degler, Estelle Freedman, and George Fredrickson were different, wonderful models of the humane academy, testimonies to the fact that one can be dedicated to research and writing about the past while maintaining a commitment to changing the present and future. Luis Arroyo provided me with a strong background in U.S. labor history, and Richard Roberts did the same for African labor history. Clay and Susan Carson pro-vided me with valuable experiences and contacts through the Martin Luther King, Jr., Papers Project. There I was fortunate to meet many valuable friends and colleagues, including Allison Dorsey, Crystal Feimster, Erica Armstrong, Katrina Nusum, Penny Russell, Pete Holloran, Karl Knapper, Megan Max-well, Stewart Burns, and Jane Benson.

Ira Berlin and Leslie Rowland helped me gain a postdoctoral fellowship at the University of Maryland. Ira graciously read several drafts of the first four chapters of this book and offered trenchant criticism. While I was at Maryland, Ira, Leslie, Bill Bravman, Robyn Muncy and Tony Speranza, Daryle Williams, and Carla Peterson were supportive colleagues and friends.

Colleagues and friends have provided unending support and helpful criticism over the long course of this project. My wonderful, sustaining writing group of Karen Dunn-Haley, Ariela Gross, Wendy Lynch, Renee Romano, Wendy Wall, and Alice Yang-Murray read numerous incarnations of the manuscript. At Emory, Margot Finn and Mary Odem gave great writing and publishing advice. I owe a special debt to Mary (and to her husband, Ralph Gilbert); she read part of the manuscript while on her honeymoon! Other members of the history department at Emory have also been unfailingly collegial. In particular I thank Matthew Payne, Leroy Davis, Jim Roark, Jonathan Prude, Dan Carter, Michael Bellesiles, Kristin Mann, Heide Fehrenbach, Jeffrey Lesser, and Randy Packard. Other Emory colleagues who lent advice and support over the years include Rudolph Byrd, Frances Smith-Foster, Mark Sanders, Kim Wallace-Sanders, Randall Burkett, Virginia Shadron, Cris Levenduski, Judy Rohrer, Julie Abraham, Amy Lang, and Cindy Patton.

During my 1998–1999 sabbatical year in New York City at Columbia University and the Schomburg Center for Research in Black History and Culture, I was fortunate to gain another circle of colleagues from whom I learned a great deal. My appreciation goes to Carolyn Brown, Martha Hodes, Jeffrey Stewart, Margaret Vendreyes, Craig Wilder, Zita Nunes, Debra King, and Colin Palmer for their fellowship. Many thanks also go to Diana Lachatanere, Zita Nunes, and Colin Palmer for their leadership of the Schomburg Center's Scholars-in-Residence program. Betsy Blackmar was my sponsor for a Ford Foundation Fellowship at Columbia University; she helped me make the most of my research year. Erica Armstrong, Martha Jones, and Adrienne Petty also provided much support and advice.

Scholars of New York City and of free blacks have been unfailingly generous. I thank Christine Stansell, Jim and Lois Horton, David Roediger, Anne Boylan, Graham Hodges, Shane White, Craig Wilder, Patrick Rael, and Michael Sappol for sharing their research and for the inspiration their scholarship provided. I also thank the Association for the Study of Afro-American Life and History, the American Historical Association, the American Studies Association, the Organization of American Historians, the Washington Seminar on American History and Culture, the Emory University African American Studies Faculty Workshop, Wesleyan University, Princeton University, the University of Maryland, the University of Michigan, and the Atlanta Seminar on the Comparative History of Labor,

Industry, Technology and Society, for giving me the opportunity to present my work to interesting, thoughtful audiences.

I could not have completed this book without many forms of material assistance. Stanford University's Graduate School of Arts and Sciences, the Stanford Humanities Center, Emory University, the University of Maryland, the Ford Foundation Postdoctoral Fellowship Program for Minorities, the Mellon Foundation, the Schomburg Center, and the Littleton-Griswold Fund of the American Historical Association have my deep appreciation. Jennifer Meares, Lisa Roy, Rik van Welie, and Scott Gavorsky provided valued research assistance. Sarah Zingarelli of Emory University's Biomedical Imaging Services and Scott Gavorsky provided inestimable help with the maps herein. I have been fortunate to work with Jim Grossman, Historical Studies of Urban America series coeditor, and Doug Mitchell, Robert Devens, Tim McGovern, Jenni Fry, and Catherine Beebe of the University of Chicago Press, all of whom have made the publishing process as trouble-free as possible.

For providing housing during the many months I spent researching and writing in New York City, I'd like to thank Alicia and James Reiger, Jill Levey-Powlen, Adrienne Petty, Julie Abraham, Neal Goren, and Carolyn Brown. Other friends had to live with me as I wrote the dissertation and the book. For their patience with a sometimes grumpy writer, I thank Marvin Peguese, Kirsten Nussbaumer, Sally Collins, Lisa Pavlovsky, and Rich Gee in San Francisco; Bill Bravman and Wendy Lynch in Washington, D.C.; Jill Levey-Powlen, Lucia Rivieccio, and Kathy Kenny in Brooklyn; and Cindy Patton, Angela Smircic, and Anne Dacey in Atlanta. A special thanks goes to John Andrews and Bill O'Brien. During the winter of 1993, when the New-York Historical Society threatened to close due to financial difficulties, John graciously shared his tiny studio apartment with me, and Bill took time from his own writing to help me take notes at the society.

Many archivists and libraries provided the raw material fundamental to this book. Thanks go to Sonia Moss of the Stanford University Interlibrary Loan office and to the staffs at the Emory University Interlibrary Loan office, the American Antiquarian Society (especially Nancy Burkett), the New-York Historical Society, the New York Municipal Archives, the New York Public Library, the New York State Library and Archives, the Schomburg Center, the Library of Congress, the Quaker Collection at Haverford College, the Friends Historical Library at Swarthmore College, the Amistad Research Collection, and the Columbia University Library.

More personally, family and friends have provided constant encouragement. I thank Alison Bailes; Allison Dorsey; Daryl Scott; Eileen McCarthy;

Carrie Bramen and David Schmid; David Goldberger; Todd Benson and Jenny Solario; Stephanie and Tony Manzella; Carole, Julio, and Michelle Baez; Cynthia Blair; Elizabeth DuPont Spencer; Judie Annozine; Alicia Cozine; Miriam Goderich; Alicia Reiger; Barbara Cutter; Suzanne Roth; Jill Levey-Powlen; Stacey Wakeley; Jeannine Verrett; and Mrs. Marianne Newman. A special thanks goes to my Atlanta family: Mary Odem, Ralph Gilbert, Felicia Gilbert, Isabelle Gilbert, and Leah Gilbert Odem. Joan Lally, Jesse Harris Bathrick, and Ilene Schroeder gave me important new strategies for thinking about my life and work. Elizabeth Baez was my central emotional support during many of the years I spent on this project. Jackie Scott contributed almost daily sustenance on all things academic and personal. Erica Armstrong encouraged me to finish it, already! Miranda Pollard coached, coaxed, and cajoled the final revisions out of me. My sisters, brothers-in-law, and nephews—Regina and David Bartholomew, Jennifer and Shane Jones, Rachel Harris, David Bartholomew IV, Reginald Batholomew, Devin Jones, and Ryan Jones—made me want to finish the book so they could read it. Most of all, my parents Merle Ann and Reginald Harris instilled in me an understanding of the importance of education and an appreciation of and thirst for knowledge. To them, this book is gratefully dedicated.

Parts of chapters six, eight, and nine previously appeared in altered form in "From Abolitionist Amalgamators to 'Rulers of the Five Points': The Discourse of Interracial Sex and Reform in Antebellum New York City," on pages 191–212 of Sex, Love, Race: Crossing Boundaries in North America, edited by Martha Hodes and published in 1999 by New York University Press, New York.

I n 1991 in lower Manhattan, construction workers and archaeologists stumbled across an unexpected treasure. Two blocks from city hall, under twenty feet of asphalt, concrete, and rubble, lay the remains of the eighteenth-century "Negroes Burial Ground." Closed in 1790 and covered over by roads and buildings throughout the nineteenth and twentieth centuries, the site turned out to be the largest such archaeological find in North America, containing the remains of as many as twenty thousand African Americans. The graves revealed to New Yorkers and the nation an aspect of history long hidden: the large numbers of enslaved African and African American men, women, and children who labored to create colonial Manhattan. The skeletons that archaeologists excavated displayed stresses associated with hard labor: bones fractured or out of alignment, made fragile through overwork, malnutrition, and disease. One child's skeleton exhibited injuries associated with carrying heavy burdens on his head. The graves also demonstrated the ways enslaved African Americans attempted both to hold on to African cultural traditions and to incorporate European traditions into their lives. Some graves contained cowrie shells; others, the remains of British and American military uniforms. The bodies faced west so that, following Christian belief of the time, the dead would arise on Judgment Day already facing Christ at his Second Coming; yet the cowrie shells were representative of the hope that the dead would return to Africa in the afterlife. Some graves were marked with a heart-shaped image—possibly an Ashanti image, signifying either *sankofa*, the need to remember the past and revere ancestors, or *akoma*, to have patience, to endure. The burial ground revealed the

1

centrality of daily slave labor to New York City's black population, but also African Americans' hopes for a life beyond slavery.[1]

The construction, destruction, and recovery of the Negroes Burial Ground, renamed the African Burial Ground in 1993, encapsulates the ways New York City's early black history has been forgotten, but also how this history may be recovered in unusual places. For many today, the quintessential images of New York City's black population come from twentieth-century Manhattan's Harlem. But the black movement to Harlem by the early twentieth century was only the continuation of a migration in which whites forced blacks northward up the island over two and a half centuries. The first free black settlements in the seventeenth century and the establishment of the African Burial Ground began this trend. With each movement of black people out of an area, new residents erased their history there, sometimes deliberately, other times incidentally. After the discovery of the African Burial Ground, archaeologists, historians, and citizens concerned with preserving New York's black history had to remain vigilant in the face of the forces of Manhattan real estate—initially, the construction of a new federal office building on the primary site, and later, the Con Edison company's disruption of an adjacent site. On both sites, construction workers using backhoes and mechanical diggers disinterred many graves, ignoring the bones they churned up in their eagerness to complete their tasks. Only with difficulty did a coalition of academics, politicians, and community activists convince the contractors responsible for these work orders of the importance of the site and the need to preserve and commemorate those buried there. By 2001, ten years after the discovery of the graves, archaeologists headed by scientific director Michael Blakey had recovered a meaningful sample of the graves for study at Howard University. An office established and headed by archaeologist Warren Barbour and ethnohistorian Sherrill Wilson in lower Manhattan's World Trade Center provided educational materials, workshops, and research updates to the general public on some of the earliest residents of Manhattan Island.[2]

In this book, I uncover the early history of enslaved and free Africans and African Americans in New York City between 1626 and 1863. To do so, I have relied not only on documents produced by black men and women, such as newspapers, literature, and organizational records, but also documents produced by whites that reveal, perhaps unintentionally, the contours of life for New York City's blacks from the seventeenth through the nineteenth centuries. As we know, black men and women left few of their own sources. But the descriptions left by non-blacks, read and interpreted carefully, can provide a wealth of information. In arenas that whites ostensibly created and controlled—courtrooms, almshouses, indeed, the very streets of the city—black people wielded admittedly limited but important influences of their own, to which whites were forced to respond and upon which they often commented. Much as the construction workers stumbled across black graves in twentieth-century lower Manhattan, the historian can stumble across black voices and actions in unexpected places in the records of old New York.

Hearing these voices and witnessing these actions reveals the importance of slavery, emancipation, and black freedom to the history of New York City. Although historians have thoroughly studied black enslavement and emancipation in the southern United States, comparable studies for northern locales are few. Before the completion of emancipation in 1827, New York City contained the largest urban slave population outside of the South. After 1827, New York City was home to one of the largest free black communities in the North. Although black people as a proportion of the total New York City population declined sharply during the antebellum period, from 11 percent in the 1790s to 1.5 percent by 1860, the black community continued to serve as an important economic, social, and cultural reference point in New York City life.[3]

Central to the story of slavery and freedom in New York City is the development of class relations and community among blacks. Rarely have historians of pre–Civil War blacks looked beyond the racial discrimination and hardships blacks suffered for signs of their attitudes about class relations and work. Historians studying the roots of class formation in the antebellum United States have only recently begun to explore the roles that the institution of slavery and racial identity played in defining class identity for blacks, whites, and other racial and ethnic groups in America.[4]

The latest works in labor history build on historian Herbert Gutman's model of class formation and identity in the United States. Gutman, drawing on the work of British labor historian E. P. Thompson, posited the existence of class identity and ideology not only on the job, but in the social and cultural expressions of workers and in their lived experience.[5] But this "new labor history" neglects the unique role that slavery and racism played for both whites and blacks in defining the American working class in the North as well as the South.[6] In particular, recent labor historians of New York City have neglected the importance of blacks and of racial politics to the construction and politics of the working class in that city. Sean Wilentz's *Chants Democratic: New York City and the Rise of the American Working Class, 1789–1850* and Christine Stansell's *City of Women: Sex and Class in New York, 1789–1860* are, deservedly, among the most acclaimed studies on the roots of the American working class in New York City. But slavery and emancipation in New York have no bearing on the class developments they describe. Black New Yorkers barely exist in these books. Both authors create a white hegemony more powerful than that which actually existed in the nineteenth century.[7] Using New York City as a case study, I demonstrate the ways northern slavery and emancipation, southern slavery, and racial identities influenced the construction of class and community for blacks and whites in the pre–Civil War United States.

By bringing the topic of class formation to the foreground in studying the antebellum free black community, this volume presents a more complex view of black community formation. In the 1920s and 1930s, the first professional black historians, such as Charles Wesley, Carter G. Woodson, Lorenzo Greene, and W. E. B. Du Bois, produced works that placed issues of class at the center of their understanding of African American history.[8] Although there has been a proliferation of works on the antebellum African American experience since the 1960s, many of these works have centered on southern slavery. Research on antebellum free blacks has focused on racial discrimination, community building, or the black elite.[9] The class analysis in such works, while present, is often subordinate to the examination of the formation of racial identity.[10] Further, these works do not examine the process of class development among blacks; they present a static picture of class relations, rather than a dynamic description of the growth of class divisions within the black community.

Although I am critical of the literature I cite above, my own work is heavily in debt to it. I draw on the theories and methodologies developed by historians of the African American and working-class experiences to explore black life in New York City. My book began as an attempt solely to study black working-class formation, but ultimately I drew on the best traditions in African American history by attempting to study that development in the context of dynamic community formation. I have looked to labor history for discussions of class formation that include economic, ideological, and cultural forces. My research strategy has been shaped by works in African American, labor, women's, and gender history. I view my work as part of a continuing and increasingly exciting discussion about the interplay of race and racism, class and gender in U.S. history.

I begin with the premise that the experiences of slavery and emancipation in colonial and early national New York City, and the ways New Yorkers interpreted those experiences, influenced the shape of labor relations there and the attitudes of blacks and whites toward black workers and their labor. The existence of slavery in New York had an indelible effect on the political and economic institutions of the city. In the colonial period, slave labor was central to the growth of the city. By the time of the Revolutionary War, slaves symbolized the condition whites most feared for themselves as workers and citizens. A condition approximating black slavery was the worst possible outcome of the Revolutionary War with Britain. But colonists' fears and critiques of their own enslavement, rooted in republican ideology, did not lead them to emancipate their own slaves during the war.

In 1785, the founding of the New York Manumission Society by middle-class and elite white men in New York City signaled a new desire to end slavery, but it took nearly fifteen years for the New York State government to agree. New York's emancipation laws were defined to free slaves carefully and thus control and contain free blacks. This was only partly to control blacks as a labor class, for increasing numbers of European immigrants gradually displaced blacks in many of the occupations they had held as slaves. Rather, the desire among different classes of whites to control blacks was based on their fears that blacks, supposedly degraded by slavery, might influence urban and state politics, whether through formal practices such as voting or informal practices such as demonstrating in the streets. Through the provisions of the gradual emancipation laws and the 1821 suffrage law that disfranchised the majority of the black community, white New Yorkers selectively enforced republican virtues. By the end of the period of emancipation in 1827, whites had legally, economically, and socially designated black people as a separate, dependent, and unequal group within the New York City community.

Despite increasing restrictions, blacks during the emancipation era established an urban presence that built upon and then grew beyond practices begun under slavery. Before the War of 1812, blacks participated in public displays of politics and culture across evolving class lines. But the rise of a new racism against blacks after the War of 1812 led to increased pressure on blacks to move out of public space and, indeed, with the formation of the American Colonization Society, out of the United States all together. The roots of class distinctions in the black community lay partially in differing responses to racism. The seeds of a black middle class were planted as some black ministers, educators, and others looked to the New York Manumission Society for support. Their coalition with the Manumission Society led to conflict between black ministers and educators and black workers over public displays, education, and blacks' work habits and religiosity. Throughout the antebellum period, debates over methods to achieve freedom for

southern slaves and racial, social, economic, and political equality for all
blacks both revealed and contributed to the evolution of class distinctions.

The rise of radical abolitionism marked another period in the evolution
of class and racial identity in New York City. Between 1830 and 1840, blacks
turned from the tactics and ideologies of the New York Manumission Society, whose members increasingly advocated colonization, to a coalition with
white radical abolitionists. Free blacks were crucial to abolitionist whites' acceptance of the doctrine that black equality was central to the goal of immediate emancipation of southern slaves. Some blacks again turned to an ideology, in this case moral perfection, that highlighted evolving class distinctions
within the black community. While some blacks, regardless of class background, subscribed to the moral and intellectual reforms promulgated by
abolitionists, others protested against the privileging of middle-class, educated blacks and their tactics for racial improvement above more grass-roots
political efforts that involved working-class blacks.

As abolitionists focused on moral improvement, other reformers took
a more pragmatic approach to the problems of the black working class. A
group of Quaker women, ideological and sometimes familial descendants of
the leaders of the New York Manumission Society, formed several organizations to aid African Americans. The most prominent of these was the Association for the Benefit of Colored Orphans, which established an orphanage
for black children in 1836. By providing education, job training, and employment opportunities, the Quaker women gave working-class black children an
alternate path of racial uplift from that advocated by the abolitionists. But
the Quaker women did not simply reform black clients. Rather, black workers transformed the orphanage into an institution that addressed their own
needs, and in the process changed the women's views of the possibilities for
racial equality.

In the 1840s and 1850s, the breakup of the abolitionist coalition allowed
the rise of a new group of black abolitionists who placed a greater value
on labor than on moral perfection as a means for the improvement of black
people. Black abolitionists distinguished between meaningful skilled labor
and "degraded" occupations such as domestic service and waiting tables.
Such distinctions grew out of an ideology about labor in the antebellum period, rooted in republican thought, which devalued personal service occupations as not providing workers with sufficient independence from employers.[11] Among blacks, such distinctions also grew out of the experience of
slavery, in which domestic and other personal servants were more subject to
the will of their masters than other workers and, at worst, were also subject

to sexual abuse. However, the majority of free black women and a large proportion of free black men continued to work in such occupations out of economic necessity. With noteworthy exceptions, most middle-class black abolitionists were unwilling to recognize the efforts these men and women made to retain their autonomy as they performed these jobs.

The occupations most criticized by black abolitionists could and did provide the basis for mutual respect between black and white workers and an alleviation, albeit temporary, of racial tensions. In 1853, for example, New York's black and white waiters joined together to ask for higher wages. Black waiters' pride in their work and their resulting belief that they deserved higher wages gained them the reluctant respect of their fellow white waiters. Black abolitionists responded by attempting to attract the black waiters into a rival race-based organization that emphasized the harmony of interest between employers and employees and encouraging black waiters to take pride in moral reform rather than manual labor. In another demonstration of the slowly growing class distinctions in the black community, most black waiters rejected this organization and pledged their support to the struggle for higher wages.

The 1853 waiters' strike was not the only instance of cooperation and contact between the black and white laboring poor. Black and white workers shared class-based neighborhoods throughout the antebellum period. They participated in social and cultural activities after work in interracial bars and dance halls and sometimes intermarried. After 1834, white journalists highlighted these relationships, creating a discourse of amalgamation that sexualized and criminalized black-white interactions in the public eye. White reformers in the 1850s appropriated and expanded on these negative characterizations, focusing on the Five Points district as the center of amalgamation, poverty, and crime in New York City.

By the beginning of the Civil War, the allure of the rich political, social, and cultural interactions that blacks could achieve in New York City had grown thin in the face of continuing poverty and increasing racism. After years of growth, New York's black population dropped precipitously between 1840 and the Civil War, from a high of over 16,000 in 1840 to about 12,500 in 1860.[12] The decrease in population was due partially to the massive influx of Irish immigrants, who competed with blacks for unskilled jobs. But it was also due to the increasing danger of kidnapping and southern enslavement that northern free blacks faced in the wake of the 1850 Fugitive Slave Law. Blacks looked beyond the boundaries of New York City to the possibility of farming communities in upstate New York, the West, and Canada. Some also embraced emigration to Liberia and the West Indies, in cooperation with the white-led American Colonization Society that had been rejected by blacks earlier in the century.

Despite the decrease in the black population, the rise of the Republican Party and its limited antislavery platform was threatening to proslavery New Yorkers and to those who opposed racial equality. Soon after the Civil War began, some white working-class New Yorkers turned their backs on the limited promise of racial cooperation and equality implied in the relationships between blacks and whites in the waiters' strike and in the Five Points. In one of the worst cases of racial violence in the nineteenth century, the Civil War Draft Riots of 1863, the antebellum period ended for blacks as it had begun soon after the War of 1812: with attempts to expunge blacks, this time by violent means, from New York's social, cultural, political, and economic life.

Four periods of black community, political activism, and class consciousness are discussed in this book: the period of slavery from 1626 to 1785; the growth of antislavery sentiment and gradual emancipation from 1785 to 1827, when blacks and whites struggled over how to define newly free blacks' economic, social, and cultural position in the New York community; the period of radical abolitionism, from 1830 through the Civil War, when blacks and some whites articulated new ideologies and tactics to address the issues of racial inequality; and finally, the period of disillusionment between 1840 and the Civil War Draft Riots, during which the enforcement of proslavery laws and racial violence pushed large numbers of blacks out of New York City.

Throughout these four periods, evolving class distinctions were evident within the black community. These distinctions were complicated by the struggle for racial equality and by the economic position of blacks. Among blacks, class was not determined only by distinctions between those who performed manual labor and those who held non—manual labor jobs, or between those who were financially stable and materially successful and those who were not. Educated blacks were often unable to sustain the lifestyle that allowed for a firm middle-class status. Further, even as blacks increasingly espoused class-based solutions to racial problems, they continued to claim racial unity. Compared to whites, cultural, political, and social markers became more important points of difference between the black middle class and the black working class than economic and occupational factors alone.

In pointing to the conflicts and compromises that black people struggled with in their communities, I seek to complicate the vision of community. Community is not a fixed entity, but a dynamic process in which individuals constantly struggle over definitions and goals. *In the Shadow of Slavery* focuses on the ways in which increasingly during the antebellum period class distinctions among blacks affected arguments about black community, particularly as expressed through political activism against racism and slavery. In seeing community, class, and political activism as dynamic, entangled processes, remade according to the exigencies of the times and the needs of the people involved, we are able to better understand how a single African burial ground can hold cowrie shells and brass buttons, Christian crosses and West African *sankofa* and *akoma*. Hopefully, then, we can do greater justice to the complex and dynamic ways New York City contained diversity across and within racial groups.

CHAPTER ONE

Slavery in Colonial New York

On the fourth and fifth of July, 1827, New York City's African Americans took to the streets, marching in processions with banners and music. Many attended church services, offering prayers and songs of thanksgiving to God and speeches praising the state legislature and white reformers. Slavery, an institution virtually as old as European settlement on Manhattan Island, had finally ended in New York State. From the time of the Revolutionary War, New Yorkers had debated ending slavery, but it took almost fifty years for them to eradicate the institution completely. Repeated attempts to pass legislation ending slavery failed in the 1770s and 1780s. New York's first emancipation law, passed in 1799, freed no slaves and granted only partial freedom to the children of slaves: those born to slave mothers served lengthy indentures to their mothers' masters, until age twenty-five if female and twenty-eight if male. Finally, in 1817, Governor Daniel Tompkins convinced the New York State legislature to end slavery completely, but even then, the legislature took the longest time suggested by Tompkins—a decade.

Slavery's long demise—indeed, slavery's long history in New York—indicates the importance of black labor to the region between 1626 and 1827. As in the South, black slave labor was central to the day-to-day survival and the economic life of Europeans in the colonial North, and no part of the colonial North relied more heavily on slavery than Manhattan. Slave labor enabled the survival of the first European settlers in Dutch-governed New Amsterdam in the seventeenth century. In the eighteenth century, the British sought to heighten white New Yorkers' reliance on slave labor and the slave trade in order to make Manhattan the chief North American slave port and economic center. As British New York became known as a center of slave labor, few European laborers, free or indentured, chose to immigrate there. Under both the Dutch and the British, slaves performed vital agricultural tasks in the rural areas surrounding New York City. By the end of the seventeenth century, New York City had a larger black population than any other North American city. The ratio of slaves to whites in the total population was comparable to that in Maryland and Virginia. In the eighteenth century, only Charleston and New Orleans exceeded New York City in number of slaves.[1]

The system of racial slavery became the foundation of New Yorkers' definitions of race, class, and freedom far into the nineteenth century. As Ira Berlin, Barbara Fields, and other historians have pointed out, the initial purpose of slavery was to secure a labor force—to "make class." But as white New Yorkers created a working class based on African slavery, they also developed racial justifications for the enslavement of Africans above all other groups of workers. Haltingly under the Dutch and more consistently under the British, Europeans defined blacks as the only group fit to be slaves amid a society with numerous racial and religious groups. The use of racial ideologies that defined blacks as inferior to other racial groups and thus deserving of enslavement condemned blacks to unequal status into the nineteenth century and beyond. Europeans did not always define the terms of racial inferiority consistently, but their reliance upon these justifications during the time of slavery meant that when blacks celebrated freedom in 1827, their struggle for equality in New York City had just begun.[2]

Enslavement dominated every facet of colonial black New Yorkers' lives—the work they did, their ability to form families, their religious practices, even how they defined themselves. But black men and women did not simply acquiesce to enslavement or to an inferior racial status. Throughout Dutch and British slavery, enslaved Africans demonstrated through their labor, their resistance to bondage, and their creation of families and communities that the racial stereotypes of inferiority promulgated by Europeans had no basis in reality. Black New Yorkers used Europeans' reliance on their labor, as well as their own knowledge of European ways, to ameliorate the conditions of slavery and to push for full freedom—through legal methods under the Dutch and, under the British, through violent resistance. Recognition of blacks' centrality to colonial New York's economic system and of blacks' continual pursuit of freedom gives the lie to Europeans' claims of African inferiority.

■ ■ ■

The first non–Native American settler on Manhattan Island, Jan Rodrigues, was of African and possibly Afro-European descent, a free man and sailor from a Dutch vessel. In 1613, Rodrigues's shipmates dumped him on the island after a shipboard dispute. Rodrigues became fluent in Native American languages, and when European explorers and traders arrived at Manhattan Island in subsequent years, Rodrigues facilitated trade relations between them and Native Americans. Rodrigues eventually married into the Rockaway tribe.[3] Rodrigues's role in trade and his marriage into a Native American tribe began the commercial and cultural exchanges for which Manhattan Island would become famous.

By 1621, the Dutch West India Company had obtained exclusive rights to settle the colony of New Netherland, including Manhattan. The first European settlers on Manhattan Island were Walloons, an oft-persecuted Belgian minority who traveled to New Netherland under the auspices of the company, for Dutch citizens had little interest in leaving the economically prosperous Netherlands for the American frontier. The company hoped that the Walloon settlements would secure its hold on New Netherland against the British, who also claimed rights to the territory during the seventeenth century.[4]

In 1625, the first Walloon families settled on Manhattan Island under the directorship of Hollander William Kieft, who renamed the island New Amsterdam. Initially, the settlers lived in makeshift shelters—trenches seven feet deep, lined with timber, and roofed with turf or bark. Late that same year, a group of Dutch builders arrived with plans for more permanent structures: a fort with a marketplace, houses, a church, a hospital, and a school within its walls. Construction began soon after Pieter Minuit allegedly purchased Manhattan Island from local Native Americans in early 1626.[5] Following the acquisition, migrants from England, France, Norway, Germany, Ireland, and Denmark joined the Walloons on the island. Although New Netherland was a Dutch colony, non-Dutch settlers at New Amsterdam probably constituted as much as 50 percent of the population, leading one observer to state that Manhattan had "Too Great a Mixture of Nations." Another estimated that the island's settlers spoke eighteen different languages.[6]

But relative to other colonies, New Netherland had difficulty attracting European settlers until the 1650s. Dutch citizens could make a comfortable living in Holland and thus had no desire to travel to the American colonies. Also, the difficulties New Netherlanders faced in the first decades of settlement frightened away the Dutch as well as other Europeans who might have been attracted to the colony. From the 1620s through the 1640s, the New Netherland colony was on the defensive against the Native Americans and the British; settlers who arrived at the colony expecting to labor peacefully instead were forced to defend themselves in violent skirmishes, if not

outright wars. The settlers also struggled economically because of misman-
agement by local directors general and the Dutch West India Company's monopoly on trade. Directors Verhulst and van Twiller conflicted with colonists
over the labor owed to the company. The company had a generous land-grant
and land-use policy, particularly for the five elite Dutch men to whom it
granted patroonships—thousands of acres of land and extensive rights over
the land's resources in return for attracting settlers to work the land. But
the company restricted settlers' and patroons' earnings from the most
profitable resource in the colony—fur—and limited the export of other
goods from the colony. These restrictions, as well as taxes on exported goods,
made it difficult for those granted land to profit from it. Out of five patroonships the company granted throughout the colony in the 1620s, only one,
Rensselaerswyck, survived. Numerous settlers returned to Europe after a
few difficult years, and some even filed suit against the company because of
the hardships they experienced. In 1630, 300 colonists lived in New Netherland, of whom 270 were clustered at New Amsterdam—not enough to make
the colony a profitable enterprise. By 1638, New Amsterdam held approximately 400 residents, but the city of Boston, founded four years after New
Amsterdam, already contained 1,000. Not until 1640, when the Dutch government removed the Dutch West India Company's trade monopoly, did
trade restrictions begin to ease in the colony; and not until the mid-1650s did
the colony attract consistent numbers of European settlers. By 1664, the end
of Dutch rule, European settlers at New Amsterdam numbered approximately 1,500.[7]

African slaves became the most stable element of the New Netherland
working class and population. The Dutch West India Company's importation and employment of most of the colony's slave labor enabled the settlement and survival of the Europeans at New Amsterdam as well as the limited economic success the colony experienced. The first eleven African slaves
were imported in 1626. The company, not individuals, owned these slaves,
who provided labor for the building and upkeep of the colony's infrastructure. In addition to aiding in the construction of Fort Amsterdam, completed
in 1635, slaves also built roads, cut timber and firewood, cleared land, and
burned limestone and oyster shells to make the lime used in outhouses and
in burying the dead. In 1625, in an attempt to diversify the colony's economy, the company established six "bouwerys," or farms, along the eastern
and western shores of Manhattan Island, just north of the settlement. By
1626, company slaves worked these farms; the produce they grew fed the
colony's inhabitants. Company-hired overseers watched the slaves during
their laboring and leisure hours.[8]

Despite the colony's reliance on slave labor, the Dutch West India Company initially imported slaves into New Amsterdam haphazardly. The company was more concerned with attracting European colonists to New Netherland than with importing slaves, and it did not want to supply New Amsterdam's merchants with surplus slaves with which they might compete with the company in North American slave markets. Until about 1640, most European settlers, reluctant to commit to permanent settlement in the colony, worked as traders and had little need for long-term, year-round assistance from slave or free laborers. They tended to hire slaves from the company or from the few private slaveowners for short periods rather than buy them. Thus, the company directed most of its slave labor to the Dutch colonies of Curaçao, Aruba, Bonaire, and briefly, Brazil; slaves arrived at New Amsterdam irregularly and sometimes accidentally. For example, settlers in 1636 bought three slaves from a ship's captain from Providence Island colony. In 1642, a French privateer dropped off an unknown number of slaves at New Amsterdam. And in 1652, a Dutch privateer captured a Spanish ship and landed its cargo of forty-four slaves at the settlement.[9]

After Holland lost Brazil to the Portuguese in 1654, the Dutch West India Company began to ship slaves to New Amsterdam more consistently, in larger numbers, and directly from Africa in an effort to develop New Amsterdam into a major North American slave port. European colonists profited from the increased importation of slaves. On the bouwerys just outside of New Amsterdam and the farms of the Hudson Valley, landowners used slaves to clear the land, plant grain crops, and take care of livestock. These farms supplied grain and livestock to other Dutch colonies and to the Netherlands. In New Amsterdam, larger numbers of wealthy merchants, artisans, and business owners bought slaves and trained them to work in their businesses. Other merchants hoped to join in the profits of the slave trade and bought slaves in order to resell them to other New Netherland residents or to other colonies. One of the largest of these shipments came aboard the *Witte Paert* in 1655. When the ship docked in New Amsterdam, residents knew of its arrival because of the stench that arose from the holds, where slave traders had tightly packed three hundred African men and women and left them to travel across the Atlantic amid their own waste. By 1660, New Amsterdam was the most important slave port in North America.[10]

African slaves constituted the predominant part of New York City's colonial working class. Throughout the Dutch period, the colony attracted few European indentured servants, especially relative to other North American colonies. Thus, the colony relied heavily on slave labor. In New Netherland and other parts of the colonial Americas in the seventeenth century, colonial governments were less concerned with defining racial difference under the law than ensuring the presence of a steady labor force. No European states formally regulated slavery in the North American colonies before the 1660s; Virginia established the first comprehensive slave codes between 1680 and 1682. Neither did colonies limit slavery to Africans—Europeans enslaved Native Americans when they could, although not other Europeans. In New Netherland, African slaves could testify in court and bring suit against whites; had the same trial rights as whites; could own property, excepting real estate or other slaves; and could work for wages. Slaves, white and black indentured servants, and free black and white workers in the seventeenth century held more rights and experiences in common in New Amsterdam, and indeed in North America, than would be true in the eighteenth and nineteenth centuries.[11]

Nonetheless, during the 1600s African ancestry became increasingly important in defining the bound segment of the working class. Although trans-Atlantic travel during this time was difficult for everyone, only African captives and European criminals and prisoners of war arrived in the New World in chains, as slaves and indentured servants, respectively. The presence of relatively few European indentured servants, criminal or not, meant that few Europeans came to the New Netherland colony as bondpersons, especially after New Netherland became more involved in the slave trade after 1640. Masters had the same control over servants during their indentures as they had over slaves. Indentured servants could not marry until their indentures were complete; masters could sell indentured servants' time to new owners as they could sell slaves; and punishments of indentured servants were similar to those of slaves. Even the fact that Africans were enslaved for life sometimes made little difference in colonies where life expectancies were short and indentured servants might not survive their seven-year contracts. In Virginia and other colonies during the seventeenth century, indentured servants worked alongside slaves; similarities in their conditions led to cooperation between European and African bondpersons in ways ranging from running away together to intermarriage. But the fact that there were only small numbers of indentured servants in New Amsterdam exacerbated the differences between African and European laborers.[12]

Practically from the arrival of the first slaves, many European laborers in New Amsterdam, feeling the pressure of a tight labor market, actively sought to distinguish themselves from slave laborers and promote their status as free workers. Most had little incentive to identify with the colony's slaves. Because free laborers earned poor wages from the Dutch West India Company, by far New Amsterdam's largest employer, many worked more than one job to survive, and even the schoolmaster took in washing. In the limited labor market, free skilled white workers particularly feared competition from slave laborers, for a slave could be purchased for the same amount as a free laborer's annual wages. This fear prompted white workers in 1628 to convince the company not to train slaves for skilled labor, as it did in other American colonies. By the 1650s, European settlers began to declare publicly that Africans were not as competent skilled laborers as Europeans. When the officers of the Dutch West India Company in Amsterdam tried to encourage the New Amsterdam settlers to train slaves as skilled workers, Director General Stuyvesant replied that there were "no able negroes fit to learn a trade."[13] Under Dutch colonial rule, Europeans of all nations united to racialize jobs and skills in Manhattan, excluding enslaved and free blacks from lucrative occupations.

But criticisms of African labor did not alone support the development of the negative racial stereotypes that enabled Europeans to justify the enslavement of Africans. New Amsterdam's slaves' religious beliefs and their access to Christianity became another way to distinguish Africans from Europeans. For much of the period before the eighteenth century, non-Christian beliefs theoretically marked those whom Europeans could enslave. Initially, Europeans justified slavery as a way to bring "heathen" Africans to Christianity. Once Africans accepted Christianity, the stated purpose of slavery was supposedly fulfilled, and blacks should have been freed. But the increased dependency of Europeans on slave labor ultimately trumped religious beliefs for most slaveholders.[14]

Christian religious leaders through the seventeenth century debated the question of enslaving Christians, including converted Africans, although they did not actively oppose slavery. Ministers and members of the Dutch Reformed Church in the Netherlands and in the Americas felt an obligation to convert slaves. In 1638, Dominie Evardus Bogardus of New Amsterdam requested that a schoolmaster be sent to the colonies to educate young Dutch and blacks in Christianity. Annually from 1639 to 1655, between one and three black children were baptized in the Dutch Reformed Church. And Dutch Reformed ministers performed marriages for a significant number of enslaved and free blacks.

By 1655, however, the Dutch church had stopped converting slaves to Christianity. According to Dominie Henricus Selyns, the slaves were not truly "striving for piety and Christian virtues" and instead "wanted nothing else than to deliver their children from bodily slavery." The Dutch church baptized only one black person between 1656 and 1664. The church's refusal to baptize slaves closed one method of Africans' assimilation as free people into the New Netherland community. Europeans depicted Africans as unable to be genuinely pious Christians and strengthened the religious foundation for preserving slavery. In doing so, they also strengthened a culturally based racial delineation between Africans and Europeans.[15]

The Dutch enslavement of Spanish prisoners of war underscored the increasing importance of race in perpetuating slavery under Dutch rule. In 1642 the French privateer *La Garce* arrived in New Amsterdam with a group of "Spanish Negroes" from a captured Spanish vessel. Despite the men's claims that they were free Spanish subjects, not Africans or slaves, the Dutch considered them slaves because of their swarthy skin and sold them.[16] By the end of Dutch rule in New Netherland, Europeans in the colony had established the racial differences between Africans and Europeans that allowed them to enslave Africans. Europeans rooted their creation of the colonial working class in seventeenth-century New Amsterdam in bound labor, particularly slavery, and increasingly defined only Africans as slaves.

Because Europeans in New Netherland in the 1600s established the relationship between racial difference and slavery gradually, the experiences of African slaves in New Amsterdam varied depending on the time of their arrival at the colony and their own prior knowledge and experiences. The first eleven slaves who arrived at New Amsterdam in 1626 have been termed "Atlantic Creoles" by historian Ira Berlin. Atlantic Creoles were men and women with cultural roots in both African and European cultures. Many spoke multiple languages, African and European, and were familiar with the customs of both worlds. Some were the descendants of African women and European men who had come to the coast of West Africa to trade in slaves and other commodities. Others were Africans who took on elements of European culture in order to better position themselves to take advantage of Africa's growing international trade in commodities and slaves. Atlantic Creoles lived in the coastal towns of Africa and in ports throughout the New World. Some traveled the seas with European explorers and traders. Many were able to use their knowledge to retain their freedom, but in other cases— perhaps with the first eleven New Amsterdam slaves—their extensive knowledge simply made them more valuable property.[17]

Of the first eleven slaves to arrive in New Amsterdam, the names of five denote a degree of mixed cultural ancestry or experience: Paul d'Angola, Simon Congo, Anthony Portuguese, John Francisco, and Gracia Angola. The last names d'Angola, Congo, and Angola indicate the birthplaces of these slaves on the west coast of Africa. For knowledgeable slave buyers, the names also suggested special skills or traits associated with Africans from those regions. Europeans characterized Angolan and Congolese slaves as having docile and complacent natures and as possessing special abilities in the mechanical arts. In fact, savvy slave traders may have renamed these slaves to lure prospective buyers. The first names Paul, Simon, John, Anthony, and Gracia denote European, and perhaps Christian, acculturation. Catholicism brought by Portuguese traders had made inroads among Africans in coastal Angola and Congo. The last names Portuguese and Francisco also indicate some degree of European acculturation. Anthony Portuguese and John Francisco may have been of mixed Portuguese or Spanish and African ancestry, or they may simply have been owned by Portuguese or Spanish slave masters before their arrival in New Amsterdam.[18]

The presence in New Amsterdam of slaves with Portuguese or Spanish connections resulted from the Dutch West India Company's aggressive attempts to gain dominance in the slave trade between Africa and the New World. Soon after its founding in 1621, the company fought the Portuguese and Spanish on land and sea, attempting to gain control of Portuguese and Spanish holdings on both ends of the route. Thus, these first slaves may have been captured during skirmishes between the Dutch and Portuguese on the coast of West Africa or in Brazil, or between the Dutch and Spanish on the island of Curaçao. Or, the Dutch may have raided a Spanish ship in the Atlantic, capturing slaves, some of which may have ended up in New Amsterdam. Additionally, any number of the first eleven slaves in New Amsterdam may have been free people, either in Africa or as sailors on the high seas, before their transport to New Amsterdam.[19]

The names of the six other slaves who arrived in 1626 apparently reflect their experiences and identities in New Netherland: Big Manuel or Manuel Gerritsen; Little Manuel or Manuel Minuit; Manuel de Reus; Little Anthony; and Jan from Fort Orange. Europeans probably gave the nicknames Big Manuel, Little Manuel, Little Anthony, and Jan from Fort Orange to the slaves after their arrival in New Netherland to distinguish among repeated first names. Jan's attribution, "from Fort Orange," refers to the fact that the Dutch West India Company sent this slave to the original company settlement on the Hudson River for a time before bringing him to the island. Minuit, Gerritsen, and de Reus bore the last names of their European masters.[20]

That both the first and last names of these eleven slaves were European does not necessarily indicate the renaming of Africans by masters as was endemic to many slaveholding societies. Slaveholders during this time, and particularly the Dutch, did not have a great interest in renaming their slaves. In fact, the repetition of first names among the eleven demonstrates that

these slaves retained names of their own choosing, regardless of the confusion that identical names may have caused their masters and other Europeans
in the settlement. These names also betoken the knowledge of multiple cultures that these particular Africans carried with them and perhaps their own
awareness of the power that could come with such knowledge. The use of
Spanish or Portuguese saints' names as first names indicates knowledge
of Christianity, which may have soothed Europeans who would have been
more fearful of "uncivilized" or "heathen" Africans. Indeed, throughout the
seventeenth century, the Dutch West India Company and individual slave
owners preferred "seasoned" or acculturated slaves to those directly from
Africa.[21]

The trust the European settlers placed in these enslaved, acculturated
men is demonstrated in the company's willingness to employ them in the defense of the colony. During New Netherland's most serious war against Native Americans, Director General Kieft's War in the 1640s, Kieft armed
slaves with hatchets and pikes to help defend the Dutch settlements. Trusting slaves with the job of executing white criminals also demonstrated the
colonists' confidence in individual Africans. In contrast to military service,
however, duties as public executioners signified slaves' low status. In Holland, the job of executioner was considered so degraded that few were willing to do it; other criminals had to be forced to perform capital punishments.
In the colonial context, slaves, who held the lowest status in the community
and who could be most easily coerced, performed these duties. Jan of Fort
Orange served in this capacity at Fort Orange before being brought to New
Amsterdam. In New Amsterdam, a slave named Pieter administered punishments including whipping, maiming, and execution.[22]

Europeans' reliance upon and confidence in Africans, despite their belief that Africans were inferior, meant that slaves exercised rights and privileges that seem unusual from the perspective of nineteenth-century or even
eighteenth-century slave systems. In addition to permitting slaves in New
Netherland to own material goods and earn wages, the Dutch West India
Company and the Dutch government allowed them to petition the government and to use the courts to settle disputes. In 1635, a group of slaves successfully petitioned the corporate headquarters of the Dutch West India
Company in Holland for wages it believed the company owed them.[23] Their
example may have inspired other blacks in New Amsterdam, slave and free,
to pursue their rights in local courts. In 1639, two slaves, Pedro Negretto and
Manuel de Reus, successfully sued Europeans for wages due. In 1643, Little
Manuel sued Englishman John Seales. Manuel de Reus and Big Manuel tes-
tified that Seales had damaged Little Manuel's cow. The court fined Seales

twenty-five guilders plus court costs and ordered payment of damages to Little Manuel.[24]

The Dutch West India Company also promoted family life among its slaves. In 1628, the company imported the first black female slaves, three women allegedly purchased for "the comfort of the company's Negro men." The company initially housed the slaves together in makeshift barracks. As the slaves married and had children, the company allowed them to form separate households. But ultimately, the colony's preference for slave men was more important than its desire to create slave families. Between 1626 and 1664, the sex ratio among slaves was 131 males to 100 females, making it difficult for men and women to marry, if they so desired. Further, individual slave owners were less concerned than the company about creating a family life for slaves. Because most colonial slaveholders owned just one or two slaves, it was unlikely that a single slave would find a mate in his or her owner's household. Individual slave owners were also more likely to sell their slaves, which meant that slaves might live in several households over the course of their lives. Director General Peter Stuyvesant stated that a group of slaves brought to New Amsterdam in 1652 had within four years been "two, three, or more times re-sold, and [had] changed masters." Even if a slave found a mate outside his or her own household, distance between households and the instability of slave ownership made such arrangements fraught with difficulties.[25]

Some masters went out of their way to ensure the marital happiness of their slaves. In 1664, Peter Stuyvesant sold the husband of a New Amsterdam slave couple to Jeremias Van Rensselaer, the patroon of Rensselaerswyck near present-day Albany. Although concern for the slave couple did not prevent the sale, Stuyvesant did "urge" Van Rensselaer to purchase the wife also, which Van Rensselaer did. And despite its rules against slave baptism after 1655, the Dutch Reformed Church supported slave marriages, performing twenty-six from the early 1640s to 1664. Slaves also formed marriages independent of the church. Indeed, of the first six recorded marriages, performed in New Amsterdam's Dutch Reformed Church between 1641 and 1643, two of the newly married were already widowers and five, widows. Probably over one hundred children were born to slave and free black couples in New Amsterdam under Dutch rule. Of these, the Dutch church baptized sixty-one.[26]

Despite the initially unreliable nature of the slave trade and the eagerness of New Amsterdam merchants to sell slaves south, the black population in New Amsterdam increased alongside the white. By 1660, New Amsterdam had the largest population of urban slaves in North America. When

Dutch rule ended in 1664, 375 blacks, of whom 75 were free, constituted about 20 percent of the population of New Amsterdam. The proportion of blacks to whites in New Amsterdam was comparable to that in the southern colonies of Virginia and Maryland. Relative to the Chesapeake colonies, however, where the imbalance between the numbers of male and female slaves was even higher than in New Amsterdam and where masters segregated black males from females on plantations, slaves in New Amsterdam had greater opportunities to form families.[27]

The variety of rights and privileges enjoyed by African slaves in New Amsterdam—relatively kind masters, relatively good opportunities to form families, and access to courts and some forms of property—did not mitigate the fundamental facts of enslavement for Africans: involuntary, largely unpaid, lifelong servitude and ultimate lack of control over one's individual and family life. Despite the ways the Dutch system of slavery may have seemed mild in comparison to plantation regimes south of New Amsterdam, the fact that New Amsterdam's slaves attempted to gain their freedom throughout the period of Dutch rule indicates the hardships blacks experienced under slavery.

Between 1639 and 1655, slaves attempted to use the Dutch Reformed Church to gain their freedom. The church's initial support of slave baptisms and marriages, and slaves' knowledge that Europeans were conflicted about enslaving Christians, led some slaves to seek freedom by converting to Christianity. Petitions for freedom always emphasized the slave's Christianity. Probably the practice of catechizing and then converting slaves led a few masters to free their slaves.[28] But throughout the seventeenth century, the Dutch were careful not to equate conversion with freedom. In 1649, several white New Netherland residents petitioned the Dutch Estates General in Holland for the freedom of several Christian African children enslaved by the Dutch West India Company. The company admitted openly to having kept enslaved several black children whose parents were free Christians, "though it is contrary to the laws of every people that any one born to a free Christian mother should be a slave and be compelled to remain in servitude." Although the company eventually freed these children, company officials were careful to state that this was done to appease their parents, who had been loyal slaves before gaining their freedom, not because the children were Christians. The Dutch Church ceased baptism of slaves in 1655.[29]

Slaves' use of government and the law led to their greatest successes in achieving freedom in New Amsterdam. They employed their knowledge of legal rights and procedures to petition for freedom. African slaves' knowledge of and belief in their rights probably came from several sources. Those who were Atlantic Creoles may have had exposure to European legal methods prior to their arrival in New Amsterdam. Just as important, however, slaves may have had a sense of their rights due to their African backgrounds. In Angola, whence many of New Amsterdam's blacks may have come, slaves could hold a variety of statuses and occupations, and many could look forward to freedom for themselves or their children as a reward for loyalty. They may have brought these expectations with them to the Americas. Finally, in New Amsterdam itself, for slaves who used the courts to protect their property rights, it was only a small step to use legal methods to pursue their own freedom.[30]

Thus, in 1644, slaves began bargaining for their freedom. In February of that year, the first eleven company slaves brought to New Amsterdam petitioned the colony's Director General, William Kieft, for their freedom and that of their families. A combination of factors made this an especially propitious time for their request. The Dutch were in the midst of Kieft's three-year war against the Native Americans. The costs of the war, combined with a severe winter, had prevented the colonists from utilizing slave labor efficiently. Further, the colonists believed they would have to rely on the loyalty of black slaves in upcoming battles. Rather than risk that these eleven slaves, and perhaps others, would join the Native Americans, the company offered the eleven what became known as "half-freedom." Kieft and the Council of New Netherland gave them certificates that "release[d] for the term of their natural lives, [the eleven] and their Wives from Slavery." The Dutch gave them land so that they could "earn their livelihood by agriculture." As a condition of their freedom, they had to labor for the company in times of need and pay an annual tribute in furs, produce, or wampum. If they failed to pay tribute or to labor for the company, they were subject to re-enslavement. Further, the condition of half-freedom could not be passed on to their children, who remained slaves.[31]

The company clearly benefited from this arrangement. Theoretically, New Netherland retained a loyal reserve labor force without responsibility for supporting them. The small amount of goods that the half-free blacks had to give the company guaranteed that they would continue to be productive laborers and would not burden the colony. And both the land grant and the retention of their children as slaves guaranteed that the half-free blacks would remain in the colony.[32] For blacks also, the benefits and limitations of half-freedom were clear. Overall, the requirements to give goods and services to the company do not appear to have been onerous. Ownership of land was a vital element of freedom for anyone in colonial America, black or white. Land provided the foundation for subsistence for individuals and families and could be the basis for entry into the market and the production of greater wealth. In the case of the half-free blacks, the land grants also provided the basis for a relatively independent community. They lived together in families with their wives, if not always with their children. The land they held, near the Fresh Water Pond, was the first geographically designated black community in New York City (fig. 1). Other black men and women, freed by the company or by individual slave owners under similar arrangements, joined the original eleven near the Fresh Water Pond so that by 1664 there were at least thirty black landowners on Manhattan Island. Travelers noted the thriving group of blacks who resided "upon both sides of [the broad way] . . . where they have ground enough to live with their families." Although the original community eventually migrated away from the stricter racial regime of the British in the eighteenth century, Europeans and African Americans continually reinscribed the area, literally and figuratively, as a center of historical importance to blacks. During the 1741 slave conspiracy, the British executed slaves there for their participation in the plot. And by the Civil War, the land was the center of the Five Points, an interracial neighborhood of free blacks and Irish.[33]

But half-freedom contained two important limitations. These limits marked the difference between African and European bondpeople. Upon completion of their indentures, the colony gave whites land and *full* freedom. Their service to the colony was rooted in their new status as citizens and was not required in the same way as that of blacks. Although they could be reindentured, such circumstances occurred only as a result of debt, and usually to individuals. But half-free blacks' service was rooted in the obligation necessary for them to retain their freedom, not to prove their citizenship. If they did not serve the colony as required, they could be re-enslaved. Additionally, the children of half-free blacks legally remained slaves. The children of indentured whites who gained their freedom were not subject to automatic indenturing. Ironically, in their petition the eleven men requested freedom because of a desire to take better care of their families, claiming that "it [was] impossible for them to support their wives and children, as they have been accustomed to do, if they must continue in the Company's service."[34] Although Kieft and the council acknowledged the family ties of the men by freeing their wives, the company's right to enslave their children indicated white colonists' limits in respecting black families as they calculated their potential labor needs.

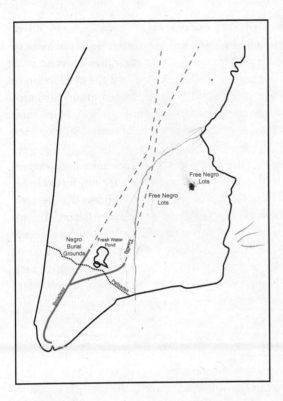

Fig. 1 The "Free Negro Lots"
in seventeenth-century New
Amsterdam. Map by Sarah
Zingarelli.

Throughout the latter half of the seventeenth century, the half-free parents of slave children attempted to negotiate full freedom for them, through baptism, petitioning, and other methods. It is unclear how many of these children Europeans held as slaves, separated from their parents. In 1649, the Dutch West India Company claimed that only three children had been separated from their parents. The company also tried to place the children on the same legal footing as their parents, claiming that they were only "to serve the Company whenever it pleased" and were not subject to permanent enslavement. Whether or not this was the practice in New Netherland for other children remains unclear.[35]

What is clear is that black parents wanted greater control over their families and less ambiguous terms of freedom for themselves and their children. Thus, throughout Dutch rule, half-free blacks continued to petition for full freedom for themselves, their children, and others in New Amsterdam. Although more privileged than enslaved blacks, half-free blacks remained tied to the slave community through kinship and friendship. Half-free blacks sometimes adopted orphaned slave children and negotiated for their freedom. In the early 1640s, Dorothe Angola adopted her godson, Anthony, after his half-free parents died. In 1661, Dorothe Angola's husband, Emmanuel Pietersen, petitioned the Director General and the Council of New Netherland to declare the boy free. Although the boy's parents had been half-free, the child was legally still a slave. Dorothe and Emmanuel wanted Anthony to be able to inherit their property, including land, upon their deaths. This was possible only if the child were declared half-free, which the company agreed to do.[36]

Even when unable to pass on their half-free status to their children, parents and guardians tried to give them the best opportunities available for a more comfortable life. Half-free black parents and guardians arranged apprenticeships for their children. Maria Portogys indentured her daughter to Maria Becker as a household servant. Susanna Robberts apprenticed her younger brother Jochim Robberts to Wolphert Webber. Although it is not clear what occupation Jochim was to learn, Webber was to pay him wages, board, and clothes and teach him to read and write. In these instances, black parents retained control over their children regardless of the legal limitations of half-freedom.[37]

Thus, under Dutch rule, enslaved and half-free black people negotiated with Euro-Americans for greater autonomy. The uneven Dutch attitude toward slavery in New Amsterdam and the knowledge of European and African ways that slaves brought to the colony enabled some blacks to successfully negotiate limited freedom before Dutch rule ended in 1664. Had the Dutch retained control of New Netherland, they probably would have increased their restrictions on the lives of slaves and free blacks, as happened in other North American colonies in the late seventeenth and early eighteenth centuries. But in 1664, the British took over the colony of New Netherland, resolving the century-long struggle between the Dutch and British over ownership of the territory. The British government awarded the colony to the Duke of York, who renamed both New Netherland and New Amsterdam New York. In 1663, just before the British took over the colony, the Dutch granted unconditional emancipation to half-free blacks in the colony, who numbered about seventy-five. Their children were probably included in this number.[38]

With British rule, slavery in New York gained a new stringency, and free blacks, too, were affected by the new rulers' desire to control slaves. British colonists' concern with regulating slavery resulted from Britain's increasing involvement in the African slave trade. The Duke of York held a controlling interest in the Royal African Company, which sought to make the New York colony a major market for slaves. Colonial officials encouraged the company's trade in New York by removing the property tax on slaves and imposing tariffs on imported slaves that favored African imports over those from other North American and Carribean colonies.[39]

While encouraging African slave imports, the British administration expended little effort to attract European free workers or indentured servants to the colony. As a result, few Europeans entered the New York labor market; rather, many attempted to establish independent farms or businesses. More Europeans went to Pennsylvania, which they perceived as having a better market for indentured servants and free laborers and, more important, better opportunities to own land. Thus, the British continued the reliance on African slave labor as the foundation of New York's colonial working class. Between 1698 and 1738, the slave population increased at a faster rate than did the white population in the colony. The value of slaves also rose with increased demand for their labor. In 1687, a healthy male slave sold for sixteen pounds; in 1700, forty pounds; and by 1720, sixty pounds. By 1760, healthy male slaves sold for one hundred pounds.[40]

In 1665, the Royal African Company's desire to increase the number of slaves in New York and its reliance on their labor led the British to create the colony's first laws regulating slavery. The creation of these laws paralleled developments in Virginia and other southern colonies, signifying the entrenchment of slavery throughout mainland North America. These laws also laid the groundwork for making slavery and African heritage synonymous, completely separating it from its previous religious justification in which, at least theoretically, any non-Christians could be enslaved. The British desire to legalize enslavement of Africans without regard to their status as Christians reflected the greater sense among the British that Africans were inferior. Most of the Africans that the British came into contact with in the slave trade were not acculturated in European ways, or became acculturated only as a result of enslavement, and then limitedly. British slave owners reinforced these ideas by largely refusing to convert blacks to Christianity, either in Africa or in the Americas, and by controlling and often limiting the degree of acculturation of slaves under their control. The experience of the Middle Passage itself—from the capture of Africans to their "storage" in slave "castles," or warehouses, on the African coast to the "tight packing" of slave cargoes en route to America—reinforced the British belief that Africans were lesser humans, subject to enslavement.[41]

New York's first laws stated that no Christians could be enslaved unless they had willingly sold themselves into slavery or had been captured in war.

Initially, Christian Native Americans and Africans were subject to the same law: they could be enslaved only as spoils of war. But increasingly the British placed Africans, Christian and non-Christian, in a class by themselves. By 1679, the provincial assembly, fearing retribution from the Native American tribes that lived in the colony, stated that no "native inhabitants" of the colony could be enslaved; Native Americans who had been enslaved outside the colony could be brought to the colony and remain slaves. But in 1706, the British excluded even this small number of Native Americans from slavery: the assembly passed a law stating that "Negroes only shall be slaves." The 1706 law also formally discounted religion in determining enslavement. The provincial assembly's law stated that "baptism shall not alter the condition of servitude of the Negro slave." This legally sundered the already tenuous connection between Christianity and freedom for African slaves. And in the same law, the British insured the hereditary nature of slavery by having children inherit their mothers' condition of slavery or freedom.[42]

Thus, by the first decade of the eighteenth century, the British had affirmed in law hereditary African slavery in the New York colony. But the economic role of slaves in the colony before mid-century was less clear. The Royal African Company and colony leaders wished to establish slaves as the leading labor force and to use New York as a major port for the shipment of slaves. But slave masters in New York City did not wish to buy large numbers of untrained or unseasoned slaves directly from Africa, as did slave masters in the southern colonies at this time. New York's economy grew slowly at the beginning of the eighteenth century and had no need for large numbers of unskilled laborers, slave or otherwise. Those colonists who did purchase slaves preferred small numbers of acculturated or skilled slaves, whom they could train for various businesses such as tailoring, carpentry, and sail making. Estate owners in rural areas of the colony who also might have bought unskilled slaves did not improve their acreage for agriculture on a large scale until later in the century.[43] Those estate owners who did wish to gain income from their land accepted European tenants, who worked the land in smaller plots or harvested timber or furs and paid fixed rents or portions of crops to the estate landlords. For example, Adolph Philipse, one of the largest slave owners in the colony, had eleven hundred European tenants on his ninety thousand acres of Hudson Valley land, but only twenty-three slaves.[44]

Thus, the Royal African Company's attempts to sell in Manhattan large cargoes of slaves directly from Africa at fixed prices, as it did in plantation areas, initially failed. Between 1664 and 1737, the company sold only 2,031 slaves there. By 1720, the New York colony contained only 5,740 slaves, compared to 12,499 in Maryland and 26,550 in Virginia. Still, New York held the largest number of slaves in the North—its closest northern rival was New Jersey, with 2,385 slaves in 1720.[45] The Royal African Company then began importing the vast majority of New York's slaves (70 percent) from the West Indies, as payment from West Indian merchants for provisions they had purchased from New York merchants. These seasoned, acculturated, and perhaps semiskilled slaves were bought by merchants and skilled trades-men in the city and by farmers on the outskirts. Between the 1720s and late 1730s, the number of slaves in Manhattan rose from under 1,400 to al-most 1,600.[46]

After 1737, the Manhattan port experienced a large increase in trade, generating a need for unskilled labor. At the same time, wars in Europe ham-pered the flow of European immigrants. The importation of slaves escalated to meet the city's demand for unskilled labor. In the thirty-four-year period between 1737 and 1771, the Royal African Company imported 4,394 slaves into Manhattan—more than double the number of slaves imported during the previous seventy-three years. Additionally, the ratio of African to Carib-bean slaves reversed after 1741: 70 percent of the imports were from Africa, 30 percent from the Caribbean. The number of slaves in the colony—just over 19,000—still lagged far behind the over 250,000 slaves in the Chesa-peake region. But New York had far and away the most slaves of the north-ern colonies—New Jersey's population was only 8,220, while Pennsylvania and Connecticut had 5,561 and 5,698, respectively. And the New York col-ony held more slaves at this time than either Georgia or Louisiana.[47] By the mid-eighteenth century, New York held the largest number of slaves of any colony north of Maryland, and Manhattan held the third largest concentra-tion of slaves in a North American city, after Charleston and New Orleans.[48]

Slaves brought to Manhattan reflected a variety of backgrounds. The Royal African Company imported slaves from the British Caribbean islands of Jamaica, Barbados, and Antigua. Dutch merchants continued to import some slaves from the Caribbean island of Curaçao. Slaves directly from Af-rica came from the Gold Coast, the Bight of Benin, the Bight of Biafra, and the Congo. Most identifiable in the historical record from their participation in the 1712 slave revolt are members of the Akan-Asante and Popo nations, but members of the Moko, Ibo, Yoruba, Adra, Jon, and Ibibio nations also ar-rived in Manhattan.[49] Between the 1670s and 1690s, the Philipse and Van Horne clans, two of the New York colony's elite families, traded with pirates for slaves from Madagascar. Between 1715 and 1717, about four hundred additional slaves from East Africa also landed in New York, when the East India Company opened its East African slave trade to private traders. The

Philipses and Van Hornes were among these private traders, and they hoped to sell the East African slaves in the Caribbean. When they were unable to do so, the excess human cargo came to Manhattan.[50] Between the 1680s and 1750, when British privateers captured free Spanish subjects during wars between Britain and Spain, they assumed these subjects to be slaves because of their dark skin and sold them into slavery in Manhattan. It is unclear how many of these so-called Spanish Negroes the British enslaved in this way, but in 1740, the Spanish government's threats to treat English prisoners of war as slaves slowed the practice, and after 1750 there were no more such enslavements.[51]

Under Dutch rule, the Dutch West India Company owned most of the colony's slaves. In contrast, ownership of slaves in British New York spread widely among the white population. From the merchant elite to small businessmen, owning slaves was a profitable enterprise. Overall in Manhattan, 40 percent of European households owned slaves, averaging 2.4 slaves per household. The ward with the highest concentration of slave owners, Dock Ward—between the East River, Prince Street, and Broad Street—contained the wharves, warehouses, and homes of English and French merchants. Seventy percent of the households there held slaves, and the average number of slaves per household was 2.2. Fifty-four percent of Dock Ward slaves lived in households containing only one slave, many of whom were female domestics. The area with the smallest percentage of slave-owning households (less than 20 percent), was the North Ward, home to less-prosperous Europeans and isolated physically and financially from the growing market in African slaves along the docks and in the markets of lower Manhattan (fig. 2). In a pattern similar to that in Dock Ward, 45 percent of slaves in North Ward lived in single-slave households.[52]

Because of the wide distribution of slaves among Manhattan's households, slaves performed every type of labor that free whites did. Particularly before mid-century, Europeans employed slave men in skilled occupations such as carpentry, tailoring, blacksmithing, shoemaking, baking, and butchering. As the need for laborers to service ships and warehouses increased after mid-century, larger numbers of male slaves were employed on the docks. Slave women, usually no more than one per household, aided white women (free and indentured) with cooking, cleaning, and child care. In artisan households, slave women, like the white women of artisan families, assisted the men in their skilled tasks as necessary. In the rural hinterlands, slave men and women performed agricultural work but also learned skilled jobs. As self-contained units, farms depended on their male laborers to be

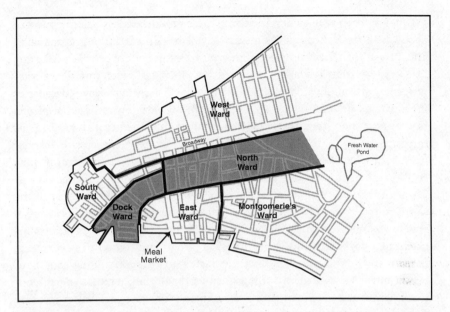

Fig. 2 Dock Ward had the highest concentration of slaves in British New York; North Ward, the lowest. Map by Sarah Zingarelli.

able to build or repair buildings, shoe horses, and perform other kinds of skilled labor necessary to operating an agricultural enterprise. Slave women might make clothing and even weave fabric. Thus, both rural and urban slaves had exposure to a variety of skilled and unskilled occupations.[53]

Slave masters in New York also devised another way to profit from their slaves: they hired them out for day labor on the docks of New York City, or to those who needed skilled labor for only a few days or weeks. By 1711, the Meal Market on the east side of Manhattan (see fig. 2) had become a daily fair for hiring slaves. Wealthier whites in Dock Ward sometimes held groups of slaves on consignment, gambling on the possibility that there would be a need for slave labor in the city or the colony from which they could benefit. While awaiting buyers, slaveholders hired out these consignment slaves for day labor, thus generating income even if a sale did not take place. In rural areas, too, masters hired out slaves to neighboring farms, or even to those needing labor in the city. Because of the types of labor usually needed, masters more often hired out slave men than slave women. Some slaves, such as Jack, owned by the Lloyd family of Long Island, lived in New York City practically as free men, hiring themselves out and returning part of their wages to their owners.[54]

As had been true under Dutch rule, white workers continued to worry about the effects of competition with slave labor. In 1686, the licensed porters of New York City complained that the employment of slaves in the markets cut into their laboring opportunities. Although New York City's local governing body, the Common Council, banned the use of slaves as porters for imported or exported goods, apparently few slave owners paid attention to the restriction. In 1691 the porters again complained that they were "so impoverished . . . they could not by their labours get a competency for the maintenance of themselves and families."[55] Skilled workers, too, feared competition from slaves. In 1737 and again in 1743, New York's coopers complained to the colonial government that "the pernicious custom of breeding slaves to trade" reduced "the honest and industrious tradesmen . . . to poverty for want of employ." They complained that New York City merchants used their slaves to build barrels for themselves and sometimes even competed with the coopers by selling the barrels to others. Although the lieutenant governor agreed with the skilled workers, they were unable to convince New York's Colonial Assembly to pass protective legislation favoring them over slave owners. Only cartmen successfully excluded blacks, slave and free, from their trade.[56]

The increased use of slave labor in the New York colony benefited slave owners at the expense of free white workers. The widespread use of slave labor was part of the reason that relatively few indentured servants chose Manhattan as a destination. Although exact numbers are unavailable for much of the colonial period, passenger lists of Europeans traveling from Europe and the Caribbean to the Americas reveal that few indentured servants listed Manhattan as their destination. Even the trade in convict servants appears to have favored the Chesapeake rather than Manhattan. New Yorkers at the time believed that the low numbers of indentured servants relative to other colonies was due to the presence of large numbers of slaves. In 1712, probably in response to fears inspired by the slave revolt that year, Governor Robert Hunter recommended to the colonial legislature "that some good law be passed, for putting slaves under a better regulation, and to encourage the importation of white servants." New York's colonial governor William Cosby said in 1734, "I see with concern that whilst the neighboring Provinces are filled with honest, useful and labourious white people, the truest riches and surest strength of a country, this Province seems regardless of . . . the disadvantages that attend the too great importation of negroes and convicts." The classification of blacks with convicts despite the fact that the colony held few, if any, convict laborers reveals the low repute in which some Europeans held slaves both with respect to their morals and as laborers. In

1757 Lieutenant Governor James De Lancey urged the colonial legislature to place a poll tax on slaves to discourage their purchase. Declining numbers of slaves would "naturally tend to introduce white servants, which will augment the strength of the country."[57] But the colony never enacted restrictions on the importation of slaves.

White New Yorkers' reliance on black labor profoundly affected the family and community lives of blacks. The wide distribution of slaves among white households meant that many Manhattan slaves lived in single-slave households, which limited their ability to form families. Black women in particular were bound to their masters' households, venturing out only to market. Black men had more mobility, traveling to and from work on the docks of Manhattan, but they did not necessarily meet black women on such journeys. In addition, in a departure from Dutch rule, and in striking contrast to nineteenth-century, southern slave masters, most Manhattan slave masters actively discouraged their slaves from marrying or having children. Urban slave owners living in limited spaces prized barren slave women and warned buyers of those women who seemed fecund. One owner offered his female slave for sale because "she breeds too fast for her owner to put up with such inconvenience." Another owner advertised his slave as better suited to the desires of New York's slave owners: "she has been married for several years without having a child." Because of the discouraging attitudes of slave masters, and perhaps also because of black women's unwillingness to bear children in such a difficult environment, the Manhattan slave community under British rule had a relatively low birthrate, despite the presence of large numbers of black women of childbearing age.[58]

New York's lawmakers also attempted to limit interactions among slaves in the city. Between 1681 and 1683, New York City's Common Council passed a series of laws restricting unsupervised activities among slaves and among slaves, whites, and free blacks. Laws prohibited slaves from leaving their masters' houses without permission, possessing weapons of any kind, and gathering in groups of four or more. The Common Council forbade whites and free blacks from entertaining slaves in their homes, selling them liquor, or taking goods or money from them. With this last restriction, lawmakers sought to prevent slaves from stealing items from their masters and others and selling them. In 1692, new laws mandated that slaves who made loud noises, played in the street on Sundays, or patronized bars receive twenty lashes, or their owners pay a fine of six shillings. In 1700, the city government reduced the number of slaves who could gather in groups to less than three and again reminded masters to control their slaves on Sundays.[59]

Through such regulations, New York lawmakers sought to control the

cultural, social, and political independence of slaves. In part, whites wished
to preserve a cultural and economic distance between themselves and slaves.
Throughout the eighteenth century and into the nineteenth, whites increasingly sought to differentiate clearly between slavery and freedom; workers
in particular distinguished themselves from slave laborers.[60] That only small
numbers of European indentured servants traveled to eighteenth-century
New York exaggerated the distinction between enslaved blacks and free
white laborers. Unlike Pennsylvania or Massachusetts, where large numbers
of indentured servants composed a vital part of the working class, few European immigrants to New York experienced bondage and thus were less likely
to identify with slaves. In this way, the labor system in eighteenth-century
New York City resembled that of the southern colonies, which also experienced the arrival of a large number of slaves at the expense of European
immigration.[61]

Distinctions between the few indentured Europeans in New York and
slaves also increased in the eighteenth century. As Europeans survived their
indentures in larger numbers, the similarities between their temporary
bondage and blacks' permanent enslavement diminished. Colonial laws after 1712 exacerbated these differences by discouraging masters from freeing slaves and prohibiting blacks freed after 1712 from acquiring land. For
blacks, the New York colony legally could not be a place of opportunity
or upward mobility. These laws tied distinctions between black and white
workers even more strongly to slavery and freedom, dependency and self-
sufficiency. Slave masters saw these racial and status distinctions as a means
to keep control over their slaves and thus encouraged the growing division
between white and black workers. White workers saw such distinctions as
preserving their own access to wage work and to land, at the expense of
slaves and free blacks.[62]

Many New York City whites, particularly slave owners, held contradictory views of the degree of acculturation and dependence they wanted of
their slaves. Slave owners at times sought to limit slaves' access to elements
of European culture that might improve their status in the eyes of the community or improve their sense of self-worth, but these limitations clashed
with the possibility that educating slaves could make them more useful and
valuable. The struggle between the Society for the Propagation of the Gospel
(SPG) and Manhattan slave masters over the religious education of slaves
demonstrates this contradiction. The first SPG minister to slaves, Elias Neau,
held the post from 1705 until his death in 1722. Neau established a school in
which he instructed slaves in the tenets of Christianity and taught them to
read and write, which was not illegal in Manhattan as it would become in

parts of the antebellum South. In fact, a few masters may have desired that their slaves learn such skills so that they could assist them in their business operations. The majority of slaves in SPG schools tended to be women; for wealthy slave owners, educating their female domestic servants became a mark of high status.[63]

But most slave masters believed that a religious education leading to the conversion of slaves at best distracted slaves from their work and at worst encouraged rebelliousness. Many slave masters were not very religious and saw little value in attending church themselves, much less sending their slaves to religious schools. Masters were also reluctant to release adult slaves from work to attend Neau's classes; most students in the schools were children too young to work. But masters' biggest fear was that education and conversion to Christianity would encourage slaves to seek freedom.[64]

In fact, a 1706 law stated explicitly that converting slaves to Christianity would not lead to freedom. Additionally, slaves were second-class citizens in the eighteenth-century Anglican church. Between 1707 and 1764, 869 slaves were baptized at Trinity Church, the main Anglican congregation in New York, but the church accepted only 19 of these as full members. Other Christian denominations in New York City had even less interest in educating and converting slaves than did the Anglicans. The Dutch Reformed Church, still present in the city despite being weakened by the British takeover, continued to disallow slave conversions. Quakers, many of whom were slave owners, did not proselytize generally and did not welcome their own slaves or other blacks into their churches.[65] But such realities did not appease the fears of slave owners. Throughout the eighteenth century and into the nineteenth, Christianity, despite its mobilization by slave owners on behalf of slavery, remained potentially revolutionary in the hands of slaves and their allies. The teaching that every soul was equal in the sight of God could lead some to claim racial equality on earth. Thus, those few adult slaves who tried to attend Neau's classes in defiance of their masters were threatened with sale out of the colony. The 1712 slave revolt further discredited Neau's efforts when two of the rebels were erroneously labeled his students. Subsequent SPG ministers had even less success than Neau in converting slaves.[66]

Although eighteenth-century slave masters often deemed Christianity too dangerous an influence on their slaves, they saw other elements of European culture as enhancing their slaves' value. Artisans were more likely to buy slaves with facility in European languages and teach them skilled crafts; New York's slaves spoke English, French, Dutch, and Spanish as well as African languages. Some slave masters encouraged the independence some slaves displayed in arranging for their own hiring-out contracts, although

such independence gave these slaves greater knowledge of their surround-
ings and opportunities to run away.[67]

Ultimately, masters could not completely control slaves' acceptance or
rejection of European culture or the uses to which slaves put their knowledge. Slaves used both European and African cultural practices in ways that
mitigated their enslavement and sometimes led to rebellion. The presence
of Africans from multiple linguistic groups led slaves to adapt one or more
European languages in combination with African languages to form a common language amongst themselves. Masters' lack of interest in exposing
slaves to Christianity gave some slaves the space to continue to follow their
African religious beliefs. Conjurers such as Peter the Doctor, a free black in
Manhattan, and Doctor Harry from Nassau, Long Island, indicate the existence of African religious beliefs and practices. These beliefs were sustained
in the eighteenth century not only by the continual influx of slaves from
Africa, but also of slaves from the Caribbean, where African traditions were
stronger than in the North American colonies.[68]

Like acculturation and education, the continued use of African names
in British New York was a double-edged sword for masters and slaves. For
the British, African names such as Ambo, Zibia, Yaff, Quam, Coffe or Cuffee, Cajoe, and Mingo underlined the cultural distinctions between Europeans and Africans and helped justify enslavement. Some African names,
such as Sambo and Quaco, evolved in the European consciousness and pro-
nunciation as derogatory. Historian Peter Wood has shown that in South
Carolina the Hausa name Sambo evolved into a derogatory term for a black
man, indicating laziness or stupidity. But among the Hausa, it was simply
the name given to the second son of the family. Similarly, Quaco was a day
name, given to men born on Wednesday, but some New York masters transformed it to Quack. Even some British names given to slaves could have been
African in origin. While some masters transformed Quaco to Quack, others
transformed it to Jack.[69] For slave masters, African names were derogatory,
or meaningless, but for slaves, such names could be valuable links to their
African past. Further, they were often the surface indications of deeper community connections among slaves in Manhattan—connections that, in the
pressure cooker that was slavery, sometimes provided the unity necessary
for rebellion.

Slave masters, more concerned with obtaining labor from their slaves
than with making them firmly African or European, did allow slaves some
leeway in self-expression. But the safety valve of manumission for good
behavior did not exist in British New York, as it had under the Dutch. As

slavery became more restrictive under the British, slaves expressed their discontent through various forms of resistance during the eighteenth century. Tensions between masters and slaves cycled up and down as masters attempted to pacify their slaves without freeing them, and slaves, frustrated by these piecemeal methods, resisted and rebelled against their enslavement. Such resistance and rebellion led to greater restrictions, as well as brutal physical punishments, until masters again felt comfortable and safe enough to offer slaves limited autonomy.[70]

Under British rule, slaves stole more cash, clothing, and food from masters' households and ran away more frequently than they had under the Dutch. In defiance of the laws, slaves continued to gather in groups and after curfew, sometimes with the aid of lower-class whites who turned their homes into illegal taverns for slaves. Laboring whites also assisted slaves in selling stolen property.[71] Individual slaves sometimes openly defied white authority. On an August evening in 1696, the mayor of New York attempted to disperse a group of slaves. When he threatened to take them into custody, one of them, Prince, struck him in the face. The mayor quickly made Prince an example: The next day, the slave was stripped, tied to a cart, and dragged around the perimeter of the city. At each street corner, he received eleven lashes.[72]

More frightening to whites than such individual acts of resistance was the threat of slave revolt. In April 1712, a group of New York City slaves attempted an insurrection. At 2 A.M. on a Sunday morning, twenty-four slaves gathered, armed with guns, axes, knives, and other weapons. The group included at least two women, one who was the wife of one of the rebels and another who was pregnant. The rebels set fire to the outhouse of Peter Vantilborough, a baker who owned two of the slaves. Through the nineteenth century, arson was an important weapon of slave rebels throughout the Americas. Residents of closely built, wood-frame cities like New York feared the destructiveness of fire. Halting the flames depended on bucket brigades of water from nearby wells or rivers, and swift action. If the winds were against them, however, such brigades could not save neighborhoods, businesses, and even whole towns from going up in flames.[73]

When whites arrived to put out the Vantilborough fire, the slaves ambushed them. In all, the rebels killed nine whites and wounded seven. But New York's colonial militia and British troops quickly outnumbered the slave rebels. The slaves tried to flee the city, but many of them were new arrivals who were not familiar enough with the area to effect a successful escape. Additionally, the rebels were unable to convince other slaves to join them once the rebellion was underway.[74] Realizing that they were to be captured, at least six rebels committed suicide. During the following investigation, colonial officials arrested seventy blacks, convicted twenty-six, and executed as many as twenty-one.[75]

The rebellion resulted from the presence of groups of African slaves in New York who had different expectations of slavery than did the British. These slaves may also have had different expectations than did the charter generations imported into Manhattan by the Dutch.[76] New Yorkers identified the majority of the rebels as Koromantine and Pawpaw Africans, part of the large groups of Africans who arrived in New York City between 1710 and 1712. Koromantine and Pawpaw Africans trained the men in their communities in the conduct of guerrilla warfare. These Africans' knowledge of slavery in Africa entailed more rights and privileges than accorded to slaves in British North America. In the Akan-Asante society from which these slaves came, slaves or their children could eventually be absorbed into the community as equals. Masters rewarded faithful slaves with the opportunity to inherit land and to work for themselves. Not every slave experienced such privileges, but the possibility of such rewards eased the condition of slavery there. Under slavery in British New York City, only a very few of the more acculturated slaves would have been eligible for any privileges. And for slaves generally, acculturated or not, there were fewer privileges in New York than in Africa. New York's slaves had little hope of escaping slavery or of being incorporated into the community as equals.[77]

African slaves' lack of privileges was not the only spark to rebellion. At least two "Spanish Negroes" who considered themselves unfairly enslaved also participated in the revolt. The British took "Hosey" (probably José) and John (probably Juan) from a captured Spanish privateer in 1706. Although the men protested that they were free Spanish citizens, their skin color led the British to dismiss their claims and sell them into slavery, just as the Dutch had done with the Spanish captives aboard the French privateer *La Garce* in 1642. For Hosey and John, the revolt was both revenge and a means to gain freedom.[78] Some acculturated black slaves also participated in the rebellion. They may have been inspired by the African and Spanish slaves or dismayed by the differences in rule between Dutch and British slave masters. At least one free black, Peter the Doctor, participated in the rebellion. A religious leader who used African practices, Peter the Doctor "gave [the slaves] a powder to rub on their Cloths" to "make them invulnerable." His participation indicates the continued presence of social, cultural, and political relationships between slaves and the dwindling free black population in Manhattan.[79]

In addition to executing numerous slaves, white New Yorkers responded to the rebellion by passing laws further limiting the activities of slaves and free blacks. The Common Council lengthened the curfew for slaves: no slave over the age of fourteen was to be on New York City streets after sunset without a lantern by which he or she could be clearly seen. Any slave breaking this law could be arrested by any white and lashed thirty-nine times. To encourage masters to enforce the law, the council fined masters of disobedient slaves and made them pay the costs of jail, court, and the public whipper.[80] New laws also made it more difficult for masters to manumit their slaves. Those wishing to free a slave had to pay a two-hundred-pound security—four to five times the price of an adult male slave, and five to six times that of an adult female slave. Ostensibly, this deposit prevented the newly freed slave from becoming dependent on the community for his or her livelihood. In fact, the law discouraged the growth of the free black community in New York.[81]

Although Peter the Doctor was the only free black brought to trial for participation in the rebellion, New York City whites linked the uprising to the example of liberty set by Manhattan's free blacks. Thus, the Common Council, in addition to limiting the number of slaves who could legally achieve freedom, took steps to limit the rights of free blacks and to limit interactions between free blacks and slaves. Slaves freed after 1712 could not own real estate. The laws penalized both free blacks and whites who entertained slaves or sold them alcohol but fined free blacks at twice the rate of whites. These restrictions, as well as the general suspicion whites held against free blacks, made New York City an increasingly hostile place for free blacks. As early as 1682, free blacks in New York City had expressed their displeasure with the British regime. When the Dutch attempted to recapture the island of Manhattan that year, some free black landowners declared their allegiance to the Dutch monarch. After Holland failed to repossess the city, a group of free blacks, including the DeVries and Manuels families, sold their land in New York and bought land outside the city, between Piermont, New York, and Harrington Park, New Jersey. Descendants of these families lived on the land through the eighteenth century. But black land-owning families who remained in New York City were not so fortunate. By 1738, Luycas Pieters, a descendant of a slave freed and given land by the Dutch, had lost his land and his freedom. He lived as an indentured servant, and his sick wife was forced to turn to the almshouse for assistance. By the time of the American Revolution, whites owned many of the "free Negro lots" blacks had obtained under Dutch rule in Manhattan.[82]

White colonists also scrutinized each other in searching for reasons behind the 1712 revolt. The government increased restrictions on white men
and women who allied themselves with slaves and free blacks after 1712,
fining whites who entertained slaves or sold them alcohol. Ministers, lawmakers, and others exhorted slave masters to gain greater control over their
slaves. Some whites accused SPG school founder Elias Neau of aiding the
insurrectionists. Although the courts never charged him with a crime, some
whites attacked Neau as he walked about New York, and masters stopped
sending their slaves to him for instruction.[83]

But as the horror of the insurrection faded from memory, slaves and
masters again created a more lax slave regime than that dictated by the laws.
Probably the small numbers of slaves in individual households created a feeling of trust alongside slave owners' dependency on slave labor. Some whites
felt comfortable allowing their own slaves certain privileges, even as they
criticized other slave owners for not maintaining control of their property.
Skilled slaves in particular achieved greater autonomy by leveraging the
need for their labor and their closeness to the artisan masters they worked
beside every day. Despite slave codes against drinking alcohol, assembling without white supervision, and theft, masters allowed skilled slaves to
indulge in these activities rather than risk having their valuable property
run away. [84]

Blacks also ameliorated their enslavement by becoming active participants in their own sales. In a number of cases slaves prevented their own
sales to new owners. Other slaves requested sales to certain owners in an
effort to be closer to wives, children, or friends. Often slaves themselves
sought out new owners, visiting potential masters and presenting their current owners with nearly completed sale arrangements. Masters granted such
privileges as an incentive to loyalty, but some owners allowed even troublesome slaves these opportunities. Esther Burr, mother of Aaron Burr, wrote
to a friend that "our Negroes are gone to seek a master. Really my dear I
shall be thankful if I can get rid of them." Individual negotiations for limited
autonomy tightened the bonds of slavery over all blacks. Few whites during
this period ever freed their slaves for "good behavior," preferring to parcel
out privileges in return for service.[85]

Blacks took advantage of other loopholes in the slave regime. When
white residents celebrated holidays such as Irish St. Patrick's Day or various
British royal holidays, slaves and free blacks used these opportunities to
gather also. Pinkster in particular became by the late eighteenth century as
much an African holiday as a European one, albeit with different meanings
for each group, with both races joining together to celebrate. Pinkster began

as the Dutch Reformed Church's feast of Pentecost, the day on which Christ's apostles received the Holy Spirit and spoke in tongues. Although the Dutch Reformed Church refused to accept black converts, this religiously based holiday became one arena in which Dutch and African New Yorkers joined together. Initially, the festival's emphasis on experiential, ecstatic religion opened a path for nonliterate blacks to participate in Protestant religion. The loose and festive atmosphere, in which whites drank and celebrated, also allowed blacks to practice their own African musical and religious traditions under cover of the festival and with the tacit approval of their masters. Blacks played drums, fiddles, and rattles, traditional African instruments of celebration. Before the Revolutionary War, blacks and whites celebrated the festival largely outside of New York City, in rural areas to which the Dutch had fled following the British takeover. In the late eighteenth century and early nineteenth, the festival was briefly popular in urban areas such as Albany and New York City. It also took on a more overtly political meaning as a "festival of misrule" in which blacks elected a man from their community governor for the day, with the power to adjudge disputes among whites and blacks. Often this "governor" was also a recognized political leader among blacks.[86]

Other holidays also served as a cover for blacks who wished to gather on their own, apart from whites. The most common "holiday" to serve this purpose was the weekly Sabbath. One New York City minister noted that while whites gathered in churches, "the Streets are full of Negroes who dance & divert themselves." Whites complained of this "profaning" of the Sabbath but were unable to control the actions of slaves without the help of masters, many of whom preferred to turn a blind eye to their slaves' activities during their leisure time.[87]

Slaves also gathered to bury their dead. Whites generally did not participate in the funerals of their slaves, although a few masters did bury their favorite slaves in the Anglican churchyard. Blacks themselves buried the vast majority of their dead in the "Negro burial ground" (fig. 3). Slaves gathered at the end of the day, after their work was done, to escort the body to the grave. Whites reported hearing drumming and chanting, no doubt African derived, at these independent ceremonies late into the night. By the 1720s, whites had become concerned about these unsupervised gatherings. The Common Council first ruled that funerals had to occur before sunset and then limited the number of mourners who could attend a slave's funeral to twelve, plus pallbearers and gravediggers.[88]

The easiest places for slaves to gather were the city's markets. As Graham Hodges has noted, West African slaves came from communities and cultures

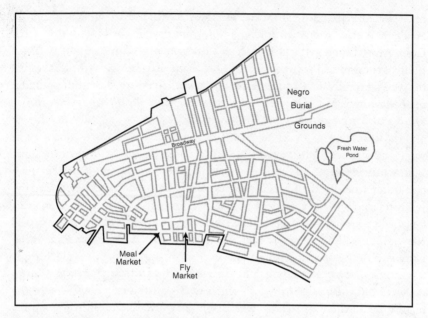

Fig. 3 Eighteenth-century New York City. Map by Sarah Zingarelli.

in which markets were important gathering places, and they brought these customs to New York. Slave women and men were able to combine errands for masters with socializing among themselves. Slaves from rural areas traveled to New York City markets to sell their masters' or their own produce. The city markets also provided cover for those slaves and whites who participated in the sale of stolen goods. Whites knew that slaves stole items from their masters and sold them in the city's markets and taverns, but many whites implicitly or explicitly encouraged the practice. Some had no problem buying from slaves, even when the goods appeared to have been stolen. Some masters may have ignored thefts from their own households, seeing it as a way to keep their slaves relatively happy. Other masters allowed or encouraged slaves to steal from others in return for a share of the proceeds. And of course, whites who served as fences for goods stolen by slaves had no reason to report the thefts.[89]

City laws dictated severe punishments for slaves who stole, including public whippings and death, but masters rarely allowed their slaves to be punished to the full extent of the law. Further, such punishments could strengthen bonds among slaves. In 1736, baker John Vaarck's slave Caesar, merchant John Auboyneau's slave Prince, and several others broke into a tavern and stole several barrels of gin, known as Geneva. Although they could have been executed for the crime, the slaves were instead publicly whipped. After their trial and punishment, the slaves became known as the Geneva Club. New Yorkers named another group of slaves the Smith Fly Boys after their participation in the theft and sale of goods near the Fly Market (see fig. 3). The reluctance of whites to prosecute these slaves to the fullest extent of the law indicates their acceptance of such forms of day-to-day resistance as a necessary price for holding slaves.[90]

Slave owners tolerated relationships that evolved between blacks and whites of similar status. Slaves worked alongside and spent their leisure time with white workers. Together, slaves, indentured servants, soldiers, sailors, and other workers frequented New York City's markets, docks, black- and white-owned taverns, and "tippling houses," private homes where individuals sold alcohol without licenses. In these places, black and white workers shared news from within the city as well as from around the Atlantic World, forging common political views as well as social networks.[91]

In 1741, a major conspiracy erupted out of these interracial gatherings. A group of African slaves, Spanish Negroes, and Irish and Anglo workers pledged to burn New York and seize the city for themselves. The conspiracy demonstrated that slaves and free workers could reach across differences in race and status to share class grievances and mobilize to overturn New York City's economic hierarchy.[92] On March 18, a slave named Quaco set fire to Fort George (fig. 4), destroying one of the most important forts in British North America and the New York colony's political and military center and ammunition storehouse. For the next three weeks a series of fires in homes, warehouses, and stables set the closely built wood-frame city on edge. The continuing threat put pressure on the government to find the arsonists. Unlike the arson of the 1712 slave rebellion, no slaves had attacked whites attempting to put out the fires. But slowly, townspeople began to suspect that the fires had been set by slaves. After one fire, coal believed to have been used by the arsonist was traced to a nearby house, casting suspicion on the slave who lived there. More damning, a white woman overheard Quaco say to two fellow slaves, "Fire, Fire, Scorch, Scorch, A LITTLE, damn it, BY-AND-BY." Finally, whites saw another slave, Cuffee, fleeing from a fire that destroyed the storehouse of his master, Adolph Philipse. His suspicious actions led the townspeople who had gathered to put out the fire to cry, "The negroes are rising!" They seized Cuffee and then began to sweep the streets of black men, arresting and imprisoning over one hundred.[93]

A four-month investigation revealed that the arson attacks were part of an extensive plan among an interracial group from the lower classes that sought to achieve greater economic and political equality. The plot centered

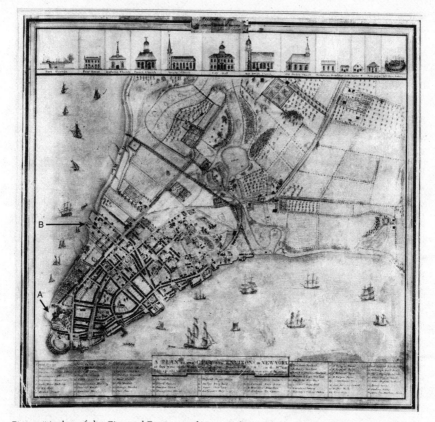

Fig. 4 "A plan of the City and Environs of New York, 1742–4," by David Grim, showing (A) Fort George, which was burned during the 1741 slave revolt, and (B) Hughson's Tavern, where the arsonists allegedly conspired. Neg. no. 3046. © Collection of the New-York Historical Society.

in a tavern owned by the Hughsons, a white family. The tavern and its patrons became the symbolic center of racial and class disorder in the city. A difficult winter on top of a five-year economic depression had embittered the suffering lower classes against wealthier whites. The Hughsons were typical of whites who had moved to New York from rural areas, attracted by the excitement of the city and hoping to make their fortunes. Although John Hughson would have been comfortable on the farm his family owned in Westchester County, his wife Sarah desired the city. On arrival, John's labors as a leather worker could not alone pay their bills; thus he and Sarah opened the tavern and sold items pilfered by slaves in an effort to become property owners. At the center of the fencing ring and the conspiracy were the slaves Caesar and Prince, prominent members of the Geneva Club. Both frequented the tavern, and John Hughson fenced small amounts of stolen goods for them. In addition, the Hughson's lodger, an Irishwoman named Margaret "Peggy" Kerry Sorubiero, was Caesar's girlfriend and was rumored to have had his child.[94]

· The fencing ring at the Hughsons' tavern provided the organizational center for the interracial band of conspirators. Within the group, the rebels also organized along lines of race and status, joining the plot to avenge particular grievances. The thirty to thirty-five Irish men and women who participated in the plot may have felt like outsiders in New York's increasingly Anglicized society.[95] For the majority of slave rebels, the specific grievance was enslavement: the conspirators hoped to become free by their actions. Slaves also resented masters who took privileges away from them. Quaco allegedly burned Fort George because his master prevented him from visiting his wife, who was cook in the governor's house inside the fort. As in the 1712 plot, African and African American slaves depended on West African religious and military practices. The slave rebels, many from the Akan or Gold Coast region of West Africa, swore war oaths "by thunder and lightning" and relied on Doctor Harry, perhaps an Akan shaman, to supply them with poison in the event of failure.[96]

Another group of slaves accused of being part of the plot were Spanish Negroes whom a British ship had captured in the Caribbean and sold into slavery in New York in 1740. These enslaved Spaniards had repeatedly declared that they were "free subjects of the King of Spain" and thus were prisoners of war, not slaves. At trial, they insisted on being called by their full Spanish names and separated themselves from African slaves, arguing that as free men, any testimony by blacks against them was inadmissible. However, the court used the testimony of black slaves and of the indentured servant Mary Burton to convict the men. One was executed, and four were banished from the colony.[97]

Although the plot was interracial in its organization, some elite New Yorkers used the conspiracy and the trial as an opportunity to argue the dangers of the slave system to New York society. New York Supreme Court Judge Daniel Horsmanden (who presided over the trials in the absence of Chief Justice James DeLancey), along with the colony's lieutenant governor, George Clarke, believed that both slavery and blacks harmed New York. Horsmanden saw slaves as "enemies of their own household," unreliable residents in New York City and in the homes of whites. Clarke viewed the large number of blacks in New York, particularly black men, as a troublesome social problem. He sided with white male skilled workers who felt threatened by competition from slave labor. New York, he stated, needed to be "replenished with white people." Both Horsmanden and Clarke saw the conspiracy and trials as an opportunity to convince white New Yorkers to rid the province of blacks, free and enslaved.[98]

In fact, the trials did rid the province of thirty slave men by execution, and over seventy slave men and women by expulsion from the colony.[99] But in general, New York's slave owners relied too heavily on slave labor to begin to end the system. Some tradesmen may have preferred to own slaves rather than hold indentured servants or apprentices who might later become their rivals in business.[100] Although some white workers may have feared competition with slave labor, it was easier for them to travel to another colony for work rather than try to fight the slave system in New York. Among those who stayed, some continued at times to ally themselves with slaves across lines of race and status. Others who remained in New York to seek their fortunes saw slave ownership as a sign of the prestige to which they aspired.[101]

Thus, rather than dismantle the slave system, New Yorkers again swung the pendulum of the law to restrict the activities of enslaved and free people. During the trials, ten tippling house owners were indicted and fined for entertaining blacks; after the trials, the Common Council passed stricter laws to regulate taverns and monitored curfews for blacks more closely.[102] The plot affected New York's blacks in a more serious way. The four-month period during which slaves accused each other of participation in the plot and the resulting death or deportation of over one hundred blacks damaged families and friendships among blacks. Slaveholders changed their patterns of slaveholding. Many were more reluctant to buy or hold on to male slaves. In 1737, there were slightly more males (52.2 percent) than females in the black population; in 1746, the first census after the conspiracy, the percentage of males had dropped to 46.6 percent. Adult women continued to form a larger percentage of the black population than men during the remainder of slavery's existence in New York, limiting blacks' ability to form families.[103]

The plot also influenced New York's slave merchants to import slaves directly from Africa. Slave masters believed that rebellious slaves from the West Indies had caused the 1741 revolt. Additionally, the increased demand for slaves in New York City in the second half of the eighteenth century could not be met by haphazard shipments from the West Indies. Between 1664 and 1737, just over 2,000 slaves were imported from Africa to New York City, and 70 percent of these were from the West Indies. But from 1737 to 1771, New Yorkers imported over twice as many slaves (4,394), 70 percent of whom were from Africa. The proportion of blacks in New York City's population remained high at almost 20 percent.[104]

Despite masters' attempts to control slaves more closely and prevent rebellion, slaves continued to agitate for greater autonomy while enslaved and for freedom from slavery. Despite laws against their gathering, slaves still frequented taverns, markets, dance halls, and other places. They continued to steal and fence goods, and in rural areas, whites claimed that bands of black people terrorized farmers on isolated properties. The number of runaways increased through the 1770s, the vast majority of whom were young males. Both acculturated slaves and slaves newly arrived from Africa tried to leave masters in their search for freedom.[105]

Beginning in the 1740s, the Great Awakening, a time of religious revival, also led New York City whites and blacks to reconsider the morality of slavery. Methodists encouraged slaves to participate in relatively egalitarian religious ceremonies, ranging from mass rallies to private prayer and reflection. According to Methodist teachings, anyone could experience Christian conversion; neither white skin, nor literacy, nor wealth was necessary. Methodist minister Francis Asbury, who preached in New York City and surrounding rural areas in the early 1770s, fostered black religiosity and encouraged masters to free their slaves. Quakers, too, began to call upon their members to free their slaves, although they did not encourage black conversion. Slaves who participated in or heard about these more egalitarian religious activities held a greater belief not only in Christianity, but also in their own right to freedom.[106]

The Great Awakening alone would not free large numbers of slaves. The New York economy relied too heavily on slavery for whites to give up the system so easily. By the time of the Revolutionary War, black bondage was firmly entrenched in the city. Between 1703 and 1771, despite the two slave revolts, the slave population had doubled in New York. Masters freed few slaves, and whites had driven free black people from the city. However, the influence of the Great Awakening convinced New York City slaves, and a few whites, more strongly of blacks' rights to freedom. This belief would play a part in making the Revolution the next great opportunity for large numbers of slaves to pursue liberty.

CHAPTER TWO

The Struggle against Slavery in Revolutionary and Early National New York

In the decades between 1741 and the Revolutionary War, some white Americans slowly and haltingly began to question the role of slavery in society. Partially in response to the Great Awakening, Quakers and Methodists began to reexamine the religious basis for the enslavement of Africans. By the early 1770s, New York's Methodists and Quakers had begun to fight against slavery within their own congregations by excluding slaveholders from their midst. Anglicans, although less overtly antislavery, continued to educate and baptize blacks, implying at least blacks' religious equality with whites. Such actions encouraged enslaved blacks to agitate for their freedom. But the attempts by religious denominations and by blacks to call attention to the wrongs of slavery had little material impact in New York before the Revolutionary War.

The political ideology of the Revolution, with its emphasis on the American colonies' enslavement to Britain, provided a secular language with which to critique the holding of blacks as slaves, one that an emerging coalition of antislavery New Yorkers could embrace across differing religious affiliations. Additionally, the practical effects of the war gave large numbers of enslaved people an opportunity to seize their freedom; both the British and American armies made limited offers of freedom to those who would fight for them, and the disorder of the war gave slaves greater opportunities to flee their masters.[1]

Ultimately, however, the Revolution did not lead to the end of slavery in New York. There were strong economic reasons for retaining slaves in New York City and the Hudson Valley immediately after the war. Slaves continued to be an important labor source for urban and rural New York

until European immigration increased in the 1790s. There were also ideological and political reasons for retaining slavery. The ideology of republicanism that emerged from the Revolutionary War depicted a society whose
success depended on a virtuous, self-sufficient, independent citizenry that
was not beholden to any social group or individual. Slaves, as the property
of masters, were symbolically and literally the inverse of the ideal republican citizen. Although the new nation celebrated colonists who resisted
"enslavement" to England as revolutionary patriots, African Americans
who sought their freedom by siding with the occupying British during the
war were considered traitors. Whites viewed even those slaves and free
blacks who assisted the colonists during the Revolutionary War as unable
to throw off the degradation of their enslavement. New Yorkers only re-
luctantly granted freedom to those slaves who fought on behalf of the new
nation.[2]

After the Revolutionary War failed to provide freedom for all blacks,
New York's blacks and a growing group of whites continued to struggle to
end slavery and, in the meantime, to ameliorate the harshest aspects of the
system. Many blacks maintained cultural independence and built community against the isolation of New York slavery through participation in Pinkster celebrations. Some slaves negotiated with masters to purchase family
members or spouses. Those able to hire out their labor for wages could buy
their freedom. Other slaves chose the path of outright rebellion. During this
period, the numbers of slave runaways again increased, and some slaves re-
sorted to arson conspiracies to free themselves and others.

The founding of the New York Manumission Society in 1785 by a group
of influential white New York City men gave enslaved black people new
allies in the struggle against slavery. The society was important in convincing white New Yorkers that blacks were worthy of freedom. Soon after the
founding of the society, a prolonged state legislative debate on black freedom
failed to produce an emancipation law. In response, the society established itself as the guardian of New York State's slaves and free blacks, providing legal assistance to those slaves sold south illegally and to those blacks held illegally in bondage. In 1787 the society founded the first of several African
Free Schools for free black and enslaved children in New York City. In addition, the society's members began producing literature that they hoped
would convince New Yorkers and others in the new nation of the evils of
slavery and of the importance of freeing their slaves.

By the 1790s, white New Yorkers' fears of an increasingly restive slave
population, reports of slave rebellions from around the New World, and
economic change in New York City, as much as the Manumission Society's

campaigns, helped foster an atmosphere receptive to the passage of New York's first emancipation law. But white New Yorkers remained unconvinced of the equality of blacks. In early republican New York, arguments for and against freedom and citizenship for blacks revolved around the degradation whites believed blacks had suffered under slavery and the resulting necessity for blacks to prove their worth as citizens. By the time the New York legislature passed its first emancipation law in 1799, theories of black dependency and degradation excluded blacks from the dominant ideology of republican citizenship. New York State had granted black people freedom, but not equality.

■ ■ ■

Quakers were the first whites in New York City to organize against slavery, but they trailed behind the antislavery activism of Quakers in other British colonies for much of the eighteenth century. Pennsylvania Quakers led the denomination's antislavery discussions. The Germantown Quakers were the first to declare their opposition to slavery, through a petition written in 1688. The majority of Quakers at this point did not subscribe to the petition, and the Quaker hierarchy denounced it. Many among the Quaker leadership held slaves and participated in the slave trade, and they were unwilling to risk their economic status. But the Germantown Petition laid the basis for future Quaker critiques of slavery by reinterpreting slavery and the slave trade as immoral in relation to Quaker religious beliefs and by elevating blacks to moral equality with whites. By the mid-eighteenth century, a new generation of Quaker leaders, many of whom were not slave owners, began to preach against slavery. Again, Pennsylvania Quakers were central to this movement. The persecution Pennsylvania Quakers suffered in the 1750s reinforced their sense of isolation from society. Their pacifist stance against participation in the Seven Years' War (1756–1763), based on religious precepts, undercut their political leadership in the colony. Such experiences strengthened the resolve of Quakers in Pennsylvania and other colonies to follow the principles of their religion more closely. By 1758, prominent Philadelphia Quakers Anthony Benezet and John Woolman had convinced the Philadelphia Yearly Meeting to direct members not to buy or sell slaves. The meeting agreed to punish those who bought slaves, declared that slaveholding members should give up their slaves, and denounced all aspects of slavery.[3]

Not until 1774 did New York's Yearly Meeting establish sanctions for those who bought and sold slaves. In 1778 both the New York and Philadelphia Quakers adopted a policy to eject slaveholders from their congregations.

In part, New York Quakers were responding to the upheaval of the Revolutionary War. As Pennsylvania Quakers had during the Seven Years' War, New York Quakers declared their pacifist principles during the Revolutionary War by refusing to participate. Taking such an unpopular stance highlighted the need to adhere to other difficult moral tenets, such as antislavery. By 1787, New York's congregations had completely divested themselves of their slaves. They were the last of the northern Quaker congregations to do so.[4]

While Quakers no longer owned slaves, they did not welcome free blacks as religious converts. In general, Quakers did not proselytize, and throughout the pre–Civil War era, Quakers, even more than other denominations, resisted bringing blacks into their congregations. They may have considered blacks unsuited for their contemplative style of worship. Like the majority of whites in American society at this time, Quakers had not yet fully embraced the idea of black equality.[5]

Methodists, on the other hand, both opposed slavery and welcomed New York's blacks into their congregations. Methodists' participation in the religious revivalism of the Great Awakening led them to preach the religious equality of all people, regardless of their status on earth. The British founders of Methodism, John and Charles Wesley, were antislavery activists themselves, as were many Methodist ministers in the British colonies, north and south. During the Great Awakening, Methodist ministers preached to interracial audiences and actively encouraged the vibrant religiosity of African Americans, slave and free. Itinerant preachers held religious gatherings in the streets of New York City and in fields and forests in rural areas. Other, more staid denominations thought that their religious authority would be threatened if they allowed the vigorous singing and dancing that occurred in such settings. But Methodist leaders such as Francis Asbury viewed the religiosity of blacks as evidence of their equality before God: "To see the poor Negroes so affected . . . to hear them sing with cheerful melody their dear Redeemer's Praise . . . made me ready to say of a faith I perceive God is no respecter of Persons." In the 1770s, Asbury counseled slave owners in New York City, New Jersey, and Long Island to free their slaves. By 1782, Methodists had voted to exclude slaveholders from their congregations.[6]

The attitudes of other religious denominations toward blacks and slavery in the New York area continued largely unchanged until the Revolutionary War. The Dutch Reformed Church used the 1742 University of Leyden dissertation of Afro-Dutch theologian Jacobus Eliza Capetein to guard against the egalitarian effects of the Great Awakening. Capetein argued that slavery saved Africans from sin by exposing them to Christianity, and that there was no explicit scriptural demand to free slaves. By the 1760s the Dutch Church in New York City began baptizing larger numbers of slaves, no longer fearful that such actions would lead to freedom.[7]

Anglicans continued to educate those slaves whose masters allowed them to attend Episcopal schools. A few male slaves received such education, but the majority continued to be female domestics. By the 1760s, however, the education of black slaves had produced a small cohort of educated black women and men who some whites believed might eventually take on leadership roles in the black community. Reverend Samuel Auchmuty allowed one of the baptized men to lead parts of the Anglican services for blacks and stated his belief that soon blacks would be able to teach their own children to read and write.[8]

Although religious denominations varied in their opposition to slavery, the Great Awakening encouraged blacks themselves to see in Christianity a message of antislavery and racial equality. The Methodist practice of allowing black lay exhorters reinforced the denomination's statements of the religious equality of blacks and whites. Neither the Anglican nor the Dutch Reformed Churches so radically supported black equality. Nevertheless, Anglicans' emphasis on education and both denominations' increasing conversion of blacks in the decades before the Revolutionary War reinforced blacks' beliefs in their own worth. Although such practices did not lead Anglican or Dutch Reformed masters to free their slaves, blacks continued to believe that joining the church should lead to freedom. Even when individual slave masters or congregations excluded blacks from religious practice, blacks developed independent beliefs about the meaning of Christianity that emphasized freedom and equality.[9]

This growing sense of religious self-worth among blacks led to an increase in slave resistance between 1741 and the Revolutionary War. Despite the harsh punishments meted out to slave conspirators following the 1741 rebellion, slaves continued to agitate for their freedom, and slave runaways multiplied. The majority of the runaways were male, but some women also ran away, as well as a few families. John Decker of Staten Island ran away "barefoot," accompanied by "a negro wench" who was "with child." Abraham ran away with Moll, "who he claims as his wife," and two children, one three years old and another five months.[10] Rural slaves fled to New York City, where they obtained jobs as mariners. Rural and urban slaves also fled deep into rural areas to sympathetic Native Americans, or to other colonies. During the Seven Years' War, New York masters feared that the French were enticing slaves to join them with promises of freedom. Slaves also occasionally fled in groups or with white indentured servants.[11]

    While neither increased religiosity nor black agitation had inspired New York's slaveholders to free their slaves in the years preceding the Revolutionary War, European philosophers initiated a new debate over the place of slavery in the North American colonies generally, and in New York in particular. During the war itself, the patriots' rhetoric of enslavement to Britain stimulated discussion about the propriety of continued slaveholding by Americans. The Enlightenment philosophy of thinkers such as Montesquieu and Adam Smith provided the basis for critiques of political enslavement to Britain and of the chattel slavery suffered by Africans. Montesquieu's *Spirit of the Laws*, published in 1748, called upon Europeans to see that slavery was detrimental to public virtue. Slavery debased the enslaved and corrupted slave owners with excessive power. Montesquieu encouraged Europeans to empathize with the condition of enslaved Africans and to recognize that slavery was not conducive to blacks' happiness or fulfillment. Adam Smith, in *The Wealth of Nations* (1776), argued that slavery was an antiquated economic system that hindered the growth of individual self-interest and was an obstacle to human progress.[12]

    Prominent New York slaveholders and patriots such as John Jay were the first to characterize Americans' relationship to Britain as "political enslavement" and to question the propriety of Americans holding African slaves. In his 1774 "Address to the People of Great Britain," Jay charged Britain with acting as an "advocate for slavery and oppression"—referring to the condition of the colonists. In 1780, although he still held slaves, Jay wrote in a private letter that unless the new country was willing to consider gradual emancipation of its African slaves, the country's "prayers to Heaven for Liberty will be impious."[13]

    But for most patriot slaveholders, including Jay, reliance on the rhetoric of slavery to explain their own condition, and even recognition of the evils of African slavery, did not lead them to free their slaves. In 1777, Gouverneur Morris tried to convince New Yorkers to include an antislavery clause in the province's first post-independence constitution. Morris was far from calling for an immediate end to slavery; rather, he asked that the constitution recommend that a future legislature "take the most effectual measures consistent with public safety, and the private property of individuals, for abolishing domestic slavery." New York City representatives rejected even this cautious statement, and the initiative languished, ignored by the rest of the convention as unimportant.[14]

    The failure of Americans to address the problem of slavery gave the British powerful rhetorical and military weapons against them during the war. Samuel Johnson chided, "How is it that we hear the loudest *yelps* for liberty among the drivers of negroes?" More dangerous to the American cause were the British offers of freedom to slaves. In 1775, Lord Dunmore, the royal governor of Virginia, promised freedom after the war to any slaves who fought for the British. Based on military service, Dunmore's proclamation only applied to male slaves. By 1780, however, Sir Henry Clinton, the British commander in chief based in New York, had expanded the offer of freedom "to every Negro who shall desert the Rebel standard," thus opening British lines to black men, women, and children. In response, tens of thousands of slaves joined the British during the course of the war.[15]

In the American colonies, blacks had been allowed to serve in colonial militia. New York excluded "bought servants" under its 1775 Militia Act but allowed free blacks to serve. But just a few months before Lord Dunmore's proclamation, General George Washington had banned all blacks, slave and free, from service in the Continental Army. By 1776, all provincial and continental armies had banned the enlistment of all blacks. But when blacks began streaming to the British Army, the Americans reconsidered their ban. In addition to the demoralizing effect of large numbers of slaves and free blacks running to the British Army, the Continental Army had difficulty retaining whites as soldiers, and provinces were not meeting the troop quotas established by the army. In 1779, the Continental Congress approved the enlistment of blacks, slave or free, in the army, over the objections of South Carolina and Georgia. By war's end, about five thousand blacks had served as soldiers in the Continental Army.[16]

Blacks served both the British and American forces in a variety of ways. Black soldiers served the British in all-black companies such as the Black Guides and Pioneers, the Ethiopian Regiment, and the Black Brigade. The British commissioned the first Black Pioneer company in New York in 1776. Two white officers led the company, but blacks filled the positions below the rank of lieutenant and ensign. In contrast, the Americans interspersed blacks among white troops.[17] Both the British and the Americans used blacks as combatants in their navies. The British in particular relied on blacks who had knowledge of the American waterways as sailors and guides. Privateers, private boats commissioned by their respective governments but not subject to their enlistment rules, also employed blacks on their crews.[18]

Neither the British nor the Americans used blacks to their full potential in the war. Although the British criticized the hypocrisy of the Americans, they were not completely committed to the enlistment of blacks in their army, or to antislavery. Throughout the war, Lord Dunmore encouraged the British to employ larger numbers of blacks, particularly in the South. But by 1779, many corps refused to employ blacks as soldiers, seeing their presence as lessening the prestige of the troops. The British also did not provide for the emancipation of the slaves of Loyalists. The Americans resisted arming their slaves for fear of insurrection; additionally, the Americans never offered slaves unconditional freedom as the British did.[19]

Both the British and the American forces more often employed blacks as noncombatants who performed the manual labor necessary for the armies. Blacks built fortifications, cleared roads, and served as foragers, spies, guides, messengers, musicians, cooks, and personal servants. Some of this work was involuntary. In 1776 in New York, as the Americans tried in vain to defend the city against occupation by the British, the Provincial Congress summoned all black males, slave and free, to the city common to build fortifications. The men were to bring their own tools—"all the shovels, spades, pick-axes and hoes they can provide themselves with." Slaves served every day, and free men, every other day. Enslaved men who remained with their masters sometimes served in the army in their masters' stead; marauding armies captured others as spoils of war and forced them to serve.[20]

When the British occupied New York in 1776, the city became a center for blacks from all colonies seeking freedom. The swelling numbers of blacks alarmed the British, but ultimately their need for labor led them to accept the aid of the growing population. The British housed black refugees in "Negro Barracks" in the city; blacks socialized at "Ethiopian balls" with British officers and soldiers. The British army also called upon blacks to labor for them. After the Americans retreated from the area in 1776, blacks assisted the British army in raiding patriot property in New York City and the surrounding rural areas. They seized supplies, particularly food, and generally helped terrorize the patriots into submission. Blacks also served in more mundane tasks. Black men helped to build fortifications and served as cartmen, woodcutters, cooks, and military servants. Black women labored as cooks, washerwomen, and prostitutes. Because the British were desperate for workers, they paid black laborers wages equal to those of whites.[21]

Whether laboring for the British or for the Americans, blacks expected freedom and equality in return for their services. At war's end, many who had served the British and were willing to relocate achieved liberty by traveling to British territories. Between three and four thousand blacks left through New York's port for England, Nova Scotia, and Sierra Leone; about one thousand were natives of New York State. Their resettlement was not easy; they faced racism in England and Nova Scotia and difficult pioneer conditions in Africa. But they believed, at least initially, that their chances for freedom and equality were greater outside the newly forming United States.[22]

The rhetoric of revolutionary Americans and the reality of blacks' service to the patriot cause led most northern states to emancipate their slaves during and immediately after the Revolutionary War. Vermont, with its tiny population of slaves, provided for immediate emancipation in its 1777 constitution. In 1780, the Pennsylvania state legislature enacted gradual emancipation. Three years later, a Massachusetts Supreme Court decision declared slavery unconstitutional in the state. In 1784, Connecticut and Rhode Island enacted gradual emancipation laws. But New York's continued reliance on slave labor in the city and in the rural Hudson Valley through the 1780s led whites to resist including general abolition in their state constitution or in legislative actions. Only those slaves who had served in place of their masters in the war were granted freedom. These men then negotiated with slave masters to free their wives, children, and other relatives, usually in return for labor or cash.[23]

By 1790, the free black population in New York City had grown to an unprecedented 1,036 out of a total black population of 3,092.[24] But slavery remained firmly entrenched in the city. The tenuousness of black freedom in New York City was revealed in 1784 when slave traders attempted to seize a group of free blacks and sell them south illegally. In response, a group of antislavery white men, a number of whom were Quakers, forged a civic organization to protect the rights of free blacks and work to abolish slavery in New York. On January 25, 1785, at the home of innkeeper John Simmons, these men held the first meeting of the New York Society for Promoting the Manumission of Slaves, and Protecting Such of Them as Have Been or May Be Liberated. The Manumission Society was the first non-Quaker organization in New York to devote itself to emancipation. Its membership included some Quakers, such as wealthy merchants William Shotwell and John Murray Jr. However, it also boasted John Jay and Alexander Hamilton as members. Although Jay and Hamilton did less of the day-to-day duties of the organization, their names lent prestige and moved the issue of antislavery from a narrowly Quaker concern to a more broadly conceived effort for the good of New York and the nation.[25]

Only two days after the founding of the organization, Quaker Edmond Prior introduced into the Assembly, or lower house, of the New York State legislature a petition to end slavery in New York.[26] Prior sparked the first extended debate on black freedom in postrevolutionary New York State, a discussion that outlined the concerns of white New Yorkers about black freedom. A committee of the Assembly considered the petition and suggested to the full Assembly that a bill be drawn up that would emancipate all blacks born "since the declaration of the independence of this State, and . . . all that may hereafter be born within this State." This bill eliminated the two-hundred-pound security deposit masters had to pay the state in order to manumit slaves. The security deposit implied that black people were unable to take care of themselves as free people; masters paid the money to the state in case the freed slaves became wards of the state. Under this emancipation bill, only if a slave were "maimed or a cripple" would the master have to pay the security deposit.[27]

On a symbolic level, this bill linked blacks' rights to freedom to the birth of the independent nation and incorporated blacks in the transformative struggle for liberty that white Americans had experienced during the Revolutionary years. Further, the emancipation of slaves without requiring masters to provide a security deposit both implied that blacks could survive in freedom and made it easier for masters to manumit their slaves voluntarily. On a practical level, however, the slaves emancipated by this bill were children, the oldest of whom would be eight years old. This seemingly meaningless gesture is partially explained by the belief of legislators and other antislavery supporters that children would not have been harmed irrevocably by slavery and could still be reformed. With "free" status and proper guidance, they would escape the alleged degradation slavery had wrought on their parents—dependency on masters and lack of appropriate religious and secular education.

The idea that black children were the blacks most worthy of freedom was reinforced in the first revisions of the bill, in which the Assembly voted to emancipate only those slaves born after the bill had been passed. This first revision also established an explicit role for slave owners in the emancipation process. Although theoretically free, black children were actually to be indentured servants to their mothers' masters until age twenty-two if female and twenty-five if male. The differing ages of freedom probably grew out of the greater value of male skilled workers, as well as the desire of owners to avoid supporting any children born to female servants.

This provision was not intended simply to compensate masters for the loss of slave labor. In fact, when one of the legislators suggested that masters be allowed to place any unwanted slave children with the overseers of the poor, thus relieving masters completely of the responsibility of slave children, the legislators denied the motion.[28] Rather, most members of the Assembly believed that masters had a responsibility both to the freed slaves and to the New York community. Masters who had previously reaped the benefits of slavery should educate black children for freedom, providing them with basic skills for survival and incorporation into the community. Indentured male and female black children were to learn to read and write; black male children were to attend nearby "writing schools" from the age of twelve until the end of their terms of service. Upon expiration of their servants' terms of service, masters and mistresses were to provide them with new sets of clothing and new Bibles.[29] Thus, black children would not be born into freedom, but into a period of extended indenture or apprenticeship. During this time, masters and mistresses would train them to be moral, upstanding, literate workers and citizens.

This system assumed black potential for improvement, but it also reinforced a belief in the inferiority of blacks. It classed blacks from birth with white indentured servants or apprentices. But white indentured servants and apprentices either had voluntarily entered into such arrangements or had been forced into them due to poverty or criminal activity. The legislators saw blacks, on the other hand, as inherently in need of the protection of an indenture. Further, the indentures for blacks did not provide the usual rewards for completing the contract—land, money, or skills. Masters could provide these things if they wished, but the legislators' intent was to ensure the moral fitness of blacks, rather than their economic self-sufficiency.

Indenturing black children and retaining black adults as slaves did not completely erase the Assembly's fears of free blacks. Although they were freeing black children who would not be eligible for the duties of citizenship or for marriage for over two decades, the assemblymen denied blacks' rights to serve on juries and in public office and restricted interracial marriage. No free blacks would be eligible to serve as witnesses in courts of law. The legislators voted down a proviso that would have allowed those blacks who had undergone the indenture process to be tested to see if they understood the meaning of the oaths they took before being witnesses. Prior to this time, there had been no racial restrictions on voting. Faced with the potential for full emancipation in several decades, however, the legislators decided that free blacks would not be allowed to vote. When Representative Peter W. Yates of Albany proposed that blacks not be taxed without their representation in the New York State government, two-thirds of the legislators voted against him.[30] Such restrictions kept free blacks close to slave status: slaves could not be witnesses in courts of law and could not vote, and taxation without representation had been a sign of white colonists' "enslavement" to England.

The Assembly's restrictions on interracial marriage provided another barrier to equal citizenship for blacks. If a black person and a white person decided to marry, they would have to pay two hundred pounds per couple, a significant sum of money. No doubt the legislators' concerns centered on the potential influence of blacks on the polity through marriage. This might occur through the indirect influence that a black spouse might have on a white voter. Legislators may also have feared that light-skinned children would pass for white, or that future "white" generations would wish to give full citizenship to their mixed-race relatives. They accounted for these possibilities by stating that mulattos and mustees (the offspring of black and Native American unions) were covered under the same laws as blacks. The provision signified the linkage between the racial category of black and lower-class status. It gave a monetary value to whiteness and to citizenship: a black person could partially buy his or her way out of his racial category, if he or she became wealthy enough. To marry into whiteness, blacks had to prove their economic self-sufficiency. The sum of money itself was the same amount that colonial slave masters had earlier been required to put in trust when freeing slaves. This same sum would be written into law as a requirement for black suffrage in 1821.[31]

The New York State Senate passed the emancipation bill but rejected all three of the Assembly's amendments against equal citizenship for blacks. The Senate's openness to black citizenship and suffrage may have been because it was elected on a different basis than the Assembly. Under New York State's 1777 constitution, only those who owned at least one-hundred-pound freeholds could vote for state senators and the governor; further, only one-third of the Senate was up for election each year. The election of state assemblymen was open to those who owned at least twenty-pound freeholds or who paid at least forty shillings per year in rent, and the whole of the assembly was reelected annually. Thus, potentially, an increase in free black voters would affect the Assembly more than the Senate. Additionally, the Assembly contained a stronger contingent than the Senate of rural slaveholders who were at best reluctant to free slaves, and were even more unwilling to admit blacks to political equality.[32]

After the Senate failed to pass the amendments to the emancipation bill, the Assembly, in close votes, agreed to drop the restrictions on black office holders and the restrictions on blacks as witnesses or jurors in courts of law. Only after a special joint meeting of the Senate and Assembly did the Assembly negate the restriction on interracial marriage. But the Assembly absolutely refused to allow free blacks to vote. So, ironically, a black person could be elected to office but could not vote to put himself into office. The legislature sent the bill to the Council of Revision with the ban on black suffrage intact.[33]

The Council of Revision, a body consisting of the governor, the chancellor, and at least one State Supreme Court justice, reviewed all bills and judged their consistency with both the constitution and the "public good."[34]

In one of the strongest governmental declarations against restrictions on black citizenship and freedom in pre–Civil War New York State, the council, consisting of Governor George Clinton, Chancellor Robert Livingston, and Justice John Sloss Hobart, declared that emancipation without full citizenship contradicted the ideals on which the United States itself was founded. This bill, they stated, "holds up a doctrine, which is repugnant to the principle on which the United States justify their separation from Great-Britain." The council specifically criticized taxation without representation, stating that the bill "either enacts what is wrong, or supposes that those may rightfully be charged with the burdens of government, who have no representative share in imposing them." [35]

The council provided a more optimistic view of the prospects of blacks in New York. The council drew on Enlightenment beliefs in the potential of all men to achieve material wealth and in the desire of all men to live in freedom and equality. Disfranchised blacks, the council stated, may "at some future period . . . be both numerous and wealthy." As such, they had the same potential as American revolutionaries to "effect the ruin of a constitution whose benefits they are not permitted to enjoy." [36] The council displayed a strong vision of the possibility of black activism in pursuit of equality and freedom.

The council also saw the effect of disfranchisement and subsequent governing of blacks without their consent as dangerous to the civic virtue and rights of white citizens. The bill created "an aristocracy of the most dangerous and malignant kind, rendering power permanent and heriditary [sic] in the hands of those persons who deduce their origin through white ancestors only." [37] The bill's disfranchisement of blacks who already held the right to vote set a precedent dangerous to all citizens, for it implied that "the Legislature may arbitrarily dispose of the dearest rights of their constituents." [38] Thus, the Council of Revision stated that for the public good, blacks should be freed and embraced as full citizens. The council recognized free blacks as political actors and stated that their rights were the same as the rights of white citizens. It rejected rule by whites alone and tied the protection of whites' citizenship rights to that of blacks.

But such appeals to a racially equal application of revolutionary ideology did not affect the Senate's stance on the bill. When the council returned the bill to the Senate for reconsideration, the Senate passed the bill without revision in a classic expression of the separation between black emancipation and black equality: the Senate saw emancipation itself as more important than the rights of free blacks to equal citizenship after emancipation. By ridding itself of slavery, the state would have erased the greater sin and preserved the virtue of whites. But the Assembly, after hearing the arguments of the Council of Revision, voted against passage of the bill. No doubt the council's scenario of future generations of enraged blacks raised the Assembly's worst fears of black freedom. The 1785 emancipation bill perished.

In the wake of this defeat, the New York Manumission Society determined to prepare both white New Yorkers and black slaves for freedom. Between 1785 and passage of the first gradual emancipation law in 1799, the society enacted a number of programs to demonstrate the viability of black freedom. The society's Standing Committee also worked to prevent the illegal sale of free blacks and slaves to southern states. Individually and as a group, the society's members published newspaper articles and pamphlets that argued for the freedom of slaves. To prepare blacks for freedom, the society, in perhaps its greatest legacy to New York City's black community, founded the African Free Schools.

The Manumission Society combined a Quaker-based religious impulse with an elite political vision rooted in emerging federalism. The society was one of a number of reform groups composed of elite men who attempted to control the city's growth and direction, "one of the municipal meeting grounds for men of wealth, influence, and power." John Jay was the society's first president and his children William and Peter were both active participants. Other members included Alexander Hamilton; John Murray Sr. and John Murray Jr., wealthy merchant Quakers for whom the Murray Hill section of Manhattan was named; and Cadwallader Colden, who had been lieutenant governor of the New York colony and served as mayor of New York between 1817 and 1821. The forty-nine most active members of the society included twenty-three merchants and ship owners, eight bankers, and eight lawyers and judges.[39]

For these men, many of whom would emerge as Federalists, slavery stood in the way of the new nation's economic growth. They followed economic theorists such as Adam Smith, who saw slavery as part of an older economic order that did not allow for the free play of individuals in the market. But Federalists (and theorists, too) were conflicted about the amount of freedom necessary for a successful economy. They feared too much freedom, believing that some people or classes did not necessarily have the self-discipline necessary to realize their full potential, and thus society's. Therefore, Federalists favored a limited freedom, guided by elites, for all, and particularly for blacks. For the Federalists, ending slavery also meant controlling black freedom.[40]

Despite the Manumission Society's vision of a controlled freedom for blacks, the society's members as well as other New York City whites found it difficult to imagine an economy that did not rest on slavery or a citizenry that included large numbers of free blacks. Throughout the colonial period, New York's economic progress had relied on slavery. In the period immediately following the Revolutionary War, European laborers did not choose to immigrate to New York City; employers still depended on slave labor to rebuild the city after the British evacuation. Releasing blacks from slavery would eliminate a part of the laboring class that employers legally dominated and could prevent from moving to other employers or other states in search of better opportunities. Additionally, slave ownership remained a mark of upper-class status in New York City. Some Manumission Society members, despite their antislavery stance, believed that black people needed inculcation in the ways of American society, and that slavery, under the proper master, was one way of doing so. Thus, the society never made emancipation of slaves a condition of membership. In the late-eighteenth century, as many as three out of ten of the society's members owned slaves.[41]

Manumission Society members' hesitancy to free their own slaves was reinforced by the reluctance of New Yorkers to legislate emancipation in the 1780s and 1790s. In addition to voting down the 1785 emancipation bill, New York strengthened its slave codes in 1784 and 1788. Realizing that the political climate did not support overt actions to abolish slavery, the Manumission Society focused more on preventing New York slave masters from selling slaves to southern and Caribbean markets than on emancipating New York's slaves. In 1788, the state legislature passed a law forbidding masters from selling their slaves out of state. The society, which supported this law, saw slave masters in southern regions as less interested than themselves in the moral education of their slaves. But loopholes in New York's laws complicated the society's efforts to prevent the export of slaves to southern markets. Slave masters could be prosecuted for this crime only if it could be proven that they had sold their slaves with the intention of export. If, however, they happened to sell the slaves to a trader, who later decided to take the slaves south, the slave master and the trader were both within the law.[42] Thus, the society's efforts relied on information from individuals who reported infractions of the law. The society also tried to prevent the clearly illegal kidnapping and exportation of free blacks.

The Manumission Society's high visibility in rescuing blacks from illegal enslavement brought another contradiction to the surface. Despite the various struggles by enslaved black New Yorkers to free themselves, whites rarely mentioned such struggles against slavery in a positive light. The Manumission Society's belief that blacks could not or should not free themselves was part of much of the late-eighteenth-century antislavery rhetoric that appeared in pamphlets, newspapers, and magazines.[43] Organized antislavery's depictions of slavery, as they aided in raising the public consciousness about its evils, also contributed to a belief in the passivity of blacks. The dominant vision of slave emancipation in the United States was not one in which slaves freed themselves, but one in which whites gave them freedom. The antislavery movement created an image of black freedom in which slaves were emancipated by white benefactors before whom they were abjectly grateful. Freed slaves in such stories often "repaid" their benefactors in some way; in one instance, a freed slave rescued his emancipator's daughter from a fire.[44] Although such depictions of black slaves combated the image of the violent black revolutionary, they created a different set of problems for free blacks' admission into early national American society and citizenship.

The assumption that blacks would become free without any agency on their part undermined their quest for equality. Enlightenment and republican ideologies of the time emphasized the active nature of man and his ability to change and improve himself and the world around him. This Enlightenment ideology was responsible in part for the Revolutionary War in America. It also was the secular aspect of the impulse that led Quakers and others in the United States and England to begin to repress the slave trade and ultimately bring about the end of slavery.[45] White Americans believed that through the Revolutionary experience itself, they had proved their worth as freedmen. As David Brion Davis states, "patriots of the Revolution tended to define liberty as the reward for righteous struggle."[46] But according to most whites, blacks experienced no revolutionary transformation. As slaves, they were the antithesis of the independent republican citizen. The large number of black Loyalists led whites to label all blacks potential traitors to the cause of American liberty. After the war, blacks' supposed reliance for their freedom on the elites who formed the Manumission Society raised fears that dependency on these benefactors made blacks unable to participate as independent citizens in a republican democracy. This reasoning corroborated assumptions widespread among whites that blacks lacked the intellectual capacity to make political choices for themselves and to fight for their own freedom.

When accounts of black agency and self-emancipation in other slave-owning areas surfaced in New York, whites viewed such actions as potentially harmful to the evolving New York community or as demonstrating the benign nature of slavery in New York. In the late eighteenth century, the most well known example of mass resistance to slavery by blacks was the

Saint Domingue rebellion of the 1790s. Accounts of the Saint Domingue rebellion focus more on the violence and disorder of the events than on slaves'
desire for freedom. These accounts brought into sharp relief the alleged lack
of slave revolts in early national New York City. In reading such accounts,
white New Yorkers could be fearful of black uprisings but also favorably
compare their own system of slavery to that of the West Indies.[47]

Within the context of late-eighteenth-century New York City whites'
skepticism over blacks' ability to achieve freedom and equality, Manumission Society members were blacks' best hope. Society members did not believe that freedom automatically transformed slaves into citizens or granted
blacks equality with whites. Rather, the society built the African Free School
to prepare blacks, particularly ex-slaves, for citizenship. The African Free
School would prevent the "rising generation" from "inherit[ing] the vices
their parents acquired in slavery" and from learning "similar [vices] themselves through want of proper education."[48] The trustees hired a white
schoolteacher, Cornelius Davis, who closed his own school for white children
and visited Philadelphia's schools for black children to get a sense of how to
teach blacks. The African Free School initially admitted boys and girls, opening with twelve students on November 1, 1787, and enrolling close to sixty
students within a year, equally boys and girls and all free blacks. By 1789,
the school began to admit slave children with the permission of their masters. In 1793, the society opened a separate school for girls, led by Davis's
wife. The Manumission Society gave no explicit rationale for opening a separate girls' school, but many, if not most, schools in the pre–Civil War period were segregated by sex. The trustees probably believed that a separate
school for girls would allow more attention to training in women's domestic work.[49] By 1834, the last year the Manumission Society administered
the schools, over fourteen hundred students were enrolled in seven different
school buildings.[50]

The Manumission Society held two closely related goals for the African
Free Schools: the intellectual and moral education of black children. Through
such education, the society sought "to turn the baser metals into gold."[51]
The schools were to prove that blacks equaled whites in intellect if given
equal opportunities. Students learned reading, writing, arithmetic, and geography; the girls also learned sewing. Manumission Society members visited the monthly examinations of the students and praised the students' ac-
complishments in newspapers and through annual public exhibitions. The
students' work "fully answer[ed]" Manumission Society members' "best
expectations" and demonstrated that blacks "[were] not inferior to those of
fairer complexions . . . in acquiring a knowledge of Letters."[52]

Even more important to the Manumission Society was the moral improvement of the children and, through them, of New York's black community.[53] To achieve an appropriate moral atmosphere in the schools, the society strictly monitored enrollment, preferring to admit those children whose families were "most regular and orderly in their Deportment." Two trustees visited each applicant's family to determine the family's moral fitness; the school admitted no child without the approval of two trustees and the schoolmaster. Through such visits, the Manumission Society attempted to use the school as a way to persuade the black community as a whole to abide by the society's standards of decorum. It hoped to do this in a more direct fashion by establishing a Committee for Preventing Irregular Conduct in Free Negroes in 1788. Although the society did not have enough personnel to staff the committee, its plans for the committee reveal the morals the society wished to impose on the black community, the same morals it tried to impose through the schools.

The committee was to register all black families whom it considered "under [the society's] patronage." Families would provide the names, ages, addresses, and occupations of their members and report any changes in their records to the committee. The schools' trustees had the right to refuse to admit any children from unregistered families. The registered families were to maintain "good characters" for "Sobriety and Honesty,—and peaceable and orderly living." They were not to associate with "servants or slaves" or to allow "Fiddling, Dancing, or any noisy Entertainment in their houses." The schools were to inform parents and students of these regulations through pamphlets. If the society thought that "a Negroe forfeited the Patronage of the Society" through immoral behavior, the teachers would post the name of the individual and the details of his or her case "in a conspicuous place" in the school, as "a warning to the Scholars" and a way to "impress their minds with Sentiments of Respect for the Society."[54] Those under the society's "patronage" were to demonstrate to other blacks, by word of mouth and by example, the benefits of following the dictates of the society. Thus, the society predicated admission to the schools on obedience to its moral strictures.

That the Manumission Society was blacks' greatest ally before the passage of the 1799 gradual emancipation law may have led some blacks to support its strictures on behavior. There were no other schools for blacks at this time. Blacks saw the African Free Schools as a path to better economic conditions for their children, and the society helped slaves attain and free blacks preserve their freedom. Still, the schools experienced declining enrollments through the 1790s, until the trustees hired free black John Teasman as "an assistant teacher or Usher" in 1797. Teasman's presence lent additional

credibility to the schools in the black community. His appointment was one
of the earliest examples in New York City of interracial cooperation between
blacks and whites in the cause of free black equality and reform.[55] Born into
slavery in New Jersey in 1754, Teasman served as usher at the schools for
two years before being named principal, a post he held for ten years. His appointment led to a renewed interest in the schools among blacks. By 1801,
attendance had increased 30 percent. Teasman also established an evening
school for black adults. The popularity of the schools among blacks led
the Manumission Society to purchase a new lot that contained several buildings for the schools' use. For some blacks the society's prohibitions were
a small price to pay for the education and greater security the society afforded them.[56]

No explicit details of John Teasman's attitudes before 1799 toward the society's moral reform agenda survive. But Jupiter Hammon, a slave on Long
Island, left a written record of support for moral reforms similar to those
of the Manumission Society. Hammon, a relatively privileged Christian
slave, advocated blacks' achievement of freedom and equality through morality in his 1786 pamphlet "An Address to the Negroes of the State of New-
York." Hammon was born in 1711, a slave of the Lloyd family of Long Island. Henry Lloyd, a prosperous merchant, educated Hammon and other
slave and white children in a school on his estate. One teacher in particular,
Nehemiah Bull, a Harvard graduate who would later become a noted New
England religious figure, influenced Hammon's religiosity.[57]

Given his literacy, Hammon may have assisted the Lloyds in the management of their business, as well as performing skilled work about the estate. Hammon also had opportunities to earn money. He worked in an independent orchard allowed him by the Lloyds and sold his produce in local
markets. He may also have been hired out to neighboring slave owners.
As far as is known, he did not attempt to buy his freedom with the money
he earned. Rather, Hammon bought books, including a Bible with psalms
that he purchased from his master. With his poem "An Evening Thought"
(1760), Hammon became the first published African American poet. He published three other poems and four prose pieces, including "An Address to
the Negroes in the State of New-York" and an address to fellow poet Phillis
Wheatley in 1778.[58] Most of his works dealt with religious themes. He probably died between 1790 and 1806.

Hammon's complicated and at times seemingly contradictory message to
New York's blacks reveals that some blacks genuinely may have viewed
moral reform as a path to freedom in this world and, just as important, the
path to salvation in the next. The majority of his "Address to the Negroes in

the State of New-York" advises blacks to conduct themselves with humility and acceptance of their fate as slaves. "Whether it is right, and lawful, in the sight of God, for them to make slaves of us or not," Hammon stated, "I am certain that while we are slaves, it is our duty to obey our masters, in all their lawful commands." He criticized the practices of "servants" stealing from masters and staying "when we are sent on errands . . . longer than to do the business we were sent upon"—time that slaves and free blacks used to socialize with each other.[59]

Hammon also encouraged greater religiosity in slaves. He based his admonitions of greater obedience on his own close readings of the Bible. He quoted from Paul's Letter to the Corinthians, "Servants, be obedient to them that are your masters according to the flesh, with fear and trembling in singleness in your heart as unto Christ," a passage popular with southern slaveholders through the Civil War.[60] Hammon also more directly addressed issues of religiosity by instructing slaves against taking "the terrible and awful name of the great God in vain" and by encouraging slaves to learn to read so that they could read the Bible and become "true Christians." For Hammon, "liberty in this world" was nothing compared to "having the liberty" to go to heaven.[61]

Toward the end of the pamphlet, Hammon did acknowledge slaves' desire for earthly liberty. "For my own part, I do not wish to be free," he stated; indeed, when his master offered him his freedom in 1780 he refused it, probably because of his advanced age.[62] But he hoped that "others, especially the young Negroes," gained their freedom, for "liberty is a great thing."[63] To change the minds of whites about emancipation, blacks, slave and free, should behave morally and circumspectly, proving their worth as free people. Ultimately, however, Hammon saw the struggle of blacks against earthly slavery as futile and put his trust in God: "If God designs to set us free, he will do it in his own time and way." However, slaves did have control over their "bondage to sin and Satan" and "[should] not rest until [they were] delivered from it."[64]

Hammon's views were probably held by only a minority of blacks. Not all slaves complied with either Hammon's or the Manumission Society's programs for achieving freedom. From the end of the Revolutionary War to the early 1800s, New York City blacks were part of the greatest round of slave resistance and rebellion the Americas had yet seen. Some were inspired by the Revolutionary War in the United States. Disappointed by the retreat of Americans on the issue of slavery in the new nation's constitution, some slaves plotted individual or group freedom. The number of runaways increased, particularly from southern plantations to those northern states where emancipation laws had been enacted. The era's greatest success was Haitian revolutionaries' defeat of the French government and liberation of the slaves of Saint Domingue by 1800. In the 1790s, the example of the Haitian revolution also inspired some slaves in the United States. Slaves throughout the United States overheard their masters discussing the massive rebellion. Along the coast from Louisiana to New York, white refugees arrived with their slaves from Saint Domingue; both slaves and masters brought stories of the rebellion. In at least one instance, in Louisiana in 1811, a slave brought from Saint Domingue, Charles Deslondes, led American slaves to rebellion.[65]

New York City's slaves did not mount massive rebellions during this period, but neither did they wait for the Manumission Society to free them. The society's efforts were only one of a range of options for blacks seeking freedom. In a few cases, the society's attempts to free blacks illegally held as slaves depended in part on blacks themselves notifying the society of their own or a loved one's condition. Thomas Day appealed to the society on behalf of his grandson, who he believed was being held illegally. Lukey, a woman born free but seized by her employer as a slave, appealed to the Manumission Society on her own behalf, gaining her freedom.[66] Free blacks held illegally may also have notified white neighbors sympathetic to the cause of antislavery and asked them to appeal to the society on their behalf.

Other slaves sought their freedom themselves. The number of runaways advertised in New York newspapers had dropped to almost none by 1785; many slaves may have believed that New York State would soon abolish slavery, as had other northern states. But as those hopes faded by the 1790s, the number of runaways again increased. Given that Pennsylvania enacted gradual emancipation in 1780, and Massachusetts, immediate abolition, and that Rhode Island and Connecticut enacted gradual emancipation laws in 1784, slaves had some choices as to where they might flee. Some no doubt remained in New York City, or came to the city from rural areas, seeing it as a place in which they could blend in amidst a relatively large black population. As in most American slave societies, New York's runaways were overwhelmingly male. Some of these men may have learned of ways to escape on the docks and in the bars of New York. The master of a runaway named Peter knew that the eighteen year old was a "great dancer" who frequented the "negro dancing cellars of Bancker street" before he ran away. But women fled also. A mulatto woman named Sukey took advantage of New York City's 1799 yellow fever epidemic to flee. Another young woman, about sixteen years old, stole a dress that had "lemon coloured diamonds scattered over a fine white [collar?] trimmed with lace" and pearl buttons before leaving the city.[67]

The form of rebellion New York City whites had always feared most was arson. After three slaves in Albany nearly burned down the entire city one winter's night in 1793, New York City whites were even more fearful, attributing a rash of fires in 1796 to enslaved "French Negroes" from Saint Domingue in collusion with native New York City slaves. Worried New Yorkers served on night watches, hoping to catch the arsonists and prevent further destruction, but never uncovered evidence of a conspiracy.[68]

Slaves in New York City and the surrounding rural areas who were unable to escape bondage attempted to mitigate the isolation and hardships of slavery through participation in Pinkster celebrations in the late 1780s and 1790s. Pinkster had not played a large role among slaves in New York City prior to this time; rather, it was a tradition of rural slaves and centered more in Albany. Its appearance in New York City at the end of the eighteenth century indicates a growing sense of community between New York City slaves and their rural counterparts. Slaves incorporated the Dutch festival into their strategies for building community to combat the isolated nature of rural slavery. Prior to the Revolution, the celebration of Pinkster was an interracial event, but in the post–Revolutionary War years, the younger Dutch saw the tradition as part of the "old ways" and let go of it, leaving slaves to play the larger role in the festival.[69] Although whites were not participating in Pinkster by the late eighteenth century, they observed and approved of the festival's continuation as a slave celebration. Slaves combined African and Dutch traditions in their version of the festival. In the spring, they elected a king to a three-day reign. As in the Dutch tradition, this king collected tributes from blacks and whites throughout the city, and for the three days of the festival he settled all disputes. Additionally, blacks performed a variety of dances during the celebration, dances that white observers considered distinctively African or "negro" in nature. These dances continued African traditions that emphasized the centrality of dance to community and religious celebrations.[70]

In New York City, blacks celebrated Pinkster in the markets. Black slaves from New Jersey who sold their wares at Bear Market joined slaves from Long Island and New York City at Catharine Market after completing their day's peddling. Together, these slaves perfected the dances for which they were known throughout New York State, with the best dancers picking up prizes of money or dried fish or eels before returning to their masters.[71] Through such approved autonomous activities, slaves and free blacks in the

1790s and 1800s could reunite briefly with family members; they could also pass along information, from gossip about friends to methods of escape from slave masters.

During this time of black unrest in the 1790s, the Manumission Society continued to petition the state legislature for gradual emancipation. Instead, the legislature passed laws strengthening slavery. In 1792, over the protests of the society, the state legislature passed a law that allowed masters to export slaves guilty of misdemeanors out of the state. Jay's election as governor that year unleashed the bitterness that many slaveholders felt toward the Manumission Society, even though Jay continued to hold slaves himself. Rural Dutch slave masters accused Jay of wanting "to rob every Dutchman of the property . . . most dear to his heart, his slaves" and of forcing slave masters to educate the children of slaves "even if unable to educate their own children."[72] In such an atmosphere, Jay was unable to convince the legislature or the public to pass a gradual emancipation law during his governorship.[73]

By 1799, however, changing economic and political conditions, as well as the continuing agitation of slaves, made New Yorkers more open to emancipation. The growing European immigrant population gave employers a new labor force, one less foreign than African slaves. The foreignness of Africans, as well as the general difficulty of holding slaves, may have been exacerbated for white New Yorkers by the influx of refugee slave masters and their slaves from the Saint Domingue rebellions. New Yorkers, like other slave owners throughout the Americas, listened in fear to the reports from Saint Domingue and wondered if the "French" slaves in their midst would incite native slaves to rebellion.[74] These factors, as much as Manumission Society attempts to encourage New Yorkers to free their slaves, led to the passage of New York's first gradual emancipation law.

The 1799 emancipation law enacted the ideas of black dependency and of blacks' need for apprenticeship discussed in the 1785 legislative debates and supported by the Manumission Society. The law's provisions for emancipation were practically identical to those of the 1785 bill, but lawmakers avoided ruling on larger issues of black citizenship, such as suffrage and interracial marriage. Under the law, children born to slaves after July 4, 1799, gained freedom. But this freedom was limited, for the law placed these children firmly under white masters' control for an extended period. The mother's owner held each newborn child as an indentured servant until the age of twenty-eight if male and twenty-five if female. Masters were responsible for educating black children in their employ. In an important difference from the 1785 bill, the law also gave masters the option of abandoning slave children to the state, which would then indenture the children to new masters under the same conditions.[75]

The emancipation law defined blacks as dependents in multiple ways. The vast majority of "free" blacks would be children. It would be twenty-five years before the first indentured blacks would be completely independent of white control of their labor. That one had to be born free suggested that black adults were unable to erase the alleged effects of slavery—dependency on white masters, as well as general immorality and lack of self-control. Further, the long period of indenture took control of black children away from their slave parents. Masters were to be their parents, instructing them in the morality and industriousness that blacks under slavery allegedly could not achieve. The status of indentured servant maintained blacks' position apart from the mainstream of white workers. By the late 1790s and early 1800s, indentured servitude as a means of upward mobility for whites was rapidly fading away. The practice of indenturing children was increasingly associated with municipal almshouses that bound out the children of the very poor to employers. Unlike previous indentures, these servants did not receive land on completion of their terms of service. In New York City, the increasing separation of homes from workshops meant that blacks bound to whites as indentured servants in the 1800s would probably work as domestic and personal servants and would not learn more lucrative skills that would enable them to gain greater economic independence in freedom.[76]

The emancipation law hindered freed blacks' attempts to become equal members of the political economy of New York City. Although it did not disfranchise blacks, it implicitly defined blacks as a special, lower class of citizens and workers who needed extra aid to achieve freedom. But despite the attempt of whites through this law to control the numbers of black adults who gained their freedom, the free black population rapidly increased in the early 1800s in New York City. As blacks left slavery, they defined their freedom in New York City in multiple ways, none of which were easily controlled by New York's whites.

CHAPTER THREE

Creating a Free Black Community in New York City during the Era of Emancipation

The gradual emancipation law of 1799 did not limit slaves' pursuit of freedom; rather, it appears to have prompted more slaves to run away from their masters and encouraged slave owners in New York City and in rural areas to enter into arrangements for manumission with their adult slaves. These newly free blacks moved into New York City, creating new cultural, social, and working lives and new forms of political activism. Free blacks moved into working-class neighborhoods and mingled in the walking city with white workers and elites. They established mutual relief societies and built churches and schools. They participated in electoral politics and in political rioting against slave owners and slave catchers. As they went about their labors in the city, black workers sang their wares to attract customers, just as white workers did. And during leisure hours, working-class blacks and whites mingled in the streets, dance halls, and grogshops of New York.

Before the War of 1812, creating access to public space united blacks across evolving class lines. Free and enslaved blacks celebrated holidays such as Emancipation Day, the ending of the international slave trade, and the founding of various mutual relief societies in public parades and ceremonies. By their very nature, such events involved a cross-section of the black community as participants and observers. Working-class blacks constructed oyster bars and dance halls for their amusement and profit, as well as contributing to the building of black institutions such as churches and schools. Although middle-class blacks may not have approved of all working-class leisure activities, they did not organize to prevent them.

The War of 1812 was a high point in black cross-class support of the various forms of the free black urban presence. Occurring in the midst of the emancipation process, this war seemed to bring more opportunity for blacks to prove their worth than had the Revolutionary War. Although some blacks again heeded the calls of the British to find their freedom with them, many more pledged themselves to the new nation. With free black men fighting of their own volition for this young country, many blacks believed whites would finally recognize their worth as citizens. The passage of a new state law soon after the end of the war, which guaranteed emancipation in 1827 to all slaves born before July 4, 1799, seemed to signify that New York's blacks had indeed proven themselves worthy of full citizenship.

■ ■ ■

Although New York's 1799 gradual emancipation law freed no adult slaves and gave freedom to the children of slaves only after a lengthy indenture, slaves throughout New York State saw the law as a sign that whites recognized black people's rights to freedom. As they had during the colonial era, some adult slaves continued to bargain with their masters about where they would be sold. Other adult slaves successfully negotiated indenture contracts with their masters similar to those of the 1799 law or convinced their masters to accept a series of cash payments in return for their freedom. Although such practices depended on the flexibility of individual slave owners, they became more common after the passage of the 1799 law, hastening slavery's decline in the first decades of the nineteenth century ahead of the schedule laid out in the law.[1]

Many slaves in New York State took advantage of a new laxity among whites after enactment of the emancipation law and ran away to New York City, where the largest free black community in the North was forming. The presence of a large, active port gave New York City a heightened visibility among the Atlantic World community of blacks. Some slaves brought to New York City by slave masters escaping the Haitian revolution successfully sued for their freedom in the courts under a 1785 law that prohibited the importation of slaves. Fugitives from the southern states also sought out New York City, perhaps having heard of the growing black community there from free black sailors who socialized with slaves in southern ports. New York's Municipal Almshouse admission records show the significant numbers of blacks in New York born outside the city. Native New Yorkers constituted the largest single group of admitted blacks; others had come from the surrounding farm towns in New York State, on Long Island and Westchester; from other mid-Atlantic states; and from the eastern seaboard slave states of South Carolina, Maryland, and Virginia. A significant minority were born as far away as the West Indies, Bermuda, and Africa. A few gave their birthplaces as "at sea," perhaps on some leg of the Middle Passage.[2]

Although some New York City whites continued to buy slaves in the first decades of the nineteenth century, the ratio of free blacks to slaves in New York City increased dramatically. In 1790, there was approximately one free black for every two slaves; by 1800, there were three free blacks for every two slaves, and by 1810, about seven free blacks for every slave. By 1810, the free black population in New York City stood at over 7,400, a seven-fold increase from 1790. As would be true for the rest of the era of emancipation, there were two black women for every black man in the city.[3]

As blacks left slavery, they sought to create urban homes and lives independent of slave owners. Those free blacks who were not live-in domestics avoided settling in areas near the eastern tip of Manhattan, where the majority of slaveholding whites lived. By 1800 they had established independent black households in the Fifth and Sixth Wards (fig. 5). Settling below Houston Street, from the Hudson River to the East River, newly free blacks rented and sometimes bought homes and established churches. By 1810, free black residences concentrated toward the western side of Manhattan, between the Hudson River and Bowery Road. Blacks in the Sixth Ward clustered around the misnamed Fresh Water Pond. In the Dutch colonial era, half-free blacks had owned lots near the pond, and under the British, the area held the Negroes Burial Ground. In the 1800s, the Sixth Ward and the Fresh Water Pond became class-defined areas in which Irish and German immigrant and Anglo-American workers as well as black laborers rented homes, but many New Yorkers continued to view the area as dominated by blacks. Wealthier New Yorkers avoided the area; its swampy land attracted malarial insects and leather tanners used the pond as a dumping site for the noisome by-products of their trade. Although the city had filled in the pond by the War of 1812, the area retained its reputation for offensive smells and diseases and was left to the poor. But for black people, it was an area in which they could settle in relative independence.[4]

Individual blacks also began purchasing property, either as residences or for business purposes. One of the most significant series of property purchases by blacks began in 1825. Andrew Williams, a twenty-five-year-old free black bootblack, bought from a white cartman named John Whitehead three lots of farmland between what is now Eighty-third and Eighty-eighth Streets and Seventh and Eighth Avenues, in Central Park. After Williams's purchase, Epiphany Davis, a laborer and trustee of the African Methodist Episcopal Zion Church, purchased twelve lots in the area. These purchases

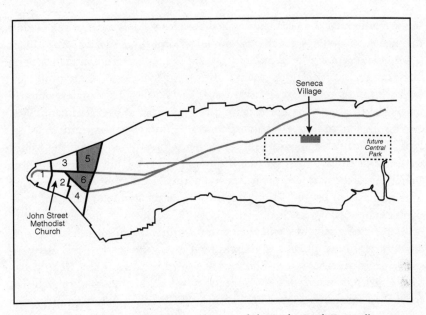

Fig. 5 Location of black neighborhoods as slavery ended. Map by Sarah Zingarelli.

inaugurated the Seneca Village community, the largest group of black land-holdings in Manhattan (see fig. 5). Between 1825 and 1832, Whitehead sold at least twenty-four, and possibly all fifty, of his remaining land parcels to black families. From the 1830s through the mid-1850s, black workers made up the majority of the Seneca Village population. By 1840, Seneca Village was home to over one hundred people, and by 1855, to almost three hundred—largely black or Irish.[5]

Seneca Village was a unique case of residential stability for black workers in New York City. Although the vast majority of the black residents worked in service trades or as unskilled laborers, they had managed to purchase land. Seventy-five percent of the families taxed in 1840 were still there in 1855. The community was also home to A.M.E. Zion and African Union Church congregations and a school. Through such institutions, as well as ties of friendship and marriage, the community sustained itself for over twenty years.[6]

The concentration of free blacks in various New York City neighborhoods did not mean that they lived completely segregated lives. Rather, pre–Civil War free blacks in New York City lived in racially integrated, working-class neighborhoods. Whites did not see residential segregation as essential to the maintenance of racial supremacy. And blacks by and large had neither the financial resources nor the inclination to form their own enclaves.[7] Black households were scattered among those of whites, with sometimes several black households per block. Many blacks occupied the cellars of buildings, with whites above. Cellar living was a legacy of New York City slavery, in which slaves usually occupied these dwellings. Damp, with bad ventilation and insufficient drainage, these residences encouraged the spread of deadly lung diseases and epidemics, illnesses that whites living above the cellars were less likely to suffer. During the 1820 epidemic known as the Bancker Street Fever, for example, in one section of the street, out of 48 blacks living in ten cellars, 33 became ill and 14 died, while the 120 whites living above them did not even get sick.[8]

Some free blacks first clustered around white institutions that were relatively friendly to them, and then around their own institutions. Between 1790 and 1810, large numbers of blacks settled near the John Street Methodist Church, a white congregation. In 1795, black members of that church split off to form their own congregation, which became the African Methodist Episcopal Zion Church. By 1810, the congregation had saved enough money to purchase property in the Fifth Ward. The site of the Zion Church on the corner of Leonard and Church Streets marked the center of another area where blacks settled, near their house of worship.[9]

Although blacks sought to form independent households in freedom, many were unable to afford single-family homes and so shared housing with non-family members. For some workers, residences were determined by their occupations. One-third of blacks between 1790 and 1810 lived with white families as domestics; the number of black live-in domestics fell gradually during the antebellum period. The spouses and children of live-in domestics saw them on scheduled days off and on holidays. A disproportionate number of working-class blacks of all occupations in antebellum New York City lived as boarders, renting single rooms in the homes of others or in larger residences designated as boarding houses. Half of black men and almost a third of black women in their twenties boarded in the homes of others, compared to approximately 20 percent of white men and 15 percent of white women. Single sailors in port lived in boarding houses near the docks. Although most black boarders lived with black families, some boarded with white families.[10]

As a last resort, and generally because of illness, some blacks moved temporarily into the Municipal Almshouse. Its segregated quarters for blacks were damp and dark, vastly inferior to those offered to whites. Throughout the antebellum years, black women and children far outnumbered black men as almshouse residents. The majority of black family groups who came to the almshouse consisted of mothers who had fallen sick and were forced to bring their children with them. The almshouse was also a haven for women during childbirth. Black almshouse residents left as quickly as possible.[11]

The majority of New York City's newly free blacks in the early nineteenth century held jobs on the lower rungs of the socioeconomic ladder, reflecting the occupations slaves held as their bondage ended. As late as 1790, artisans were the most numerous slave owners in New York City and held the second-largest number of slaves. In artisan households, which combined workshops and residences, male slaves learned skills that could fit them for movement into skilled jobs as free laborers.[12] In the early years of emancipation, before the War of 1812, a few black males used the skills they learned under slavery to establish themselves as artisans in freedom. In 1800 forty-two, and in 1810 seventy-five free black male heads of households were listed in city directories as artisans, with jobs as carpenters, coopers, cabinetmakers, upholsterers, sailmakers, butchers, bakers, shoemakers, tailors, hairdressers, and tobacconists. Some black women worked as seamstresses and milliners. New York City's free blacks were twice as likely to possess skilled jobs as their contemporaries in Philadelphia.[13]

During the emancipation era, a few blacks ran businesses that provided a secure income. For example, by the beginning of the nineteenth century, blacks dominated the chimney sweeping trade (fig. 6). White workers had little interest in the work, either as master sweeps or as child apprentices. By the late 1810s there were 60 master sweeps, including at least one woman, and 150 sweeps who worked under them, the vast majority of whom were young male children. Chimney sweeping was steady work: laws passed by New York's Common Council in the 1790s made it mandatory that residents keep their chimneys swept in order to prevent fires in the city. Some master sweeps opened offices and were listed in city directories, a sign of their wealth and status; others simply walked the streets with their workers, crying "Sweep O!" to attract householders.[14]

Black New Yorkers also contributed to the burgeoning entertainment business of New York. Black-owned oyster cellars, restaurants, and dance halls were popular with black and white New Yorkers. On weekends, some black working-class New Yorkers transformed their rented apartments into oyster cellars and dance halls. Thomas Downing's Oyster Bar on Broad Street and Cato's Tavern just outside the city catered to New York's white political and economic elite and were among the best-known restaurants in antebellum New York. Downing's survived until the Civil War. Black entrepreneurs also opened pleasure gardens, outdoor cafés where patrons could socialize,

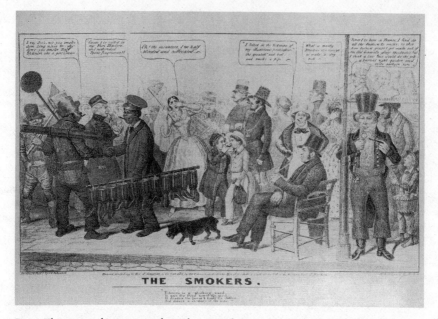

Fig. 6 This antismoking cartoon from the 1830s depicts a black bootblack and a black chimney sweep among the people found on antebellum New York City streets. Courtesy of the American Antiquarian Society.

drink cool drinks, and eat ice cream. Pleasure gardens were particularly popular during the summer months. Those who could afford to traveled to cooler rural areas during the hot weather, but the gardens gave those forced to remain in New York some relief from the heat and crowds of the city. However, this range of entertainment excluded middle-class and aspiring middle-class blacks. The elite restaurants or pleasure gardens run by blacks would not have survived had they offered interracial seating. The informal, sometimes interracial, and often temporary oyster cellars and dance halls of poorer working-class black New Yorkers would likely have been unappealing to those of middle-class or aspiring middle-class status.[15]

To provide entertainment for a wider range of black New Yorkers, retired ship steward William Brown opened New York's first pleasure garden for African Americans in 1820. Known by disparaging white New Yorkers as the "African Grove," Brown's pleasure garden offered blacks one of the few permanent recreation spots not affiliated with a church or mutual aid society.[16] Little is known about Brown's life before his arrival in New York. He may have been born in the Caribbean, though there is no indication as to whether he was born slave or free. Brown retired to New York City in 1816, having traveled the Caribbean and Europe. He rented a house on Thomas Street, in present-day Greenwich Village, and opened the pleasure garden in its back-yard. At the time, Thomas Street was on the outskirts of New York City. Because this area was not as heavily settled as lower Manhattan, property there rented cheaply.[17]

Complaints from white neighbors forced the closure of the garden in 1820, but Brown, not to be dissuaded from his quest to provide entertainment by and for black New Yorkers, opened a small theater in an upstairs apartment of the Thomas Street house in 1821, which survived until 1823. For the first year of its existence, the troupe, which Brown sometimes called the American Theater, performed Shakespeare and plays written by Euro-Americans. In mid-1822, Brown and the troupe produced "The Drama of King Shotaway," believed to be the first play written by an African American. Brown's theater closed in 1823 due to white hostility, but not before it had provided a valuable training ground for internationally renowned Shakespearian actors Ira Aldridge and William Hewlett.[18]

Despite the success of some black entrepreneurs, most blacks during and after the emancipation era found themselves in unskilled, low-paying jobs. Concomitant with the passage of New York's emancipation laws, European immigration and burgeoning industrialism changed the position of artisans and thus of blacks, slave and free, in the economy. Artisan slave-holding declined in the 1790s as the arrival of large numbers of European immigrants made it more cost-effective for artisans to hire cheaper wage labor than to own slaves or indentured servants and be responsible for their food and lodging.[19] At the same time, slaveholding among elites in New York City increased as they began to build elaborate homes that required greater upkeep. Slaves performed meaningful tasks in these new homes as part of the household economy, but they were also a form of what historian Shane White has called "conspicuous display," a sign of wealth. Whites did not view slaves' new tasks as central to the emerging industrial economy. Increasingly, slave women outnumbered slave men in New York City, feminizing the black labor force and perhaps causing further devaluation of black labor. Whites increasingly viewed the work black slaves performed, like white women's domestic work, as on the periphery of the industrializing economy.[20]

The compression of free black men and women into a limited range of occupations in antebellum New York was a legacy from slavery, particularly from the form that slavery took in New York City during its final decades.

The vast majority of free blacks in New York City at any one time in the antebellum period were, on the basis of occupation and income alone, part of
the working class. However, whites excluded blacks from both the declining
artisan trades and the burgeoning metropolitan industrial economy of New
York City. Thus, the development of the black working class and of black
class consciousness differed from that of whites.

Most free blacks, male and female, worked as domestic laborers beginning in 1800, in private homes, hotels, and boarding houses. Black men
worked in other service occupations, such as waitering and barbering; and as
casual laborers. Black women took in washing. Black men and women also
worked as fruit and vegetable peddlers. Perhaps the most steady and high-
est-paying work available to black working-class men, and to a few women,
was maritime work. Most black seamen obtained jobs as stewards or cooks
on inland, coastal, or trans-Atlantic voyages; a few black women worked as
chambermaids on steamboats. Although such jobs paid comparatively well,
black maritime workers had to endure long separations from their families;
additionally, their families ashore had to contend with long stretches of time
between paychecks.[21]

The low- or irregularly paying occupations that most black adults held
meant that children in families served as an important source of additional
income. Boarding house and restaurant owners often hired children as helpers. A six-year-old black boy waited on Englishman Henry Bradshaw Fearon
during tea at his boarding house. The child was part of a retinue of sixteen
servants, of whom only one was white. The others were the servants of the
boarding house, and the slaves of southern visitors to New York City.[22] Black
child laborers also dominated chimney sweeping. Children, who were small
enough to fit into chimneys to clean them, were especially needed. Chimney
sweeping was steady, but dangerous, work. Sweeps were subject to broken
bones, misshapen limbs, and "Chimney Sweeper's Cancer" and were sometimes mistreated by sweep masters.[23] Like other forms of child labor, sweeping limited the children's ability to gain an education.

Many of the jobs that black workers held were ones that white workers
feared and despised. As slavery ended, blacks were no longer automatically
accepted in the skilled workshops of employers who had formerly owned
them, if indeed blacks wanted to hold such jobs. As one employer said
of his former slave, "The laws set him free and he left me—now let the
laws take care of him."[24] That blacks sought autonomy and that whites
were bitter about black freedom led to blacks' exclusion from many skilled
workshops. As free competitors with whites in the job market, free blacks
were bound to lose out as white workers refused to work with them and

employers easily found wage laborers among the increasing numbers of European immigrants.

Black workers did not simply acquiesce to whites' understanding of their occupational roles. Rather, they claimed varying levels of autonomy in the occupations to which they were limited, negotiating with their employers for their own and their families' needs. The struggle for cultural and individual autonomy was most difficult for live-in domestic workers. Everyday tensions between live-in domestics and employers sometimes erupted dramatically into arson during the emancipation years, a carryover from methods of rebellion under slavery.[25] But most domestics mediated in less dramatic ways between their desire for autonomy and stability for themselves and their families and the labor needs of the families they served. Some live-in domestic servants managed to convince their employers to help them pay to board their young children with neighbors. A few, such as John Pintard's servant Hannah, were able to persuade their employers to allow their young children to live with them or to hire relatives or friends. When Hannah left her position, Pintard hired Tamar, a woman who had worked for him eight years previous and whom he trusted. Tamar capitalized on this trust and Pintard's need by insisting that Pintard hire her daughter Nancy as well, thus increasing the communal wages in her family. Other domestics may have received lesser benefits, such as leftover food or cast-off clothing. Such negotiations for the benefit of their families mitigated, to a degree, domestic servants' lack of autonomy.[26]

Black men and women also actively sought jobs that provided greater autonomy than domestic service. Washerwomen collected laundry at various households but washed the clothes in their own homes. Some washerwomen supplemented their income by taking in the children of domestic workers and other parents who worked outside the home, either on a daily or a long-term basis. Male and female fruit peddlers, ragpickers, cartmen, and day laborers also retained a relatively independent existence. The price of such independence, however, could be unreliable income that threatened economic independence.[27]

Although sailors' lives could result in long separations from families and less attention to communal ties and responsibilities, black sailors often retained strong connections to their land communities. Black sailors tended to be older than their white peers, and more black than white sailors supported wives and children with their earnings. Black men sometimes attained a greater degree of equality and freedom as sailors than they could on land. This sense of equality combined with relatively high and stable earnings to enable black sailors to provide well for their families when in port. One sailor, a widower named William Smith, earned enough money to purchase "a lot of ground in Harlaem" and to pay the twelve dollars a month required for the board of his four children while he was at sea.[28]

The difficulties of sustaining family life on meager incomes meant that many of New York's black workers were part of networks of family, neighbors, and friends that provided emotional and material support. Such networks were particularly important for domestic servants and sailors with children. Domestic and maritime employment, the backbone of the black working class, could take parents from their own homes for months or even years at a time. Further, black working-class parents were subject to higher than average illness and mortality rates. Thus, black parents relied on paid and unpaid boarding situations to help take care of their children. Possibly half of black children between the ages of ten and fifteen lived away from their parents during the antebellum era. Although separation of families in this fashion was emotionally wrenching, the relationship between parents and those who boarded their children could be mutually advantageous. Such relationships may have reinforced cultural and community ties among blacks. By not placing their children in white-run institutions, such as the Colored Orphan Asylum (founded in 1836), or apprenticing them to chimney sweeps, parents had more flexibility to visit their children or to take them home if their employment situation changed. Boarding also created an alternative to domestic work for some black women. But boarding arangements were also subject to the whims of New York employers and to the high disease and mortality rates that plagued the black community. As unemployment, illness, or death befell their guardians, children were shunted from home to home. Families with whom children boarded sometimes forced them into wage work or begging to help pay for their keep, or sent them to the Municipal Almshouse.[29]

To prevent such misfortunes, blacks built on these informal networks to create more stable forms of institutional relief. Churches were the first of these institutions to provide material aid to working-class blacks. Between 1796 and 1826, New York City blacks founded four Methodist Episcopal, three Protestant Episcopal, and two Baptist congregations, as well as one Presbyterian (fig. 7). Black people formed separate congregations largely because established churches refused to admit blacks as equals. Black congregations largely followed the beliefs of white parent denominations in catering to blacks' spiritual needs. But in separate congregations, black churchgoers could focus more on the material needs of believers than white parishes would. These churches became central institutional structures through which money could be collected and food, clothing, and other necessities of

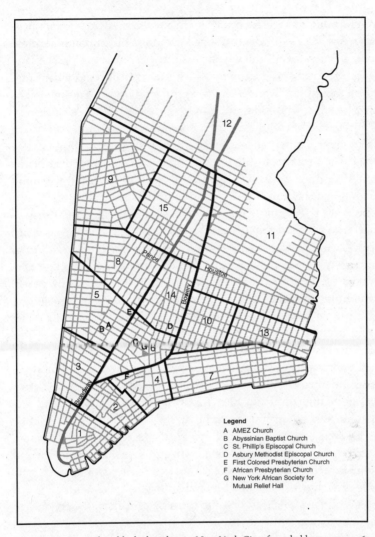

Fig. 7 Locations of six black churches in New York City, founded between 1796 and 1826, and the African Society for Mutual Relief Hall. Map by Sarah Zingarelli.

life bought and distributed. The ministers of the various churches often joined across denominational lines and with whites to participate in programs for the betterment of the black community.[30]

Black congregations also pooled resources to purchase property that served community needs. The African Society, the first known black religious organization in New York City, came together not only to provide a

place of worship, but also a place of burial. In 1795, the African Society petitioned New York City's Common Council for money to purchase land for
a church and a cemetery. White developers were encroaching on the land
containing the Negroes Burial Ground, which had existed from British colonial days. That same year, Peter Williams Sr. led a group of blacks out of the
John Street Methodist Church; they formed the African Methodist Episcopal Zion Church in 1796. Williams's group joined with the African Society
to purchase a lot at Church and Leonard Streets, on which they built the
A.M.E. Zion church in 1801. In 1807, another group of New York City blacks
formed the Abyssinian Baptist Church with the assistance of Reverend
Thomas Paul, founder of the First African Baptist Church in Boston.[31]

After the War of 1812, black religious congregations and secular organizations continued to solidify their standing in the city through the purchase
of property. Black Episcopalians from the Trinity Episcopal Church began
meeting separately in 1809. In 1819, they were able to form St. Phillip's congregation and erect their first church building on Collect Street, with newly
ordained deacon Peter Williams Jr. as their first pastor. Born in New Jersey,
Williams grew up in New York, the son of ex-slave Peter Williams Sr., then
a successful tobacconist and the sexton to the predominantly white John
Street Methodist Church. Williams Jr. attended the African Free Schools and
later studied under the Episcopal theologian John Henry Hobart. In 1826,
Williams was ordained an Episcopal priest. He remained pastor of St. Phillip's and retained a high profile in New York's black community and the radical abolition movement until his death in 1840.[32]

Despite his son's high profile in the Episcopal church, Peter Williams Sr.
remained active in both the African Methodist Episcopal Zion Church and
the white John Street Methodist congregation. Until 1820, Zion Church continued under the governance of the Methodist Episcopal denomination. An
all-black board of trustees controlled the church's property and day-to-day
operations, but a white minister, William Stillwell, oversaw the congregation. That year, amid controversy within white New York Methodist congregations over the distribution of church funds and the degree of control
Methodist elders had over individual congregations, Stillwell led a group of
disgruntled white congregants out of the Methodist denomination. Fearing
that a new white minister might attempt to control them more tightly, the
Zion congregation decided to withdraw from the Methodist denomination
and form its own church. James Varick became Zion's first bishop, holding that post until his death in 1827. He was replaced by Christopher Rush,
who held the position until 1872 and also became the first historian of the
denomination.[33]

The Asbury Methodist Episcopal Church had separated from Zion in 1813 under the leadership of William Miller and Thomas Sipkins. The congregation purchased a meeting house on Elizabeth Street, which was destroyed by fire in 1827. For several years after that, the congregation met in various rented locations before an individual donated a permanent building to them. The Zion and Asbury Churches as well as Philadelphian Richard Allen's A.M.E. Bethel Church had a competitive relationship for much of the early 1800s. Allen had founded an independent congregation in Philadelphia in 1794 and by the early 1800s had a small following in New York as well, although this congregation initially did not have its own church. Allen established a separate black Methodist church in New York in 1820, under the leadership of former Zion and Asbury member William Lambert. Allen hoped to increase his influence in New York and eventually combine Zion and Asbury with the new Bethel Church. However, Allen antagonized both the Zion and Asbury Churches, who saw him as encroaching upon their territory. Additionally, Allen did not intend to break with the white Methodist establishment, which Zion and Asbury ultimately did. The three churches did not differ in their doctrines, however, and thus eventually established friendly relationships. Asbury, the weakest of the three, aligned itself with Bethel for a time in the early 1820s, and by 1843 had been absorbed by Zion.[34]

In 1821, Samuel Cornish organized New York's First Colored Presbyterian Church; the Presbyter of New York formally installed him as its pastor in 1824. Cornish emigrated to New York City in 1820 after a childhood spent in Delaware and an education in Presbyterian theology gained in Philadelphia. Cornish originally came to New York as a missionary under the auspices of the Presbyterian Missionary Society to serve in the Bancker Street area, where a number of free blacks were settling. The society expected Cornish to establish a mission church and hold Sunday services, Sunday school for adults and children, and weekday prayer meetings. He also visited black families in the area to ascertain their levels of religiosity and morality and to encourage them to join the church. Within a year, Cornish's mission efforts created enough support among blacks to establish the First Colored Presbyterian Church. By 1824, Cornish's congregation numbered several hundred, with about eighty who were full members of the church, and the Presbyter of New York appointed him pastor. Cornish also spearheaded the construction of a thirteen-thousand-dollar brick building for the new congregation. Cornish raised some of the costs through donations from whites, but the rest was held as debt, which ultimately led to the loss of the building by 1826. Unable to raise money to pull the church out of debt and suffering from illness, Cornish resigned from the pastorate in 1828 and was replaced by his protégé, Theodore S. Wright. Not until 1831 was the congregation again able to purchase a church.[35]

Although educated black ministers and businessmen led these churches, the labor of black workers provided part of the material and financial basis for them. George Lyons, a whitewasher, "applied the first coat of paint on the first edifice" of St. Phillip's Protestant Episcopal Church in 1819.[36] Other "menial" workers saved enough money to purchase land for the A.M.E. Zion and African Union churches in Seneca Village.[37] The educated ministers who led these churches were often only a generation away from slavery and often continued to live economically precarious lives. Such common experiences among ministers and congregants no doubt influenced the social missions of these churches.

During and after the emancipation period New York's blacks also established numerous mutual aid societies. Many of these societies were linked to the newly founded black churches through leadership and ideology. These societies functioned as early forms of workers' compensation insurance for black workers. It is difficult to know how many of these societies existed in New York City during the antebellum period. Although a few left records in the form of acts of incorporation or constitutions, it is possible that many were never incorporated or existed only for a few years before disbanding. Philadelphia had sixteen male societies and twenty-seven female societies in 1830, and it is likely that there were at least as many in New York.[38]

With the exception of one, the African Marine Fund, all of these societies were segregated by sex. Founded to help members and their families in times of material need, the organizations also served to establish and reinforce community norms and values. The models for such societies had both African and Euro-American roots. In many West African societies, sex-segregated societies enforced community norms. Both the importation of slaves into New York in the mid-eighteenth century and the recent influx of slaves from the Haitian revolution may have reinforced these societal practices among New York's African Americans.[39]

The bylaws of these societies reveal the values important to some in the growing free black community. Blacks founded the first and longest-lived mutual aid society, the New York African Society for Mutual Relief, in 1808. Later organizations, such as the African Marine Fund, founded in 1810, and the New-York African Clarkson Association, founded in 1825, had guidelines similar to those of the Society for Mutual Relief. The Society for Mutual Relief was established to alleviate the economic difficulties of blacks and out of a "desire to improve our condition," meaning the moral condition of blacks. Eight ministers were among the society's members, demonstrating its strong link to New York City's black churches. The society limited its membership to "free persons [who were invariably male] of moral character" between the ages of twenty-one and forty. The society charged its members an annual fee and twenty-five cents in dues per month. After one year of paying dues, a member became eligible for compensation. After ten days of proven illness that prevented him from work, the sick member and his family would receive two dollars a week from the society for as long as three months, after which the sum was reduced to twelve shillings a week for six months, and then a sum of money such as "his case considered with the state of the funds shall appear to [the society] to demand." Other organizations, such as the African Clarkson Association, devoted their funds totally to those left widowed and orphaned by the deaths of their members.[40]

Mutual aid societies founded by black women aided those working women with children whose husbands had died, were invalids, or had deserted them. For example, a washerwoman named Susannah Peterson was one of the two hundred members of the Benevolent Daughters of Zion. Her son drowned as he attempted to save the lives of three boys who had fallen through the ice on a frozen pond. Susannah's son had been a major support of the household, which included his three siblings, the five-year-old daughter of a friend of Susannah's who had died, whose father refused to provide support for the child, and Susannah's own invalid husband. Susannah had paid an entrance fee of one dollar as well as one shilling per month to the Benevolent Daughters of Zion. Now, in her time of need, she was entitled to an allowance of twelve shillings a week for six weeks; any amount after that time would be subject to the ability of the organization to pay.[41]

The membership of these mutual relief societies reveals several important points about evolving socioeconomic classes among blacks. The participation of relatively educated men, such as ministers, caterers, restaurateurs, and other small businessmen, indicates the precariousness of life for the nascent black middle class. At the same time, the multiplicity of mutual aid societies and the variety of their membership reveals competing views among blacks about the labor they were forced to perform. Job and business opportunities were limited, and blacks developed interpretations of the status of some occupations that differed from those of whites. But even during the emancipation era some blacks recognized that certain jobs and businesses were of less social value than others. For example, in comparing the list of known black master chimney sweeps with that of the New York African

Society for Mutual Relief, there is no overlap.[42] Perhaps the harsh conditions to which masters exposed sweeps' apprentices, and that the Manumission Society was highly critical of the sweeps, kept them out of black New Yorkers' charter mutual relief society, even though economically sweeps were among the better-paid black New Yorkers. The "better sphere of life" to which members of the New York African Society for Mutual Relief aspired included moral as well as economic goals. The presence of separate mutual aid societies, perhaps aimed at different segments of the black community according to occupation, such as the African Marine Fund, may have allowed some to separate their moral aspirations from their desire for care during illness or for a proper burial.

Of the churches and mutual aid societies, the New York African Society for Mutual Relief was most successful in acquiring and retaining property. The society bought its first lot of land on Orange Street in 1820. The lot already contained a boarding house, the rent from which paid for the mortgage. Behind the rental property, the society erected a meeting hall that it used for its own events and rented to other organizations. The society also acquired other rental properties, which throughout the antebellum period provided the organization with income beyond the dues collected from its members.[43]

The creation of religious, social, and economic institutions reflected the new independent public and political roles blacks moving from slavery to freedom created in New York City. The growth of black public celebrations and parades was another visible sign of this transition. By 1800, free blacks had turned from the slave celebrations of Pinkster, sanctioned by the white community, to a new tradition of black parades.[44] Public parades arose among whites in American cities during and after the Revolutionary War as a sign of citizenship. Aligning themselves with the evolving traditions of the new nation, free blacks challenged their exclusion and the absence of anti-slavery ideals in the new nation's definitions of freedom and citizenship.[45] From 1800 through 1830, New York's black inhabitants increasingly celebrated their important holidays with parades. Such processions usually revolved around black freedom and were highly ritualized, with elaborate costumes and banners. One year after the passage of the 1799 emancipation law, blacks paraded in the streets in celebration.[46] After its founding in 1808, the New York African Society for Mutual Relief celebrated its anniversary with elaborate processions "through Broadway, across the park and back to its hall, where the occasion terminated in an oration and grand dinner. The old banner 'Am I not a Man and a Brother?' was borne through the streets, preceded by the Grand Marshal Samuel Hardenburgh, a magnificent black man, mounted on horse back, with a drawn sword in his hand."[47] Through these all-male parades, blacks laid claim to their rights to political, and sometimes economic, equality. Riding on horseback, wearing military-style uniforms and carrying swords, the parading black men displayed their historic partic-ipation in the Revolutionary War. This history, and thus blacks' claim to po-litical equality, was being taken away from them throughout the emancipa-tion period by whites who refused to recognize them as full citiens. When the Wilberforce Philanthropic Society, a mutual aid organization named for the British antislavery activist William Wilberforce, carried its funds in pa-rade "in a sky-blue box" with a gilt key, its membership was proudly and publicly proclaiming the ability of blacks to be economically independent and frugal on behalf of the black commonwealth—thus proving that blacks, too, could be independent equals in the larger society.[48] In these parades, black women and children cheered from the sidelines. Unlike Pinkster cele-brations, in which women as well as men danced, parades expressed an in-creasingly common practice of equating black public citizenship with mas-culinity. Black men displayed their achievement of full manhood and thus the black community's rights to full citizenship through the parades' visual assertions of black men's ability to lead and protect the black community.[49]

Speeches given by community leaders following the parades reinforced the processions' visual themes. Although white newspapers rarely reported on these black parades or speeches, except to caricature them, blacks and their white allies reprinted the speeches that followed the parades, and some-times the order of the procession and ceremonies themselves, thus preserv-ing some of the sentiments of the celebrations.[50] On January 1, 1808, the day when the slave trade between the United States and Africa became illegal, Peter Williams Jr. gave "An Oration on the Abolition of the Slave Trade" at the African Methodist Episcopal Zion Church. He gave his speech amid hymns and prayers of thanksgiving, as well as sermons and other speeches delivered by black ministers and others. Probably because he had been a stu-dent at the African Free Schools, publisher and Manumission Society mem-ber Samuel Wood printed his oration. Williams's speech served to prove the value of the school as well as the potential of blacks as independent citizens.[51]

Like their white counterparts, black parades and celebrations also re-vealed the divisions in the black community. In 1809, for example, blacks held three separate celebrations to commemorate the abolition of the slave trade. On January 2 of that year, three men preached celebratory orations in three different venues. Two of the speeches, those of William Hamilton and

Joseph Sidney, were part of celebrations sponsored by mutual relief organizations. Hamilton's was sponsored by the New York African Society for Mutual Relief, and Sidney's, by the Wilberforce Philanthropic Society. The third speaker, Henry Sipkins, was part of the celebration sponsored by the A.M.E. Zion Church. Although Sidney expressed regret over the fact that there were three celebrations instead of one for such an important anniversary in the black community, none of the speakers directly addressed the division. Part of the reason for the division was that Joseph Sidney had planned an explicitly partisan speech supportive of the Federalists. Although Henry Sipkins's political affiliation is unknown, one of the leaders of the New York African Society, John Teasman, was active in the Democratic-Republican Party by 1807. White artisans opposed to black political equality dominated the Democratic-Republican Party. Teasman joined the organization to force debate on racial issues within it. Few if any other blacks followed Teasman into the party, but he remained popular in the community. Hamilton and Sipkins probably split from the original celebration in order to be able to express their divergent views freely, without directly confronting the well-liked Teasman.[52]

All three speeches reveal the optimism of blacks in this period. A carpenter, William Hamilton, speaking at the Universalist church, stated that not only had the international slave trade ended and gradual emancipation in New York State begun, but the condition of free blacks in the United States was "fast ameliorating." "Science has begun to bud with our race," he said. "Soon shall our tree of arts bear its full burthen of rich and nectarious [sic] fruit, soon shall that contumelious assertion of the proud be proved false . . . that Africans do not possess minds as ingenious as other men."[53] In praising the Manumission Society for establishing the African Free Schools, Henry Sipkins, speaking at the A.M.E. Zion church, noted that some blacks had already made "considerable attainments in literature, and become worthy members of civil society."[54]

Such speeches were also calls to action. A founding member of the New York African Society for Mutual Relief, Hamilton had entitled his speech "Mutual Interest, Mutual Benefit, and Mutual Relief" and sought to encourage blacks to organize against poverty through mutual aid societies. The Society for Mutual Relief had only been in existence at this point for "three quarters of a year" but had already gained more members than previous such societies, he stated. Hamilton drew a careful line between mutual relief and dependency. Participation in the society's programs did not cause members to become "beggars to the society for relief in times of sickness"; rather, each person in need would be given his or her proper due, as the society's duties described. The success of the Society for Mutual Relief could serve to reinforce in whites' minds the ability of blacks to be free and independent citizens.[55]

Of the three speeches delivered in honor of the anniversary of the abolition of the slave trade, Joseph Sidney's speech before the Wilberforce Philanthropic Society was the least conciliatory to potential white listeners. Like Sipkins and Hamilton, Sidney urged his audience to express gratitude to the Manumission Society as well as "God . . . our kindest benefactor." But Sidney eschewed recounting the history of the African slave trade. Rather, he conceived that his "more immediate duty" was to speak to the complete abolition of slavery in the United States. Sidney called for gradual emancipation of southern slaves. "Immediate emancipation," he said, "is an event which we cannot reasonably expect; and, perhaps, ought not to desire." Southern slaves, "in a state of deplorable ignorance," "uneducated . . . and unacquainted with every thing except the plantations," were not ready for freedom. However, the example of the northern states demonstrated the safety of gradual emancipation.[56]

In the meantime, northern free blacks had the responsibility to bring about southern emancipation through wise use of the vote. Unlike the other two speakers, Sidney explicitly took on electoral politics by calling for blacks to support the Federalist Party. His support of the Federalists was based on two issues. Sidney tied the commercial success of the country to the leadership of Federalists, "the immortal Washington, the Father of his country. [Alexander] Hamilton, [John] Jay, [John] Adams . . . [Rufus] King . . . together with most of our old revolutionary officers and soldiers . . . attached themselves to this party." This group, a "distinguished band of patriots . . . gave to commerce every possible encouragement." "So long as Federalists remained in office," he stated, "so long this country enjoyed an uninterrupted state of increasing prosperity."[57]

But with the success of the Democratic-Republicans and the rise of Jefferson to the presidency in 1800, "the tide of prosperity soon ceased to flow, and all our goodly prospects vanished." The Democratic-Republican Party consisted of "a set of ambitious, designing and office-seeking men," who had emerged from their "native cave of filth and darkness." Among them, Sidney claimed, were "a number of abandoned printers, mostly foreigners." The Democratic-Republican Party and President Jefferson had also "bestowed high dignities on foreigners" by placing them in office in place of the "real patriots and statesmen" whom Washington had appointed.

Most important for Sidney, however, the Democratic-Republican Party was clearly linked to the southern slaveholding states. "The great hotbed of democracy is Virginia, and the other southern states. . . . And these are the very people who hold our African brethren in bondage." These people "are the enemies of our rights." Jefferson, "the great idol of democracy," continued to hold slaves; in contrast, Washington had freed his slaves (although Sidney neglected to mention that this did not occur until after Washington's death).[58]

In addition to voting, parades, and speeches, blacks displayed a more direct political presence through demonstrations and rioting against those who attempted to circumvent the emancipation laws. In August 1801, 250 blacks attempted to rescue twenty slaves whose owner, Madame Jeanne Mathusine Droibillan Volunbrun, had sold them south to Norfolk, Virginia. Although the Manumission Society had entered legal proceedings against Volunbrun, it dropped them out of fear that the release of the slaves would encourage further disorder and rioting. The slaves were sent south. In 1819, a crowd of blacks attempted unsuccessfully to rescue a Virginia runaway slave, Thomas Hartlett, from a slave catcher, John Hall. And in 1826, blacks waited outside city hall to hear the disposition of a case in which an entire family faced being returned to slavery. When the slave catcher won his case, blacks pelted him and police attempting to stop the riot with bricks, sticks, and stones.[59]

Newly free black men and women also made their mark in the streets during work and leisure hours. Chimney sweepers' cries in the early morning hours attracted customers. Throughout the day peddlers cried their wares, and in the early evenings black "tubmen," workers responsible for cleaning out the city's privies, sang bawdy songs to cheer them through the malodorous work.[60] During leisure hours, blacks shaped a burgeoning nightlife in dance halls and grogshops near Bancker Street. Working-class whites were onlookers and sometimes joined blacks in these activities, attempting to imitate the complicated dances performed by blacks on the docks and in the evolving interracial dance halls.[61]

The early emancipation era from 1800 to just after the War of 1812 was a time of optimism for black New Yorkers. The number of free blacks in New York City continued to increase as masters released their slaves from bondage ahead of the schedule laid out in the emancipation law. Blacks during this time displayed a conscious political activism as well as a social and cultural presence in the city. The new black public life, particularly the parades and celebrations that followed, was the basis of community for all blacks, who participated across class lines in feasts to honor the formation of the Society for Mutual Relief or the passage of emancipation laws. Other free blacks were both regular church participants and frequenters of the dance halls and grogshops of Bancker Street.[62]

Reform-minded whites continued to assist blacks in attaining a foothold in New York City through education. The Manumission Society expanded its schools, and during this period, several groups of white women founded schools. In 1815, Quaker women founded the New-York African Clarkson Society, which opened a mission school for black women. And in 1817, the interdenominational Female Union Society for the Promotion of Sabbath Schools, run by Johanna Bethune (wife of revivalist Divie Bethune) and staffed almost wholly by white women, opened several Sabbath schools that taught men, women, and children to read and write. Although these schools were open to all, blacks took the greatest advantage of them; in many cases over 50 percent of the pupils in these schools were black.[63]

The War of 1812 presented opportunities for blacks despite the economic difficulties that resulted from the embargo on international trade. The federal government initially banned black men from military service but asked them to perform war-related manual labor, such as building fortifications in and around New York City. Now that most blacks in the city were free, such labor could be freely given, rather than compelled by masters. In August 1814, a "Citizen of Colour" encouraged his fellow black men to volunteer to work on fortifications in Harlem Heights and Brooklyn. Perhaps in reference to the actions of Loyalist blacks during the Revolutionary War, "Citizen of Colour" saw the participation of blacks as "an opportunity of shewing . . . that we are not traitors or enemies to our country." Participation in the war effort would also show gratitude toward the state of New York, which had "evinced a disposition to do us justice" and "discard[ed] that illiberal, misguided policy, which makes a difference of complexion a pretext for oppression." "[N]o man of colour, who is able to go, [should] stay at home," "Citizen of Colour" concluded.[64]

In response to this call, about a thousand black men, "patriotic sons of Africa" according to the *New York Evening Post*, accompanied by "a delightful band of music and appropriate flags," crossed over from Manhattan to Brooklyn Heights to work on the fortifications there, while others labored in Harlem.[65] In October, the federal government lifted the ban on black soldiers, and New York blacks formed two regiments. The opportunity for black men to serve during the war again held out the promise of full participatory citizenship for the community as a whole. Throughout the war, black men could serve on navy ships and on privateers. Of black U.S. naval men captured and sent to Dartmoor prison in England, the largest number were from New York State.[66] With such proof of their worthiness as citizens, free blacks felt they had reason to hope for greater equality, and slaves, for full freedom.

Such hopes were seemingly validated in 1817, when the New York State legislature, at the urging of the Democratic-Republican Governor Daniel Tompkins, voted to emancipate all New York slaves by July 4, 1827. Tompkins argued that "most colored persons born previously to the 4th of July, 1799 . . . will have become of very little value to their owners. Indeed, many of them will by that time have become an expensive burden." Thus, manumitting these slaves would interfere with the property rights of slaveholders only "in a very small degree" and would still "be consistent with the humanity and justice of a free and prosperous people."[67] All slaves born before 1799 gained their freedom in 1827. The youngest slaves freed by the law would be twenty-eight years old, the same age as those males freed by the gradual emancipation law. These younger black people would still be able to work for a living. The oldest freed blacks, however, would be at the mercy of the community. Those children born to slave mothers between July 4, 1799, and March 31, 1817, would continue to serve as indentured servants under the terms of the old law. Those born to slave mothers after March 31, 1817, would be completely free at the age of twenty-one.[68] Thus, potentially, slave masters retained access to the labor of blacks as late as 1848, when the last black children, if born to slave women before July 4, 1827, would be free of indenture. Under this new law, slave parents might gain full freedom before their children.

Some families may have made choices like that of a slave woman named Isabella, who later became anti-slavery activist Sojourner Truth. Isabella had bargained with her master, John Dumont, to earn her freedom a year earlier than 1827 through extra labor on his farm in Ulster County. When Isabella injured her hand, Dumont withdrew the agreement. Isabella decided to work for Dumont for six months past the original date of July 4, 1826, and then leave, taking only her youngest child, the baby Sophia, with her. Her three other children remained with her husband Thomas on the land of her former slave master, bound to serve out their indentures. Had Isabella remained, Dumont might have given her and her family a cottage to live in, but her four children would still have been bound to serve Dumont until 1840 for the oldest, and 1847 for the youngest, and subject to resale to new masters much as slaves had been. Isabella chose to travel to the nearby Van Wagenen family, who opposed slavery; they bought her and Sophia from Dumont. Perhaps she hoped to negotiate freedom for all her family members, but she was only able to do so for one, Peter, and only after a protracted court battle. By 1828, for reasons that are unclear, Isabella had returned Sophia to the

Dumont household. Isabella and Peter found freedom in New York City, but they had left the rest of their family behind in Ulster County.[69] The emancipation law still privileged white slaveowners' needs or desires for slave labor over the freedom of black workers and the needs and desires of black families.

CHAPTER FOUR

Free but Unequal:
The Limits of Emancipation

On July 5, 1800, New York City blacks gathered to celebrate the first anniversary of the successful passage of New York State's first emancipation law. Although the appropriate day of celebration would have been July 4, both the Democratic-Republican Tammany Society, made up of white artisans, and New York's white merchants had established the Fourth of July as a celebration of white American freedom only, preventing blacks from celebrating their own emancipation as well as the nation's.[1] Thus, for almost thirty years, many black New Yorkers celebrated their emancipation on July 5, with a large parade ending in a ball and dinner.

From the beginning of the emancipation era, various groups of whites attempted to limit free blacks' access to political, social, and economic equality. Many working-class whites feared and despised black workers, seeing them as representative of the worst fate that could befall them: lives as menial, low-paid wage slaves. Working-class as well as many middle-class and elite whites believed that free black people were unable to overcome either their own inherent inferiority or the legacy of slavery and live as equals in a republican society. Even Manumission Society members were conflicted as to the degree of equality blacks could achieve in New York City.

After the War of 1812 and the passage of the 1817 emancipation law that promised freedom for all New York slaves in 1827, white animosity toward blacks increased. Economic difficulties in the wake of the War of 1812 led to greater poverty for both blacks and whites, and white workers feared competition with blacks even more. Crime pamphlets more pointedly depicted the alleged dangers to the city of grogshops, dance halls, and oyster bars that catered to working-class blacks. Middle- and working-class whites excluded blacks from mainstream civic celebrations and threatened blacks' parades with jeers, mockery, and violence. Central to this time of disappointment for blacks was the disfranchisement of the majority of the state's black men in the new 1821 constitution, even as white men gained universal suffrage. State legislators focused on the alleged immoral and dependent behavior of New York City blacks to demonstrate that blacks should have to prove their political equality before gaining the right to vote.

For New York City blacks, these setbacks raised questions as to the best path to equality. After losing suffrage in 1821, one group of blacks, some of whom had been instrumental in the fight for blacks' equal access to public space before the War of 1812, turned to more conservative ways to demonstrate black equality. They joined with the New York Manumission Society to regulate the activities of free blacks, seeking again to prove blacks worthy of citizenship. By 1828, a year after the completion of the emancipation of New York's slaves, New York City's blacks ceased parading as a united group, signaling a new attention to moral reform and circumspect behavior among blacks as a path to political equality. Debates over moral reform and the nature of black political activism became central to the definition of class in the antebellum free black community. Such debates set the divisions between working- and middle-class blacks on a new ideological plane, one that would define class and political struggles in New York's black community through the Civil War.

■ ■ ■

From the beginning of the emancipation era, whites had ambivalent feelings about the free black urban presence. Part of whites' discomfort with free blacks grew out of the ways republican ideology implicitly and explicitly defined blacks as unequal. Republican ideology defined the best citizens as men whose public, political virtue was based on their economic independence. Such independence would allow these virtuous men to exercise the duties of citizenship for the public good. The initial formulations of republicanism based economic independence in ownership of land. In the late eighteenth and early nineteenth century, white male urban workers began redefining ideal republican citizens as craftsmen who performed "honest" work with their hands. These workers partially defined their virtue in opposition to elite men whom they termed nonproducers, such as bankers and Federalists. These men, white workers claimed, gained their wealth by exploiting others.[2]

Women were also important to definitions of the ideal republican citizen. As wives and daughters, they depended on husbands and fathers for their well-being. Middle-class and elite white women were able to carve out a space for themselves as "republican mothers" and wives, who prepared their children in the ways of virtuous citizenship and kept a moral domestic space for their husbands. Working-class white women, on the other hand, found it more difficult to achieve the moral status and political influence implied by republican motherhood, if indeed they desired this status. That most of these women needed to work for wages in order to help support their families, and that many rejected evolving middle-class norms of behavior for women, excluded them from virtuousness as defined by the middle class; their working-class fathers and husbands often did not respect them much more.[3] Theoretically, though, even working-class white women could remake themselves as virtuous, if limited, republicans, and middle-class reformers offered to show working-class white women ways to achieve such a transformation.

Blacks had a more difficult time achieving equality under the terms of republicanism. Blacks' prior enslavement devalued them in the eyes of whites. There were no alternative roles possible for "slaves" in republican ideology. Slaves were the main symbol of dependency and thus lack of virtue, particularly after the Revolutionary War, with its emphasis on freedom from "slavery" to England. Additionally, the unskilled, low-status, low-wage jobs at which most free blacks worked devalued them as much in the eyes of whites as did the legacy of slavery. Whites believed that blacks who had been enslaved and who in freedom held jobs as servants were the most degraded of workers and the farthest removed from the ideal republican citizen. Additionally, whites often conflated the status of free blacks and slaves, conferring the alleged negative attributes of slavery—dependency and immorality—onto free blacks as well. In New York City, of those black domestics who lived in, one-third were employed by households that owned slaves. Thus, in the minds of their employers and many other whites, the lines between slavery and freedom for these blacks blurred during the emancipation period. Also, the intimate role that domestic servants played in the households of their employers supposedly rendered servants dependent on their employers not only for jobs, but for political guidance. In a sense, domestic servants, male or female, were like wives and children, dependent on the master of the house for political protection and therefore unable to vote. For these reasons, domestic servants were not candidates for full republican citizenship.[4]

The employment of black domestics by Federalists and other elites impugned the political virtue of all blacks in the eyes of whites. But black men's and women's roles as domestics affected whites' views of blacks differently. Whites excluded black women from the best of women's roles in the new republic, republican wives and mothers, because of their history of slavery and their continued servitude to others, rather than to their own families. Additionally, for women working in the households of others, away from the watchful eyes of their families, such servitude could imply a lack of sexual virtue. But even if freed from association with domestic servitude, black women would not attain the status of full citizens or represent the virtue of all blacks because they were women.

The position of black male domestic servants affected the definition of the black community more directly. The responsibility for control and political representation of women in the early republic fell most fully upon men. But whites believed that black male domestic servants' labor made them dependent and feminized, and thus incapable of being true republican citizens. Black men's roles as domestics devalued claims of independent black political activism, particularly when those men were domestics in the homes of Federalists. In the eyes of whites, the black population as a whole was feminized, first because there were more women than men in New York City, and second because black men held a disproportionate number of jobs as domestics.[5]

White workers also feared blacks as symbolic of disquieting changes in the newly industrializing nation. In the early 1800s, changing work processes limited increasing numbers of white male workers to unskilled, low-paying jobs. Master mechanics began abandoning the apprentice and journeyman systems, hiring unskilled laborers to perform piecework to produce goods. Unskilled men, but especially women and children, put together shoes, clothing, and other articles in large supervised workshops (soon to be known as sweatshops) or at home. Employers paid these workers stingily for their labor so that they could compete nationally and internationally and gain greater profits.

These practices led to deskilling among white male apprentices and journeymen who formerly would have been trained to become masters themselves. Instead of preparing these men to own independent shops, masters used them as cheap, unskilled labor. These young men increasingly worked under masters long past the age at which their predecessors would have opened their own shops, for their wages no longer enabled them to save enough money to do so. The Embargo Act of 1807 further clouded their chances for advancement and independence. When merchants were forbidden from trading with Britain, the major market for American goods, workers lost jobs. In New York by 1809, over a thousand men were imprisoned for debt; half of these owed only a week's wages.[6]

Although free blacks were not heavily involved in the new piecework system, their history of enslavement and their current concentration in low-status jobs such as domestic work, chimney sweeping, sailing, and wai-tering represented symbolically and literally the worst fates that could be-fall white workers. Blacks themselves symbolized enslavement. Chimney sweeps' sooty appearance and resulting depiction as "black" in British and American accounts no doubt kept whites away from the occupation. Sailing, another occupation that employed large numbers of blacks, was seen as re-sembling slavery. Sailors since the eighteenth century had been referred to as children and as slaves and carried reputations of immorality and de-pendency. The discipline aboard ship, especially flogging and impressment, could be interpreted by those on land as depriving sailors of independent po-litical thought. The boarding houses and grogshops that sailors frequented on land were often characterized as places of immorality. Further, the large number of blacks who entered the maritime trades in the late eighteenth and early nineteenth centuries may have degraded the profession in the eyes of whites.[7]

In menial jobs that both blacks and whites held, workers occasionally or-ganized across racial lines. In 1802, black and white New York sailors went on strike for a raise from ten dollars to fourteen dollars a month. In 1853, black and white waiters joined to form a waiters' union and also went on strike for higher wages. But in general New York City's white workers ex-cluded blacks from most jobs in which unions formed and excluded both skilled and unskilled blacks from their organizing activities. Thus, whites ex-cluded blacks from the evolving definition of working-class republicanism and from the practice of white working-class organizing.[8]

Manumission Society members tried to elevate blacks and the work they performed in the eyes of the New York community. Beginning in the 1790s, the society attempted to halt the devaluation of black male labor by encour-aging apprenticeship programs with skilled master craftsmen for black boys. In 1793 the society placed an article in the New York newspaper the *Argus*, urging whites and the small group of free black skilled workers to take in free black children as apprentices. In doing so, skilled workers would "raise the *African* character more" by "rescuing blacks from the state of servitude, to which they are now universally condemned."[9] Ironically, Manumission So-ciety members themselves contributed to the deskilling of New York's black men, for they owned slaves as domestic servants.

Manumission Society members also encouraged the placement of equal value on the different kinds of work blacks and whites performed. In this, the elite, Federalist-dominated Manumission Society's views of labor differed from that of the predominantly Democratic-Republican white working class.

In 1808 and again in 1814, Samuel Wood published a picture book for children entitled *The Cries of New-York*. This book depicted a variety of jobs performed by blacks and whites throughout the city. At the heart of the book was an attempt to prevent both the poor and the wealthy, black and white, from disparaging honest labor. Wood stated, "We are formed for labour; and it is not only an injunction laid upon, but an honour to us, to be found earning our bread by the sweat of our brows." He criticized wealthy whites in particular for relying on others' labor, comparing them to "hogs" by using a story told by Benjamin Franklin in slave dialect: "Boccarorra (meaning the white man) make de black man workee, make de horse workee, make de ox workee, make eberting workee; only de hog. He de hog, no workee; he eat, he dring, he walk about, he go to sleep when he please, he libb like a gentleman."[10]

Wood and other Manumission Society members found even child labor potentially uplifting. In Wood's book, a white girl sold radishes and a young black girl assisted her mother in selling pears. Such labor brought "honest" income into poor families; other forms of labor, such as domestic work, could bring greater morality by exposing blacks to white families. In 1805, John Jay went so far as to suggest that free black children be bound out as domestic servants to whites, who were "better qualified" to give them moral education than their own parents.[11]

Wood's book criticized the employment of boys as chimney sweeps— the only labor he depicted boys performing. Such boys "ought to be employed in getting learning, to qualify them to be useful to others, and comfortable to themselves."[12] Although the criticism of the employment of child sweeps was in part due to the danger of the work, Wood's emphasis on education for young black boys indicates the Manumission Society's gendered concepts of work for boys and girls, and thus men and women. As future heads of household and future citizens, boys needed education more than girls. Boys had the greatest potential for proving the equality of blacks as a whole.

The Manumission Society's support of blacks probably further distanced black workers from the heavily Democratic-Republican white workers. Although New York's white artisans had supported the Federalists and George Washington in the 1780s, by the early 1800s many had begun to turn away from the Federalists to ally with the Jeffersonian Democratic-Republicans. The elitism of Federalist party leaders, who wished to control the lower classes more than give them a free voice in politics, was a major factor in the defection of white workers from the party. Alexander Hamilton's belief that

"Mechanics and Manufacturers will always be inclined with a few exceptions to give their voices to merchants in preference to persons of their own professions" encapsulated the hopes of the majority of Federalists for elite rule. Additionally, the Federalists reneged on promises to control international trade through a tariff that would have favored New York's manufacturers. By 1794, a group of New York artisans had formed a Democratic Society, which criticized nonproducers such as bankers, merchants, and speculators as anti-republican and elevated small independent producers as the basic building blocks of a virtuous society.[13]

Although a number of blacks were artisans before the War of 1812, white Democratic-Republicans made no attempt to appeal to them politically. Because of the role of the Federalist Party in securing emancipation for New York's slaves and the Democratic-Republican Party's ties to the slave south, New York's blacks largely supported the Federalists. The Democratic-Republican Party in New York City exacerbated this antagonism by focusing on blacks as a key voting bloc that could prevent a Democratic-Republican ascendancy in local and state politics. Democratic-Republican inspectors at polling booths attempted to dissuade blacks from voting by harassing them for proof of their freedom. In 1811, the Democratic-Republican-dominated New York State legislature made such harassment legal by passing "[a]n Act to prevent frauds at election and slaves from voting." Blacks who wished to vote first had to obtain proof of their freedom from a "supreme court justice, mayor, recorder, or judge of any court of common pleas" in the state; pay that person to draw up the necessary certificate; and then bring this proof of their freedom to the polls. When a close Assembly election in 1813, in the midst of war, was declared in favor of the Federalists, Democratic-Republicans blamed the victory on the three hundred black New York City voters.[14]

During this era, larger numbers of free blacks also pursued informal means of political and social expression: parades celebrating emancipation, the end of the slave trade, and the formation of mutual relief organizations; political discussions amid the socializing in bars and dance halls; and occasionally riots against those who attempted to circumvent laws forbidding the sale of slaves south. Before the War of 1812, blacks' best allies, the predominantly Quaker membership of the New York Manumission Society, frowned upon many of the signs of independent black social and cultural life, from bars and dance halls to parades and other festivities in celebration of Emancipation Day and other black holidays. In 1799 and 1806, the society reprinted Jupiter Hammon's "Address to the Negroes in the State of New York" in an attempt to encourage blacks toward more circumspect behavior.

The African Free Schools' trustees also tried to use the institution and its black principal, John Teasman, to control black public life. When the trustees named the ex-slave John Teasman principal in 1799, enrollments increased dramatically. Part of the reason for the increase was that Teasman was already a community leader. He was a central figure in organizing parades celebrating emancipation and in the founding of the New York African Society for Mutual Relief. But throughout Teasman's tenure as principal, the trustees attempted to get him to cease his participation in organizing parades. Finally, as founding member and vice president of the Society for Mutual Relief, Teasman played a central role in organizing the society's first anniversary celebration in 1809. When the Manumission Society objected to the planned parade and requested that the mutual relief organization not process, the membership refused. Shortly after this parade, the trustees fired Teasman from his position as principal. In his place, they hired white educator Charles C. Andrews at twice Teasman's salary. In response, attendance at the schools dropped as parents transferred their children to two schools Teasman and his wife opened under the auspices of the Society for Mutual Relief.[15]

The Manumission Society's concerns were rooted in its fears and objections to any public displays, not simply those of blacks. The society was composed of Federalists, who feared "mob rule," and Quakers, who believed in plain, circumspect behavior. The society was not alone in such beliefs. Excessive drinking and socializing disturbed middle-class employers' sensibilities and, they believed, disrupted the labor discipline of workers. In the minds of city officials and reformers, and sometimes in reality, such activities were associated with criminal activity. Domestic workers and others who had access to the goods of their employers stole clothing and other items that could be sold for cash. Drinking and socializing, reformers argued, led to prostitution and violence. Manumission Society members and other reformers were concerned about such activities among both black and white workers.[16] As we have seen, after blacks attempted to rescue the slaves of Madame Volunbrun, the Manumission Society stopped its own legal proceedings against the slaveholder, for fear of further inciting blacks to protest.

Crime pamphlets depicted the confusion and anxiety that some white New Yorkers felt as the free black population rapidly expanded in the years before the War of 1812. In colonial times, religious agencies distributed accounts of crimes and executions widely to the general public. The early 1800s saw the rise of a secular literature of crime in addition to the religious writings. A wide variety of authors ranging from lawyers to judges to journalists produced this literature. In urban areas, these pamphlets focused on legal judgments and secular morality as much as explicitly religious judgments.[17]

In New York City, some of these new crime narratives also divided crime and criminals along racial, national, and class lines. Individual accounts characterized the alleged dangers posed to the New York City community by free blacks, European immigrants, or white workers.[18] For blacks, these crime narratives were part of the attempts of white New Yorkers to characterize and define black freedom and the role free blacks would play in the city.[19] Before the War of 1812, these pamphlets depicted a relatively fluid attitude, or at least a debate, as to the degree to which blacks would approach equality with whites. At the same time, however, these pamphlets ultimately limited the vision of black freedom. The pamphlets depicted blacks almost universally as workers. Although free, these workers might not always be dependable. This literature depicted other groups negatively also, but the depictions of blacks and assumptions about blacks' morality under freedom held special importance in whites' discussions of black citizenship in the era of gradual emancipation.

The crime pamphlets linked black crime to the usual sins of the early nineteenth century, such as drinking and adultery, but they also charted the emergence of whites' belief that a particular culture among free black workers led to urban chaos. In 1811, the trial of James Johnson for the murder of Lewis Robinson was printed for its moral lesson against "the effects of unbridled passion and of the destructive and odious crime of DRUNKENNESS."[20] This crime took place in one of the cellar dance halls that were part of the urban culture blacks were developing in freedom. On the evening of the murder, Johnson and his wife had transformed their home into a combination oyster cellar, dance hall, and bar for their own profit and for the amusement of their working-class black neighbors. When Mrs. Johnson denied credit to Robinson, who had not paid his previous bill, Robinson stepped on her toe. Mrs. Johnson then said of her husband, "Jim is no man, or he would not see me insulted," whereupon Johnson began fighting with Robinson, fatally stabbing him. Johnson had also been seen earlier "playing with the bosom" of Robinson's wife, which contributed to the altercation.[21]

One of the defense lawyers, Hopkins, in asking for clemency for Johnson, suggested that Johnson's wife provoked him to kill Robinson by questioning his manhood and calling on him to protect her honor. Although men of all classes might wish to respond to such a call, "higher education" enabled middle-class and elite men to "control the workings of natural passion." But among working-class men, "the pride and point of honor lies in their courage and strength. . . . [S]uch a cry, in such a moment, must have greatly aggravated his passion."[22] Hopkins's argument both appealed to the cross-class belief in female honor and established Johnson's response as one of a working-class person in particular. Among laborers, and in this case black laborers, pride derived from the demonstration of strength and action, not from restraint.

But ultimately free black, not working-class, culture was on trial here. Another of the defense lawyers, Griffen, asked the jury to uphold respect for different cultural standards among members of other races by requesting that "the dancing of these black people . . . not be urged to the prejudice of the prisoner." Griffen's argument suggests the presence of criticism of emergent urban black culture in the New York City community. "This man, it is true, is poor and humble, but in this happy country, the law respects the rights of the lowest as well as the highest; and whatever man can feel, or be concerned for, is at stake with him. He has a right to your humanity," Griffen stated.[23] Unfortunately, however, Griffen's arguments contributed to the depiction of working-class men and women, in this case black working-class men and women particularly, as being less in control of their passions and less adapted for citizenship. In contrast to defense arguments, prosecutor and Manumission Society member Cadwallader Colden focused not on the culture of working-class blacks, but on the definition of premeditation and on whether Johnson intended to kill Robinson. The defense's plea for respect of different cultural practices failed to win over the jury. The court convicted Johnson of murder and sentenced him to death.

Other crime narratives focused on crimes committed by whites against blacks. These obliquely addressed issues of citizenship for blacks. New York slaves under the British and Americans in the eighteenth century could not testify against whites, although free blacks could. Rarely were whites brought to trial for wrongs against slaves or free blacks, although of course slaves and free blacks were prosecuted for crimes against whites. But gradual emancipation brought an increasing number of blacks, mostly free blacks, to court as plaintiffs. The presence of blacks in court on their own behalf became familiar by the late 1820s.[24] But in the early years of gradual emancipation, there was some confusion over the growing role of blacks as plaintiffs. The three cases discussed below show this transition and confusion. The first, the 1809 Amos and Demis Broad case, is evidence of the difficulties of defending enslaved and indentured black people against abuse by their masters. The second and third, the Dunn and Little cases of 1808, depict the problem the courts had in adjudicating the gender and sexual roles of newly free blacks in relationships with whites. All three cases dealt with the problem of blacks' changing status as legal actors during the emancipation era.

In 1809, husband and wife Amos and Demis Broad were brought to trial for assaulting two of their "slaves," Betty and her three-year-old child Sarah. Amos Broad was an upholsterer and Baptist evangelist.[25] Under the terms of the 1799 emancipation law Sarah was legally an indentured servant, not a slave, but she was referred to throughout the trial as a slave, indicating the limits of the law in changing whites' views of blacks.

The Broads severely abused Betty and Sarah. On one occasion, Amos Broad forced Betty to strip, beat her with a "bunch of rods" while naked and then sent her out into the snowy yard for half an hour in the dead of winter, threw several bowls of water on her, "and kept her there till the water froze into ice upon her." On Christmas Day, Demis Broad took away Betty's clothes and ordered her to build fires in the home's fireplaces while naked. Both husband and wife kicked and beat three-year-old Sarah. Amos Broad rubbed Sarah's face "so violently upon the carpet as to hurt it very severely and occasion much blood to flow." On another occasion, Amos Broad "with one kick" sent the child flying across his store. Demis Broad threw a cane knife at the child, leaving a large gash in her forehead. The Broads gave neither Betty nor Sarah sufficient food to eat; white servants in the Broad household often shared their food with them.[26]

These same servants were the main witnesses against the Broads at trial. Of the nine witnesses "for the people," and against the Broads, four had worked for the Broads as servants; two of them left their jobs so that they might testify fully and truthfully, without fear of reprisal. These women gave the most complete descriptions of the cruelties to which the Broads subjected Betty and Sarah, and in one instance encouraged another servant to admit that she, too, had witnessed the beatings.[27] Their testimony led to the conviction of the Broads. The court released Betty, Sarah, and a third black woman, Hannah, from service. Amos Broad served four months in prison and paid a fine of 1,000 dollars. Upon his release from prison, he had to pay an additional 2,000 dollars as a bond against his good behavior. At the plea of the Broads' defense lawyer that the Broad children not be punished, the court did not sentence Demis Broad to prison so that she could return home to take care of the children; she paid a fine of 250 dollars.[28]

The Broad trial unraveled the belief that New York slavery was more humane than other forms of slavery. The Broads' punishments—the loss of their servants, their fines, and Amos's prison sentence—were to send a message to other masters that the courts would not tolerate such abuses. Had

Broad been a good master, he would have retained the right to these women's labor. His punishment served to demonstrate that slave owners did not have complete power over their slaves. Additionally, the trial showed the important role of community feeling against abuse of slaves. This community feeling could be backed up by the power of the law. The Broads' white servants modeled the community at the trial by playing an instrumental role in the conviction of the husband and wife. The Broads' trial and punishments set the limits of abuse of slaves and indentured servants by masters. More generally, the trial set out new ideas of whites' attitudes and responsibilities toward blacks: whites should testify against injustices against blacks, even when such testimony could cost them their jobs.

For some, defining limits on the conduct of whites also raised questions as to the role of blacks in the polity. The prosecution attorney, Manumission Society member William Sampson, lamented the fact that blacks could not testify themselves, but had to rely on the community: "The master's authority—the silence which fate, for I will not call it law, imposes on the slave, who cannot be a witness to tell his own complaint; gagged, and reduced to the state of a dumb brute, that must suffer and be silent—the want of sympathy among those who are more apt to construe murmurs into crimes, than to hear them with compassion—all these are weighty obstacles to justice." [29] His arguments may have swayed those in antislavery circles of the wrongs in not allowing enslaved blacks to act as witnesses for themselves but did not lead to a reconsideration of the testimony of slaves in court by the general public. Particularly in republican New York, whites considered the testimony of slaves too untrustworthy. Indeed, throughout the trial whites stated that not only the law kept these "slave" women from speaking on their own behalf. Rather, slavery had so degraded them that they could not tell the truth, even to protect themselves: kept under the thumb of their owners, "not only terror prevented the complaints of the slave, but . . . they were forced to deny the very violences of which their bodies bore testimony." [30] Such inaction confirmed some of the worst republican fears of enslavement. If slavery destroyed blacks' own self-interest, they could not possibly begin to think of the broader interests of the commonwealth.

The Broad case may have imparted a greater degree of humanity and sympathy to slaves in the eyes of whites, but it reinforced the idea that enslavement degraded blacks, and that blacks needed whites' protection. Ultimately, the Broad case served to ameliorate the worst abuses of the dying slave system, rather than to encourage destruction of the system itself. When Governor Daniel Tompkins suggested, in January of 1812, that the state legislature consider emancipating all of New York's slaves, the state

Assembly replied that such a law would "violate the private rights [and] dis-
turb the quiet of the community." Here, clearly, black slaves were not part
of the community but were the property of the white community. Whites
needed to continue their protection and gradual moral education of blacks.
The Assembly stated that the legislature's commitment to ending slavery
could best be shown by continuing the process of gradual emancipation and
by "passing laws for the amelioration of the condition of the African race,"
as it had in the past.[31]

Both the governor and the legislature agreed to continue government
protection of blacks by passing a bill that would prevent masters from exporting their slaves as punishment for crimes. In doing so, the legislature
recognized the limited ability of slaves to defend themselves against abuses
of the law. The previous law encouraged masters to accuse slaves of crimes,
particularly those slaves they could not sell easily in the state because they
were older or handicapped in some way. Those slaves could then be sold to
traders, who could take them to other areas, particularly out of state, where
their medical history was unknown. But according to Governor Tompkins,
the old exportation law also unjustly punished slaves, who did not have as
developed a moral sense as free people. Slaves should not be punished more
severely than free people for crimes such as theft, for slaves were "poor, un-
tutored, unrefined and unfortunate victims." "The servant 'that knew not,
and did commit things worthy of stripes, shall be beaten with few stripes.'"
Thus, the governor and the legislature reinforced the idea that adult slaves
were less morally developed than free people. Ameliorating their condition
was important, but freeing these blacks would disrupt the property rights of
slaveholders and also unleash upon the community a group of people with
low moral knowledge, leading to chaos.[32]

By the War of 1812, despite the passage of the gradual emancipation law
over ten years earlier, there were only partial indications of community sentiments among whites against the enslavement of blacks. However, whites
were investigating the limits of their own behavior toward blacks. The published accounts of the Dunn case (fig. 8) and Little case also focused on the
conduct of whites toward blacks. Both cases involved white men accused of
physically abusing free black women.

In 1808 the court convicted Captain James Dunn of raping a black
woman, Sylvia Patterson, the wife of James Patterson, a wood sawyer. The
prosecutor "blush[ed]" as he informed the court, "the defendant is a white
man." During the course of the trial, the prosecutor revealed Dunn's guilt
of "numerous crimes" of rape and described him as "perpetually skulking

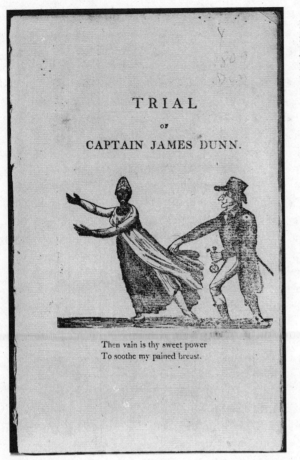

Fig. 8 Cover illustration from *The Trial of Captain James Dunn*. Neg. no. 74182. © Collection of the New-York Historical Society.

after negroes, and after the wives of those in the humble and industrious walks of life." Dunn's actions exposed his "infamous character," "meanness," and "avaricious disposition."[33]

Dunn's pursuit of black women in particular impugned his reputation. Although the prosecutor acknowledged the possibility that Dunn pursued white working-class women (the raceless "wives of those in the humble and industrious walks of life"), the prosecutor focused on Dunn's pursuit of black women. This inclination was not only because "no white woman that had the least regard for herself would have anything to do with him." Rather, Dunn's "avaricious disposition" led him to pursue black women—his greed for sex and his belief (and the prosecutor's) that black women would be more willing than white. Although the prosecutor presented the Pattersons as moral and upstanding in their desire to preserve their marriage, and a white neighbor described Mrs. Patterson as "always dressed genteel," the sexual morality of black women generally was disparaged in the case. In the end, the court convicted Dunn. As was typical of sentencing in rape cases at this time, regardless of race, Dunn was ordered to pay a low fine of one dollar plus court costs to Mr. and Mrs. Patterson.[34]

Also in 1808, William Little, a white medical doctor, was accused of beating his wife, Jane, a black woman. The *New York Commercial Advertiser* initially reported the case in considerable detail that June; this account was published in pamphlet form a month later. Both versions are somewhat tongue-in-cheek. While acknowledging that wife beating was wrong, the accounts also had to explain why Dr. Little, a middle-class white man, had married a black woman. On one level, Jane Little's race did not mitigate the seriousness of the crime. According to both accounts, when William Little was put on trial, "expectation stood on tip-toe" to learn why Little had beaten his wife, "an operation so long exploded and justly condemned in the practice of the medical society." The court's sympathy was ready for a "fair patient"—in other words, a white female victim. But the court was, at best, startled by the appearance of Jane Little: "she came forth—not *fair* like the swan upon the lake, but like the raven glossy; as black, and to the full as comely." In response to the court's snickers at the idea that Jane Little was the "weaker vessel," defense lawyer William Sampson defended interracial marriage: "every man must follow his own pleasure . . . neither philosophy nor religion have forbade such mixtures." Further, Sampson stated, the marriage was truly one of passion, and to prove this he read from love letters between William and Jane. In the newspaper account, the trial ended with the defense attorney pleading with Jane to forgive William, which she did. The two left arm in arm, amid the laughter of the court.[35]

For Little's defense attorney, Sampson, the trial was less about the interracial marriage than Jefferson's 1807 Embargo Act against exporting goods to Europe. As a result of the embargo, Little's debtors could not pay him, and thus he could not pay his own debts. This cycle had driven William Little to such extremes of financial distress that he had taken out his frustration on his wife. "That villainous embargo" had "destroy[ed] the best of tempers, and sour[ed] the milk of human kind." Even Petrarch might have beaten his Laura, "if there had been a vexatious embargo in his day, which made those who never before bestowed upon their wives but kisses and caresses, give them blows."[36] By depicting William Little as one victim of the embargo among many, his defense lawyer hoped to gain sympathy for him.[37]

By comparing Jane and William to Petrarch and Laura, the classic Renaissance Italian literary lovers, Sampson held them up as a couple like all others, downplaying the interracial aspect of the marriage. But the pamphlet account of the trial described Jane Little's gender identity as less than ideal. The title of the pamphlet described her as a "black *Lady*," with "Lady" italicized. A fuller account of the Little story than had appeared previously in newspapers reinforced the inappropriateness of using the word "lady" to describe black women and particularly Jane Little. Jane Little apparently was not the "weaker vessel," but gave as good as she got. Sometime after the dismissal of the charges against William Little, Jane and William "had a pretty severe battle, which terminated in favor of the *mistress*." The use of the word "mistress" to describe Jane echoed rumors that the marriage was not real, but that William Little kept Jane as his mistress.[38] Letters from William to "his lady" written after this second fight depicted Jane as the aggressor: "Jane—you know that I can prove by Mr. H——, who took or pulled you off of me when you was a beating me as hard as you could on my breast; and I kept my bed all the next day. I was so hurt that I was obliged to bleed myself. T—— T—— held you one night for some time (you were so crazy mad) from beating me." And William stated, "I hope you will not forget my twice throwing your hatchet into the street, so as you should not hurt me."[39] Such actions depicted Jane as at best a coarse working-class woman, at worst a masculine, and emasculating, wife.

The reason for Jane's anger was that William had lost to creditors the property that she had brought to the marriage—several houses and a garden. Again, William blamed the embargo for his difficulties. But just as important in this context is the fact that William had not taken the reins of his marriage—he had not taken control of the property that Jane had brought to the marriage, as was his right as a husband.[40] His letters to her are full of apologies for having lost the property, assurances that he never wanted to touch her property and had not married her for it, and promises to repay her by working not only as a doctor, but also on a farm, "for a dollar a day," and to bring her the money every Saturday night.[41] Such pleading for what was his right as a husband presented William as less than manly in the context of the times.

Thus, in depicting interracial marriage, the newspaper account and trial pamphlet presented the possibility, through the defense lawyer Sampson, that interracial marriages could be loving, like traditional ones. But the letters reprinted in the pamphlet, allegedly written by William Little to his wife, undercut this view by depicting William as a weak, ineffectual husband: unable to make a living at his occupation, beaten by his wife, and forced to work as a common laborer to pay his debts. Additionally, Little had not properly taken the reins of his marriage—he had not taken possession of his wife's property, and perhaps by implication, had not taken possession of his wife sexually—after all, Petrarch never achieved Laura either.

The Dunn and Little trials, as well as the Johnson murder trial, affected whites' views of the marital relations among blacks, too. The focus on women in the Dunn and Little trials (as well as the Broad case) reflected the fact that black women outnumbered black men in New York City by a large margin—two to one. Thus, in the eyes of whites, citizenship for New York City's blacks was tied to the conduct of black women, despite republicanism's and the black community's emphasis on manhood as the basis of citizenship. But these cases perhaps implied a lack of manliness on the part of black men. In the Johnson case, the fact that Johnson had to be cajoled into defending his wife from Robinson, and that he tried to prove his manhood by flirting with Robinson's wife, rendered the sexual basis of his citizenship problematic. Similarly, Jane Little's ownership of property and her marriage to a white man perhaps reflected something lacking among black males in the community. Whites controlled the distribution of these trials, and among whites the conduct of these black men and women negatively affected the attempts of New York City blacks to attain equal citizenship.

After the War of 1812, white criticism of black public life grew sharper and more explicitly linked to issues of equal citizenship for blacks. Despite financial difficulties in the decades after the War of 1812, New York City's free black population continued to grow, to build institutions, and to purchase property. By 1820, the free black population stood at 10,368. Additionally, the state legislature's decision to free all slaves as of July 4, 1827, raised fears among whites that New York City's black population would continue to grow and dangerously influence politics there.[42]

Some white critics of black public life disparaged blacks' activities as weak attempts to behave as equal citizens. William Brown's pleasure garden and his theater troupe were favorite targets of Manuel Mordecai Noah, a newspaper editor hostile to black equality. Noah's newspapers, the *National Advocate* and the *New-York Enquirer*, major vehicles for antiblack invective after the War of 1812, focused on Brown's pleasure garden and theater troupe as two of many ways newly free black New Yorkers were putting on airs. In his descriptions of the garden and its patrons, Noah sought to undermine both blacks' amusements and intellectual pursuits. According to Noah, Brown founded his pleasure garden because the increasing numbers of free blacks, as well as their "high wages, high living, and the elective franchise,"

made it necessary that blacks "have a place of amusement for them exclusively." Noah described the patrons as "black beauties," largely male and
female domestic workers, who "'[made] night hideous'" and imitated their
employers in clothing and in politics. "Harry," asks one patron in Noah's description, "who did you vote for at de election?" Harry replies, "De federalists to be sure; I never wotes for de mob." According to Harry, "Our gentlemen"—meaning his employers—"brought home tickets, and after dinner,
ve all vent and voted." [43] Such images raised the greatest fears of Democratic-
Republicans regarding the supposed political corruption of the alliance between Federalists and blacks.

Whites again linked black public life to criminal activity in the postwar
period. The most renowned postwar trial, the case of Rose Butler, demonstrated the dangers of black crime to white middle and elite classes. This was
a danger that cut across party lines. In the publicity surrounding Butler's
trial and execution, enemies of emancipation and of black equality reinforced
the idea of the black urban presence as dangerous if not carefully managed.
Of the crimes committed by blacks that whites publicized during the period
of emancipation, none was more emblematic of whites' fears of emancipation or received more attention than the Rose Butler case.

In 1819, the New York City Court of Oyer and Terminer convicted Rose
Butler of arson, a crime particularly associated with slave conspiracies in
New York, and sentenced her to death by hanging. Rose Butler herself epit-
omized the emancipation process that many New York City blacks had experienced. She was born in November 1799, in the rural town of Mount
Pleasant in Westchester County, and thus was part of the first generation of
blacks born "free" in New York State. Under the gradual emancipation law
passed that year, she owed twenty-five years of service to the Straing family. In 1809, the Straing family sold her indenture to Abraham Child of New
York City. When Butler was sixteen, Child sold her indenture to William
Morris of New York City. [44]

The primary reason Butler gave for her crime was revenge for repri-
mands from the mistress of the house, Mrs. Morris. Apparently, Butler set
the fire in league with two unnamed white men, who had convinced her to
burn the house for her revenge. After her arrest, Butler would not identify
the men. While she was in jail, the Morris house completely burned to the
ground, which the *Evening Post* interpreted as an attempt by these same
men to relieve her of guilt in the first case of arson. However, the governor only delayed her sentence several weeks, in order to give her time
to name the men, which she again refused to do. On July 9, 1819, after a

procession through the streets of New York City, and before a crowd of several thousand, Butler was hanged for the crime of arson. Her alleged accomplices were never brought to trial.[45]

Rose Butler's case was perhaps the most well known court case in New York City involving a black person during the era of emancipation. Over forty years later the historian of New York's markets, Thomas DeVoe, recalled the execution as "one of the most prominent transactions of my boyhood."[46] The case was a cause célèbre for those who wished to lecture the working classes, but particularly blacks, on their behavior, as well as for the smaller number of people who for a variety of reasons opposed the death penalty. The minister John Stanford published in pamphlet form the "authentic" account of Butler's story amid strong support for her execution. Stanford was the official missionary of the Society for Supporting the Gospel among the Poor of the City of New York. In this role, he was chaplain to the city's prisons, almshouse, and hospital, a position he held until the early 1830s.[47]

In Stanford's account, Butler's acts grew not simply out of her frequent conflicts with her employer, but also out of her position as part of an urban network of theft and disorder that involved lower class blacks and whites. According to one of the women assigned to take care of her while she was in prison, Butler talked of when she lived with Abraham Child, her first master in New York, and stated, "I was in the constant practice of stealing, and giving the articles to a coloured woman in the neighbourhood, who sold them for me." At first taking thread and silk from Child's store, she moved up to stealing cash and larger items directly from Child. "Emboldened" in her theft because she was never caught, when Butler went to live with Mrs. Morris she "continued pilfering whatever [she] could lay [her] hands on." This included one theft of three hundred dollars in silver. Butler's loot went toward gifts of cash and clothing to an aunt, who was also a domestic servant in New York City but who, according to Butler, did not realize that the money had been stolen from Butler's mistress. Butler also spent the money on amusements for her friends: "I went a carriage riding with [my aunt] and several others, and paid all the expences. On the 4th of July I went with some girls, on board the steam-boat, on a party of pleasure, and paid the charges; and $15 of it I spent at Mrs. Bundys, at Corlaer's [sic] Hook, on a frolic! It was in this manner I squandered away the money I had stolen—in frolicking and rioting in the dance-houses and other places at the Hook."[48] Corlear's Hook was at the eastern-most end of Manhattan. During the era of emancipation, free blacks, slaves, and white workers drank, danced, and fenced stolen goods together in the dance halls, bars, and brothels that had been built up among the shipyards and docks there. As a result, "the Hook" was one of the areas of New York City that reformers throughout the antebellum period focused on and popularized as examples of the increasing dangers and immorality of the city.[49]

In using Rose Butler's activities as an example, however, Stanford and others also expressed and addressed a specific group of anxieties about blacks and freedom.[50] Slaves had been allowed certain illicit freedoms by their masters during the slavery era. Some masters looked the other way when slaves got drunk or stayed out late. Others ignored thefts or even shared in the proceeds from stolen goods. Such liberties were necessary, some owners felt, in order to obtain satisfactory service from their slaves. Despite frequent complaints from individuals, the establishment of fines to those who provided slaves with alcohol, and the censure of the New York City government by the Supreme Court of Judicature for its lack of control over slaves, enforcement of the laws controlling the behavior of New York City's slaves remained uneven and lax throughout the colonial period.[51]

Under the gradual emancipation laws, the purpose of which was in part to prepare blacks for freedom, the continuation of lax control over black indentured servants increased anxiety among whites. If employers allowed blacks to behave this way as indentured servants, how would they fit into society as free men and women? In Rose Butler's case, the laxity of her employers "emboldened" her to the point of arson—one of the most feared crimes in New York City. That Butler had set fire to an inhabited house reinforced the idea that those complicitous in their servants' crimes, whether through carelessness or deliberate inattention, did not only endanger the working class, as in the murder of Lewis Robinson. The chaos produced by recalcitrant servants could also enter the businesses and homes of their middle-class and elite employers.

According to Stanford's account, Butler's experiences and lack of guidance turned her into a hardened, unrepentant criminal.[52] Some in New York attempted to present a different picture of Butler. Quaker anti–death penalty activist Dorothy Ripley, who visited Butler the night before her execution, found a sorrowful and repentant young woman who begged God's forgiveness and claimed to have been repentant of her crime for two weeks. Ripley castigated ministers such as Stanford for allowing the death penalty to continue through their lack of faith in the ability of humans to reform. Criminals could and should be reformed. Ripley's argument that Butler had effected her penitent transformation alone, without the help of the skeptical ministers, suggested that blacks could achieve morality independent of guidance from New York's moral elite.[53] Others objected to the taking of a life for a crime against property. Johnny Edwards, a scale-beam maker, working-class evangelist, and antislavery activist, "exerted his whole energies in her cause; in the streets, markets, and churches his whole saying was, 'Blood for blood—but not blood for fire.'"[54] Edwards's activism linked the concerns of newly free blacks with those of the white working class. One of the few white workers who publicly supported antislavery activity, he does not appear to have had a large following in New York.

Evidence is less clear on whether blacks protested Rose Butler's execution. The *New York Evening Post* reported, "we hear that threatening letters *(of the rising of the colored people)* have lately been sent to the Mayor, if the execution should be carried into effect." But after Butler's execution, an article in the *Columbian Spectator* stated the belief that "the colored people of this city, being convinced of the enormity of the crime, are generally reconciled to the fate of Rose Butler." Probably both accounts held some truth. No doubt some working-class blacks were angered, as was Johnny Edwards, over the execution of Butler when no one had actually died in the fire. However, the four unnamed black ministers who participated in the procession to Butler's hanging may have had a less angry response to her death, seeing it as a just verdict under the laws of the state, and were perhaps more concerned with how Butler's actions would affect the wider case to be made for black equality.[55]

The Rose Butler case was central to the discussion in New York over the moral equality of newly free blacks during the emancipation era. The statements of Ripley and Edwards indicated a persistent belief among some whites of the possibility of equality for free blacks in New York City. But Stanford's view that the actions of blacks needed to be guarded over during and perhaps after the emancipation era reflected the more general sentiment among white New Yorkers toward free blacks.

Whites' increasing lack of faith in blacks' abilities to live as independent free men and women in New York City fueled the debates over black suffrage and the nature of black citizenship held during the New York State Constitutional Convention of 1821. The convention met in Albany to draft a new constitution for the state, the first since 1777. One of the central issues for the 1821 convention was the range of property requirements for suffrage. The 1777 constitution had no racial restriction on voting. Rather, property requirements limited the electorate: the election of state senators and the governor was limited to those who owned at least one-hundred-pound freeholds, and the state assembly was elected by those who owned at least twenty-pound freeholds or who paid at least forty shillings per year in rent. Local governments might also set their own property requirements for voting.

After the War of 1812, an influx of residents into upstate New York from states that had no property requirements for voting provided the impetus for revising New York's suffrage requirements. These new rural residents viewed the property requirement for the vote as undemocratic, but they did not necessarily want to extend suffrage to blacks. Representatives of the rural constituencies at the constitutional convention expressed a fear of New York City's free black population. By 1821, the complete freedom of black slaves under the 1817 emancipation law was only six years away. New York City's free black population had almost tripled, from 3,500 in 1800 to 10,368 in 1820. More important, 35.4 percent of all blacks in the state resided in New York City, as opposed to only 8.5 percent of all whites. For many, New York City's black population represented that of the state as a whole.[56]

Some legislators compared New York City to London, which was known for its "rotten boroughs," electoral districts in which aristocrats bought the votes of the poor. On this basis, New York legislators opposed universal suffrage for working-class whites as well as blacks, claiming that all poor people might have their votes bought by the wealthy. Chief Justice Ambrose Spencer expressed his belief that the agricultural interests of the state should have control of the government, and that no urban workers should be allowed to vote.[57] But others argued that blacks in particular were more likely to sell their votes. Samuel Young of Saratoga County stated that blacks were "prepared to sell their votes to the highest bidder."[58] General Erastus Root of Delaware County declared that if blacks were given the vote, "a few hundred free negroes of the city of New-York" would have the power to "change the political condition of the whole state." "This species of population" would follow "the train of those . . . whose shoes and boots they had so often blacked," rather than vote independently.[59] This characterization placed black workers, even as free laborers, on a lower level than white workers, one of dependence, degradation, and mistrust. Black men were not comparable to women, another large class of dependents, for women were "the better part of creation." Legislators' praise of women was directed at white women; they did not discuss black women during this debate at all. Several conventioneers put blacks on the mental and political level of children, who "are deemed incapable of exercising [suffrage] discreetly, and therefore not safely, for the good of the whole community."[60]

Erastus Root's anxiety about "this species of population" demonstrates the distinction between emancipation and equality for blacks in New York.

Root had been one of the strongest legislative proponents of emancipation for blacks in 1799.[61] But by 1821, many white supporters of emancipation had become disillusioned with the process of black freedom. Although some saw racism as limiting the opportunities and achievements of free blacks, many more blamed blacks themselves: their alleged immorality, lack of work ethic, and lack of intelligence.

Those in favor of black suffrage tried to refute such arguments. Peter Jay of Westchester County, son of John Jay, reminded the delegates of the positive reasons behind New York's gradual emancipation laws. Blacks, he said, were not "naturally inferior"; rather, slavery had made them so: "The day you make a man a slave takes half his worth away." But blacks' degradation due to slavery, Jay argued, was "fast passing away" through the efforts of schools and other programs enacted by reformers for their uplift. Jay also reminded the delegates that the convention had been formed not to disfranchise anyone, but to extend suffrage.[62] Robert Clarke of Delaware County stated that blacks had proven themselves worthy of citizenship through service in the Revolutionary War and the War of 1812. Further, Clarke argued, blacks were not the only group potentially subject to becoming followers of the aristocracy. He claimed that there were "many thousands of white ambitious fawning, cringing sycophants, who look up to their more wealthy and more ambitious neighbours for direction at the polls, as they look to them for bread."[63]

Such arguments were not strong enough to prove blacks equal to whites in the eyes of the legislature, which voted to raise the property requirement for black men to 250 dollars. White men who served in the militia or paid taxes could vote without a property requirement. By 1826, the legislature had removed both militia service and tax requirements for white men, who then voted based on age, citizenship, and residence.[64] Chancellor Kent of Albany said that the property requirement "would not cut [blacks] off from all hope" of full citizenship. Rather, it would improve them by making them "industrious and frugal, with the prospect of participating in the right of suffrage." The requirement's tendency to encourage moral reform among blacks also "might in some degree alleviate the wrongs we had done them"— the wrongs of slavery and its resultant moral degradation.[65]

According to whites, the property requirement would provide additional impetus for blacks to improve themselves. Like the gradual emancipation law's period of indentured servitude, the higher property requirement of the new constitution essentially forced blacks to serve an apprenticeship to political equality. But the property requirement also went farther than the emancipation law's provisions for blacks. Blacks, to prove their worth as citizens, could not simply be born in New York, or simply be industrious workers. Through acquisition of property, blacks had to achieve middle-class status in order to vote. Those blacks who did achieve this status allegedly would have proved their independence beyond a shadow of doubt. At the same time, such proof reinforced the idea that "unimproved" blacks were inferior to any whites. Through this law, the legislature drew an indelible line between blacks and whites of all classes. The law devalued blacks in comparison to whites, for white men gained the vote despite their occupations and wealth or lack of it. The law also continued the belief that black workers, like slaves in republican ideology, could not think for themselves, but were under the influence of whites.

By 1826, only sixteen blacks in New York County were eligible to vote; by the Civil War, that number had grown only to an estimated three hundred, out of a population of over twelve thousand.[66] Some of those blacks eligible to vote in the antebellum period were residents of Seneca Village. Although depicted at the time and remembered later as a community of dissolute persons, Seneca Village gave a group of black workers the opportunity to achieve some of the goals of citizenship required by the 1821 suffrage law and esteemed by the wider community: property ownership and residential stability, which allegedly led to political independence.[67] The mere existence of a Seneca Village, however, could not erase the negative stereotypes of blacks in the minds of white New Yorkers.

The 1821 constitution legally enacted the devaluation of blacks as political and moral community members that had been in force since the end of the War of 1812. This devaluation had focused on black conduct, as depicted in the Rose Butler case and in the principal New York City newspapers. This constellation of efforts against blacks led some black and white reformers to focus on the conduct of blacks, and particularly black workers, as a way to prove black equality. Joining with the members of the New York Manumission Society, a small number of black ministers and reformers began to characterize all public displays, whether the formal parades celebrating emancipation, riots against slaveholders, or the revelry of the docks and dance halls, as inappropriate and damaging to the cause of equality. In the conflicts over the public displays of free blacks during the emancipation period were the seeds of divergent black middle-class and working-class political and social cultures.

That racism limited many educated blacks economically creates a complex problem for historians attempting to define separate black working and middle classes during this time. For most Americans, the antebellum period was a time in which class definitions developed amid rapid economic change.

Financial stability based on new, nonmanual occupations partially defined the new middle class. By the 1830s, some members of this evolving economic category also derived their identity and authority from the moral reform movements that developed during and after the Second Great Awakening. From this segment of the white middle class would come part of the impetus for 1830s radical abolition.[68] At the same time that nonmanual occupations were becoming a sign of middle-class economic stability, those who held skilled working-class jobs found it increasingly difficult to support their families, or found that such jobs were simply disappearing due to industrialization.

The place of New York City blacks amid these evolving economic trends was complicated by the racial division of labor in the city. Men emerged from slavery with some manufacturing skills, such as tailoring or shoemaking, but these became increasingly irrelevant in the antebellum period. Employers excluded black men and women from the emerging sweatshops and from what remained of the skilled labor opportunities. Further, blacks at all educational and skill levels were consistently underemployed throughout the antebellum period. Thus, many blacks with middle-class educational experience held manual labor jobs or were married to those who held such jobs. Presbyterian minister Samuel Cornish was also a shoemaker. Peter Williams père et fils were tobacconists, and Peter Williams Sr. also served as the sexton to the John Street Methodist Church. William Miller, minister and ultimately bishop in the A.M.E. Zion Church, was a carpenter. Some of those who began the emancipation era straddling the line between the working class and the middle class were ultimately able, through savings, business acumen, and desire, to place themselves firmly in an economic middle class. Thomas Downing, for example, owned a highly successful restaurant, which his son George inherited. But most other "middle-class" blacks were defined less by their economic wealth than by their educational level and participation in moral reform activities.

By the early 1830s, those blacks who moved, or aspired to move, out of the working class were often linked to reform movements aimed at their community and also united with whites to improve the material condition of free blacks through education and other programs. For these reformers, the creation of class divisions within the black community was a by-product of the process of remaking the race. Middle-class blacks felt a responsibility, due to the ties of race and their own experiences, toward their working-class brethren that went beyond the paternalism of white reformers. Middle-class blacks attempted to impart reform ideology to the black working class in the

belief that it would aid in racial uplift. But increasingly during the antebellum period, ideas of racial uplift through moral reform would be associated more with the growing middle class than the working class, and would become a source of division within the black community.

In New York City, the ideological roots of the antebellum black middle class lay in the alliance of black reformers and white Manumission Society members in the 1820s and 1830s. The most visible black reformers in this alliance were Peter Williams Jr., founder of St. Phillip's Episcopal Church, and Samuel Cornish (fig. 9), founder of the First Colored Presbyterian Church. These leaders, together with the Manumission Society, continued to redefine the limits of acceptable behavior for blacks and to heighten the connection between moral uplift and material aid for working-class blacks. Apart from white influence, precedent for such efforts among blacks existed in the formation of the New York African Society for Mutual Relief in 1808, which Williams had helped organize. Membership in the society depended on moral uprightness as much as on the ability to pay dues. Applicants to the society had to be recommended by members, and the application voted on by the whole membership. Widows of members received twenty dollars per year, contingent on their "widowhood" and "good behavior." Other New York mutual aid societies followed the model of the Society for Mutual Relief.[69]

There was a practical reason for seeking out those of "good behavior." In such a network, members depended on each other's reliability. The survival of mutual relief societies hinged on the degree to which they were able to attract financially stable, or at least responsible, members of the black community. In writing the history of the New York African Society for Mutual Relief in 1892, member John J. Zuille noted that its membership consisted of those "aiming at a better sphere of life." The membership rolls included ministers, teachers, and restaurateurs, indicating the fragile economic base of many "middle-class" blacks. One way these blacks were able to secure their economic base was through adherence to moral reform programs.[70]

The moral strictures that the Manumission Society encouraged were not completely foreign to blacks. Prior to the War of 1812, the Society for Mutual Relief had maintained a connection with the black community as a whole through participation in public parades around emancipation. Peter Williams Jr., a student of John Teasman, had been central to such public displays as a speaker and as a member of the society. In the 1820s, however, the rise of a new morality concerning public displays caused divisions both within the Society for Mutual Relief and in the black community generally. By the late 1820s, Peter Williams Jr., Samuel Cornish, and other aspiring middle-class blacks had joined forces with the Manumission Society to restrict all forms of public display among blacks and then to establish forms of surveillance over the black community.

The attempts to dismantle the Emancipation Day parades in 1827 were among the first major conflicts between older black traditions and the new moral reform activism. The 1827 celebration was particularly important, as it was scheduled for the day on which slavery legally ended in New York State. The new coalition of black and white moral reformers wished to limit Emancipation Day celebrations to indoor, minister-led events affiliated with churches. By focusing on churches as the center of the day, only the more educated and religious could participate actively in the celebrations; others were reduced to observers or nonparticipants. The discussion over the Emancipation Day celebrations reveals some of the conflicts among blacks as to what the community's public presence should be, as well as the beginning of class tensions among New York City's antebellum blacks. The discussion also makes clear the ways black middle-class ideologies were initially influenced by black leaders' perceptions of antislavery movement concerns. Such self-conscious interaction between black and white reformers, and the adaptation of black reform methods to white reformers' plans, would continue through the 1830s and into the 1840s. But such interdependence did not represent the simple hegemony of whites over blacks. Rather, black and white reformers together developed plans and methods to address the issues of free blacks, who were largely working class, drawing on a variety of moral, intellectual, religious, and pragmatic concerns to create programs that black leaders thought would help increase the status of all blacks.

Planning for the Emancipation Day celebration began in late April 1827, according to Samuel Cornish and John Russwurm's *Freedom's Journal*, New York City's and the nation's first black newspaper. As coeditors of *Freedom's Journal*, and as reformers, Cornish and Russwurm stood together in their desire to control the shape of the Emancipation Day celebration and the public demeanor generally of New York City blacks. They reported "cheerfully" on an Albany, New York, meeting led by black minister Nathaniel Paul concerning Emancipation Day celebrations there. Paul shared their fears about the role of free blacks and the meaning of citizenship for them. In Albany, stated Cornish and Russwurm, Reverend Paul had been "of great utility in improving the morals and conduct of that class of the community, which has been but too long neglected." Paul had worked "to prepare men for the rational enjoyment of liberty" by giving them "a just sense of their own rights," as well as "the duties which they owe to the community."[71]

Paul pledged a "virtuous course of conduct" for the Albany celebration, in which newly freed blacks would express "[their] gratitude to Almighty God, and [their] public benefactors." Albany blacks would celebrate emancipation on July 5, as they had since 1800 when they first paraded in celebration of the law. By 1827 the celebration of emancipation on the fifth was an explicit admission of blacks' lack of citizenship rights: the "4th day of July is the day that the National Independence of this country is recognized by the white citizens." This was not the moral indictment that Frederick Douglass and other radical abolitionists would later make of the hypocrisy of celebrating Independence Day in a country in which slavery was still legal. Albany blacks simply "deem[ed] it proper" to celebrate emancipation on the fifth.[72] Probably contributing to their desire to hold the celebration on the fifth was a fear that whites, celebrating drunkenly on the fourth, would be more likely to attack blacks in the streets. This had been a fear since the early 1800s, one that the Manumission Society had used to try to convince blacks to stop parading completely. Before the War of 1812, such arguments did not sway blacks, but in the increasingly hostile postwar atmosphere, some blacks began to shy away from any public expression.

Nathaniel Paul's plan to hold the emancipation celebration on the fifth was subsequently adopted in New York City at an organizational meeting led by free black carpenter William Hamilton and secondhand clothing store proprietor Thomas L. Jennings. The members of the meeting asked New York City's blacks not only to hold the celebration on the fifth, but also to "abstain from all processions in the public streets on that day," thus preventing "the least tendency to disorder" as blacks expressed their "gratitude for the benefits conferred . . . by the honorable Legislature of the State of New-York."[73] The fear of New York City's black leaders regarding public processions had several sources. One was the very real concern that a public celebration of black freedom would result in counter-demonstrations and riots by whites. Just as important, however, was the impression that blacks would make on the city in their new freedom. Despite the steady increase of the free black population of New York City during the twenty-seven years of gradual emancipation, the day itself symbolized the final leap toward freedom and set the stage for the role of free blacks in the new society. According to the reform-minded, public demonstrations endangered blacks' attempts to achieve full citizenship rights.

Thus, New York blacks' Emancipation Day plans acceded to the white community's, and particularly white workers', views of the limits of black citizenship. During the Jacksonian era, public displays of citizenship in the form of parades, festivals, and, more sinisterly, mobs, would be a sign and celebration of white working-class citizenship. Increasingly, the white middle class abandoned the streets and demonized such public displays. Black reformers encouraged blacks, too, to move out of the public space being conquered by the white working classes. The celebration supported by Cornish, Russwurm, and others pointed to a middle-class-based way of defining black celebrations, and thus for blacks to deal with urban life: with speeches, prayers, and hymns, all performed indoors, in churches and meeting halls.[74]

Cornish and Russwurm also displayed their worries about street politics and culture and its propriety for blacks in their suggestions for the Emancipation Day speakers. They called on New York Manumission Society members to use the occasion "to suggest the future conduct and pursuits of the emancipated."[75] Cornish and Russwurm then offered their own suggestion: the speaker or speakers should dwell on agricultural pursuits, a theme that

would recur throughout the pre–Civil War era among black and white reformers. Ignoring the fact that many free blacks had fled the country for the
community of the city, Cornish and Russwurm predicted that blacks would
succeed best in the country, for they already knew that business. "Should
these people be left to flock into our large cities, with their minds uncul-ti-
vated, and without having learned to provide for themselves, it is much to be
feared, that many of them will fall victims to temptation, and its consequent
evils." But in the country, Cornish and Russwurm believed, "they will be
likely to succeed, and become useful citizens."[76]

Not all agreed with these Emancipation Day plans and the cautious attitude toward citizenship for blacks they suggested. Some blacks continued to
organize a parade for July 5. A week before the planned celebration, "R."
wrote to express his "feelings of the deepest regret" over the intention to
split the emancipation celebration into two parts, one a church service, the
other a parade. Doing so divided the black community. R. encouraged a compromise. The celebration should be held on the fourth, as an expression of
blacks' full citizenship and stake in American society: "The event celebrated
by whites, is the one in which we are interested, and have cause to rejoice, as
well as they," he stated. But, recognizing the fear that celebrating blacks
would "be in danger of being molested by vagabonds among the whites,"
blacks should dispense with the procession: "Of what use to us are processions? . . . [H]ave they not . . . a tendency to injure us, by exciting prejudice,
and making the public believe we care for nothing so much as show?" R.
urged the newly freed blacks not to offend their "earthly benefactors," including those of the Society of Friends, who tended to "heartily disapprove
of our making a street parade. . . . Most of the Societies of colour have refused to join in the contemplated procession, and it ought to be made public,
that at the first general meeting held to make arrangements for the celebrating of this Jubilee, the majority were opposed to any such measure." These
societies included not only churches, such as the Asbury Methodist Church
and Samuel Cornish's Presbyterian Church, but also the African Society for
Mutual Relief, formerly a leader in public processions in the city.[77]

The 1827 opposition to public parades was linked to the identification of
some blacks with moral reform movements that in the 1830s would increasingly attempt to chart and restrict the uses of the streets. Cornish, Russwurm, and others were first among a growing group of black reformers who
aligned themselves with a more middle-class comportment. However, black
reformers were ambivalent about criticizing black behavior in particular. In
the same issue of *Freedom's Journal* in which R. entered his protests against

parades, the editors defended the rights of the lower classes of blacks to parade, against the suggestions of whites. An editorial from the white-owned
New York Morning Chronicle had expressed doubts that blacks would be able
to have an orderly celebration, and fears that emancipation would increase
the numbers of black "dandies" and criminals in New York. Cornish and
Russwurm responded, "We are no friends to public parades, and have long
since entered our *protest against them.* Yet we hold, that our brethren (when
they see proper) in common with the rest of the community, have a right to
indulge in them." Further, Cornish and Russwurm emphasized that "Broadway, the Bowery, &c. exhibit too great a mixture of white and coloured
dandies, equally rude, and destitute of the courtesy and respect due to their
superiors." By calling attention to the behavior of blacks and whites of
the same class level, Cornish and Russwurm attempted to recast the problem from one of race to one of class in the eyes of the white community. To
do so would not only address the fact that whites were imperfect also, but
could also elevate in the eyes of whites those blacks who were more circumspect in their behavior. However, such efforts to force the white community to acknowledge class divisions within the black community were often
unsuccessful.[78]

Ultimately, blacks held two Emancipation Day celebrations. Despite their
support of the rights of blacks to parade, Cornish and Russwurm joined the
African Society for Mutual Relief and other individuals and organizations
in a celebration on July 4, 1827, in the safety of the society's meeting hall.
The celebration was an opportunity to praise the black community's benefactors: "The portraits of Jay, Clarkson and Thompson, which adorned the
walls of the church, recalled to our minds, former times, when these philan-
thropists particularly exerted themselves in behalf of our oppressed race."
The celebration also promoted the moral reforms of charity and temperance.
The editors of *Freedom's Journal* attempted to ease the divisions in the community revealed in the discussions over the Emancipation Day celebration:
"We are brethren by the ties of blood and misfortunes, and we can perceive
no sufficient reasons, why matters of a trifling nature, should cause so much
excitation and division among us," they stated.[79]

On July 5, between three thousand and four thousand blacks marched in
celebration with music and banners, ending at the A.M.E. Zion Church for
speeches. Whites did not disrupt the festivities.[80] Perhaps because of the success of the parade in 1827, blacks paraded again the following year. Samuel
Hardenburgh led a procession of New York and Brooklyn societies through
the streets, accompanied by music. Hardenburgh, a member of the Society
for Mutual Relief, would support the rights of blacks to parade in the streets

for the next six years, both in New York City and as a delegate to the National Conventions of the Free People of Color, which debated this issue
in 1834.[81]

Cornish and Russwurm applauded the orderliness of the Manhattan celebration, but they sternly criticized an additional public emancipation celebration held in Brooklyn the following Saturday. "Nothing serves more to
keep us in our present degraded condition, than these foolish exhibitions of
ourselves," they declared. Chiding both the leaders of the parade for setting
a bad example and the "lower orders" for following the parade, Cornish
and Russwurm said of the Brooklyn celebration: "We have heard of officers
high in authority scarcely able to bear their standards—of the insolence of
certain Coloured females, and the debasing excesses committed on that ever
memorable day. . . . [N]othing is more disgusting to the eyes of a reflecting
man of colour than *one of these grand processions,* followed by the lower orders of society." In particular they criticized the purchase of secondhand
army uniforms and "horse trappings," "that we may appear as Generals or
Marshals, or Admirals on these occasions, complete and appropriate laugh-
ing stocks for thousands of our citizens." Spending money on such clothing
"profit none of us," they argued. "Has any man yet been held in estimation
on account of his *fine dress?* is it [a] mark of *prudence* to put all our earnings
upon our backs? and finally, from this imprudence, to be *unprovided* with
food, and *clothing,* and *fuel,* during the chilling blasts of winter?"[82]

Such criticisms echoed those of the Manumission Society, which blacks
earlier in the emancipation period had rejected. Now, some black leaders
openly agreed with the society. This new group of black leaders no longer
viewed as subversive or uplifting the sight of blacks marching in the clothing of an army that they could not participate in as equals. But for supporters of parades such as Samuel Hardenburgh, these displays maintained the
visibility of the black presence in New York. Brooklynites calling themselves
"Freemen" denounced Cornish and Russwurm's criticisms as "prejudice and
misrepresentation." Blacks could "afford a holiday without depriving ourselves of fuel and clothing for the winter." As to the charge of "excesses," the
Freemen replied, "It may . . . be true that some 'debasing excesses' took place
on that day, and it would be very extraordinary if such should not occur
among a vast concourse of people. Who ever witnessed any celebration in
this country without some 'excesses'? Mr. Rushman [*sic*], might with as
much propriety censure the civil authorities for all excesses on the celebration of our national independence. They are unavoidable, and the 'Brooklyn
Society' are not to be held answerable for the conduct of a mob who might
have been permitted to follow at their heels."[83]

The 1828 Emancipation Day parade was one of the last of the antebellum era in New York. Pressures from within the black community, generational changes in black leadership, and increasing verbal and physical hostility from whites led to the decline of these elaborate celebrations by the early 1830s. Increasingly, public celebrations of emancipation and black equality were led by the radical abolitionists, who limited the participation of the masses in favor of controlled celebrations that extolled moral reform and antislavery sentiments in more conservative fashion.[84]

The debate over the Fourth of July Emancipation Day parades reveals the struggles within the black community over the public roles blacks should take in the city, and over the definition of black citizenship. Some black reformers felt, as did whites, that newly free blacks required preparation for citizenship. Controlling blacks' public parades was only one element of blacks' and whites' new reform efforts. In early 1828, barely six months after the complete emancipation of New York's slaves, "several respectable men of Colour" met with the New York Manumission Society to implement ways to increase the attendance of black students at the schools. These black and white men implemented a revised version of the registry system that had been suggested by the New York Manumission Society in 1788 but which the society had been unable to implement. They divided the city into seventeen districts and dispatched two black men to each to obtain information on black families, including "condition, occupation, number of children under five years of age, with such other particulars as may be deemed desirable, to be known" by the Manumission Society. Peter Williams was chairman and Samuel Cornish was "general agent" of this home-visiting project. Other participants in the effort to enumerate black families and enroll their children in the African Free Schools included John Russwurm, coeditor of *Freedom's Journal* and one of the first black college graduates in the United States; Thomas Jennings, proprietor of a secondhand clothing shop; real estate dealer Thomas Jinnings; carpenter William Hamilton; and Thomas Sipkins—all members of the New York African Society for Mutual Relief and part of the black community's emerging middle class.[85]

Through the efforts of these black reformers and the Manumission Society members, material aid became more central to the school's efforts to reach greater numbers of New York City blacks. Two weeks after their initial meeting, Peter Williams and John Russwurm met again with members of the Manumission Society, this time to form the African Dorcas Association, the purpose of which was to provide clothing for needy children attending the African Free Schools. The Dorcas Association not only gave children an incentive to attend the school, but also gave black women, who were

excluded from the census activities of the school, an opportunity to participate in the moral reform activities of the Manumission Society. Meeting
weekly, black women repaired and distributed used clothing to needy children of the African Free Schools.[86]

The trustees of the African Free Schools also gave monetary prizes to
top scholars. Throughout the school year, students received tickets worth
one-eighth of a cent for good behavior and attention to studies. Teachers
took away tickets as punishment for bad behavior. At the Annual Public Days
of Examination, the best scholars received prizes of fifty cents.[87] Through
such incentives, black and white reformers hoped to attract and retain poorer
black children to the school by providing needed cash and garments, particularly in winter months when their parents had greater difficulty finding
work and may have been tempted to hire out their children.

Material incentives to keep children in school were not simply manipu-
lative stratagems to encourage moral reform. In providing cash and clothing
incentives to black children and parents, the Manumission Society and its
black supporters were responding to the exploitation of working-class black
children, most explicitly those in the chimney-sweep trade. The majority
of child sweeps in New York were black boys between the ages of four and
ten. Apprenticed to sweep masters by parents desperate for income, they
climbed down chimneys to scrub the flammable soot off the walls. Constant
contact with and inhalation of soot and ash resulted in skin and lung diseases. Climbing down narrow chimneys led to broken and permanently damaged bones. Some children became trapped in chimneys or fell off roofs during the dangerous work. The early morning hours of the job kept these
children from obtaining an education, and sweepmasters improperly dressed
and fed child sweeps. Manumission Society members successfully requested
that the New York City Common Council pass a series of ordinances that
protected the health and welfare of child sweeps more closely.[88] Further,
through its contacts with the Pennsylvania Society for the Promotion of
Public Economy and the London Society for Superseding the Necessity of
Climbing Boys (both Quaker-based organizations), the society received information on the latest innovations in chimney-sweeping machines that
they hoped would decrease the number of child sweeps.[89]

Black sweep master Adam Marshall joined the Manumission Society in
these reform endeavors. Marshall was at the forefront of the technological
changes supported by the society: he had obtained a new sweeping machine
that eliminated the need for child labor and had opened a shop on Duane
Street. In 1816, Marshall recommended to the Common Council that the
sweeps' method of obtaining customers through street cries be stopped. He

stated that "there are a number of offices for chimney sweepers now established," to which those interested in having chimneys swept could go. In doing so, Marshall aligned himself with middle-class reformers, but possibly for the purpose of alleviating the competition to the machine he owned. In December of 1817, the Common Council passed a series of laws regulating the sweep trade. The council established a superintendent of sweeps, who employed and licensed the master sweeps, regulated the use of child labor, and ensured that all houses with chimneys were swept. The ordinance also stated that because "the present practice of chimney sweeps in making an outcry particularly disturbs the sick," the city would pay those who informed on noisy sweeps two dollars; the reported sweep master could lose his or her license.[90] But repeated petitions against the new law by black sweep masters (who included three women) led to its alteration. Probably they were less successful financially than Marshall and thus unable to rent office space or buy mechanical sweepers. In their petition, they stated that "the means of gaining a living for [our]selves and [our] families is very much lessened" by this ruling. Three months after the initial ruling, the Council stated that sweeps' cries were only forbidden in the First, Second, and Third Wards, where many of the city's wealthiest families lived.[91]

It is difficult to know the degree to which the ordinances and machines prevented the use of black child labor. Although sweeps were not allowed to cry in parts of New York, those who could not establish offices simply traveled to other parts of the city, or to Brooklyn, where there was no such ordinance, to ply their trade. Further, the efforts of the Manumission Society and others who wished to protect children from dangerous labor were double-edged. Certainly black parents agreed with the goals of the society as far as protecting their children from the risks associated with chimney sweeping. However, the Manumission Society was unable to counteract the forces that limited economic opportunity for black families and led them to such forms of labor for income. As late as 1859, reformers reported the presence of child sweeps and their deaths from the dangerous work.[92]

Preventing harmful child labor practices and educating children were only two of the Manumission Society's goals for its schools. The society and its supporters also hoped to be able to influence the parents of the children in its schools. This had been a goal of the society virtually from the founding of the African Free Schools.[93] The cooperation of black ministers and reformers after 1820 provided the Manumission Society with a way into the private lives of the families of the students of the schools that it had never had before. It gave black leaders and the Manumission Society greater influence over the political, cultural, and social expression of those ex-slaves seeking to improve their economic status. In a handbook for parents published in 1818, the trustees laid out their conceptions of the best ways for black parents to raise their children, for "their and *your* present good, and consequent future happiness." The trustees acknowledged that parents of African Free School students were those most concerned with the well-being of their own children: "Who, we would ask, can or ought to feel more concern, that a child should be 'trained up in the way he should go,' than the parents of such a child?"[94] But the trustees also placed themselves in a position of guardianship over both parents and children, instructing parents in their conception of the proper way to raise their children. Parents were to set a good example for their children by attending church services and reading the Bible with them. As good disciplinarians, parents were to give commands "with prudence and moderation, and . . . enforce them with a becoming resolution," but were never to correct children in anger. They were also to teach children basic habits of cleanliness, as well as that stealing, "profane language," and cruelty to animals were wrong.[95]

Parents were also to train their children in industrious ways by finding "employment for their children, at a suitable age." Such early employment would prevent *"close confinement at maturer age in a state prison or house of correction."* For the Manumission Society, employment was crucial to maintaining the progress blacks began in the schools. "It has been a subject of much regret to the Manumission Society," the trustees stated, "that many of the children who have been educated in [the] school, have, after leaving it, been suffered to waste their time in idleness, to mingle in bad company, and to contract those various habits, which are calculated to render the subjects of them pests to society." Such actions brought "scandal upon the school itself" and "frustrat[ed] its grand object, which is, to improve the condition of your children by making them good citizens, and intelligent members of Society."[96]

However, black parents, and particularly ex-slaves, rarely had the contacts to provide their children with what the society considered suitable employment. Thus, the trustees asked that the parents leave to them "the power of putting out to trades or service, those children who may have received their education at the school . . . it being understood that the parents shall, in every case, if they desire it, be previously consulted."[97] This course of action was a recognition of both the power that the school trustees might wield over potential employers of black children and the trustees' perceptions of the responsibility of black parents. In selecting employers, the trustees assured parents that they would "have a single eye to [the children's] welfare, and be careful that they are put with persons of kindness and humanity.

During their apprenticeship, or term of employment, the trustees will act as the guardians of their rights." In providing such apprenticeships, the trustees saw themselves as continuing the "parental care" that they had exercised over the children while in school. The trustees' parental care would also teach the children the lessons of employment: the necessity for the children to learn to "demean themselves with fidelity and industry in their several employments." Further, the children should be proud of any employment, for "there is no disgrace incurred by the pursuit of any honest calling, however humble." Thus, employment for children would teach them to be responsible employees who submitted to any type of honest labor. And although the trustees stated that they would "effectually resist and cause to be punished those acts of oppression that may be practised upon" the black workers, ultimately the trustees, not the children or their parents, were to judge what were oppressive labor conditions.[98]

Such restrictions probably in the end made the scholars and parents of the African Free Schools a self-selected group. They were willing to abide by the rules of the Manumission Society and of the growing cadre of black reformers. They were perhaps themselves aspiring middle class. In this way, the African Free Schools became a vehicle for the production of black reformers in New York City. Throughout the antebellum period, graduates of the African Free Schools assumed visible leadership in New York's radical abolitionist, religious, and reform movements.

Through the Manumission Society, black reformers gained their earliest experience in cooperating with white reformers over issues of black poverty and reform. Through alliances with white middle-class and elite reformers and through their own concerns for the future of their race, a small group of New York City's free blacks began to develop a distinct set of agendas and identities for themselves during the era of emancipation. At times, they attempted to impose these agendas, such as moral reform and education, upon the black community as a whole, and particularly upon New York's black laboring poor. Their class-based conception of moral stewardship for the black community would continue to be shouldered by succeeding generations of middle-class and aspiring middle-class blacks throughout the antebellum era. For many, such stewardship would become a marker of middle-class status in a community where the material base of that status was difficult to obtain.

Between the Revolutionary War and 1827, white residents of New York debated the meaning and limits of black freedom and citizenship. They rooted their efforts to end slavery in Enlightenment beliefs in the perfectibility of their society and of individual men and women. However, whites' belief that blacks could escape the degradation of slavery was limited. In the eyes of whites, the "badge of servitude" of dependency and immorality that marked blacks under slavery did not completely disappear upon freedom. The 1799 gradual emancipation act reflected these beliefs through the establishment of special programs to reform the labor habits of free blacks, as did the white discourse on urban black culture and black crime. These ideas reached their culmination in New York in the state legislature's disfranchisement of the vast majority of free blacks even as it enacted universal white male suffrage.

Thus, full freedom for New York's slaves did not result in equality. Hampered by the continuation of indentures and job discrimination and its resultant poverty, blacks lived on the margins of the growing New York City economy. But despite these hardships, New York City, with large numbers of blacks in close proximity, provided unparalleled opportunities for community, freedom, and political activism for blacks, particularly for those escaping the isolation of rural areas. Slaves who had become free workers were vital to the creation of black religious and social institutions during this time. They also created informal networks among themselves that aided their economic and political survival, as well as a multifaceted public presence through political and social parades, through actions against slavery, and in dance halls and grogshops.

By the end of the era of emancipation, black and white reformers, responding to attacks on black life by those who saw free blacks as unfit to survive in the United States, increasingly labeled such manifestations of black public culture as harmful to the cause of black equality and freedom. Some blacks, however, retained a skeptical view of reform methods, whether promulgated by blacks or whites, and their ability to address such issues as employment and slavery. Increasingly in the antebellum period, dissension from moral reform in the black community was associated with workers and the poor. When black middle-class leaders frowned upon street culture and demonstrations, working-class blacks continued to use them to raise consciousness and achieve their objectives, particularly since the 1821 suffrage law locked them out of traditional politics. In such divisions lay the ideological basis of class distinctions within the black community.

CHAPTER FIVE

Keeping Body and Soul Together:
Charity Workers and Black Activism in
Post-emancipation New York City

In 1832, Charles Andrews, the white principal of the African Free Schools, "severely caned" a young student named Sanders for calling a black male visitor to the school a gentleman. The caning highlighted the struggles between blacks and the New York Manumission Society over the place of blacks in New York City. By the mid-1820s, prominent members of the society had begun to support the American Colonization Society's programs for sending free blacks to Africa. The Colonization Society publicized free blacks' difficulties with poverty, crime, and white racism to demonstrate that blacks could not survive in the United States and that blacks' true home was in Africa. Members of the Manumission Society founded the New York City Colonization Society in 1817 and were instrumental in founding the New York State Colonization Society in 1829. The African Free Schools began to train blacks for emigration to Liberia. The New York Manumission Society's support for colonization encouraged other state manumission societies to lend their support as well.

The Manumission Society's support for colonization led New York City blacks to question the society's commitment to their political and economic well-being in New York. With few exceptions, black commentators adamantly opposed the Colonization Society's policies as racist. But blacks continued to support the African Free Schools, until Andrews caned Sanders. The caning echoed the punishments of slaves. Terms such as "gentleman" or "lady" implied middle-class economic status, as well as proper morals. For some blacks, aspiring to or achieving middle-class status was one of the best ways to prove the equality of the black race. Andrews's refusal to recognize a black man as a gentleman (and by extension, black women as ladies) demonstrated to blacks that by the 1830s the Manumission Society had given up on its goals of incorporating blacks into American society as full citizens.

Black activists' response to the caning demonstrated their increasing lack of deference toward whites attempting reforms on their behalf. Although disillusioned by Andrews's actions, blacks did not reject the schools. Rather, they sought a greater role in the institution founded on their behalf. Blacks demanded Andrews's resignation and the installation of a black principal. Although the Manumission Society acquiesced to this demand, it turned over control of the schools to the New York Public School Society soon after. Manumission Society members were apparently unable to work with blacks as equals. Black men and women continued to play important roles in the African Free Schools as teachers and principals, but the Manumission Society's influence among black New Yorkers collapsed in the 1830s, and the organization folded in 1849.

The end of the Manumission Society's influence in the New York City free black community, as well as the political activism of blacks themselves, led to two new but largely separate efforts by whites to address the issues of material and political inequality facing black New Yorkers. Two new groups of reformers, female charity workers and male and female radical abolitionists, rose to power in the 1830s. Both groups grew out of the Manumission Society and the New York City Colonization Society, but blacks played crucial roles in shaping the goals of each. The rise of radical abolition in the 1830s (see chapter 6) led to a new intensity in the fight against racism and southern slavery. The radical abolitionists' rejection of colonization, their advocacy of immediate emancipation for southern slaves, and their promotion of racial equality stemmed from the influence of blacks on white leaders such as William Lloyd Garrison and Arthur and Lewis Tappan.

But the radical abolitionists were never as concerned with the material condition of northern free blacks as black people would have liked. White radical abolitionists never consistently funded programs or institutions to address the poverty of free blacks in New York City, or in the North generally. Instead, it was the wives and daughters of Manumission Society members who founded new charity organizations in the late 1830s to address the problems of poverty in northern black communities. The female managers of the Colored Orphan Asylum and the Colored Home, founded in 1836 and 1839, respectively, largely avoided the growing radical abolitionist struggle against southern slavery and for black equality, and a few were Colonization Society supporters. But as with the Manumission Society, middle-class and working-class blacks persuaded the asylum's managers to adjust their conceptions of the needs of blacks.

This influence is most clear in the case of the Colored Orphan Asylum. The asylum's all-male advisory board included former Manumission Society members and Colonization Society members. In its early years, the asylum followed the model of the Manumission Society's early treatment of black children. The asylum's managers did not have particularly high expectations for their students. These women saw themselves as training blacks to be content with lives as servants and menial laborers and to see such jobs as worthy and meaningful.[1] But blacks did not simply accept the goals these women had set for them. Indeed, middle-class black reformers publicly criticized the managers for not having higher educational and occupational objectives for black children, and for their association with those who favored colonization.

Despite the criticisms of middle-class blacks, working-class blacks adopted the orphanage (as well as the Colored Home) into their own strategies for survival. The orphanage provided much better material care and education than did the Municipal Almshouse, where orphaned black children were otherwise forced to reside. But despite the relief the women provided, black working-class parents and children demanded that the women go beyond their initial, limited plans for the orphanage's clients. Black parents called on the orphanage to address the needs of the children of widowed working mothers as well as of children who had lost both parents. Throughout the antebellum period, parents and relatives who placed their children in the orphanage, as well as the children themselves, continued to resist managers' limited expectations for the children in their care. Blacks' activism on this issue led to changes within the institution and informed the women's views of blacks: in the mid-1840s, the women replaced the orphanage's white doctors, who supported colonization, with black radical abolitionist James McCune Smith; throughout the antebellum period, the women admitted many more children of single parents ("half-orphans") than orphans; and in individual cases, the managers were forced to acquiesce to the power of parents and children who sought to move beyond the limits of the orphanage's goals and take greater control of their own lives.

Blacks in the 1830s increasingly exercised their power to influence organizations founded on their behalf. The orphanage provided a valuable service to black families who were unable to keep their children due to poverty, work, illness, or death, but simple material charity and moral lessons were not enough for many blacks. They sought to make the providers of these services understand the larger struggles over race and class that were at stake for them in New York City, and sometimes they succeeded. In the wake of the demise of the Manumission Society, the asylum managers were probably all too aware of the vulnerability of their project to the desires of their clients. New York City blacks' rejection of the Manumission Society had resulted in the downfall of the society's activist agenda. Whereas the men in charge of the Manumission Society could return to other public roles after the society's dissolution, the orphanage provided its female managers with one of their few opportunities for institutional influence and power, and perhaps even for independent income. As these middle-class white women interacted with middle-class and working-class blacks, each group constantly renegotiated its perceptions of the goals and needs of working-class blacks for mutual beneficence.[2]

■ ■ ■

During the 1820s and early 1830s, members of the New York Manumission Society had become increasingly frustrated with the conditions of free blacks in the city. Some of their frustration grew out of the inability of black workers, and particularly the graduates of the African Free Schools, to obtain jobs commensurate with their education or skills. The African Free Schools successfully attracted students through the 1820s. In 1822, enrollment peaked at eight hundred students and ranged between six hundred and seven hundred for the remainder of the decade, forcing the Manumission Society to open a second school to accommodate the demand. Charles C. Andrews, the white principal who replaced John Teasman in 1809, presided over this surge in enrollment. Andrews was by all accounts a dedicated educator who also brought a great deal of positive publicity to the schools. He invited members of the Common Council and newspaper reporters to school programs, which generated good press for the schools. This positive publicity enabled the society to build new school buildings in neighborhoods formerly hostile to the schools (fig. 10).[3]

The success of the schools was evident in its top graduates. A small number of students whose parents were willing and able to allow them to remain at the schools for the full array of courses available received an education that prepared them for college and other advanced degrees. Many black leaders of the radical abolitionist movement of the 1830s and 1840s obtained their early education at the African Free Schools in the 1820s and 1830s. James McCune Smith went from the African Free Schools to receive a medical degree from Glasgow University in Scotland in 1832. Smith returned to New York City in 1837 to practice medicine and become involved in the radical abolitionist movement. Henry Highland Garnet attended the African Free

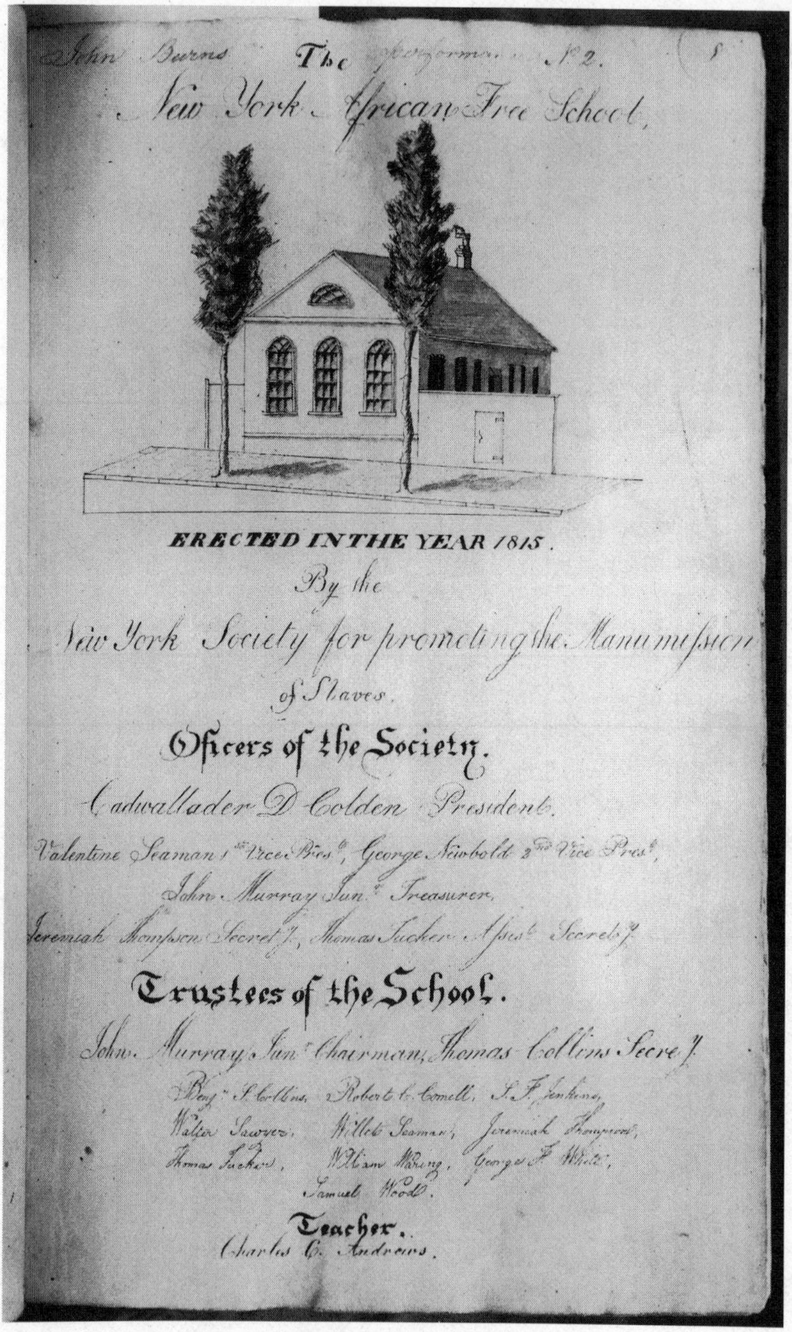

Fig. 10 Drawing of the African Free School, no. 1. Neg. no. 59134. © Collection of the New-York Historical Society.

Schools before graduating from the Oneida Institute and returning to New York in the 1840s as a Presbyterian minister, abolitionist, and city missionary to Manhattan's poor blacks, as did Alexander Crummell, who became an Episcopal minister.[4] Other graduates of the schools included Congregationalist minister and abolitionist Samuel Ringgold Ward; engraver Patrick Reason and his brother, educator Charles Reason; and internationally renowned Shakespearian actor Ira Aldridge.[5]

But the majority of students only obtained a basic education before seeking out working-class jobs. These students, despite their education, often experienced the same difficulties as uneducated black New Yorkers in finding skilled jobs. The Manumission Society members and schoolteachers were all too aware of the obstacles their students faced. As Andrews stated in 1830, "It may afford some relief . . . to learn that a few have obtained trades of the following descriptions; viz. Sail Makers, Shoe Makers, Tin Workers, Tailors, Carpenters, Blacksmiths, &c." But most students experienced "difficulties" that "attended them on account of their color." Whites tried to prevent them from "obtaining a thorough knowledge of the trades, or . . . [from] finding employ in good shops; and a general objection is made, by white journeymen to working in the same shop with them." As a result, "many of our best lads go to sea," and others worked as "waiters, coachmen, barbers, servants, laborers, &c."—jobs that the Manumission Society and Andrews considered menial, and that may have paid less well and less regularly than skilled jobs.[6]

The Manumission Society's concern in the 1830s that its male students achieve skilled jobs signified a slight change in its members' attitudes toward blacks. In the 1790s and early 1800s Manumission Society members had been largely concerned with ensuring blacks' appreciation for any type of paid labor. But by the late 1820s the society, as expressed in the words of Charles Andrews, had begun to realize that education without hope of advancement was discouraging to many blacks. Many blacks realized, stated Andrews, that "they can do just as well, in all the stations filled by those whom we educate, and get as much wages as they can, and are as well off without education as with it. Hence the great indifference which prevails among them to the acquisition of knowledge."[7] Although Andrews and the society were concerned about elevating blacks intellectually, they also worried that blacks might turn away from moral education. A large class of immoral blacks would threaten the safety of the city.

The Manumission Society's failure to convince other white New Yorkers that blacks should be given equal opportunities to succeed economically, as well as its own fears that racism among whites would lead blacks to turn away from moral education, led the society by the mid-1820s to support privately the American Colonization Society's programs to send blacks to Africa. The American Colonization Society, founded in 1816 in Washington, D.C., reinforced the belief among many whites and some blacks that blacks could not achieve full citizenship in the United States. Some white colonizationists blamed the racism of whites, who they believed would never, or only very slowly, learn to accept blacks as equals. "No individual merit can elevate the black to the condition of the white man; no path of honourable distinction is open to him; no post of honour or usefulness is within his reach," stated the society's *African Repository and Colonial Journal* in 1825. The racism that prevented blacks from achieving economic and political success negatively affected blacks' moral state. Blacks had no motive to seek "virtuous exertion and industry," and became "degraded, and conscious of [their] hopeless degradation . . . [sank] into poverty and vice." The Colonization Society compiled statistics, sometimes erroneous, that claimed that the proportion of blacks in prisons, almshouses, and mental hospitals was far greater than their proportion in the general population. The society specifically targeted and publicized the conditions of free blacks in cities. They believed that "a great portion of [blacks in cities] are found in abodes of poverty and vice, and become the tenants of poorhouses and prisons."[8] These examples of poverty demonstrated that freed blacks could not compete in the economy alongside whites. According to colonizationists, repatriation to Africa was best. Africa would give blacks an opportunity to grow morally and economically without the hindrance of white racism. Some believed that blaks could prove their equality with whites by Christianizing native Africans and building up the economic infrastructure in Africa. Once blacks in Africa demonstrated their true abilities, whites in America would realize that slavery and racism were wrong and would welcome blacks in America. Other supporters of colonization argued that the possibility of sending freed blacks to Africa would increase voluntary emancipation in the southern states and ultimately end slavery.[9]

In 1817, a group of New York City men met in the mayor's office to form an auxiliary society to the American Colonization Society. The founders included John Murray Jr., the treasurer of the New York Manumission Society, and several other members of the Manumission Society. Although the auxiliary society soon lapsed for lack of funds, New York Manumission Society members continued to solicit support for colonization from the American Convention of Abolition Societies, an organization of state manumission societies of which it was a member. Until the late 1820s, the American Convention consistently voted against supporting colonization "without an immutable pledge from the slaveholding states of a just and wise system of gradual emancipation." But in 1826, the American Convention began to waver in its stance. That year, delegates from the New York Manumission Society again suggested that the convention reconsider supporting colonization. The New York delegates put forth resolutions that the American Convention should recommend to Congress "the gradual, but certain, extinguishment of slavery, and the transportation of the whole coloured population, now held in bondage, to the coast of Africa, or the island of St. Domingo." Although the American Convention would only agree to request "an adequate portion" of federal money "for the voluntary removal of such slaves as may hereafter be emancipated," this was a turning point in the convention's support of colonization. In late 1829, the American Convention for the first time linked the success of southern emancipation to African colonization. The convention stated that voluntary emigration of blacks to Africa and federal funding for such programs would encourage at least some southerners in states with large numbers of slaves to free their slaves, secure in the knowledge that the newly free blacks would not try to achieve political or economic power in the United States. Although the American Convention did not believe that "the whole coloured populaton" would be removed from the United States, they did think that "partial emigration may greatly aid the cause" of emancipation.[10] At the same meeting, the New York Manumission Society also promoted the colonization of free blacks in Texas as the best way to "produce any sensible diminution of [free blacks] in the old states." Because Texas was near "those states which are overcharged with the descendants of Africa," it would be much less expensive to export blacks there than to Africa. Support for colonization among New Yorkers also grew stronger in the late 1820s. In 1829, a group of white men met in Albany, New York, to form a new state colonization society. In 1831, another group, including members of the Manumission Society, formed a New York City Colonization Society.

A few blacks supported colonization, but the vast majority of New York City blacks opposed it, and many heaped scorn on its supporters, white and black. When black newspaper editor John Russwurm accepted the position of administrator of Liberia's school system, he was subjected to "violent persecution" by "the most influential" among blacks—including, no doubt, his coeditor at *Freedom's Journal,* Samuel Cornish, a staunch opponent of colonization.[11] As did free blacks in other cities, in 1831 New York City's blacks held a public meeting to denounce the colonization scheme. "A number of gentlemen in this city" hold "mistaken views with respect to the wishes and welfare of the people of this state, on the subject of African colonization," the meeting's organizers stated. A recent address from the New

York Colonization Society contained "opinions and assertions regarding the people of color" that were "as unfounded as they [were] unjust and derogatory to them" and tended "to excite the prejudice of the community." Blacks resolved to "protest against" the assertions that the "colored population are a growing evil, immoral, and destitute of religious principles." Such assertions, as well as the colonization movement itself, were part of an "unholy crusade against the colored population of this country" and "totally at variance with true Christian principles." Blacks at this meeting claimed "*this country, the place of our birth, and not Africa,* as our mother country."[12]

Although the New York Manumission Society's support of colonization seeped into the African Free Schools, blacks continued to support the schools. In 1829, principal Charles Andrews and the schools' trustees agreed to educate two young men for teaching positions in Liberia. Andrews's support of colonization grew out of his frustration with racism against blacks in the United States. Attempts to place school graduates in apprenticeships had ended in failure. One of the students Andrews helped to go to Liberia, Isaac Moore, had been unable to find an apprenticeship in New York or Philadelphia. Moore himself "resolved to leave the country and go to the Colony of Liberia."[13] But even the most outspoken critics of colonization continued to support the African Free Schools. Education was an important goal for blacks of all classes. Although New York City blacks established schools in connection with churches and independently, none had the resources that the Manumission Society could bring to black education. Black reformers such as Samuel Cornish, Peter Williams Jr., and William Hamilton encouraged blacks to continue to work with the African Free Schools to obtain needed education. By the early 1830s, their efforts, combined with those of principal Charles Andrews, resulted in doubled attendance. The Manumission Society opened four more schools between 1831 and 1832.[14] But this period of cooperation between black and white reformers on behalf of the African Free Schools was short lived. The controversy which arose after Charles Andrews's 1832 caning of Sanders led to demands for the principal's resignation.

Albro Lyons Sr. later recalled the incident. Lyons was a pupil in the African Free Schools when "a knock came to the door, [and] a lad by the name of Sanders . . . was directed to ascertain who the visitor was." Sanders stated that "a colored gentleman" wished to speak with principal Charles Andrews. Andrews received the visitor "very cordially." After the visitor departed, "Andrews caned the lad severely for having called a colored person a 'gentleman.'" Andrews's use of the cane may have been a result of his British background, but during this time, most American educators were turning away from corporal punishment as a means to discipline students. Caning held overtones of the punishments meted out to slaves, sailors, and other lower-class persons. The word "gentleman," on the other hand, implied education, morality, and nonmanual labor—characteristics of the middle-class and elite status that some blacks hoped to obtain through the African Free Schools. Andrews's punishment of Sanders asserted that blacks could never be gentlemen. Even with each other, Andrews's actions implied, blacks in the United States should *only* envision themselves as workers, and not as gentlemen or ladies.[15]

For blacks, this incident revealed that Andrews held limited expectations of economic and social success for his students and for blacks generally. Outraged by this event, a group led by carpenter William Hamilton, porter Henry Sipkins, and restaurateur Thomas Downing demanded that Andrews be fired.[16] Black support for Andrews's firing revealed that some blacks conceived of middle-class aspirations and achievements as a way to redeem the race's degraded status. The need for blacks to demonstrate middle-class achievement in order to achieve racial equality was established by the 1821 suffrage law that required blacks to own property in order to vote and reinforced by colonizationist whites who stated that black poverty indicated blacks' unfitness for full U.S. citizenship. Additionally, for some, middle-class status increasingly implied upright morality. Gentlemen (and by extension, ladies) were not sexually promiscuous, did not drink immoderately, and attended church regularly. These moral attributes constituted important parts of citizenship for middle-class blacks and whites. (These attributes were in opposition to some parts of the public political culture of many working-class whites, many of whom favored drunken celebrations of political holidays.) For blacks, the African Free Schools were one way through which their children could obtain an education that could move them beyond their own status as ex-slaves and menial workers and into the middle class—intellectually and morally. Although Sipkins was a porter, a lower-status occupation, and Hamilton was a skilled laborer, their membership in the African Society for Mutual Relief and their activism in churches and in the community more generally were rooted in these evolving middle-class values of education and morality. For them, and perhaps for working-class blacks as well, Charles Andrews's disciplinary action against Sanders confirmed that the Manumission Society had given up on the project of educating blacks for the purpose of achieving equality in New York City.

In demanding Andrews's resignation, however, blacks did not reject the schools. Rather, they tried to reshape the schools for their own goals and needs. They demanded that the Manumission Society dismiss Andrews and replace him with a "gentleman of color," John Peterson. Peterson was a graduate of the schools and had been trained for two years by Andrews before becoming a teacher there in 1826.[17] The trustees of the African Free Schools named Peterson as Andrews's replacement on May 1, 1832. By 1833, in the seven African Free Schools, all but one of the teachers were black, and 1,439 students had enrolled in the schools, an all-time high.[18]

This tension over the leadership of the schools led the Manumission Society trustees to consider relinquishing control of the schools. A cut in the New York City Common Council's funding to the schools increased the society's desire to end their administration of them. Despite the renewed support of the schools by the black community and the support of the wider New York City community, in January 1833 the Common Council cut the funds supplied to the schools for the upkeep of school buildings and for teachers' salaries to an amount that would cover only the teachers' salaries. The Manumission Society could not support the schools' upkeep on its own, and so empowered a committee of trustees to find a solution that would enable the schools to continue to operate with the least disruption.[19]

For some time, New York's Public School Society had been interested in acquiring the African Free Schools. The Public School Society received the vast majority of the money allocated from the Common Council's School Fund and educated over 1,400 students yearly. Thus, the Manumission Society decided to sell the school property and transfer its authority over the schools to the Public School Society. On May 1, 1834, the trustees of the Manumission Society ended their most successful venture.[20]

Some trustees joined the Public School Society to facilitate the transfer of the schools. The Manumission Society as a group branched out into other charitable and educational endeavors involving the city's African Americans, largely in an advisory or financial role. Although it had been unable to sustain the schools, the Manumission Society still held a fair amount of money in its coffers, particularly after the sale of the school property. Operational until 1849, the society continued to provide legal assistance to blacks accused of being fugitive slaves. The society also functioned as a foundation to which new or financially troubled white organizations interested in aiding New York's free blacks applied for advice and funding.[21] In this role, the society aided a new group of female reformers in establishing charitable institutions for New York City's free blacks. Many of these new reformers were the wives and daughters of Manumission Society members. In 1836, these women organized the Association for the Benefit of Colored Orphans, which founded the Colored Orphan Asylum. In 1839, the women founded the Colored Home to care for elderly, sick, and indigent blacks who were without homes or families. Of the two institutions, the Colored Orphan Asylum was the more well known and controversial.

On a spring day in 1834, Anna Shotwell and Mary Murray decided to take a walk along Cherry Street in lower Manhattan. On this day, they noticed two rather disheveled black children sitting on the stoop of a dilapidated two-story brick building. They asked the black woman who leaned out of a window above, "Are these your children?" "No," the woman replied. "They are orphans; I'm caring for them until the municipal authorities find them permanent homes." Shotwell and Murray gave the woman some money for the care of the children and promised to visit again soon. When they returned, four new children, plus the original two, were sitting on the stoop, all neatly dressed. The black woman explained that the money had enabled her to take in the additional children.[22]

   According to the orphanage's records, this incident was the catalyst for the founding of the Association for the Benefit of Colored Orphans. The story implies that these two Quaker women had simply stumbled across one of the informal networks of family, neighbors, and friends that working-class blacks in New York City's neighborhoods struggled to establish and maintain to take care of their children in the wake of New York's gradual emancipation. But Shotwell and Murray in fact had previous experience with the problem of black poverty in New York City before their spring stroll. The two women came from the same tradition of Quaker benevolence, and even the same families, as the founders of the all-male New York Manumission Society.[23] Anna Shotwell's father was William Shotwell, a member of the society; her niece Mary Murray was the granddaughter of John Murray Jr., the society's treasurer for over thirty years.[24] Shotwell and Murray had also come of age in a community of religious women who, beginning in the 1810s and 1820s, participated actively in educating the black community. Women in the Society of Friends were among the first to establish nonsectarian public schools for the education of the poor and blacks during the era of emancipation.[25] Like other benevolent women of their time, the managers of the Colored Orphan Asylum (fig. 11) blurred the boundaries of separate-spheres gender ideology. They called on their moral authority as middle-class and elite women to take them out of the home and into the heart of the problems of the burgeoning city. Through the establishment of the orphanage, they moved beyond domestic moral authority into the financial, legal, and

HEROINES OF A CENTURY AGO

A trio of the founders of the Colored Orphan Asylum

Center—Anna H. Shotwell

Left—Hannah Shotwell   *Right—Mary Murray*

Fig. 11 Portraits of Colored Orphan Asylum founders Anna and Hannah Shotwell and Mary Murray, reprinted from *From Cherry Street to Green Pastures: A History of the Colored Orphan Asylum at Riverdale-On-Hudson,* published in 1936 to celebrate the orphanage's one hundredth anniversary. Neg. no. 74633. © Collection of the New-York Historical Society.

political responsibilities of what middle-class ideology defined as the male sphere of activity.[26]

Mary Murray and Anna Shotwell determined to build an institution specifically for orphaned black children. There were three different orphanages receiving municipal funding at the time, but none of them accepted black children. Those black children who had no friends or relatives to take care of them ended up at the Municipal Almshouse. They resided alongside adults, and the almshouse provided no education for them. Such practices denied black children the protection of childhood accorded to white orphans. Before 1831, white children were kept separately from adults in the almshouse. Overcrowding, the susceptibility of the children to epidemic diseases (particularly opthalmia, a form of conjunctivitis), and the lack of education led the Common Council in 1831 to establish the Department for Children at Long Island Farms in Queens County. By 1834, all white children who previously would have been almshouse residents were instead housed at Long Island Farms, and after 1848 at new buildings built on Randall's Island.[27]

For two years, Shotwell and Murray tried to convince the New York City government to grant them funds for their project, but as with other orphanages, the Common Council refused to do so.[28] In 1836, the Quaker women formed a privately funded organization, the Association for the Benefit of Colored Orphans, with fourteen other women and five male advisers. The association elected Martha Codwise first directress and Sarah Hawsehurst (also a Quaker) second directress, while Anna Shotwell and Mary Murray served as secretary and treasurer, respectively. The women then spent the next six months procuring funding and supplies, finding a house for the orphans, and informing the black community of the association's existence.[29]

In May of 1837, the managers were ready to admit "under their protection not exceeding five Orphans" and to open a day school. The sewing committee had completed 113 garments. The managers had received donations in kind ranging from knives and forks to furniture to andirons to a "key" of potatoes. The women had canvassed the neighborhood, informing black families with children that the day school would be available to them. Receiving an enthusiastic response, the managers had purchased school furniture "at a reduced price." The orphanage was ready to receive its charges. On June 9, 1837, four-year-old Sarah Williams entered the asylum as the first orphan. "She was soon neatly equipped from our little Store," wrote Anna Shotwell, "and bears a very prepossessing appearance." [30] Within the first six weeks, the managers easily exceeded the five-orphan limit suggested to them by the advisory board.

In July, Shotwell, Murray, and Hetty King visited the commissioners of the municipal almshouse and proposed to them that the black orphaned children there, who were "represented to be in a most neglected and suffering condition," be admitted to the asylum. The almshouse commissioners agreed, and that same day the three women took away five children. Unable to find a coachman who would drive the black children, the three women each carried a child and walked back to Twelfth Street with the other two in the summer heat, a distance of over twenty blocks.[31]

The women founded their orphanage during a particularly violent time in New York City's racial history. Over three days in 1834, whites had attacked the homes, churches, and businesses of black and white radical abolitionists. According to rioters, abolitionists were promoting "amalgamation," or interracial socializing and marriage. But the rioters were also attacking the political and economic power that blacks might gain through alliances with middle-class and elite whites. The riots were the worst in antebellum New York City. They discouraged most white and some black New York City abolitionists from pursuing political and social equality for blacks in New York City.[32] The riots may also have been the reason behind the refusal of other orphanages to integrate, as well as the reluctance of the Common Council to fund the Colored Orphan Asylum for ten years, despite the fact that the asylum had relieved the city of providing for the 141 children taken from the Municipal Almshouse.

For the first decade of its existence, the association relied on donations in money and in kind from the managers' friends and relatives; benefactors such as the Manumission Society; the ministers of the Episcopal, Presbyterian, Baptist, and Methodist churches, as well as "the coloured ministers of this City"; and individuals who donated money and goods as word spread about the orphanage. These donations enabled them, with some difficulty, to purchase their first building in 1837, a house on West Twelfth Street, near Sixth Avenue, and to procure furnishings, clothing, food, and other necessities for the orphanage.[33] When a fire destroyed this first building in 1842, the city relented its stance against funding the orphanage and donated to the asylum twenty lots of land located between Forty-third and Forty-fourth Streets and Fifth Avenue in Manhattan. In 1845, the Common Council also agreed to pay for one hundred orphans at fifty cents a week each, "provided the whole number of inmates amount to one hundred fifty, and in proportion for any less number."[34] By 1843, the women had built a spacious structure on Fifth Avenue (fig. 12) that would be home to the orphans until the Draft Riots of 1863. Capable of housing 150 children, the building stood as

Fig. 12 The Colored Orphan Asylum building on Fifth Avenue, completed in 1843 (detail). Neg. no. 74635. © Collection of the New-York Historical Society.

a potent symbol of white benevolence toward blacks. By 1863, 1,257 children had passed through its doors.

The asylum's reform activities on behalf of blacks challenged what many white New Yorkers believed should be the status quo for black children, the black community, and white women. In her work, historian Lori Ginzberg paints a rosy picture of the ease with which elite women moved into the public sphere through the work of benevolence. Ginzberg sees "conservative and prosperous" female reformers, such as the women who founded the asylum, as dependent on political favors and financial funds from their social class. "Unchallenged in their efforts to organize benevolent institutions," these women "clung . . . tenaciously to the rhetoric of silent, sentimental female benevolence."[35] The women who founded the Colored Orphan Asylum did receive funds and approval from members of their social class, if that social class is narrowly defined as other conservative Quakers and evangelicals. But at least initially, the New York City government denied the asylum access to municipal funds. Despite the female asylum managers' elite racial and class status, the municipal government's denial of funds to the orphanage accorded with its policies toward charitable organizations founded by blacks, such as mutual aid societies, which also did not receive municipal funding during this time. Additionally, some whites criticized the women for overstepping gender and racial boundaries. Some anti-abolitionist whites conflated the activities of the orphan asylum with those of radical abolitionists, despite the women's repeated attempts to dissociate themselves from the "exciting questions that have lately agitated the public mind, in relation to the colored race"—questions regarding, among other things, the existence of interracial radical abolitionist organizations and the abolitionists' goals to end racial prejudice and slavery immediately.[36]

Further, in the eyes of some whites the women's work in the orphanage took them away from their own white families, as well as from the benevolent work that poor whites needed. One critic, Marie Hankins, invented a character called Mrs. Biffles to stand in for female reformers who worked on behalf of blacks (figs. 13 and 14). "Go to Mrs. Biffles in your own character, as an honest white man or woman, and you will receive no favors at her hands," Hankins stated. Mrs. Biffles "neglected" her own home: her children "grew up like weeds," and her husband "seldom had buttons on his linen." When a "half starved, and ragged white boy" called at Mrs. Biffles's home to request aid, he was greeted by "Mrs. Biffles *adopted* favorite little African," who informed the white boy that Mrs. Biffles "wouldn't do nuffin for you, 'cause you are not *colored* enough. . . . White people can help demselves, *missus* says . . . de Lord lubs his dark skinned children de best."[37] Such arguments pitted black and white poor people against each other.

Despite such criticisms of their work, the female managers of the Colored Orphan Asylum persevered. Part of their strength came from the fact that the Quaker community generally was more accepting of women's public roles than were other groups. But not all of the managers were Quakers. A major part of the women's strong belief in their project grew out of their conviction that women had a unique role to play in addressing the moral problems of society. Through the establishment of institutions that embodied women's ability to make personal connections with poor clients, women could make more effective moral reforms than could bureaucratic organizations such as the Municipal Almshouse. In their annual reports, reprinted in New York City newspapers, the asylum managers responded to those who criticized them by arguing for the appropriateness of their roles as moral reformers. "[The managers] cannot believe," they stated, "that the most fastidious will consider their attempt at work unnecessary in itself or inappropriate to their sex. It rests on the immovable basis of Christianity and is upheld by every consideration of public safety and justice." More particularly in the case of the orphanage, the emphasis on women's control was based in the nineteenth-century middle-class

MRS. BIFFLES.

Fig. 13 In her 1860 book *Women of New York,* Marie Hankins invented "Mrs. Biffles,"
a reformer who neglected her own family and poor whites in order to care for blacks.
Neg. no. 75074. © Collection of the New-York Historical Society.

belief that women should have primary responsibility for forming children's
characters.[38]

The female managers and their predominantly female staff performed
most of the work of the orphanage. The male advisory committee, which
consisted of husbands, relatives, and friends of the women, was simply
that—an advisory committee, which dispensed advice on legal and financial
matters, advice the managers sometimes ignored in the interest of their own
vision of the orphanage.[39] Repeatedly through these years, the advisory
committee told the women that they had taken in too many children for their
facilities and funding; and repeatedly the women ignored these warnings,

56   Women of New York.

with whom they are associated, while they be-
moan the woes of some oppressed race, sect or
body, and even worship its unworthy members
to an abject and servile degree.

As Mrs. Biffles pretends to be such a devout
philanthropist, people very often send *white*
objects of charity to her dwelling, and we could

Fig. 14 Here, a "half-starved, and ragged white boy" is turned away by "Mrs. Biffles *adopted favorite little African*" in Hankins's *Women of New York*. Neg. no. 75073. © Collection of the New-York Historical Society.

working harder to procure more funding and larger facilities, rather than turning away children.

The managers hired a male superintendent and a male doctor, but the rest of the employees, including teachers, a matron, and servants, were women. In establishing the office of superintendent, the managers seem to have considered the necessity of a male role model for the boys they would take in. The rules and regulations of the asylum designated the superintendent as "he." With his assistant, the superintendent was responsible for the boys outside of school hours. He also made purchases, but only under the direction of the all-female purchasing committee. However, the earliest mention in the minutes of a male superintendent is in 1856, and he is unnamed. Prior to that time, women served in this post. Even when a man did hold the post, however, he had little power. The matron, designated as female in the rules, was to "exercise a general supervision of the Institution." She held the keys to the storerooms, engaged domestics, and was responsible for the house and the children. She answered only to the Executive Committee.

The asylum served as a source of employment and income for many single women over the years, including the managers themselves. Although the staff's salaries were discussed openly in the managers' minutes, the salaries that the managers received are alluded to only once. In July of 1848, Anna Shotwell had to take over the nursing duties after the nurse left suddenly. Shotwell had previously received eight dollars a month for her work with the Sunday School; as a nurse, she received nine dollars a month and was relieved from her Sunday School duties. This reluctance to reveal their payment for duties may well have been a way to preserve their moral status as benevolent middle-class women, rather than as women working for wages.[40]

Although some New York City whites saw the women as radically threatening the racial and gender hierarchies in the city, black middle-class reformers were less convinced of the women's desires to improve fundamentally the conditions of New York City's black children or the black community. Some of the conservatism of the New York Manumission Society's founders toward blacks lingered in the Association for the Benefit of Colored Orphans. Like the Manumission Society, the Association for the Benefit of Colored Orphans began as an organization *for* blacks, not led with or by them. The vast majority of the staff whom the managers hired were white. Until his death in 1840, black Episcopal minister and community leader Peter Williams attended the orphanage on religious matters, but he did little more. Initially, black reformers publicly supported the women's effort to aid "dear parentless children." But the Manumission Society's distribution of a sum of money that New York City lawyer William Turpin bequeathed for the "education and benefit of colored people" led to conflict between black reformers and the managers of the Colored Orphan Asylum. [41] Turpin's executors, Israel Corse, a member of the New York City Colonization Society, and Arthur Tappan, a former Colonization Society member who was now a radical abolitionist, disagreed on how the money should be distributed. Initially Tappan, as well as Philip Bell and Samuel Cornish, the editors of the black newspaper the *Colored American,* believed that Turpin intended the money be donated to the Phoenix School, which abolitionist blacks had founded to provide black children with a classical education. When Corse and Tappan gave the money to the asylum instead, black reformers criticized the limited goals of the asylum. "It is . . . a branch of the Alms House," stated Cornish and Bell.[42] Another article in the *Colored American* claimed more pointedly that the orphanage's managers "entertain[ed] . . . contracted views" of the expectations of blacks and "opposed . . . the colored man's *social and civil* elevation, as to his classical intelligence. The most they wish for the colored man is, that he may be a free 'hewer of wood, and drawer of water.' They neither seek nor wish to elevate him to posts of honor, of trust, or of profit."[43]

The asylum's managers responded to the conflict over the Turpin legacy by giving half of the money they received to the Phoenix School. But middle-class blacks continued to be wary of the orphanage's goals because of its continued association until the early 1840s with the American Colonization Society. The white physicians who took care of the children in the orphanage, James MacDonald and James Proudfit, were members of the American Colonization Society. In detailed published reports of the children's health, MacDonald and Proudfit claimed that blacks' "peculiar constitution and condition," as well as environment and poverty, were the reasons for their high morbidity and mortality rates. Although the doctors did not elaborate on these "peculiarities," colonizationists often made arguments that blacks' respiratory systems differed from those of whites. Such "innate" differences, rather than blacks' actual living conditions or poor nutrition, accounted for blacks' higher rates of illness and death from tuberculosis and other infectious diseases. These supposed physiological problems supported colonizationists' views that blacks should be returned to Africa, where the warm climate better suited them.[44] After MacDonald distributed his first report in 1839 in New York City newspapers, black abolitionist and medical doctor James McCune Smith (fig. 15) responded in the *Colored American.* MacDonald claimed that black children were more subject to death from teething than white, but McCune Smith cited citywide statistics that demonstrated that many more white children died from teething than black, both in number (235 to 7) and in terms of their proportions in the population. On the subject of blacks' supposedly weaker respiratory systems, McCune Smith quoted a British medical expert who stated that "predisposition to consumption" was caused by "bad formation of the chest, particularly,

Fig. 15 James McCune Smith, medical doctor and abolitionist. Engraving by Patrick Reason. Neg. no. 74638. © Collection of the New-York Historical Society.

smallness of the transverse, but above all, of the antero-posterior diameter." McCune Smith stated that "the colored people of this city . . . have singu-larly well-formed chests. To those who doubt this fact, we recommend a visit to Zion's Church on Sunday next, where they will find, for this statement, 'confirmation strong as proof of holy writ.'"[45]

It is unclear if the women agreed with the views of the doctors in their employ. In the organization's unpublished minutes, Anna Shotwell observed that "all the children that have died in the asylum have previously to their admission been of the most neglected class." Their diseases were caused by "want and neglect, abuse and inheritance" and "were not incurable." Despite

Shotwell's assumption that some of the children's diseases were inherited, her statement that the diseases were not incurable reveals the managers' belief that environmental factors, not inherent physiology, caused the high morbidity and mortality rates of the children.[46] However, the women did not publicize this belief; rather, only the male doctors' views of the health of the children were reprinted in the asylum's annual reports and in black and white newspapers.

Occasionally the managers did work with radical abolitionists on issues of slavery that affected children in New York City. On one occasion in 1839, the New York Committee of Vigilance, a radical abolitionist group led by African Americans, brought a West Indian slave child, John Tomate, to the asylum. John's mistress brought him to the Committee of Vigilance because of a spinal injury that made him unfit for work.[47] On another occasion, when a French ship wrecked off the coast of Long Island in October 1854, the ship's captain brought Dongo and Kelo, two African boys, to the asylum for medical attention. The asylum's managers convinced the ship's captain to allow them to keep the two children, as "fears were . . . entertained that if taken away by the Captain the boys were liable to be sold as slaves." Kelo soon died, but Dongo, whom they believed to be the son of a king in Africa, quickly learned to read and write. Impressed by his ability, the managers wished to place him "in some school where particular regard will be had to his religious welfare as well as a liberal education afforded." Their highest hopes for him were that he return to "his country and to his father's dominions" as a missionary to bring to his "benighted countrymen the glad tidings of Salvation."[48] Radical abolitionists would not have disagreed with this goal.

Additionally, fugitive enslaved children and the children of southern slaves also found their way to the orphanage during the pre–Civil War era. Twenty-eight of the 1,257 children admitted to the orphanage between 1837 and 1860 can be identified as former southern slaves or children of southern slaves. In the orphanage's first year of operation, 1837, six of the children admitted had been born in the South. Jacob Becket Lee was the eight-year-old son of a fugitive slave from Virginia. Jacob Sr. had been apprehended by his master in New York and carried back to slavery. Jacob's mother, Maria Lee, died of cholera in New York in 1833. Maria Weeks, a friend of Jacob's mother, brought him to the asylum.[49] Soon after Jacob's arrival, the managers admitted Jeremiah and Adaline Rawle, ages eight and six, and their cousin Wiley Rawle, age three. The children were part of a group of forty slaves from Virginia who were liberated under the will of their deceased master. The group had arrived in New York in the autumn of 1837 "in destitute circumstances." The managers felt that these freed slaves' circumstances upon arrival in the city "were so helpless and distressing that they could not close the doors of the Asylum against them."[50]

The managers' sympathy for the former slaves did not, however, signal the beginning of an involvement in radical abolitionism. They stated firmly that "it is not the intention of the Committee [of Admission] that they shall form a president [sic] for the admission of others under similar circumstances."[51] The managers' impartiality on these questions extended to the point of accepting slaves brought in by their masters. There was little comment in the minutes on the circumstances under which these slave children came to the asylum. In 1857, for example, six children came to the orphanage from Cuba. Ranging in age from six to eight, these children were the slaves of "Esetvan Santa Cruz de Oviedo who has on his plantation 800 to 1000 slaves." No explanation was given as to why Oviedo chose these children out of all of his slaves to receive an education in the United States, but possibly they were his children. In listing their parents, each child had a different woman's name in the space provided for mother, but no mention of the father; each child's last name was listed as Oviedo, implying ownership, but also fatherhood. Perhaps naïveté played a role in the managers' initial acceptance of the children, for these women were not proslavery, nor would they have favored or supported illicit sexual relationships between masters and slaves. The children remained in the asylum only two months before being returned to their guardian, again without explanation.[52] The managers never permanently crossed the boundaries of their type of reform into radical abolitionist circles, but when asked for help, they did provide sanctuary, within the limits of their own more conservative antislavery sentiments.

From the perspective of middle-class blacks, the major event that established trust in the managers was their employment of James McCune Smith as the orphanage's doctor in 1843. The hiring of McCune Smith was a major break in the orphanage's dependence on their white male advisers, whose views were increasingly more conservative than those of the women themselves. McCune Smith built ties between the orphanage and the black community. Black churches began to hold fundraisers for the orphanage, and the orphans gave special recitals specifically for the black community. McCune Smith's appointment signaled the managers' slowly expanding vision of the various roles of which blacks were capable, as well as an end to their close association with the colonizationist views of the New York Manumission Society, even though some managers remained supportive of colonization, and none of the managers ever openly embraced radical abolitionism.

The managers' shift in attitude toward blacks during the antebellum period reflected not only the influence of educated middle-class blacks such as

McCune Smith, but also the self-sufficiency and agency of working-class black parents and children. Throughout the association's existence, potential clients worked to convince the women of their needs and desires. In one instance, they may have succeeded in changing the policies of the orphanage. In their original discussions about establishing the orphanage, the women believed they would focus on black children who had lost both their parents, or "whole orphans." But the mission of the society soon spread beyond whole orphans to include the children of widowed parents, called "half-orphans," and some children who were not orphans at all. Although it was common during this time for orphanages to admit half-orphans as well as children who had lost both parents, in this case single black parents themselves, probably women, asked that their children be admitted to the asylum while they performed the "days work from home" that "enabled [them] to provide for [the] support" of their children.[53] By 1838 there were only twelve full orphans in the asylum. Two children were not orphans at all, and twenty-one were half-orphans. In 1840, only one orphan was admitted, along with six non-orphans and twelve half-orphans. In 1850, out of a total of sixty-one children admitted, only nine were orphans; the remainder comprised thirty-four half-orphans, two non-orphans, and sixteen children of uncertain parentage. And in 1860, out of seventy children admitted, seventeen were orphans, forty-two were half-orphans, and eleven were of uncertain parentage.[54]

Working-class blacks shaped the orphanage in other ways, too. In describing their work to the New York community in their published annual reports, the managers sometimes portrayed themselves as the active participants, rescuing children from neglectful parents or guardians or removing them from "scenes of misery" such as sweeping chimneys, begging, scavenging, "and other modes of eking out a scanty subsistence." In these accounts, poverty forced some parents to place their children in occupations that the asylum managers (like the Manumission Society members before them) viewed as immoral and dangerous. In other cases children left alone after the death of parents and relatives were subsequently taken in by neighbors or friends who placed them in these occupations to help support themselves and their guardians. According to the managers, the parents of one five-year-old boy placed him with a family who transferred his care to the next occupants of the apartment when they moved. These new caretakers "employed him in begging" before he came to the asylum.[55]

There is little doubt that on their walks in New York City the women occasionally met black children whom they encouraged to enter the asylum, or that the managers' friends, city magistrates, or managers of other institutions brought children to them. However, the black parents, relatives, guardians, neighbors, and friends of the children themselves brought the vast majority of children to the orphanage. In the asylum's first year of operation, half of the children were brought there by blacks who knew them. In 1840, 1850, and 1860, the number of children brought in by blacks ranged from over three-fifths to over three-fourths.[56] Most of these children were half-orphans whose surviving parent was ill, indigent, or working at a job that prevented care of the child. These figures reveal the great degree of concern that black parents and guardians, as well as neighbors and others, had for these children. They also reveal the trust that some working-class blacks had of the orphanage as a safe place for their children.

Single parents who asked that their children be admitted as half-orphans were to sign agreements that effectively gave the managers control of the children and of their future indentures. Although parents had to pay fifty cents a week for each child boarded, the managers waived the fee for parents who were unable to pay. The orphanage only accepted children whose parents were "decent and respectable." Parents had to give "satisfactory testimony" that the children were not born outside of marriage and that one parent was dead "or considered so in law." If at the time of indenture (usually when the children were between ten and twelve years of age), parents wished to retrieve their children, they had to have paid the board "punctually," and they had to "satisfactorily prove" that they were "in a situation to extend a parental care over" their children.[57]

Black parents exercised as much control over their children as they could within this system. In doing so, parents forced the managers to adapt to their perceptions of their children's needs. For example, not all of the signed agreements between parent or relative and the admitting manager followed the exact formula described above. Rachel Johnson placed her children Amanda and Hamilton in the orphanage in July 1844. She agreed to pay three dollars a month for their care, leaving the children "under their control . . . unless I remove from the city of New York, when it is agreed that they shall be surrendered to me." William A. Smith, a sailor, was able to afford to board all four of his children in the orphanage, at the rate of twelve dollars a month. His agreement reveals his middle-class aspirations for his children. Smith allowed his daughter Jane to remain in the asylum until age eighteen under the condition that "the managers educate her for a teacher." Unlike many of the other single parents who placed their children in the orphanage and could only mark an X for their signatures, Smith signed his agreement in his own shaky hand.[58] It is impossible to generalize about the literacy of the parents because of the small number of parental agreements extant. But according to the existing agreements, many of the parents who were most assertive at the time the managers admitted their children were literate in some sense, as they were able to sign their own names.

But the signed agreement was not the last word for many parents. Although parents signed control of their children over to the managers, many parents continued to take an active interest in their children's lives in the orphanage. When visiting their children, parents asked questions about the management of the orphanage and sometimes criticized the matron, as a new set of rules added to the bylaws in 1838 indicates. The rules instructed the managers "to express to the parent or guardian their entire confidence in the matron and their resolution to support her authority." Parents who used "a disrespectful language to the matron" would not be allowed to see their children until they apologized. The orphanage limited parents' visits to three hours once a month, no doubt to prevent the parents from disrupting the routine the orphanage was establishing with the children. Managers who served on the Visiting Committee, which regularly inspected the orphanage, were to be present on parents' visiting days to address any concerns the parents might have about their children. Finally, "no child" was "permitted on any pretence whatever to go beyond the front door without consent of the matron"—even with his or her parent. Despite these rules, some parents continued to interfere with the women's control over their children and, if dissatisfied, took their children away, with or without the permission of the managers. For example, Eliza Giles's mother took her away from the asylum in 1845. Eliza's mother may have had too close a look at the asylum—she was an employee at the time that she "quit without permission."[59]

The managers did dislike some parents, which sometimes affected their decisions to return their children. When Minerva Rawle, a fugitive slave from Virginia, asked that her children be returned to her in March 1839, the managers refused. She "was a vicious and ignorant woman, and from her ingovernable temper became exceedingly troublesome to the inmates of the asylum," they wrote of her. On visiting her residence, they determined that it was unsuitable for her children and decided to bind them out to employers in rural areas of New York State. For Minerva Rawle, who had managed alone to bring her children, if not her husband, with her from Virginia slavery into "freedom" in New York City, this must have seemed the ultimate irony. The managers noted dispassionately that she died that summer. As in this case, the managers' belief that they knew what would best benefit the children was sometimes at the expense of the parents' wishes.[60]

The overwhelming majority of single parents who brought in their children were single mothers, most of whom appear to have been domestic servants. Some of these parents may have been encouraged or coerced to bring their children to the asylum by their employers, who wanted access to black women's labor without the problems of family ties. Employers sometimes paid the board for the children of their employees. When Rosanna Peterson placed her two children, Richard and Mary Robinson, in the orphanage in 1843, her employer, Mrs. Teboult, promised "to be security for the payment [of the board] as long as [Rosanna] may be continued in her service." Many domestic servants may have attempted, and preferred, to board their children with trusted friends or relatives. Friends and relatives did not limit visits between parents and children. But when these arrangements fell through, these children, too, sometimes ended up at the orphanage. When Hester Williams Isaacs's employers took her as a servant on their travels to Europe, she left her two-year-old daughter, Frederica Matilda Isaacs, at board with Hester Burgoyne of Thompson Street. When Burgoyne was "unable to keep her any longer," she brought Frederica "temporarily to the Asylum, until something should be heard of the mother." Unfortunately, Frederica died of scarlet fever two years later, before her mother returned from Europe.[61]

The orphanage was a more stable option than some of the situations in which domestic servants left their children—with guardians who died themselves or lost their jobs, or in the Municipal Almshouse. But none of these solutions addressed a fundamental issue: the continued devaluation of the black family in New York City in favor of the domestic labor needs of white families. Antebellum domestic service jobs for black women in New York City echoed the separation of families under both southern and New York City slavery. Radical abolitionists publicized the negative effects of southern slavery on black families, in which masters sold slaves apart from spouses and children, through the publication of antislavery tracts and slave narratives at this time. In eighteenth-century New York City, slave masters considered female slaves who had children less valuable and sold them out of the city if they became pregnant. The managers of the orphan asylum, of the same economic class as the employers of domestic servants, never addressed this issue; in some ways, they aided those who employed domestic servants in slighting black family ties by taking in the children of these servants. As in the case of Minerva Rawle and her children, the managers may have seen their care of black children as better than that of some black parents. The orphanage, in its efforts to serve the needs of the black community, sometimes reinforced the idea that keeping black families intact was less important than fulfilling white middle-class families' needs for domestic labor.

The managers of the Colored Orphan Asylum practiced what historian Christine Stansell has called "corrective domesticity": the restructuring of the lives of the asylum children through the rules and regulations of "the family," as the managers sometimes referred to the orphanage. The women sought to inculcate lessons of cleanliness, religiosity, and general morality in these children—lessons they may have believed the children's parents or guardians had not imparted to them.[62] Upon arrival, the matron or the managers thoroughly washed the children, comfortably dressed them, and combed their hair. The managers then introduced them to the other residents, whom they "reminded of their obligations to fulfill the law of love toward their new companions" and encouraged "to endeavor to remove the unpleasant feelings peculiar to their new situation." Each day began with a reading from the Bible before breakfast. During the day, the orphans attended school, along with any children from the neighborhood who attended as day pupils (figs. 16 and 17). After supper, the matron read from the Bible again, and the children recited the Lord's Prayer. In keeping with Quaker religious practices, the children observed an interval of silence before each meal, to offer up their own private thanksgivings to God. The orphans also attended a Methodist Sunday school.[63]

Sickness and death were ever-present realities in the orphanage. The children, particularly those who had spent time in the almshouse before coming to the asylum, suffered from seasonal diseases such as whooping cough or influenza, and some died. The managers used occasions of illness or death to reinforce the Christian lessons they taught the children. When ill or on their deathbeds, the children were encouraged to think of religious matters. The managers also designed a funeral ritual to ease the grief of the children and to reinforce religiosity. A funeral would not be performed for at least a day following a death, giving the managers, matron, and teachers time to prepare the children emotionally and spiritually for the event. As many managers as possible attended the funeral, increasing the sense of family for the residents. A minister, sometimes the black Episcopal minister Peter Williams Jr., led the service, giving "very appropriate advice" to the children. The children then formed a procession and, accompanied by their matron and teacher, "followed their little companion to the grave."[64]

These rituals seemed to provide the children with some comfort. As nine-year-old Anne Williams lay on her deathbed after eating poisonous berries, she said, "I hope I shall go to the good place." Eight-year-old Margaret Johnson said to the matron attending her deathbed "that she was willing to die now and that she should go to heaven where there were only good little girls." These rituals also soothed the managers, who in the first year

Fig. 16 Schoolroom at the Colored Orphan Asylum. Neg. no. 59133. © Collection of the New-York Historical Society.

alone witnessed the deaths of nine children, and in some years as many as twenty. "Let us remember that a sparrow falleth not to the ground unnoticed and renew our diligent and watchful care over their survivers [sic]," they wrote.[65]

Those children who survived the childhood diseases and whose parents did not remove them from the orphanage were indentured from between the ages of ten and twelve until the age of twenty-one. Of the 1,257 children admitted into the orphanage between 1837 and 1863, the managers placed 347 in indentures. Of these, 264 indenture records for 205 children survive, not all of which are complete. The asylum's use of legal indentures continued the practice of indenturing indigent or orphaned children that had been common since the mid-eighteenth century. In indenturing blacks, the managers also echoed the provisions of New York's gradual emancipation laws, whereby masters were to provide limited education and religious guidance. But unlike New York's gradual emancipation laws, the children received a sum of money

Fig. 17 Children posed in the courtyard of the Colored Orphan Asylum. Neg. no. 59126.
© Collection of the New-York Historical Society.

upon completion of their indentures—fifty dollars for girls, one hundred
dollars for boys. Like many middle-class reformers of the mid-nineteenth
century who had come to view the burgeoning city with horror, the managers placed a premium on getting the children out of the city, into the countryside. Only eight children were indentured in New York City, and one in
Philadelphia. The majority went to farming towns surrounding New York
City, in Westchester County and Long Island, as well as in New Jersey and
Connecticut. The managers sent a few of the children as far west as Ohio and
Illinois, and as far north as Vassalboro, Maine. The managers indentured
one child, David Shutt, to Edward Mole, a German citizen. Mole requested
"a dark boy" whom he could take to Cologne and give a good education and
a trade, but he returned Shutt to the orphanage before his term of service
ended.[66]

The managers' practice of indenturing children continued their concern with shaping them into independent, moral adults. In choosing families or individuals to whom to indenture the children, the Indenturing Committee was to make sure that the employers would "exercise a Christian care" over them. The managers gave each child a Bible in which they inscribed the name and address of the manager who had particular responsibility for the child during the time of his or her indenture, along with a hymn book and "one or more religious books." State law required employers to continue the children's education in a limited way by allowing them to attend school three months of the year. Each employer had to submit an annual report of the child's progress to the Association for the Benefit of Colored Orphans.[67]

No precise account of the jobs performed by indentured children survives. These records may have been lost. More likely, however, the managers were less concerned with the specific skills children learned than with their development into moral citizens. They stated that "they have never formed for the children . . . any higher earthly anticipations than those which belong to a life of upright and independent labor; and to impress on their minds a sense of the real dignity and happiness belonging to such a condition." The majority of the girls appear to have been placed in indentures as domestic laborers, and the boys, as helpers on family farms. The managers sought skilled training only for the "most promising." One child learned to make candy. Edward Hicks was indentured to the Boston firm of Hutchins, Brown, and Company, Merchants, in 1857. Sarah Williams, the first child admitted, completed her apprenticeship to a tailor in 1851. One boy learned the house-carpenter's trade; another, the tinnery business. Another option for the "most promising" was to remain at the orphanage as members of the paid staff, an opportunity the managers always offered to girls.[68]

The majority of the children initially accepted the indentures offered them, whatever the position, but most children do not appear to have completed their indentures. Although it is difficult to determine with accuracy the disposition of all the indentures, of the 205 children indentured between 1837 and 1863 whose indentures were recorded, only 23 children completed their indentures; 141 indenture agreements were unfulfilled for a variety of reasons. This latter number includes 37 children whom the managers indentured a second or even a third time; only 3 of these children completed their second or third indenture. For 100 children, it is unclear whether they completed their indentures.[69] Sometimes the children resisted being placed in the country, far from relatives in New York and friends and siblings in the orphanage. Mary Wales was placed in the orphanage along with her brother,

William, in 1841. Together they had survived neglect and abuse before an aunt brought them to the asylum. In 1848, the managers indentured Mary to Robert Post of Southampton, Long Island; her brother stayed behind at the orphanage. While on Long Island, Mary "bore a good character, but being homesick and wanting to see her brother . . . she was induced to set fire to a barn!!" Unfortunately, her actions did not result in a reunion with her brother. The managers removed her from the indenture and sent her to the House of Refuge, New York State's institution for juvenile delinquents. Her brother later went back to their father. The managers indentured James Hitchcock to Mr. Denison of Mount Bethel, Warren Township, New Jersey. Two days later Hitchcock returned to the orphanage, saying he "would rather die than stay there in such a lonely place."[70]

Forty children actually ran away from their employers—some repeatedly. In addition, 14 indentures ended because of misconduct on the part of the children. Although Mary Wales was the only child to burn a barn, employers returned other children to the Asylum for infractions such as stealing, "gross misconduct," "unfavorable acts," or simply unsatisfactory work. Of these children, the managers sent 3 to the House of Refuge and 1 to the state prison.[71]

Not all indentures ended unhappily. Some of the employers practically adopted the children. Twelve-year-old Mary Jackson was indentured in 1850 to a Mrs. Penfield of Fairfield County, Connecticut. Mrs. Penfield brought Mary on trips to New York City for cultural enrichment, which the managers considered "an act of great kindness." "T. H. F." wrote that he had spent four months with his employer's father "in the city." He had charge of the two sons of his employer, one of whom loved him "more than any one," and he was teaching two girls who were servants on the farm how to read. Further, those children who did not complete their indentures were not always to blame. Of the 141 incomplete indentures, 17 were forced to leave because the employer moved and did not want to take the child along, or because the employer died. In 3 cases, the children charged their employers with mistreatment or abuse, and the managers ended the indentures. Five children became too ill to work, and their employers returned them to the orphanage.[72]

The managers and employers did not always understand the ties of family and community that pulled some children back toward New York City. After three successful years on an indenture in Tiego County, New York, eighteen-year-old William King left his employers, giving, according to them, "no sufficient cause for his leaving but his own determination." In 1853, Anna Shotwell offered seventeen-year-old Benjamin Bowen the opportunity to go to England to be a machinist. Benjamin had spent his time of indenture with Shotwell in Morrisania, New Jersey. She had secured for him money, clothes, and passage to England when Benjamin "was ungrateful enough to leave without [her] approbation." Shotwell found him painting houses with his uncle in Williamsburg, Brooklyn.[73]

Parents might also use the time of indenture to reunite with their children. Many parents approved of the indenturing process but still kept an eye out for their children. Ten-year-old Moses Brooks was apprenticed to Roderick N. Morrison of Castleton, Staten Island, in 1839. When Morrison became dissatisfied with Moses's work, Moses's father, Noah, a laborer, took his son home. Other parents negotiated with the managers to have their children indentured in New York City so they would stay close to family. If a child behaved badly during an indenture, the managers would sometimes send him or her home to a parent or guardian. When ten-year-old Elizabeth Dennis's employer returned her to the asylum for "not giving satisfaction," the women returned Dennis to her father, barber Amity Dennis, so that he might "attempt her reformation." Parents also used the indenture as an opportunity to remove their children from the influence of the orphanage. The father of Abijiah and George Norton "enticed away" his children from their indentures in 1863, while George was apprenticed to Anna Shotwell herself.[74]

On one level, the managers of the orphanage performed a great service to the black community. Throughout this period, black reformers and, more rarely, white abolitionists decried the lack of skilled training and job opportunities for blacks due to the racism of employers in New York City. The orphanage was perhaps the only organization that managed consistently to place black children in apprenticeships of any kind during this time. But the women's success lay in the fact that they placed children outside of the city. Further, the managers were reluctant to see the majority of the children as completely independent workers beyond the level of menial jobs. In their second annual report, the managers stated that "nothing more than elementary instruction is of course practicable, but it is hoped that the sound principles and industrious habits which it is intended they shall form will fit them faithfully to fulfill their duties as apprentices or servants."[75]

But the managers' own initially conservative estimates for the children's futures were changed by their experiences with the children and parents themselves. Children and parents often asked for more from the asylum than "elementary instruction." For those children who completed their indentures, the training and the money that they received were the basis for independence and even movement into middle-class status. At least two girls requested help from the managers in their efforts to attend Oberlin College so that they could be trained as teachers. Stephen Russel used his money to purchase a house and garden for 150 dollars, which he then rented for 25 dollars a year. Francis Potter reunited with his mother and brother and moved to Boston following the end of his indenture in 1861. There, he entered the hair-dressing business as an apprentice to the deacon of the Twelfth Baptist Church of Southac Street. He wrote to the asylum managers in 1862 for the money that remained for him in the asylum's bank; his employer was leaving for the East Indies and was willing to sell his business and all his supplies to Potter. In his letter, Potter promised to visit the asylum whenever he was in New York. His mother sent "her warmest regards" to the managers. All of these stories were printed in the managers' annual reports as examples of the positive work they had performed.[76]

The Association for the Benefit of Colored Orphans did not attempt radical change of the class position of New York City's blacks. It did not petition New York City's skilled tradespeople to give black children jobs. But the managers tried to give black orphans some of the same privileges of childhood accorded to white orphans. Before the asylum's founding, white orphaned children were sent to asylums that met their special needs as children, but black children were sent to the almshouse and placed with adults, an explicit denial of their childhood. The Colored Orphan Aslyum's managers, within the limits of their own racial and reform ideology, attempted to fashion a new vision of black childhood, as well as change actual living conditions for working-class blacks.

Throughout this endeavor, blacks forced the managers to adapt their racial and reform ideology to address the needs and aspirations of the very community the managers sought to change. Middle-class blacks criticized the managers' initial reliance on the limited racial visions of the Manumission Society and the New York Colonization Society. Some parents and children rejected the women's efforts because the managers interfered with the children's ties to relatives and community. Other parents and children used the asylum as a stepping stone to independent working-class, or even middle-class status. The managers' limited views of the importance of black family life did at times have a negative impact on the clients they served. But the limited goals of the orphanage, in combination with the efforts of blacks themselves, allowed for concrete achievements and a degree of autonomy for some members of New York City's working-class black community.

While offering material and educational assistance, the women who ran the Colored Orphan Asylum were publicly silent on issues of political and

social equality for blacks. On the other hand, the rise of the radical abolitionist movement in the 1830s gave blacks a new group of allies in the political arena. Although these reformers advocated stricter attention to morals,
they initially included immediate abolition and full citizenship rights for
free blacks as part of their goals. By taking up the topic of the economic and
political position of free blacks in New York City, this movement challenged
the status quo established under emancipation and in some ways proved
more threatening to the evolving racialized class order than had emancipation itself.

CHAPTER SIX

The Long Shadow of Southern Slavery: Radical Abolitionists and Black Political Activism against Slavery and Racism

In the 1830s, a new coalition of black and white middle-class reformers challenged the racial order of the nation. These "radical abolitionists" called for an immediate end to southern slavery, unlike the gradual emancipation that whites had enacted in the North, and without plans to colonize free blacks. Radical abolitionists also pledged to fight racism by elevating "the character and condition of the people of color" so that blacks could "share an equality with whites, of civil and religious privileges." The activism of New York City blacks, together with blacks from other cities, inspired much of the radicalism among whites on the issues of slavery and racism. Free blacks' vociferous opposition to colonization in the 1820s and 1830s, as well as their establishment of annual national conventions in 1830, led some white supporters of colonization, such as William Lloyd Garrison, to rethink and then reject colonization as a solution to America's problems of slavery, racism, and black poverty. White abolitionists were also inspired by the religious revivalism of the Second Great Awakening. Arthur and Lewis Tappan, who came to New York City from New England, were among those whose intense religious experiences motivated them to work to expunge the sins of slavery and racism from the nation. For the Tappans, Garrison, and other white radical abolitionists, the struggle against slavery and racism was part of a larger struggle for the moral perfection of the United States. Slavery and racism were the most degrading of a host of sins of which they hoped to cleanse the United States, ranging from intemperance to sexual promiscuity to nonobservance of the Sabbath.[1]

Blacks agreed that slavery and racism were immoral, but their opposition to them came from the direct threat these sins caused to their well-being. In

New York City the racism of northern whites limited blacks' abilities to educate themselves and find well-paying jobs. As debilitating to blacks was the long reach of southern slavery. Fugitive slaves fled to New York City seeking freedom, and New York City blacks welcomed them into their communities. But southern slaveholders and their agents also traveled to New York in search of their former slaves. As southerners sought fugitives, all blacks, regardless of their status, were subject to capture, for it was whites' words against blacks' that they were free.

The interracial radical abolitionist coalition offered blacks powerful new allies in the struggle against slavery and for racial equality. The unprecedented racial equality preached and practiced by white radical abolitionists led blacks to support the organized abolition movement across evolving class lines. New York City middle-class black reformers who had cooperated with the Manumission Society during the emancipation era, such as Samuel Cornish and Peter Williams Jr., united with white middle-class abolitionists such as William Lloyd Garrison and Lydia Maria Child nationally and the Tappan brothers in New York City. Working-class blacks, too, found ways to contribute to the new movement. The tactics of the abolitionist movement, such as the creation of local auxiliary organizations both before and after the organization of the interstate American Anti-Slavery Society; the focus on individual contributions to the struggle against slavery, ranging from prayer and individual moral reform to raising money through sewing bees to the boycotting of products produced with slave labor; and the respect that white abolitionists and particularly William Lloyd Garrison held for black opinions on colonization and antislavery, led many blacks to pledge their support to the new movement.[2]

The radicalism of the abolitionist movement led to opposition from proslavery, colonizationist, and racist whites of all classes. These groups feared the power of the new abolitionist coalition to upset the racial hierarchy north and south. New York City had important economic ties to the South, and merchants feared the alienation of southern slaveholders. Working-class whites feared losing jobs to blacks and resented the efforts of the abolitionists and other evangelical reformers to impose a new morality on them. In New York City, these whites also feared the economic and political power of reformers like the Tappans, who represented a new middle class whose vision of economics, politics, and morality potentially threatened their livelihoods. Anti-abolition whites attempted to discredit the abolitionist movement by charging abolitionists with encouraging amalgamation, or racial mixture that included socializing in integrated settings, casual sex, and intermarriage. The charges of amalgamation highlighted some whites' fears that blacks would achieve economic and political power in New York City through association with abolitionist whites. Such fears resulted in the 1834 anti-abolition riots, the worst riots in antebellum New York City.

The 1834 riots cooled the radicalism of New York City's abolitionists. Black middle-class abolitionists refocused their efforts on the moral and material reform of the black community. White abolitionists who had not anticipated the violence with which their calls for racial equality would be met backed away from addressing the material problems of northern free blacks to focus on eradicating southern slavery. The abolitionist movement also divided over the ways blacks should work against slavery and for racial equality. Some of these divisions were class based. Because anti-abolition, colonizationist, and racist whites used the poverty of many free blacks and their allegedly immoral activities to support arguments for racial inequality, black and white middle-class abolitionists focused on working-class blacks as crucial to solving the problems of racism in the North and slavery in the South. For these abolitionists, the end of slavery required not only that southern slaveholders realize their own sinfulness, but also that free blacks demonstrate their moral worthiness and equality. Thus, middle-class abolitionists focused on converting all blacks to the evolving middle-class ideals of moral and social improvement, such as classical education, temperance, and religiosity. Middle-class abolitionists also tried to control the participation of the black masses in the struggle to protect fugitive slaves in New York City. Middle-class abolitionists advocated nonphysical ways to fight against slavery and for racial equality, such as moral suasion, nonresistance, and legal action. Abolitionists should convince others of the sinfulness of slavery through propaganda campaigns, petitions to government, and refusal to participate in economic systems that upheld slavery. Physical or defensive force should not be used to protect fugitives. Rather, blacks accused of being fugitives should fight for their freedom only through the courts. These were tenets of abolitionist activism aimed at everyone regardless of class or race, though in some cases, abolitionists explicitly attempted to limit the participation of blacks whom they deemed uneducated or unruly.[3]

Abolitionists, black and white, were participating in the process of defining middle and working classes, consciously and unconsciously. In their own eyes, they advocated a new moral standard for all, regardless of class. But the rejection of their moral ideologies by both black and white working classes, albeit for different reasons, meant that they developed new meanings of what it meant to be middle class, based on morality as well as economic success.[4] When dealing with the economic, political, and social problems of blacks, both white and black abolitionists tried to conflate class and racial identities. By advocating certain ideological stances as best for blacks as a race, abolitionists tried to remove the class implications of such ideologies. Both black and white abolitionists advocated moral and intellectual reform out of a sincere belief in its efficacy for solving the problems of race in America. But black middle-class abolitionists occupied a special relationship to the reforms aimed at the black working class. The fate of the black middle class or aspiring middle class was bound inextricably with that of the black working class in a society that saw all blacks as inferior and defined that inferiority partially in class terms. Black abolitionists, reacting to the race- and class-based assumptions of inferiority promulgated by the society at large, sought both to control the black working class and also to define themselves in relation to that class. Discussions of the problems of working-class blacks were often cloaked in the unifying language of racial community. Black middle-class reformers thus attempted to create a united black community that would be a reproduction of themselves: their own moral, political, social, and intellectual goals and desires. This kind of black community, they believed, could not be denied equality in the United States.

Middle-class abolitionists' advocacy of certain tactics heightened class divisions among blacks. The solutions to racial inequality promulgated by both black and white middle-class abolitionists were increasingly markers of ideological differences between the black middle class and working class. A few blacks began to question the prescriptions for success spelled out by abolitionists. Some simply claimed working-class identities and pleasures privately, implicitly challenging moral perfectionism as the only way to prove black equality. Others, such as the porter Peter Paul Simons, publicly attacked moral suasion, nonresistance, and intellectual elevation as ways to achieve racial equality. Simons advocated manly physical struggle and greater public roles for women, forcing more conservative black middle-class abolitionists such as Samuel Cornish to defend their political methods. Some black middle-class activists, most notably David Ruggles, founder of the New York Committee of Vigilance, attempted but failed to find a middle ground between the tactics of middle-class radical abolitionists and those of black workers in order to create a more inclusive movement against slavery and for racial equality. These tensions over the best tactics to fight slavery and racism were mirrored in the larger abolitionist movement and resulted in the split in the abolitionist forces by 1840.

■ ■ ■

For free blacks across the North, 1829 was a turning point to greater radicalism. That year, the American Convention of Abolition Societies openly declared its support of the American Colonization Society. In Cincinnati, Ohio, a three-day riot by whites who feared the increase in the free black population that had occurred there in the 1820s drove two thousand blacks out of the city to Canada. In September of that year, David Walker published his *Appeal to the Coloured Citizens of the World*. Walker, a runaway slave from North Carolina who had settled in Boston, set off a storm of fear among southern whites as his pamphlet, with its fiery call for physical action by blacks to achieve racial freedom and justice, turned up in the hands of free blacks and slaves there. Not all parts of Walker's argument appealed to reform-minded blacks and whites. Black and white reformers, particularly religious leaders, probably agreed with Walker's call to educated "men of colour" to "enlighten your brethren!" But blacks and whites questioned Walker's justification of the violent uprising of southern slaves, even as a last resort against whites who refused to cease their abuse of blacks. Still, the increase in support for colonization, the Cincinnati riot, and Walker's pamphlet called blacks to action and increased the number of whites sympathetic to immediate abolition and antiracism.[5]

For a few years prior to 1829, blacks in New York, Philadelphia, and Baltimore had toyed with the idea of holding a "national" convention of free people of color to address the pressing issues of the day: emigration to Canada or Liberia as well as the struggle for black freedom and racial equality in the United States. The events of 1829 spurred them to action. In September 1830, Philadelphian Richard Allen, founder and bishop of the A.M.E. Bethel Church, called a meeting to form an organization that would improve the condition of blacks in the United States but would also buy land and aid in the settlement of free blacks in Upper Canada. The majority of the delegates to the convention came from Philadelphia. Allen's desire for leadership and tight control of the convention echoed his attempts to gain control over New York City's black Methodist churches in the 1820s and discouraged the attendance of New Yorkers such as Christopher Rush, Samuel Cornish, and Peter Williams. But free blacks from Maine to Virginia watched with interest the first attempt by blacks to achieve an organized national presence. Although the convention movement largely reflected the goals and aspirations of black middle-class leaders throughout the antebellum period, it also served as a forum for cross-class debate of the issues of moral and economic improvement, emigration, and blacks' role in the abolition of southern slavery.[6]

In 1831, the convention reassembled in Philadelphia with a broader platform of goals and broader geographical representation. (Allen had died

a few weeks prior to the meeting.) New Yorkers Samuel Cornish, Peter
Williams Jr., Henry Sipkins, William Hamilton, and Thomas Jennings were
active participants, their numbers equaling that of the Philadelphians. In addition, delegates from Maryland, Delaware, Long Island, and Virginia attended and were joined in subsequent years by delegates from upstate New
York, Connecticut, Rhode Island, Massachusetts, New Jersey, Ohio, Maine,
and Washington, D.C. White antislavery activists William Lloyd Garrison of
Boston, Arthur Tappan of New York, Benjamin Lundy of Washington, D.C.,
and Simeon S. Jocelyn of New Haven, Connecticut, also attended the 1831
convention. All had recently or were soon to reject colonization and convert
to the doctrine of immediatism, which called for the immediate abolition of
slavery, without guarantees of compensation to slave owners, colonization of
freed blacks, or any form of "apprenticeship" freedom for former slaves.[7]

The desires of free blacks and the perfectionist beliefs of religious re-
vivalists like Charles Grandison Finney inspired this new group of white antislavery activists. Although William Lloyd Garrison was deeply affected by
the religious revivalism of the 1820s and 1830s, his position against colonization also grew out of his contacts with the black Baltimore community
while he assisted Lundy with his newspaper, the *Genius of Universal Emancipation,* in the late 1820s. In 1831, soon after he founded his own newspaper, the *Liberator,* Garrison traveled to black communities in half a dozen
cities, including New York, pledging to devote his life to the service of blacks
who had suffered at the hands of whites for so long. Additionally, Garrison
publicized what he had learned on this tour about blacks' anticolonization
views in his 1832 work *Thoughts on African Colonization.* In the first half
of the book, Garrison repudiated his previous alliance with the American
Colonization Society. He devoted the second half of the book to blacks'
thoughts on colonization, as expressed in anticolonization meetings and resolutions in Philadelphia, New York, and other cities. Garrison's willingness
to listen to blacks' thoughts about their own destiny and to allow them to
shape his views on colonization, slavery, and racial equality led blacks to embrace Garrison wholeheartedly. Blacks provided the majority of the funds
for the *Liberator* in its first years of existence and peddled the newspapers in
cities across the North.[8]

In contrast, the conversion to the cause of immediatism of New York
merchant Arthur Tappan and, later, his brother Lewis was based more on perfectionist religious ideology than on contacts with free blacks. Perfectionist
reformers believed that the world around them could achieve moral perfection, free from sin. Eventually, the Tappans came to believe that slavery was

the greatest of sins in the United States, but they were also concerned with other evils such as alcohol and prostitution. Their belief in perfectionism did not necessarily lead to greater faith in the abilities of blacks to survive in the United States. Although Arthur Tappan's visit to the Convention of the Free People of Color in 1831 was a turning point in his awareness of the conditions and aspirations of northern free blacks, he did not openly reject colonization as a solution to slavery until two years later. The temperate Tappan's disillusionment with the American Colonization Society stemmed partly from his knowledge of blacks' opposition to colonization, but also from the fact that rum was the Colonization Society's chief import into Liberia. When the society refused to stop shipping spirits to Liberia, Tappan resigned. Throughout the 1830s, both Arthur and Lewis Tappan held a more conservative attitude toward methods of achieving the abolition of slavery and the equality of blacks than did Garrison. Arthur Tappan initially favored an apprenticeship system to ease the transition from slavery to freedom in the South, such as the British had implemented in Jamaica and similar to gradual emancipation in New York. The New York–based antislavery newspaper founded by Arthur Tappan and Charles Denison, the *Emancipator*, was less fiery in its rhetoric than Garrison's *Liberator*.[9]

The range of opinions between Garrison and the Tappans would be both a strength and a source of division in the national antislavery movement after 1834.[10] In 1831, however, the formation of the interracial but white-dominated American Anti-Slavery Society was still a few years off. Blacks were more organized in their goals regarding slavery and racism than were whites. What Garrison, Arthur Tappan, and the others brought to the 1831 black convention was the possibility that they could provide money and property for the conventioneers' plans to educate blacks. The white activists suggested that blacks and whites work together to create a college "for the liberal education of Young Men of Colour, on the Manual Labor System." This manual labor school would combine moral and intellectual uplift with practical means to alleviate economic distress among laboring blacks, much as the African Free Schools had. "Young Men of Colour" educated on the manual labor system were to obtain both a classical education and "a useful Mechanical or Agricultural profession." Such education would help alleviate the "present ignorant and degraded condition" of free blacks and "elevate the general character of the coloured population." Blacks and whites would work together on the project, but blacks would control the school and form a majority of the school's trustees. The school was never built. But the discussion around the manual labor school plan, as well as the reasons for its failure, reveal the evolving class and race ideologies of this new interracial coalition, which in a few years would lead the most radical attack on slavery and racism New York and the United States had yet witnessed.[11]

The manual labor school model on which the conventioneers based their plans was not initially designed to outfit individuals for careers as manual laborers. American theological seminaries adapted the manual labor school from European models, hoping this method of education would strengthen the bodies of students without impairing their mental abilities. The manual labor system theoretically would enable poorer students to work their way through school by farming, making and selling furniture, and perhaps even constructing school buildings. Middle-class abolitionists in the early 1830s turned to the manual labor system because they thought that the instruction of middle-class students in manual labor would alleviate the middle class's growing distaste for physical labor. For middle-class abolitionists, the manual labor school was a way to decrease evolving class divisions and instill respect among the middle class for all in society.[12]

By 1834, most American educators had begun to question the combination of manual and intellectual pursuits in schools. "The calling of the laborer is as honorable, useful and important as that of the student, but these two callings do not require the same kind of training, either physically or intellectually; nor is the physical system of the student to be kept in the same condition with that of the laborer," stated one.[13] On a more practical level, students who had hoped to work their way through school often did not have the mechanical or agricultural experience to do so successfully. But the manual labor system remained popular through the 1850s at abolitionist schools such as the Oneida Institute in upstate New York and Oberlin in Ohio.[14]

Neither mainstream nor abolitionist manual labor schools were designed to prepare their students for manual labor occupations, but the dual nature of education (manual and mental) inherent in the structure of the manual labor system particularly suited black and white reformers' goals for free blacks. At the 1831 convention, both blacks and whites saw the school as a way around the exclusion of free black male workers from skilled apprenticeships in the North. The school could employ skilled craftsmen who would train blacks outside of the racially exclusive apprenticeship system in northern cities. But providing intellectual and moral education to blacks was just as important to supporters of the school. The children of the poor would "receive a regular classical education, as well as those of their more opulent brethren." The school would also provide an institutional basis for inculcating morals into free blacks. For middle-class blacks, the "present ignorant and degraded condition" of many working-class blacks reinforced the racist perceptions of blacks held by proslavery and colonizationist whites. Black reformers recognized that blacks had had few opportunities "for mental cultivation or improvement" but saw blacks' lack of education as detrimental to the fight for racial equality.[15] The black conventioneers identified the school as a way to combat whites' claims of black inferiority.

The abolitionists' focus on moral and intellectual training also reflected a desire to give blacks opportunities to move beyond working-class status. Black leaders of the 1830s believed that blacks' low economic and social status reinforced whites' racism. The American Colonization Society's negative characterizations of northern free blacks as poor, as well as disproportionately criminal and reliant on public funds, encouraged this belief. In New York in particular, the 1821 suffrage law that gave political equality to blacks who proved their worth by achieving 250 dollars in property also implied that racism could be erased by movement beyond a lower-class status. These images and realities, combined with white workers' refusal to work with blacks in skilled jobs, led the conventioneers to focus their energies on providing blacks not only with skilled training, but with something beyond skilled training—the intellectual skills and moral conditioning that they saw as necessary to move blacks economically, socially, and politically out of the realm of workers, into a more middle-class status. For New Yorkers, this would increase the number of black men who could participate in society as full, voting citizens.

The convention's focus on improving blacks' morality and class and citizenship status meant that the manual labor school project focused on the education and occupational training of young men. The all-male conventioneers never referred to the education of women in connection with the project. Many conventioneers may have felt that black women had already achieved a greater degree of morality than black men. Black women numerically dominated black church congregations, and in 1833 the conventioneers noted that "societies for mental improvement" had been established "particularly among the females." But more important, women could not bring full citizenship status to the black community because no woman could vote. And to the degree that citizenship also implied public participation in political debate, many conventioneers may have believed that women should not speak in public.[16]

Such beliefs were shared by blacks in Boston, who had driven writer and orator Maria Stewart from the city in 1833. Stewart's experiences in Boston and her migration to New York City illustrate the limits black people placed on black women's political activism. She and her husband, James, a ship's outfitter with a substantial income, were associates of David Walker. After

James's death in 1829 and Walker's in 1830, Stewart's religious commitment deepened, inspiring her to begin to work for greater justice and equality for blacks. In 1831, she went to the Boston offices of William Lloyd Garrison's *Liberator* and presented Garrison with her first manuscript, a political essay encouraging blacks to demand their rights. Garrison was immediately drawn to Stewart and published many of her writings in his newspaper and later in pamphlet form. By 1832, Stewart had begun to deliver her addresses before secular, "promiscuous" audiences (audiences containing men and women). In both her writings and her speeches, she made women's rights central to the struggles for black freedom and equality. But by 1833, the black comunity's criticism of her outspokenness led Stewart to flee Boston, finding "no use for me as an individual to try to make myself useful among my color in this city." Stewart settled in New York, worked as a schoolteacher, and participated in black women's literary and benevolent societies. She may have lectured occasionally in the city, but the *Colored American* did not cover these events. Her public silence, whether real or created by New York City blacks' conservative attitudes to black women's participation in political activities, appears to have been typical of many of New York City's black women. Black women were active in separate benevolent and literary societies in New York, but until the 1850s black men excluded them from public political leadership.[17]

Blacks did believe that women had an important role in improving the morality of the black community. In the 1830s, black male reformers and black women themselves created roles for black women as teachers in black schools and as organizers of benevolent and literary associations. These roles paralleled the mainstream emphasis on women's roles as inculcators of moral values in children and ultimately in the wider society. Women did this through moral example and direct instruction in the domestic sphere. The domestic sphere also extended to associational gatherings on behalf of benevolent or intellectual causes, and these associations brought black women into the public sphere, albeit in initially proscribed ways. Black women were central to the first religious congregations but did not function as ministers or deaconesses in organized churches. Rather, women founded benevolent and literary societies under the umbrella of black congregations, and sometimes with the explicit leadership of men. In 1828, Peter Williams Jr. chaired the inaugural meeting of the African Dorcas Association and John Russwurm served as secretary. African Free Schools principal Charles Andrews had already drawn up a constitution for the association, which was to be composed of "Female[s] of Colour of a good moral character." Manumission Society members lectured the meeting, which included women, on the need for the association, which would provide clothing for needy African Free Schools students. Four men, including Samuel Cornish, took the names "of all who feel desirous of joining the new Society." Subsequently, the women elected their own officers and members and submitted notices to black newspapers announcing their meetings and encouraging cash and clothing donations, but they appear to have retained a male advisory board.[18]

Six years later, the founding of the Ladies Literary Society of the City of New York displayed the increased self-confidence of black women in public organizing. This confidence grew out of women's involvement in the Dorcas Association; the two organizations shared leadership. Henrietta Ray served as secretary to the Dorcas Association as Henrietta Regulus; in 1834, she served as first president of the Ladies Literary Society. The Literary Society reflected the increased public speaking roles of women. Literary societies generally, black and white, allowed both men and women to practice the arts of written and oral expression. Members might read books or their own essays aloud, or even perform musical or dramatic pieces. These activities resembled familiar domestic-sphere activities, in which women might read aloud or perform for each other or for family members. Literary societies stretched the boundaries of the domestic sphere. Female literary societies allowed women to speak publicly, first among themselves, and then in front of audiences of men and women. Newspapers advertised their activities, inviting an unknown public, not simply family and close friends, to witness their readings and performances. Both men and women attended the third anniversary of the Ladies Literary Society, in which women gave addresses and performed music, poetry readings, and dramatic dialogues. The activities themselves, as well as their extensive coverage in Cornish's *Colored American,* contrasted markedly with those of the African Dorcas Association a few years before.[19]

Black reformers believed that black women's participation in literary and benevolent societies and maintenance of sheltered nuclear households could help all blacks achieve equality. But these activities and household practices were largely the domain of the middle class. For black reformers, the occupational and domestic lives of working-class black women could not move blacks ideologically or economically into the middle class or aid in the ideological struggle for black citizenship. Blacks and whites continued to view as degrading the domestic work most black women performed. Although sewing could lead women to own independent businesses as seamstresses or milliners, for most women needlework led them to labor at piecework, at home or in sweatshops. Theoretically, wages from such work might aid black families in improving their economic status, but in reality, employers paid black and white women's work so poorly that their wages barely covered the basic necessities.[20]

At home, poor black women and their families relied on interfamilial networks of aid; their families were not sheltered in nuclear households. Living practices in which families shared apartments with single boarders or in which parents boarded their children with neighbors while they worked were common. Households were not delimited by biological ties, nor families by household spaces. Middle-class blacks were not immune to such arrangements. Henrietta Ray lived with Samuel Cornish and his wife for several years while her husband Charles worked as an agent and traveling reporter for Cornish's *Colored American*. Other black activists also traveled as agents or lecturers for the abolitionist cause, leaving families at home. But middle-class blacks saw such arrangements as temporary and did not judge them as they did working-class living arrangements. Working-class blacks' living situations were subject to intrusions by reformers such as Samuel Cornish, who visited black families to judge their fitness as part of the enrollment process of the African Free Schools. Working-class black families may have desired more privacy, or at least the ability to choose, but the fiscal fragility of their lives limited their options.[21]

The black male delegates to the Convention of the Free People of Color ascribed to middle-class views of men's and women's roles. They sought to make black men the sole breadwinners in their families. Black women should use their domestic skills to improve their own families, rather than working for white families at the expense of their own. These ideals were nearly impossible for the majority of black families to achieve—including the families of conventioneers themselves. But the convention's focus on elevating the citizenship status of blacks through middle-class methods meant that the male conventioneers ignored the education of black women as part of the manual labor school project.

Although blacks from New York and Philadelphia shared the leadership of the Convention of the Free People of Color, New Yorkers dominated the leadership of the manual labor school project. The black delegates from Philadelphia had been relatively successful in carving out a niche in the urban economy there. Convention delegates such as William Whipper and James Forten parlayed their skills as woodsawyers and sailmakers into substantial fortunes. Robert Purvis inherited a large sum from his white father, a cotton broker who had moved from Charleston, South Carolina, to Philadelphia with his mulatto wife and children in 1819. Further, the link between property ownership and voting in Philadelphia was not explicit as in New York. Under Pennsylvania's Revolutionary War–era constitution, anyone who paid a certain amount in taxes could vote, resulting in access to suffrage for 90 percent of Pennsylvania's men. When Pennsylvania legislators revised the constitution in 1838, they kept tax payment as the basis of suffrage, but excluded blacks completely. Thus, white Pennsylvanians excluded blacks from the polls by threats and physical force before 1838, and by race afterward.[22]

In contrast, none of the New York delegates, with the possible exception of restaurateur Thomas Downing, were as wealthy as the Philadelphia delegates. Although both cities contained large numbers of poor blacks who needed skilled training, the New York delegates appear to have been more understanding of the difficulties of life for poor blacks than the Philadelphians, probably from personal experience. Samuel Cornish, general agent for the school, and members of the New York–based Executive Committee (Peter Williams Jr., Philip Bell, Thomas Downing, Peter Vogelsang, and Boston Crummell) were middle class or aspiring to that status. But few professional New York City blacks in the 1830s were able to maintain a middle-class standard of living without resort to some form of manual labor. The lives of some of these men were a mixture of middle-class status or aspirations and working-class occupations. Samuel Cornish had been the pastor of a black church as well as a founder of *Freedom's Journal* and its successors, the *Rights of All* and the *Colored American*. But Cornish opened a shoemaker's shop in 1836 to augment his income. Philip Bell was coeditor of the *Colored American* and kept an intelligence office, which for a fee matched up employers seeking domestic servants with employees. But he also peddled coal to make ends meet. Boston Crummell, the father of Alexander Crummell, the black minister and leader, harvested and sold oysters. He was prosperous enough to contribute funds to the founding of *Freedom's Journal* and, it was rumored, to hire a white teacher to tutor his children outside of their classes at the African Free Schools. But his occupation ranked low in terms of social status.[23] Perhaps because of their own precarious financial situations, these men sought to remove blacks from reliance on casual or unskilled labor. Such labor was poorly paid and would not help blacks attain the property necessary to vote. Additionally, wary whites of all classes continued to view unskilled or casual labor as degrading; thus, such labor was ideologically harmful to the cause of black equality.

Although New York's blacks may have seen in the manual labor school an opportunity for the elevation of the black community beyond the working class, the reasons behind white support of the school were not the same. New York merchant Arthur Tappan's support of the manual labor school project was part of his evolution from colonizationist to radical abolitionist, and his views on labor were bound up in that transformation. As a supporter of colonization in the late 1820s, Tappan was also a founding member of the short-lived Society for the Encouragement of Faithful Domestic Servants in New-York. Not coincidentally, the organization formed in 1826 as slavery drew to an end in New York, and as the first wave of Irish immigrants entered the city and moved into domestic work. The society's organizers felt that "the number of faithful and respectable servants in our city, has, latterly, been quite inadequate to our wants." Reasons for this shortage included "the very genius of our government," a veiled reference to emancipation. Additionally, though, domestics may have tried to find jobs that paid better, that gave them greater independence, or as the society noted, jobs "which the pride of servants leads them to consider as being more reputable than their own." Domestic work was difficult and dirty; additionally, female and male domestics feared physical and sexual abuse in the intimate home environment.

But most trying to employers was what they perceived as their servants' "love of incessant change," or the movement of domestics from household to household in search of better situations. Servants changed jobs for many reasons, including better wages, family obligations, or illness. Female domestics may have sought other jobs after marriage or opted to stay home with their own families. But the primary concern of Tappan's organization was the disruption to middle-class households caused by domestics' alleged "love of change," rather than the conditions that led to such change. As the society stated in its first annual report, "we are very dependant upon our Domestic Servants for a large share of our daily family comforts . . . *bad* Servants are alone sufficient, if not to destroy, at least to mar, much of the calm happiness of domestic life." The society tried to discourage domestics from leaving their jobs by rewarding "faithful and respectable" servants with cash prizes and public recognition. The society also established an intelligence office to assist both "masters and servants" in obtaining mutually pleasing situations. Through such rewards, the society hoped to inculcate domestic servants with pride in their work, even though it was humble. "There is nothing inherent in republicanism," the society stated, "which incapacitates the humble in life from filling the unobtrusive, but not unimportant, station of servant, with proper humility and faithfulness. Such a person forms one of the connecting links by which society is bound together, and the meanest link in the chain is of cardinal importance to the rest." [24]

Tappan remained on the board of managers of the Society for the Encouragement of Faithful Domestic Servants until it dissolved in 1830. But Tappan's concern with inculcating workers with morality, good work habits, "loyalty," and acceptance of low-paying, low-status occupations continued. Tappan supported an apprenticeship system for freed southern slaves, which would perform the same end of teaching newly free workers habits of industry. Thus, Tappan's support of the manual labor school project may have come mostly from a desire to form loyal, moral workers, and less from a desire to elevate blacks to the middle class. Tappan's goal to educate blacks did not necessarily mean that blacks should move beyond the working class.[25] Probably none of the other white supporters of the school were initially concerned with such issues either.

The goals of the various constituencies in support of the manual labor school project in the 1830s were not forced to a resolution in practice, however, for the school was never built. Garrison, Arthur Tappan, and the other white visitors to the 1831 convention gave the black conventioneers one year to raise the twenty thousand dollars necessary for the establishment of the school in New Haven, Connecticut. Tappan also bought land for the school near Yale University. But a protest rally of seven hundred of New Haven's white residents against the school stalled the project in 1831. Samuel Cornish and his agents continued to collect money for the school but were unable to find a new site on which to build. Most predominantly white towns in the northeast feared that the establishment of black schools would increase their black populations. Additionally, Arthur Tappan retreated from full support of the project, skeptical that other communities would welcome the school if the "friendly, generous, pious and humane" residents of New Haven had not. The newly formed New England Anti-Slavery Society also attempted to raise funds for the school, but was unsuccessful.[26]

Divisions among blacks as to the purpose of the school also contributed to the downfall of the project. In 1834, black Philadelphians took over leadership of the school project. William Whipper, Robert Purvis, James Forten, and other Philadelphians were less concerned with the material elevation of blacks than with the moral reform not only of the black community, but of the entire nation. Whipper led the establishment of the American Moral Reform Society, which at the 1835 convention gained control of the manual labor school project. The Moral Reform Society's control of the school project led to a greater concern with the personal morality of blacks. The Philadelphians believed that moral improvement was the best way for blacks to improve their status. Although morality and economics were related in the minds of New Yorkers, the emphasis of the Philadelphians on individual moral reform provided fewer options for collective or material means to provide working-class blacks with employment. Samuel Cornish said of the society that they were "vague, wild, indefinite and confused in their views."

Not opposed to moral reform, Cornish noted that the Cranberry Moral Reform Society, auxiliary to the American Moral Reform Society, had in its constitution made "definite" plans to reform "the people of color of Cranberry" by giving "the rising generation a good education, and instructing them in some useful occupation; second, by the general diffusion of useful knowledge among all classes of adult persons; third, by promoting among us the moral virtues of Christian graces, and the refinements of civilized life." Cornish and other black New Yorkers linked material improvement to moral improvement more strongly than most Philadelphia leaders.[27]

Additionally, the Philadelphians who founded the American Moral Reform Society did not want to build a school that would serve only blacks. Conventions, schools, and other organizations and institutions that invited only blacks to participate reinforced the lines of race, and thus racism. Despite the fact that blacks had far less access to skilled training than whites, the Moral Reform Society voted in 1836 that any schools the society tried to establish should not be designated solely for "the free people of color," but should address "the white as well as the colored community." Black improvement should be subsumed in the improvement of all of American society. Additionally, the words "of color" and "colored, implied degradation" and should not be associated with institutions and other efforts made by blacks for their improvement. The Moral Reform Society's refusal to address problems specific to blacks led many blacks to reject the society and refuse to give funds to the school.[28]

The Moral Reform Society also contributed to the foundering of the black convention movement after 1835. The Philadelphians and New Yorkers had struggled throughout the 1830s over leadership of the convention movement. In 1836, the Moral Reform Society scheduled its first meeting in Philadelphia at the same time that New Yorkers in charge of the black convention had scheduled the annual meeting in New York. Although the New Yorkers ultimately did not hold a meeting that year, they also refused to attend the Moral Reform Society's meeting. Such infighting led to the collapse of the convention movement. As the Moral Reform Society alienated blacks, and the convention movement collapsed, the manual labor school project lost a stable source of black support. The national effort for a black-controlled manual labor school lay dormant until the revival of the convention movement in the 1840s. At that time, a new set of more secular leaders and concerns would animate the discussion.[29]

As the national manual labor school project and the black convention movement foundered, New York City blacks established local societies and schools to work toward the original goals stated in the convention's support of the manual labor school project: moral, intellectual, and occupational training for blacks. The most successful was the Phoenix Society, established in early 1833 by Samuel Cornish and his protégé, Theodore Wright. Wright, as with so many other black New York educators and reformers, had attended the African Free Schools in the 1820s. After completing his studies at the Princeton Seminary, he succeeded Cornish as pastor of the First Colored Presbyterian Church in New York City in 1828.[30] African Methodist Episcopal Zion bishop Christopher Rush was named president of the society, and Samuel Cornish acted as general agent. White reformer Arthur Tappan acted as treasurer and provided financial support. The Phoenix Society would provide blacks of all ages with guidance in "morals, literature and mechanical arts," through education, cultural activities, job training, and employment assistance. Plans included lecture series and circulating libraries, employment centers to assist young men in finding apprenticeships and long-term employment, and material aid in the form of clothing or food to the more destitute. The society opened a high school for young men in 1833 and one for young women in 1836. The African Dorcas Association collected and repaired used clothing to distribute to poor children attending these schools, as they did for poor children attending the African Free Schools. The Phoenix Society also sponsored an Evening School for Colored People, and eventually a Sabbath school taught by Lewis Tappan. These schools rented rooms, including some in the Broadway Tabernacle, which New York evangelicals associated with revivalist Charles Finney and radical abolitionism built in the 1830s to replace the smaller Chatham Street Chapel. The school for young women was more successful in attracting students than was the school for young men, enrolling thirty-five at its height. This was probably because adolescent boys in black families could earn more money working than adolescent girls. Thus, families were more likely to allow girls to attend schools for longer periods than boys. But neither high school sustained steady enrollments, and by 1838 both schools had closed for lack of funds.[31]

Following the closing of the schools, the Phoenix Society continued as one of several literary societies in the city. These literary societies were usually single-sex. The Phoenix Society welcomed "young men, from fifteen years old and upwards," as did the Philomathean Society and the short-lived Union Lyceum. The Ladies' Literary Society welcomed married and single women. Both male and female societies featured a range of lectures, musical performances, and poetry recitals by members and guests. The Phoenix Society's 1841 lecture series featured among its twelve speakers John Peterson, a black New York City school principal, speaking on geography, and James

McCune Smith speaking on the "Circulation of the Blood." At an anniversary meeting of the Ladies' Literary Society, members composed their own speeches and dialogues on such topics as "the improvement of the mind" and "on First Appearance in Company" (probably a series of examples on how to introduce oneself properly at social occasions). Membership in such societies ranged from those who "had considerable advantages of education" to those who had less education but sought to "improve their leisure hours." But middle-class, educated blacks, and particularly black ministers and their wives, dominated the leadership of such societies. Cornish, Rush, Wright, and Peter Williams Jr. continued to lead the Phoenix Society. Henrietta Ray, the first president of the Ladies Literary Society and a deeply religious woman herself, was the wife of Charles B. Ray, who worked as a traveling reporter for the *Colored American* before becoming a Methodist minister (albeit after Henrietta's death). As with plans to build black schools, the literary societies encouraged moral reform as well as intellectual growth.[32]

The emphasis New York's black reformers placed on education grew out of two concerns: improvement of their own condition and the abolition of slavery and racism. On the one hand, northern blacks needed to improve their economic, political, and moral condition for their own survival. "If there is any one thing which we can do more than others, in the elevation and enfranchisement of our colored people, it is education." Reformers repeatedly urged blacks of all classes, but particularly the lower classes, to obtain education. They feared that blacks had been "too negligent on this subject" and had not taken sufficient advantage of the multiple opportunities of receiving education available to them, from private and public schools, to free Sabbath and evening schools, reading rooms, and literary societies. Although at times black reformers focused on the education of black men as crucial, as in the case of the manual labor school project, women's moral and intellectual education too was important, so that they could fulfill roles as teachers and as mothers.[33]

New York City's free blacks were also under pressure to prove the success of northern emancipation. Exclusion from schools and skilled training prevented northern blacks from displaying their full moral, intellectual, and economic potential and thus proving unequivocally that blacks could live as free and equal citizens in the United States. But institutions such as the Phoenix Society schools and manual labor schools could provide the opportunity for blacks to prove they were equal to whites. New York City supporters of these schools sought in particular to create a black working class along middle-class lines. The combination of moral, intellectual, and skilled-labor education would result in a class of artisan scholars who possessed high-status skilled jobs and in their spare time read and discussed literature, art, and the sciences as well as the pressing political issues of the day. They would be much like their middle- and upper-class brethren. Additionally, the Phoenix Society hoped that some of its students would be prepared to enter middle-class professions. Such achievements would not only improve the conditions of free blacks, but also prove the correctness and possibility of the goal of immediate emancipation of southern slaves.

Black reformers' establishment of free black uplift and immediate emancipation as interrelated goals became a central part of the goals of the American Anti-Slavery Society (AASS), formed in December of 1833. In its constitution, the society pledged to "elevate the character and condition of the people of color, by encouraging their intellectual, moral, and religious improvement, and by removing public prejudice."[34] Radical abolitionists acknowledged that the "removal of public prejudice" involved the education and improvement of whites. But blacks would also have to prove their equality. For middle-class abolitionists, black and white, the simplest way to do this was to adhere to middle-class norms of moral perfection. Abolitionists repeated the dictum "Every coloured man has it in his power to promote emancipation, by his *Example*" to blacks of all classes.[35] But reformers aimed their efforts particularly at working-class blacks, whose habits colonizationists held up as a sign of the inability of all blacks to participate as equals in American society. Both black and white abolitionists encouraged temperance and education for blacks. AASS conventioneers encouraged blacks in other cities to follow the example of New York blacks and form Phoenix societies for their moral and intellectual improvement.

The American Anti-Slavery Society emphasized mass mobilization of antislavery support. In the first three years of its existence, the society distributed over a million pieces of antislavery literature and submitted nearly six hundred thousand antislavery petitions to Congress, signed by nearly one million people. Southern congressmen found these petitions so threatening to slavery that they successfully passed a gag rule that tabled all antislavery petitions automatically and prevented congressional debates on slavery. Undeterred, abolitionists continued public discussion of slavery at the local level. Radical abolitionists addressed their efforts to everyone so that by 1837, men, women, and even children, black and white, had formed over one thousand local antislavery societies, with a combined membership of two hundred thousand by 1840. Abolitionists wished to eradicate the sin of slavery from the nation; to do so, they sought to demonstrate to individuals how the choices they made in their daily lives could either uphold slavery or help to end it. The clothes one wore, the foods one ate, where one chose to spend money, for whom one chose to vote, and where and with whom one chose to pray were all part of the struggle against slavery. Free produce campaigns encouraged consumers to avoid buying slave-produced goods such as sugar and cotton. Men should vote only for political candidates who opposed slavery. Those who could not vote, namely, blacks and women, should sign the petitions that antislavery societies continued to send to Congress, despite the gag rule, and to state legislatures. Women organized antislavery sewing bees and sold their creations to supporters of abolition at antislavery fairs; the proceeds funded antislavery speakers and the publications of the local and national societies. Abolitionists encouraged even the poor and children to contribute to antislavery causes through "penny-a-month" campaigns. And if nothing else were possible, the abolitionists encouraged antislavery prayer. Chistians should "come out" of, or leave, religious denominations that continued to characterize slavery as God's will.[36]

North and south, many whites found the radicalism of the abolitionists disturbing, even if they themselves opposed slavery. As the anti-abolitionist and colonizationist New Yorker David Meredith Reece said of the radical abolitionists, they were "not the creed and practice of Jefferson, Franklin, Rush, and John Jay, of the old school, for those laboured for *gradual* abolition, and were clearly right." Yet, the radical abolitionists were gaining power and support at the same time as those members of the old antislavery school who had converted to colonization were unable to raise money for their cause.[37]

In New York City, blacks and whites, men, women, and children all formed local abolitionist societies. Among white societies, many of the new radical abolitionists had previously been colonizationists. As abolitionists, their criticisms of southern slave labor now assailed one of the cornerstones of New York City's economy. As southern newspaperman J. D. DeBow stated, New York was "almost as dependent on Southern slavery as Charleston itself," and the city far outstripped Boston and Philadelphia in its reliance on southern trade. New York producers sold clothing (including the "negro cloth" that slaves wore), shoes, and luxury items south. Southerners shipped cotton, tobacco, turpentine, pork, and other raw goods and produce to New York. The New York port served as a center from which merchants shipped cotton as well as other southern goods to points up and down the East Coast and to Europe. New York also served as the central point through which European goods were shipped south. Southern ports such as Charleston, Savannah, Mobile, or New Orleans often shipped goods directly to Europe themselves, but New Yorkers managed early in the nineteenth century to establish the New York port as a major force in shipments between the South and Europe. Ships filled with goods from the South landed on the wharves of the East River, where they were reloaded onto ships bound for Europe. New York shippers collected heavy tolls on these goods. New Yorkers also established shipping lines in southern ports and thus profited from shipments that went directly from southern ports to Europe. New Yorkers were able to do this because most southerners were fully absorbed with the wealth to be made through agriculture and the slave trade. Antebellum writers estimated that New Yorkers earned as much as forty cents on every dollar's worth of southern cotton sold. New Yorkers sold southerners between 76 million and 131 million dollars in merchandise annually. New Yorkers also held part ownership in southern factories, plantations, and slaves through business and family connections. Finally, wealthy southerners and New Yorkers socialized together. Many southern merchants and planters made annual trips to New York City to purchase goods, and some brought their families with them, viewing such trips as social and cultural as well as business opportunities. Southerners also vacationed in New York state resorts, such as Saratoga Springs. The reliance of New York's economy on the southern trade meant that working-class whites also depended on the continuation of the slave labor system.[38]

In New York City, proslavery, colonizationist, and anti-abolitionist whites' attacks centered on Arthur and Lewis Tappan. Migrants from New England, the Tappan brothers were the most visible of a new generation of radical, moral perfectionist reformers in New York City who sought to expunge a range of sins from the nation, from prostitution in northern urban centers to drinking to nonobservance of the Sabbath to slavery in the South. But even before the Tappans converted to radical abolition, New York City elites had begun to view Arthur Tappan as a threat to their way of life. As leader of New York City's Magdalen Society in 1831, Tappan linked economics and morality in a harsh criticism of city elites' participation in prostitution. The Magdalen Society, an organization to reform prostitutes, initially gained the support of a range of the city's religious, social, and political leaders. In the wake of Charles Grandison Finney's first New York City revival in 1829, some reformers had begun to address the issue of prostitution, particularly in the Five Points area. Princeton divinity student John McDowall spent a year leading prayer meetings in New York City brothels before founding the New York Magdalen Society in 1830 to organize the reformation of prostitutes. Lewis and Arthur Tappan were among the leaders of the society and the most generous contributors to its House of Refuge for reformed prostitutes. Under Arthur Tappan's presidency in 1831, however, the

society's efforts to reform prostitutes became a discussion of the moral standards not only of wayward women, but also of some members of the city's
elite. In the 1831 annual report, using statistics gathered by McDowell and
written under Tappan's leadership, the Magdalen Society charged that New
York City contained ten thousand prostitutes, and that the clients of prostitutes belonged to some of the city's most prominent and respectable
families.[39]

Some New Yorkers were outraged at what they saw as the slandering of
New York and its best families by an upstart group of New England reformers. But members of New York's best families were not just clients to prostitutes, they were entrepreneurs in the business of brothels. John Livingston, brother of founding father Robert R. Livingston and one of the most
successful landlords in New York, built his wealth through brothels. John
Delaplaine, an importer; George Lorillard, a tobacco entrepreneur; and Matthew Davis, a Tammany Hall politician, all profited from prostitution. In
fact, a coalition of these wealthy and politically powerful men had already
defeated several proposals before New York's Common Council to raze
houses of prostitution in the Five Points. The Magdalen Society's annual report pamphlet threatened to mobilize a new alliance to eradicate the brothels. City elites and politicos quickly responded. Former mayor Philip Hone
and General Robert Bogardus, Manhattan's wealthiest real estate speculator,
held anti-Magdalen meetings, railing against the "social influence of New
Englanders in the City." Newspapermen and Tammany leaders James
Watson Webb, editor of the *Morning Courier,* and Mordecai Noah fanned
the flames against the Magdalen Society and Arthur Tappan. Newspapers
from Webb's *Morning Courier* to the *Working Man's Advocate* denounced
Tappan, and there were rumors that angry men would physically attack him
and his home. Surprised and fearful of the repercussions of his activism, Tappan quickly withdrew from the society, which dissolved within the year.[40]

The new public discussion of sex and morality in New York City continued in connection with the abolitionist movement.[41] The Magdalen Society
controversy did not explicitly touch on issues of interracial sex. Two years
later, however, the Tappans' embrace of radical abolition, and the formation
of the American Anti-Slavery Society, resulted in the centering of amalgamation, or interracial socializing and sex, in New Yorkers' political land-
scape. Unlike the word "miscegenation," which Democrats invented in 1863
for the express purpose of demonizing black-white relationships and dis-
crediting the Republican Party, the word "amalgamation" has a history beyond American nineteenth-century racial politics. In Europe and the United
States, "amalgamation" described the blending of any two or more distinct

groups of people through intermarriage or through nonsexual cultural exchanges. The British in 1775 used the word to describe the earlier historic
mixture of Normans and Saxons. In the United States in 1811, the Emperor
of Russia asked John Quincy Adams whether immigrants to the United
States "all amalgamate well together," implying an acceptable intermixture
of people. But by the mid-1830s, the use of the word "amalgamation" in the
United States chiefly suggested negative attitudes about black-white sexual and social relationships, from intermarriage to casual sex to dancing and
other forms of socializing. The offspring of interracial sexual relationships
were also held up to adverse scrutiny.[42]

The abolitionist controversy of 1830s New York City was central to this
redefinition. In the 1830s, black and white abolitionists made interracial
cooperation a hallmark of their efforts. Black and white abolitionists attended political meetings together, worshiped together, and sometimes visited each others' homes. Within abolitionist organizations, such actions
were not without conflict. The Ladies' New York City Anti-Slavery Society,
for example, refused to allow black women to join, and throughout the antebellum period, as Theodore Wright stated, white abolitionists struggled to
"annihilate, in their own bosoms, the cord of caste." But as anti-abolitionist
whites recognized, the professed principles of the abolitionists had the potential to upset the power balance between the races in New York City, as
well as to threaten the business relationships between southerners and New
Yorkers.[43]

The abolitionists' political tactics and goals blunted the attempt by some
whites to remove New York's blacks from the political process by denying
them the vote, and indeed from the polity completely by colonizing them in
Africa. In their actions and words, abolitionists expanded the meaning of
politics by relying on moral suasion and by questioning universal white
manhood suffrage and even the Constitution as the best examples of democracy and equality. Abolitionists also demonstrated that political tactics
previously deemed fit only for whites could in fact be used by blacks also.
Abolitionists presented forums in which black men (as well as black and
white women) discussed the political issues of the day as equals with white
men, and black and some white abolitionists worked to obtain equal suffrage
for blacks. The most radical abolitionists, such as William Lloyd Garrison,
blurred caste lines between blacks and whites even more. When visiting
black organizations, Garrison often said that he visited "as a black man" or
spoke to blacks "as one of you."[44] Such actions did not simply reduce white
abolitionists to the level of blacks, as some anti-abolitionists charged, but
raised the possibility of blacks' equality to whites and forced the questioning

of the nation's political process. In New York City, the interaction between the wealthy Tappans and blacks particularly disturbed white workers. The Tappans were representative of the new capitalists who stripped workers of lucrative skilled jobs and attempted to reform them during their leisure hours. Some white workers supported the antislavery movement and other reforms promoted by the Tappans, but for many, the Tappans' association with blacks, and their admonishments to white workers to support moral reform and racial equality, were unwelcome attempts to change white workers' way of life, with little in return in the way of increased economic or political opportunity.[45]

Although black and white abolitionists did not intermarry in New York City or elsewhere, some abolitionists did attempt to redefine public attitudes toward interracial sex in two major areas: they favored the legalization of consensual interracial unions, as might occur among free blacks and whites in the North; and they opposed those that were forced by southern slaveholders on slaves. In Boston in 1832, white abolitionists William Lloyd Garrison and Lydia Maria Child began a highly public campaign to repeal the Massachusetts law that forbade interracial marriage. In Child's words, "The government ought not to be invested with power to control the affections, any more than the consciences of citizens."[46] Lydia Maria Child, in her 1833 *Appeal in Favor of that Class of Americans Called Africans*, was the first abolitionist to denounce in print the rape of slave women by slave masters. Other abolitionists followed suit. At the first anniversary meeting of the American Anti-Slavery Society, held at the Chatham Street Chapel in New York in 1834, delegate James Thome of Kentucky related his observations of the "[y]oung men of talents and respectability, fathers, professors of religion, ministers—all classes!" who consorted with slave women and contributed to the "overwhelming pollution!" of the South.[47] As had been true with the Magdalen Society, abolitionists were again openly attacking the sexual practices of elites. That women, too, were joining the discussion made the attack even more disturbing to the middle and upper classes.

Probably all abolitionists opposed sexual relationships between slaves and slave masters, and some became comfortable speaking against such relationships in public. But few abolitionists sustained as strong a commitment to interracial marriage as did Child and Garrison. In New York City in the late 1820s, black reformers denied that respectable blacks would wish to marry whites or participate in other forms of interracial socializing but admitted that "dissolute" blacks were indeed guilty as charged. Samuel Cornish and John Russwurm also blamed whites for initiating the contact by frequenting black neighborhoods. They stated, "Our streets and places of public amusement are nightly crowded" with white prostitutes and their white male clients. In an article in *Freedom's Journal,* a black writer calling himself Mordecai responded to charges by the racist and colonizationist newspaper editor Manuel Mordecai Noah that blacks wished to marry whites: "I am not covetous of sitting at the table of Mr. N——, to hold [him] by his arm in the streets,—to marry his daughter, should he ever have one—nor to sleep in his bed—neither should I think myself honoured in the possession of all these favours." [48] Arguments by blacks against interracial marriage sought to uncouple the link between black equality and interracial sexuality. According to these writers, interracial socializing was not "respectable" and thus not a suitable goal of blacks seeking political equality.

The attitudes of abolitionists toward interracial socializing, sex, and marriage were thus far from simple approval. For the vast majority of abolitionists, black and white, their support of political and even social interracial interactions did not mean that they wished to intermarry, and indeed abolitionists stated repeatedly that they did not wish to. Yet abolition's opponents in New York City, many of whom had earlier opposed the Magdalen Society, now sexualized and redefined the issues of immediate emancipation and black equality as the desire of abolitionists to encourage amalgamation in New York City. The abolitionist coalition did participate in controversial actions: they cooperated with British abolitionists and held up Britain's record of antislavery as a positive moral example, which angered the strongly anti-British New Yorkers; they advocated temperance, which angered some workers; and they called for strict observance of the Sabbath, which angered some businessmen. But the abolitionists' alleged support of amalgamation became the most provocative rallying point for anti-abolitionists, leading to the violent riots of 1834. The riots distorted the abolitionists' call for moral change into imagined sexual relationships between black and white abolitionists. For supporters of slavery and racial conservatives, charges of amalgamation were a means to discredit abolitionists' demands to end slavery and include free blacks as equals in the political and economic life of the city.

Soon after Arthur Tappan's defection from the colonizationists to the abolitionists in 1833, white New Yorkers who supported southern slavery and black colonization attacked the emerging abolitionist coalition. In October 1833, a mob encouraged and led by *New York Courier and Enquirer* editor James Watson Webb attempted to disrupt the organizational meeting at Clinton Hall of the New York City Anti-Slavery Society, a local precursor to the American Anti-Slavery Society. The abolitionists, fearing such activities, had vacated the hall early. The rioters proceeded to hold a mock meeting in which they seized an elderly black man, named him Arthur Tappan,

PRACTICAL AMALGAMATION (Musical Soirée)

Fig. 18 This anti-abolition cartoon was one of a series that depicted the political activism of abolitionists as leading ultimately to intermarriage. Courtesy of the American Antiquarian Society.

and forced him to preside over the meeting and make a speech. When the man declared, "I am a poor, ignorant man . . . but I have heard of the Declaration of Independence, and have read the Bible. The Declaration says all men are created equal, and the Bible says God has made us all of one blood. I think . . . we are entitled to good treatment, that it is wrong to hold men in slavery," the mob interrupted him, denouncing immediate emancipation and "immediate amalgamation" before dispersing.[49]

The incident was only the first in a series of public altercations linking immediate emancipation, racial equality, and amalgamation. Throughout early 1834, New York newspapers printed numerous articles about the "fanatical" abolitionists and their opposition to colonization, and white editors frequently linked the abolitionists' goal of immediate emancipation to amalgamation (figs. 18 and 19). James Watson Webb's *Courier and Enquirer* led the attack on the abolitionist coalition. During the annual meeting of the American Anti-Slavery Society, held in New York in May 1834, Webb and other anti-abolitionist newspaper editors raised the possibility of black annihilation or amalgamation as reasons to support the colonization of blacks and

THE FRUITS OF AMALGAMATION.

Fig. 19 An anti-abolitionist depiction of a content interracial family at home. A man resembling abolitionist William Lloyd Garrison stands in the doorway, arm in arm with a black woman, as a white manservant prepares to offer tea. Courtesy of the American Antiquarian Society.

to denounce immediate abolition. As "Quo" wrote in the *New York Journal of Commerce* (which ironically had once been owned by the Tappans), slavery in the United States could end only in "Colonization, Amalgamation, or Annihilation" of black people. Annihilation would occur after full emancipation because "the free blacks do not increase at all; on the contrary, they dwindle away. . . . They have not within them that stirring spirit which stimulates the white sons . . . to penetrate the West, and . . . people the world with intelligence and enterprise." Of the supposed alternative, amalgamation, Quo stated, "There will never be an honorable and virtuous amalgamation of the races. . . . A deluge of pollution must engulph our country, at the thought of which the heart sickens." [50] Quo offered the solution to the problems of annihilation and amalgamation: colonization. But according to Webb's *Courier and Enquirer*, abolitionists prevented colonization from occurring. They "enticed" blacks to stay in the United States with "the prospect of being speedily admitted to a social equality with the whites." Abolitionists, the paper stated, "invite the blacks to dine with them; send their children to school with them; and, what we know to be a fact, invite and encourage them to seat themselves in the same pews with white ladies; to thrust themselves into their places in steamboats, and to obtrude their aromatic persons in places whence the customs of society, and, let us add, the instincts of nature, have hitherto banished them."[51]

These debates over the place of blacks in society sparked physical confrontations between blacks and whites that led to full-scale rioting in early July.[52] The July riots began with the harassment of black and white abolitionists by a crowd of "hundreds of young men" who disrupted the abolitionists' Fourth of July celebration in Chatham Street Chapel. On July 7, a black celebration of New York's Emancipation Day in the same chapel was disrupted by members of the Sacred Music Society, who claimed they had rented the chapel for the same night. The interruption ended with blacks routing the musicians from the church, amid epithets and broken furniture. News of the incident spread on July 8, and between July 9 and 12, whites rioted, destroying the homes of white abolitionist Arthur Tappan and the homes and churches of black Episcopalian minister Peter Williams Jr., white Presbyterian minister Samuel Cox, and white minister Henry G. Ludlow of the Spring Street Church, as well as homes and businesses of blacks who lived in the interracial Five Points area.[53]

The three days of violence constituted the largest riot of the antebellum years in New York City. Although blacks had been the victims of mob violence before, this was the first time the issue of amalgamation was the explicit concern and rallying cry. The riots were so violent not simply because of the explosiveness of the amalgamation issue itself, but because this was an issue, and abolitionists a population, against which members of all classes of white New Yorkers united. Because working-class blacks and whites shared neighborhoods, particularly in the Five Points area, where much of the disturbance was centered, the meanings of black citizenship and amalgamation were of particular concern to them. Working-class whites wished to demarcate themselves politically and economically from blacks. Many of the rioters were skilled workers who feared the economic as much as the social effects of the new regime represented by the Tappans. The rioting continued with the approval of anti-abolitionist newspaper editors, police, and elites. The union of these groups with the white working classes led to an intense level of destruction.[54]

The charge of amalgamation focused the rioters' hostility, but the riots revealed fears of increasing black political and economic power. Rioters destroyed Arthur Tappan's house because allegedly he had entertained blacks there. Mobs attacked Peter Williams's and Henry Ludlow's churches because of rumors that the ministers had performed interracial marriages. Riotous crowds struck twice at Samuel Cox's church. Cox had denounced the practice of segregating black churchgoers in "negro pews" and had described Jesus Christ as a dark-skinned man. Gangs of men attacked black residences in the interracial Five Points area fairly indiscriminately, but singled out some examples of black affluence for special harassment. Mobs destroyed the African Society for Mutual Relief Hall and a black-owned barbershop and physically assaulted a black barber from another shop. Isaiah Emory, a black shopkeeper, received a threatening note. Another black storekeeper feared that two brick houses he owned would be destroyed.[55] The working-class white mobs displayed a mixture of fear about interracial sex, antipathy toward sharing neighborhood space with blacks of any class, and particular resentment of attempts to elevate blacks to equal standing either with themselves or with middle-class white abolitionists, whether through intermarriage, through rhetoric, or through the efforts of blacks themselves.

The abolitionists were unprepared for whites' violent denunciation of black citizenship rights in the 1834 riots. The riots led New York City abolitionists to tone down the radicalism of their claims for immediate emancipation and black equality. On Saturday, July 12, following the dispersal of the rioters, white abolitionists Arthur Tappan and John Rankin, on behalf of the Executive Committee of the American Anti-Slavery Society, posted handbills throughout the city that stated, among other points, "We entirely disclaim any desire to promote or encourage intermarriages between white and colored citizens." Despite the abolitionists' repeated petitions to Congress against slavery, the abolitionists also stated their support of states' rights to decide the fate of slavery, claiming that abolitionists did not "ask of Congress any act transcending their constitutional powers; which the abolition of slavery by Congress, in any state, would plainly do."[56] Soon after, white abolitionists also beat a fast retreat on some aspects of the issue of black equality. On July 17 and August 19, Tappan, Rankin, and other abolitionists (including black abolitionist Samuel Cornish) stated again that they had not encouraged interracial marriage. But the abolitionists also defined additional limits on action for the cause of black citizenship and equality, in particular withdrawing from a defense of black use of public space. They refuted rumors that prior to the riots, abolitionists had encouraged blacks to take over the streets and search for white women. They stated that they had not "encouraged colored men to ride up and down Broadway on horse back or, . . . put themselves forward in public parades," nor had they encouraged "'fifty of those' colored lads 'who belonged to a Sabbath school before the abolition measures commenced' to 'parad[e] [in] the street with their canes and dandy dress, [and seek] white wives.'" Those who spread these rumors had used them to exaggerate the distinctions between older methods of social reform for blacks and the new radicalism of the abolitionists, and they had invoked sexuality to provoke fear of the new movement. Under the new moral reform regime, the anti-abolitionists claimed, blacks were running amuck. To combat these ideas, abolitionists retreated more firmly into moral reform ideology. They also disavowed blacks' public parades, even more strongly than Samuel Cornish and Peter Williams had in 1827, thus effectively giving over the streets to whites.[57]

The abolitionist response to the riots confirmed the power of the mob and the weakness of black claims to racial equality, middle-class standing, and political power within and outside of the abolitionist movement. In strongly rejecting interracial marriage, New York's black and white abolitionists implicitly disassociated themselves from William Lloyd Garrison's continuing campaign to repeal the Massachusetts law against interracial marriage. Abolitionists through the Civil War drew a distinction between opposition to legal restrictions on interracial marriage and their own personal actions. But in the wake of the 1834 riots, the Tappans and other New York abolitionists, both black and white, did not risk such a complex statement, instead rejecting the possibility of intermarriage completely.[58]

Further, white abolitionists, with the possible exception of William Lloyd Garrison, began to draw distinctions between blacks and whites that depicted blacks as a group as unlettered, even as white abolitionists continued to associate with middle-class blacks in their organizations. Such distinctions defined the limits of black equality, and the limits of white abolitionists' role in helping blacks achieve equality. For example, Bostonian Lydia Maria Child wrote in 1834, "On the subject of equality, the principles of the abolitionists have been misrepresented. They have not the slightest wish to do violence to the distinctions of society by forcing the rude and illiterate into the presence of the learned and refined." Abolitionists only wished to give blacks the same rights enjoyed by "the lowest and most ignorant white man in America." But the lowest white man increasingly saw himself as by definition above the level of blacks. Further, Child's statement implied that all blacks, to a degree, were "rude and illiterate." The views of Child and other white abolitionists, as historian George Fredrickson has noted, "could be used to reinforce the unfavorable free-Negro stereotype that was promulgated by colonizationists and defenders of slavery."[59] Thus, because white abolitionists themselves reinforced views of blacks as inferior, their attempts to grant social and economic equality to New York's blacks were in disarray.

Black abolitionists, too, retreated from the radicalism of interracial political activism. On July 14, white Episcopalian bishop Benjamin Onderdonk ordered black Episcopalian minister Peter Williams Jr. to either step down from the American Anti-Slavery Society or resign his position as minister. Williams not only left the society, but denied that he had played an active role there. Although elected to the Board of Managers at the society's inaugural meeting, Williams claimed that he "never met with that Board but for a few moments at the close of their sessions, and then without uttering a word." Williams also claimed that when he was elected to the Executive Committee at the AASS meeting held in New York in May 1834, he had "replied that I could not attend to it, and have never attended but on one occasion." The procolonization newspapers of the city published Williams's retreat from the AASS "with unfeigned pleasure."[60]

For black reformers such as Williams, the solution to the abolitionist controversy was for blacks to focus on the reform of the black community, without the physical presence of white abolitionists. White abolitionists were best equipped to pursue the freedom of slaves and the political rights of free blacks; and black abolitionists were best equipped to prepare blacks for freedom and equality. In the wake of the 1834 riots Williams said that he wished the American Anti-Slavery Society "all success" in ending southern slavery, but that his own role, as a black reformer, "was exclusively . . . to labor to qualify our people for the enjoyment of these rights." Samuel Cornish was more blunt when he stated that "white men are not calculated to judge of the abilities and adaptedness of colored men. . . . [Y]ou know our coloured population but in certain spheres of life. The intelligent among us, can descend with them into their different walks and associations, and therefore can better estimate them under their various circumstances."[61] Williams and Cornish saw themselves and other middle-class, educated blacks as a bridge between the black community and racial equality. Their education and morality meant they understood what black people needed to do to achieve equality in the eyes of whites; and the ties of race gave them a special understanding of the conditions, needs, and desires of blacks. In the black neighborhoods and churches, they had more day-to-day contact with blacks than white abolitionists. But they, too, viewed the mass of blacks as inferior to whites, and perhaps to themselves, and believed that blacks needed preparation and education for citizenship. Thus, their overall goals did not differ essentially from those of white abolitionists: classical education, moral improvement, temperance, and other ideals were part of the moral-reform, middle-class agenda for improving society overall.

The increasing conservatism of black and white abolitionists in the wake of the 1834 riots complicated enactment of the American Anti-Slavery Society's credo of racial uplift. For black abolitionists, conservatism meant less emphasis on interracial interactions and greater support for black education—occupational, intellectual, and moral. But for white abolitionists, greater conservatism led to a retreat from funding practical reform efforts to address the material and educational needs of northern free blacks; instead, the American Anti-Slavery Society focused on ending southern slavery. The New York abolitionists led this change in focus. As historian Aileen Kraditor has pointed out, abolitionists such as the Tappans, in calling for racial equality, had been "more radical than they realized. . . . [T]heir demand for the abolition of slavery linked with the establishment of political and civil equality of the races would require an alteration in American society more drastic than they thought or were by temperament prepared for." Thus, in the wake of the 1834 riots, the first commitment of white abolitionists such as the Tappans was to the eradication of slavery. The existence of racial prejudice was troublesome, but not as troubling as slavery, and "while accepting both . . . goals of . . . emancipation and eradication of race prejudice . . . [they] wished to demonstrate to the potentially friendly sections of the white population that abolition was compatible with most customs and institutions. . . . [T]hey were willing to accept partial gains as steps toward the ultimate goals." White abolitionists also believed that if slavery ended, racism, too, would fall, and the condition of free blacks would improve. Abolitionist Gerrit Smith, of Peterboro, New York, stated that "until this slavery ceases— this enslaving of a man simply because he has African blood in his veins— the free colored population of this country will not be able to exchange their present debasing mockery of freedom for freedom itself." This belief that only the end of slavery would end white prejudice allowed many white abolitionists to stop working to improve the conditions of northern free blacks.[62]

As a result of these reconsidered goals, black and white abolitionists began to part ways. Black abolitionists continued to believe that the improvement of the condition of northern free blacks was as important as the abolition of slavery, and that the two goals were interrelated. They needed American Anti-Slavery Society funds to assist them in their uplift programs for free blacks. But the AASS refused to fund such programs. Of the society's thirty-eight traveling agents, only three were assigned to "the interests of our free colored brethren," and in 1838 the society reassigned these three agents to other duties. In 1836, black New York abolitionist Theodore S. Wright asked each of the local auxiliary societies to appoint standing committees that would introduce "our colored brethren to the useful arts" and hopefully establish contacts between blacks and "such mechanics as are willing to teach them trades, and treat them as they do their other apprentices." But the local societies concentrated their efforts in Ohio or among black communities of Upper Canada, away from the East Coast cities where the abolitionist leadership was centered, and where black problems were among the most acute. Both in New York City and nationally, white abolitionists' aid to free blacks, and particularly working-class blacks, was characterized by a lack of serious, stable funding to schools and other projects that would improve blacks' conditions and by an emphasis on individual moral and intellectual uplift rather than material means to improve blacks' status.[63]

By the late 1830s, some blacks had become disillusioned with black and white abolitionists' methods of pursuing black freedom and equality. They were critical of the ways middle-class abolitionists, black and white, tried to reshape the racial identity of blacks as a group along middle-class lines. Although these black critics were not always working class themselves, the criticisms of those like black porter Peter Paul Simons and middle-class grocer David Ruggles allowed for greater discussion of class distinctions in the black community and greater involvement by the mass of blacks in the abolitionist struggle. They challenged moral reform, skilled labor training, and classical education as inadequate solutions to the problems of racism and poverty in New York City and slavery in the South. Accepting the goals of immediate abolition of slavery and racial equality for blacks, they subtly or explicitly criticized the means. The Stewards' and Cooks' Marine Benevolent Society, for example, freely served alcohol at its annual gathering, toasting with wine the temperance advocates William Lloyd Garrison and Arthur and Lewis Tappan for their assistance with abolition. Reporting on this event, a *Colored American* editor, either Samuel Cornish or Philip Bell, stated his belief that "the angel of temperance could wink" at this "indulgence" among "men, spared by the perils of the sea [and] united after long separation."[64] But Bell and Cornish viewed other objections to moral reform as more threatening to the cause of racial equality. Peter Paul Simons openly condemned the moral reform approach to black problems in several speeches to black benevolent societies in the late 1830s.[65] In his speeches and interactions with other abolitionists, Simons proudly clung to his own working-class identity, encouraged blacks to utilize their own collective resources, and criticized what he saw as the class-, color-, and education-based prejudices of some middle-class black leaders. His outspokenness created enemies amog middle-class reformers such as Samuel Cornish and Philip Bell.

In an 1837 speech before the Daughters of Wesley, a black women's benevolent society, Simons criticized those tenets of moral reform that asserted female inferiority and the inappropriateness of women's activism in the public sphere. Although seeing benevolence as the "brightest gem that adorns the female character," he also asserted women's intellectual equality with men and criticized men and women who saw women as inferior: "those females who considers there gudgement [sic] less, ought to be outcasts of all popular societies; for there [sic] influence might excite the same opinion, of self incapability in many a promising damsel, and I sincerely contend, that where a female feels this inferiority, she is but a dead member to the intellectual and cultivated society of mankind." [66]

Simons submitted the speech to the *Colored American* for publication, but editors Samuel Cornish and Philip Bell refused to publish it, allegedly because it would take too long to edit. An angry Simons charged the editors with "Prejudice against COLOR." He claimed that Cornish and Bell had not printed his speech because he was not part of the "straight haired gentry" or a college graduate. Simons distributed these charges in letters he mailed to black New Yorkers. To prevent further charges of color prejudice, Cornish and Bell printed the speech without editing it. In a subsequent edition, Bell discredited the speech and its writer in an editorial. Bell stated that Cornish had considered the speech "not worth publishing" and that he himself had thought the speech "worthless trash." Bell claimed that the speech was unintelligible and that Simons's audience "could not understand it any more than if it had been Greek." [67]

Some of Cornish's and Bell's criticisms of the speech were true. In written form, the speech is difficult to follow, full of unnecessarily long words and awkward phrasing. But Simons was probably partially correct in raising the charge of "color prejudice" against the editors. To claim "color prejudice" was not simply to talk about skin color, but to allude to the class divisions among blacks, which sometimes followed skin color, as well as beliefs about who was worthy of leading the community. Samuel Cornish had previously displayed a certain snobbishness toward the efforts of working-class blacks to rise to positions of leadership in the black community. In an obsequious letter written to the trustees and faculty of the African Mission School at Hartford in 1829 and reprinted in his short-lived newspaper the *Rights of All*, Cornish "begged leave" to suggest to the school administrators that they not admit any adults "whose dispositions, associations, and talents are not peculiarly adapted to the work, whatever may be his moral and religious character." More particularly, Cornish questioned "the propriety of taking up young men who have spent twenty or twenty five years as common servants. Their minds scarcely can have escaped the contracting influence of their servile condition, they must be ignorant of the interests of their brethren, and destitute of the nobler feelings of the soul."[68] No doubt Simons's occupation as a common laborer, and the possibility that he was self-taught, made him less reliable as a leader in Cornish's eyes.

Cornish and Bell's need to either edit Simons's speech or prevent its publication entirely was also an attempt to prevent embarrassment to the newspaper itself. White newspaper editors read black newspapers and sometimes reprinted and criticized the articles blacks wrote, interpreting the articles as inferior or as examples of blacks "putting on airs." The possibility that Simons's article could be used as another example of the ineptitude of blacks in running their own affairs, or their attempts to "put on airs" by using words that whites claimed blacks barely knew the meaning of and could not pronounce, no doubt led the editors to want to suppress the speech.

But Simons's speech was also threatening to the editors because of its political message. It contained a more powerful and forthright assessment of women's roles and abilities than the rather formulaic praise of women's mutual aid societies generally found in Cornish's and Bell's newspapers. Some middle-class black reformers in the 1830s believed that the opportunity to provide their wives with a sheltered home environment could erase some of the stigma of slavery. Slave owners blurred blacks' gender roles by forcing women to do men's work, such as fieldwork, and men to perform domestic service. Additionally, slave masters often prevented women and men from caring for their own homes. In New York City, such blurring or eliminating of traditional gender roles continued under freedom when men labored as sailors, away from home for months or years, and women worked as domestic servants, forced to leave their own families to someone else's care. Cornish particularly championed traditional gender roles for black men and women as an aspect of moral reform. An article in the *Colored American* described the ideal roles of men and women:

> Man is strong—Woman is beautiful
> Man is daring and confident—Woman is deferent and unassuming
> Man is great in action—Woman in suffering
> Man shines abroad—Woman at home

Such ideals bore little resemblance to the lives of most black women, who worked outside the home to supplement the meager incomes that men earned. Cornish and Bell may have withheld Simons's speech in part for its potentially inflammatory rhetoric about the place of women, not only in the home, but as public participants in the political and social concerns of New York's black community.[69]

The circumstances surrounding the printing of Simons's speech in the *Colored American* provide one of the rare instances for an analysis of the differing meanings of literacy and education among different sectors of the black population. Simons, a laborer, stated implicitly that his achievement of literacy was not part of the creation of a leadership elite based on education, and he did not use his education to exclude from political power those with less education. But some blacks, particularly those of or aspiring to the middle class, viewed education as a passport to leadership and a lack of education as a disqualification.

Simons and the *Colored American* editors came into conflict again in 1839. In a speech before the African Clarkson Association, Simons attacked the political usefulness of moral and intellectual reform for the black community. He stated that "moral elevation . . . has now carried its good to a climax." The high level of moral elevation that the black community had achieved contributed to an enervation of the community's self-respect and pride. The emphasis on morality led to "blind submission" and "soft manners when . . . addressing those of pale complexions." These submissive attitudes were the "roots of degradation" of the black community, not blacks' alleged immorality and lack of education. For Simons, "moral elevation" was "designed expressly . . . to hinder our people from acting collectively for themselves."[70]

Simons also saw "intellectual elevation" as of limited use in the struggle against slavery and racism. Many who were educated and held positions as preachers still worked at menial jobs. Further, the educated created "classes of distinction" and looked down upon those who held laboring jobs, despite that, according to Simons, "the majority of the means among us, you will find among the laboring class." Both moral and intellectual elevation, as defined by middle-class abolitionists, disrupted the unity necessary to the black community in its struggle against racial prejudice and slavery. Simons ended with a call to death-defying action on behalf of the rights of blacks. "Physical and political efforts are the only methods left for us to adopt," he stated. For Simons, fighting to the death affirmed the Christian belief in the afterlife. He stated that "if our forefathers held the truths of immortality of the soul before their eyes," they would have fought to the death, and "there would have been no such thing as African slavery, for they all would have died one by one, before they would remain one day in the clutches of captivity." In words reminiscent of David Walker's fiery appeal ten years earlier, Simons called free blacks to demonstrate "ACTION! ACTION! *ACTION!* and our will to be, or not to be . . . this we must physically practice, and we will be in truth an independent people."[71]

Although Simons's speech echoed the call to action of David Walker's *Appeal*, Walker had preserved a leadership position for educated men and had encouraged moral and intellectual improvement. Walker called for slaves to seize their freedom by violent action only as a last resort. During Walker's life, he and Cornish were colleagues, with Walker serving as the Boston agent and occasional correspondent for Cornish's *Freedom's Journal*. Although Cornish approved of Walker's stands on intellectual and moral improvement, he did not support Walker's advocacy of slave rebellion, even as a last resort. Cornish was committed to the radical abolitionist tenet of non-violence, as was Philip Bell. In the *Colored American*, the editors attempted to diffuse the implications of Simons's speech. Forced to print it by the Committee of Arrangements of the African Clarkson Association, they included it as a paid advertisement. Cornish and Bell hastened to assure their readers that they did not support Simons's critiques of intellectual and moral elevation. "A miserable people shall we be indeed, when we learn to despise or ridicule moral and intellectual elevation," they stated. "A miserable people are many of us now, who delight in traducing the wise and good among us, and in making efforts to bring their *well directed, sacrificing efforts* into disrepute."[72] But Simons's speech indicated that for some blacks the time for Walker's last resort to violent action was approaching. Many blacks, even some black reformers, were disillusioned with moral and intellectual improvement as the central method to achieve black freedom and equality.

As Peter Paul Simons attacked the moral and intellectual exclusivity of organized abolition, David Ruggles and the New York Committee of Vigilance maintained that the abolitionist tactics of nonresistance and legal redress were not the sole defense of blacks accused of being fugitive slaves. In 1835, David Ruggles and other blacks founded the Committee of Vigilance, which drew on the devices and resources of both working-class and middle-class blacks and whites. During its seven years of existence, the Committee of Vigilance presented an alternative vision of black activism and citizenship, combining the abolitionists' sometimes abstract call for black equal rights with the concrete issue of kidnapping to create a mass movement among New York City's blacks. Ruggles's vision of black citizenship and mass power threatened not only anti-abolition whites, but also the New York Manumission Society and black and white radical abolitionists.

The fugitive slave issue blurred the boundaries of slavery and freedom for New York's blacks. This issue affected working-class and poor blacks as it affected no other group of New Yorkers. Between the passing of the federal

Fugitive Slave Act of 1793 and the better-known Fugitive Slave Law of 1850, black and white New Yorkers debated, in the courts, newspapers, and streets, the rights of fugitive slaves and free blacks against those of southern slave-holders and slave catchers, who sought and seized fugitive slaves and some-times captured free blacks and classed them as slaves. The 1793 Fugitive Slave Act enforced the fugitive slave clause of the Constitution, which stated that fugitive slaves were not "discharged from such service or Labour" that they owed in one state because of the laws of the state to which they escaped. Thus, northern states had a legal responsibility to return escaped slaves to their masters in the South. But the 1793 law left it up to local courts to de-cide enforcement. In New York State, this left legal loopholes, which both proslavery and antislavery forces tried to exploit.

Between the passage of New York state's 1810 emancipation law and 1841, southerners could bring their slaves into the state for up to a period of nine months without threat of having the slaves freed. Once the grace period expired, the state's legislature and higher courts often went out of their way to free eligible slaves. But slaves had to find their way to the courts in order to press for their freedom. Further, local governments were not as open to blacks seeking freedom. Local authorities rarely required slave masters trav-eling with their slaves in New York to prove how long they had been in residence. In New York City, law enforcement officers and courts were noto-rious for their zealousness in upholding the claims of slave masters who wished to keep their slaves, or who traveled north to seek fugitive slaves. And both state and local agencies were required by federal law to return any proven fugitive slave to his or her master upon proof of ownership, regard-less of the length of the fugitive's residency in the state.[73]

Before the completion of emancipation in 1827, blacks and white anti-slavery activists were more concerned about the attempts of New York's slave owners to recoup their imminent losses by selling their slaves south in eva-sion of the emancipation law of 1799 than with the status of fugitive slaves. In their efforts to prevent the sales of New York State slaves, the lawyers of the Manumission Society generally found the local courts and magistrates helpful. But once New York's emancipation was complete, threats to the freedom of New York's blacks, as well as to the fugitive slaves who made their way north in a steady stream, became more pressing. The clear direc-tive of the 1793 law, combined with the zealousness of some New York City law enforcers who made a profitable business of slave catching, resulted in a very real threat to the freedom of black New Yorkers. In December of 1828, *Freedom's Journal* warned that "[t]he business of arresting our brethren as runaways is still daily occurring in this city. . . . [W]e have heard, that a Slaveholder, has hinted the determination of himself and others to have *five hundred* at least, out of this city, during the *winter*." [74]

From the 1790s to the early 1830s, the New York Manumission Society had provided legal aid to fugitive slaves and to free blacks accused of being fugitives. But as with the African Free Schools, the Manumission Society's link to the American Colonization Society and its conservative stance on southern emancipation made it ineffectual in the eyes of many blacks in the 1830s. Many Manumission Society members pledged to uphold the 1793 Fugitive Slave Act that radical abolitionists and blacks clearly opposed. At least one Manumission Society member acted as a lawyer on behalf of southerners attempting to retrieve their slaves. As had been true in the 1790s, when the society refused to exclude members who were slaveholders, the society did not discipline this member.[75] As the Manumission Society receded in importance, the radical abolitionists began to address the new challenges facing fugitive slaves and free blacks in 1830s New York.

By the 1830s, City Recorder Richard Riker and Third Ward Constable Tobias Boudinot had become the most well known members of what blacks and white abolitionists called the New York Kidnapping Club. Riker and Boudinot were responsible, along with Daniel D. Nash, John Lyon, and two Virginians, Edward R. Waddy and F. H. Pettis, for re-enslaving fugitives as well as enslaving some free blacks. Nash, Lyon, Waddy, and Pettis acted individually or in concert as agents for slave owners, advertising their services in southern newspapers and seizing suspected fugitives on the streets of New York. They then appeared before any federal or state judge, or more likely the local magistrate and known southern sympathizer Riker, to offer oral or written proof that the person was a slave. If the judge believed the proof, the slave catcher took the person south. Anyone interfering with this process was liable to a five-hundred-dollar fine, a suit for injuries, or both.[76]

There were many reasons why New York City's black working class particularly identified with the issue of fugitive slaves. The anonymity of life among the largest community of blacks in the North attracted many fugitives, and the majority of those who came to New York City entered the community of workers. In addition to these fugitive southern slaves, black workers in New York included former New York slaves and those who still had enslaved kin in the South. Working-class blacks' jobs often entailed high visibility in public places frequented by southerners. In hotels and restaurants, black workers served southerners, who often brought their enslaved personal servants north with them on their travels. Those black men who worked the docks often saw ships at anchor in the harbor with illegal slave

cargo aboard. At home, a more open street culture during domestic and leisure activities left working-class blacks more exposed to kidnappers than
were middle-class blacks. Hannah Conyers, a seven-year-old child whose
parents had sent her to a public pump to collect water, disappeared; her parents believed she had been kidnapped by slave traders. A French family held
ten-year-old Jane Green for two months, hoping to sell her south. Francis
Dallam of Baltimore claimed fugitive slave Dorcas Brown, who had been a
domestic for three years in New York City; despite Brown's New York employer's offer to buy her freedom, Dallam returned with Brown to Baltimore.
Sailors who journeyed south both before and after the passage of South Carolina's Negro Seamen Acts in 1822 were at the mercy of the crews with
whom they shipped not to sell them ashore for a handsome profit, as happened to James Emerson. Black working-class men, women, and children,
whether fugitives or free, were therefore particularly vulnerable to being
kidnapped and sold into slavery. Although high-profile abolitionists or community leaders who were fugitives were also open to this risk, these blacks
were often surrounded by powerful whites, who could provide hiding places
or money to send them as far away as Canada or Europe. The travails of
working-class blacks in particular were often uppermost in the minds of abolitionists concerned with kidnapping.[77]

The informal and formal community networks and institutions that
blacks established during this period to meet the necessities of life also provided the basis for blacks' day-to-day political action in the struggle against
slavery. Black workers took fugitives into their homes and communities,
providing food, shelter, and clothing. The African Society for Mutual Relief
built a hidden cellar beneath its hall where fugitives could hide. Although
some whites were also involved in these activities, most escaped slaves
turned to those most like themselves, trusting the visible tie of race and the
relative anonymity provided by communities of working and poor blacks for
guidance to safety.

Not all blacks could be trusted. Some saw an opportunity for money in
turning in other blacks to slave catchers. A fellow fugitive from Baltimore
told Frederick Douglass upon his arrival in New York that "the black people
in New York were not to be trusted. . . . [T]here were hired men on the look-
out for fugitives . . . who, for a few dollars would betray [fugitives] into
the hands of slavecatchers."[78] But throughout the antebellum period, the
vast majority of fugitive slaves placed their trust for day-to-day subsistence
and survival in other blacks. Harriet Jacobs fled the South in 1842, passing
through Philadelphia and Brooklyn before arriving in New York City. After
reuniting with her daughter and other friends who "had left the south years

ago," she found employment as a nursemaid in New York City.[79] Although she kept her fugitive status secret from her employers, she participated in the "many impromptu vigilance committees" established for fugitives in New York: "Every colored person, and every friend of their persecuted race, kept their eyes wide open. Every evening I examined the newspapers carefully, to see what Southerners had put up at the hotels. I did this for my own sake. . . . I wished also to give information to others, if necessary; for if many were 'running to and fro,' I resolved that 'knowledge should be increased.'"[80] Some blacks used physical force to protect themselves and others from those seeking fugitives and to protest court decisions that resulted in the enslavement of blacks. When police officers arrested Peter Martin, he "made a vigorous resistance, and wounded one of the officers, but was overcome by superior force, and carried to Bridewell [prison], covered with blood and bruises." When a magistrate ruled that fugitive slave William Dixon be returned south in 1837, a black mob took matters into their own hands. As police led Dixon down the courthouse steps, a crowd surrounding the courthouse attempted to rescue him, giving him a knife and a dirk to aid in his escape. Police soon recaptured Dixon, who later won his freedom on appeal.[81]

Middle-class abolitionists focused on legal efforts to protect fugitive slaves. Radical abolitionists were nonresistants—that is, they avoided physical confrontation in their efforts to attain freedom for fugitives. Many also objected to the purchase of slaves' freedom. To some blacks, such attitudes limited the methods open to fugitives and free blacks to retain their freedom. David Ruggles's New York Committee of Vigilance attempted to utilize the resources of blacks themselves, alongside the opportunities for political action and legal services that white radical abolitionists offered. The committee attempted to shape a political organization with more cross-class unity and participation from members of the black community, and with less focus on moral and intellectual elevation. Under the leadership of the fiery Ruggles (fig. 20), the Committee of Vigilance incorporated the methods and abilities of blacks of all classes. But Ruggles's willingness to use extralegal methods to rescue fugitive slaves and kidnapped blacks resulted in division within the organization and his ouster in 1839 by more conservative forces led by Samuel Cornish.[82]

Ruggles structured the committee's activities to involve large numbers of the New York City black community. An Executive Committee of eight black men included Ruggles, Theodore Wright, ex-slave and restaurateur Thomas Van Rensellaer, Samuel Cornish, British-born abolitionists William Johnston and Jacob Francis, and grocer James W. Higgins. The committee employed a paid agent, usually Ruggles, to seek out fugitives and offer them

David Ruggles,
leader of New York City's
Vigilance Committee.

Fig. 20 David Ruggles, founder of the New York Committee
of Vigilance. Courtesy of the Amistad Collection, Tulane
University.

shelter and legal aid. The Executive Committee facilitated the legal work
necessary to free fugitives by forging ties with white abolitionists as well as
some Manumission Society members who were sympathetic to their cause
and had legal expertise. But the Committee of Vigilance was not simply
a top-down organization. In addition to the Executive Committee, the organization formed an Effective Committee, which consisted of one hundred
men and women, each of whom was to collect dues from ten to twelve of
his or her friends. This was a much larger number than participated formally
in either the antislavery societies or the national black conventions. In this
way, the organization involved almost 10 percent of the black community,
which numbered between thirteen thousand and sixteen thousand at this
time. The Effective Committee also spread news of the Committee of Vigilance's activities through word of mouth. More formal methods of keeping

the community informed of important news and events were the Executive and the Effective Committees' monthly meetings and anniversary celebrations. Ruggles also publicized the exploits of the New York Kidnapping Club, the successes of the Committee of Vigilance, and the plight of free blacks and fugitives through newspaper articles in the *Emancipator*, the *Colored American*, and in his own short-lived newspaper, the *Mirror of Liberty*, between 1835 and 1841. Newspaper publishers expected that these newspapers would be read aloud in meetings, workplaces, and neighborhoods and passed along to others. In this way, the names and tactics of members of the Kidnapping Club spread throughout the community. The committee used the courts, the streets, and the press to enable blacks of all classes to save themselves and others from slave catchers. The committee saved approximately 1,373 fugitives and free blacks from slavery. In its most important legal victory in 1840, with the help of Manumission Society lawyers, the Committee of Vigilance won the freedom of William Dixon, and thus the right to trial by jury for fugitive slaves in New York.[83]

The Committee of Vigilance had the support of William Lloyd Garrison and other white abolitionists. But most important, it had the support of free blacks themselves. Thomas Van Rensellaer, chair of the organization in 1836, stated, "The colored people of the city [are] awake. . . . [I] never saw them pay in their money so freely and so promptly as to this committee. [I suppose] that the reason [is], that this [is] *practical* abolition."[84] David Ruggles himself drew many blacks to the Committee of Vigilance. Despite his nominal position as secretary, most within and outside the organization recognized him as its driving force. Born a free man in 1810 in Norwich, Connecticut, he came to New York at the age of seventeen and within two years had established a grocery business. In 1833, he gave up his business to become a traveling agent for the *Emancipator*, a position he retained until he founded and became the agent for the New York Committee of Vigilance.[85] By the age of twenty-five, he was one of the most well known black leaders in New York City. Abolitionist Frederick Douglass, describing his arrival in New York City as a fugitive slave in 1838, stated that "Mr. Ruggles was the first officer on the underground railroad with whom I met after reaching the north, and, indeed, the first of whom I ever heard anything."[86]

Ruggles was a man of action. In 1836, in attempting to rescue slaves from a Brazilian ship docked in New York, Ruggles was jailed and accused of assisting a slave to escape and of inciting a riot. His fiery temper, pointed newspaper articles, and most of all his dramatic attempts to rescue fugitives drew the wrath of New York's proslavery whites. When Ruggles brought suit against a man illegally holding a black person enslaved in New York, the *New*

York Express stated that Ruggles's efforts to free the slave would "embarrass trade." The *New York Gazette* also displayed disgust with Ruggles's flouting of the fugitive slave laws and his transgression of racial boundaries: "Negroes with a white skin [meaning white abolitionists] are disgusting enough . . . but for native born citizens of the United States—without the advantage of black blood—to be harassed in this way by the genuine soot, is a little more, we trust, than will be submitted to." [87] Ruggles's actions also furthered divisions between New York Manumission Society members and abolitionist activists. When a newspaper mistakenly identified Ruggles as secretary of the Manumission Society, a member of the society pointedly replied, "Ruggles is a colored man, and is Secretary of a Vigilance Committee of colored persons in this city . . . who have no connection whatever with the Manumission Society." [88]

Within the Committee of Vigilance, divisions erupted over the definition of "practical abolition." In late 1836, the committee agreed to the resolution that "while we the people of color, are deprived of that *bulwark of personal freedom,* a trial by jury, it is vain to look for justice, in the courts of law." The committee resolved to continue to fight for this right through legal means, such as petitioning the legislature and bringing new court cases before judges in hopes of a positive ruling. [89] But after the negative verdict in the 1837 William Dixon case and the mob actions that followed, the committee divided over the use of physical force to defend fugitives from reenslavement. Samuel Cornish renounced the crowd's tactics. He advised the "thoughtless" and "ignorant part of our colored citizens" to leave the care of such cases to the "intelligent and efficient Vigilance Committee" and its "eminent lawyers." He singled out "those females" who "so degraded themselves" for "everlasting shame" and "[beg]ged their husbands to keep them at home for the time to come." Cornish thus defined the Committee of Vigilance as an organization for the educated to aid working-class blacks, rather than an organization in which working-class blacks might participate. Blacks should avoid "going to the Courts at all, or assembling in the Park, on the occasion of fugitive trials—you can do no good, but much harm." [90]

In contrast, Ruggles, in the wake of a trial later that year which failed to protect a black person from re-enslavement, proposed a resolution that the committee "cannot recommend nonresistance to persons who are denied the protection of equitable laws when their liberty is invaded and their lives endangered by avaricious kidnappers." This statement tacitly endorsed the direct action some blacks took in New York and other cities to rescue those accused of being slaves. Committee members and ministers Theodore Wright, Charles B. Ray, and others opposed Ruggles's proposal as "inconsistent with the peace principles advocated by the members of the [American Anti-Slavery Society], and to the spirit and tendency of every other resolution." After a heated discussion and three separate votes on the resolution, "the chairman decided it carried to rejection."[91] The struggle among the Committee of Vigilance members reflected struggles within the wider antislavery movement. An angry mob had killed Illinois abolitionist newspaper editor Elijiah Lovejoy just a few weeks prior to the vote. Some abolitionists believed that Lovejoy, in his final hours, had betrayed abolitionist principles by physically defending his printing press against the mob, but neither Garrison nor the Tappans, both strong nonresisters, condemned Lovejoy. Without doubt, Ruggles, Ray, Wright, and Cornish were aware of the heated debates over nonresistance both before and after 1837. Ray, Wright, and Cornish's belief that blacks should be nonresisters reflected their strong support of the nonresistance element of abolitionist moral reform, but their promotion of nonresistance also resulted from their reluctance to approve the use of public space and mass power by blacks as methods of displaying and achieving political citizenship and racial equality. Pragmatically, black mob actions could lead to worse violence against blacks, as they had already witnessed in the 1834 riots and in the death of Elijiah Lovejoy.[92]

Unfortunately, though, other tensions tore the Committee of Vigilance apart by 1840 and permanently damaged Ruggles's standing among other reformers in New York City. In 1838, John Russell sued the *Colored American* and the Committee of Vigilance for libel and won a judgment of 220 dollars. In 1837, Ruggles gave Cornish a letter that accused Russell of assisting in kidnapping three black men and placing them aboard a ship headed south, and the *Colored American* published the letter. Russell, a black man, owned a boarding house for black sailors; such an accusation could have destroyed his business. The judgment and legal fees resulting from the suit, totaling almost 600 dollars, bankrupted the Committee of Vigilance and severely damaged the finances of the *Colored American*.

Cornish blamed Ruggles for sending him the letter without checking to see if the information was correct. Cornish stated that he had always questioned Ruggles's "judgement" and "prudence" and believed that his assistance to fugitives was harmed by Ruggles's attraction of "public fame" through his activities. Despite their differences, Cornish stated that he had "defend[ed Ruggles] against those who would have EATEN HIM UP." But the fiasco of the false accusation ended the collegial relationship between Ruggles and Cornish. Despite Ruggles's leading role in forming the Committee of Vigilance and attracting large numbers of blacks, Samuel Cornish forced his resignation in 1839. The committee's activities lapsed until the formation of a state committee in 1848 with the Quaker abolitionist Isaac Hopper at its helm. The presence of Quaker leadership insured quieter, legalistic methods of rescuing slaves. Ruggles himself, who was going blind, lived in poverty in New York City until 1842, when Lydia Maria Child invited him to Northampton, Massachusetts. There, he founded the first hydropathic (water cure) center in the country after a course of treatment partially restored his eyesight. He remained in Northampton until his death in 1849.[93]

Meanwhile, William Seward's term as governor of New York between 1839 and 1843 provided abolitionists and blacks throughout the state with stronger legal tools in their struggles on behalf of accused fugitives. During his campaign, Seward, a Whig, had given no hint of his support for blacks' rights. Once in office, however, Seward signed into law a series of bills passed by the Whig-dominated legislature that gave fugitives in New York State greater rights than ever before, and more rights than blacks had in any other northern state at the time. In 1840, Seward signed a law guaranteeing alleged fugitives a jury trial, taking the power to return blacks to slavery out of the hands of proslavery individuals like Richard Riker. Additionally, county district attorneys had to defend accused fugitives in court. Finally, those bringing alleged fugitives to court had to provide a "penal sum" of one thousand dollars as guarantee against court costs in case the person seized was not a slave.

Another law Seward signed that year allowed the governor to appoint agents to negotiate the rescue of free blacks kidnapped and sold south. Until the Civil War, New York governors used this law to help illegally enslaved free blacks return to their homes in New York. In 1841, Seward signed legislation that repealed the law allowing southern slave masters to bring and retain their slaves in New York state for nine months. With this law, slaves brought to New York with their masters gained their freedom as soon as they touched New York soil. (Slaves who came to New York without their masters as runaways, however, had to be returned to their masters under the fugitive clause in the federal constitution.) Seward also openly refused to extradite to southern states black and white men accused of assisting slaves escaping slavery, gaining the enmity of many slaveholders. In four years, Seward and the state legislature expanded the rights of fugitives as far as was legal under the federal constitution.[94]

The 1830s tested the limits of radicalism of both black and white abolitionists. Middle-class abolitionists displayed the limits of their activism most clearly in their attitudes toward the actions and needs of the black masses. The ways abolitionists addressed the material needs, legal rights, and political participation of working-class blacks were rooted in their own evolving middle-class interests. Further, white abolitionists' focus on southern slavery, their own prejudices, and their fears of the racism of other whites led to a faltering of the project of full racial equality for free blacks by 1840.

By the end of the 1830s, some blacks believed that the abolitionists' methods were inadequate to address the material needs and political desires of the mass of blacks. Despite attempts to silence Peter Paul Simons and David Ruggles, both men had pointed the way to alternative political actions on behalf of abolition and black equality that could involve greater numbers of blacks across class lines. After 1840, changes within the abolitionist movement allowed a more secular black leadership to gain influence and build on these ways for abolitionists to reach out to black workers.

CHAPTER SEVEN

"Pressing Forward to Greater Perfection":
Radical Abolitionists, Black Labor, and
Black Working-Class Activism after 1840

In late April 1840, only a few weeks before the American Anti-Slavery Society split into Garrisonian and Tappanite factions, the New York City government fined black New Yorker Henry Graves for using his handcart without a license. Graves paid the fine and the following day applied for a license. A cross-section of white supporters, including merchants, cartmen, doctors, and lawyers, signed his petition for application—but none were white radical abolitionists. Mayor Isaac Varian refused Graves's request, fearing that "white men following the same business would mob the colored ones."[1] Graves was one of several black men who had unsuccessfully applied for carting licenses over the past four years. William Hewlett was denied a license in 1836. He had worked as a porter, owned property, and had references from forty firms. Although he could have lived on the income from his property, he wished to perform manual labor. Anthony Provost was denied a license in 1839. After he operated without a license for a while, city officials fined him and "forced [him] to take himself to more menial employment."[2] The cartmen's occupation was lucrative, but also one of the most racially restrictive in New York City. Ties of kinship in which licenses were passed down from father to son, as well as a rhetoric of manhood that implicitly excluded black men, prevented blacks from obtaining occupations in this field. The New York City government supported the white cartmen in their clannishness by refusing to license blacks.[3]

The actions of Graves, Hewlett, and Provost were part of a new activism among blacks, independent of white abolitionists, to address the problems of racism, under- and unemployment, and poverty in the black community. After the abolitionist schism of 1840, larger numbers of blacks were more

openly critical of middle-class abolitionists' focus on moral reform and intellectual improvement as the only paths to equality for free blacks. Many
blacks were dismayed by the increasing focus of white abolitionists on the
problem of southern slavery at the expense of addressing northern racism
and the conditions of free blacks. Blacks continued to see the struggle against
slavery and the struggle for racial equality as linked. But white antislavery
activists increasingly separated the two struggles. In formulating plans to
address white racism and free blacks' poverty and lack of citizenship rights,
black abolitionists in the 1840s largely had to rely on the limited resources
of blacks themselves. In some cases, blacks also turned to nonabolitionist
whites, such as the businessmen who supported the cartmen, or the women
who ran the Association for the Benefit of Colored Orphans.[4]

A new group of black reformers animated the struggle for black equality in the 1840s. Their efforts at uplift moved beyond moral reform and intellectual improvement to seek more pragmatic methods of improving the
condition of free blacks. This was not a revolution in thinking about black
workers, but rather a shift in emphasis. Black reformers shifted from moral
perfectionism to examine labor as central to the black community's efforts at
uplift. The reasons for this shift were rooted in the new black leadership of
the 1840s. Like 1830s reformers, many of the most prominent black abolitionists and reformers of the 1840s had extensive contact with skilled and
unskilled working-class jobs, and some continued to be workers or had relatives who were workers, despite their own middle-class aspirations, education, and activities. But unlike 1830s reformers, black abolitionist-reformers
in the 1840s publicly claimed their slave- or free-labor past as an integral part
of their identities. Although their jobs may have been tainted by slavery
or experiences with racism, physical labor itself was meaningful and contributed positively to their moral characters. Black reformers of the 1840s
brought their experiences as laborers to the discussion of the destiny of the
black community. They saw in meaningful labor a path to equality, one just
as powerful as moral reform. Indeed, manual labor could lead to moral reform and thus redeem the race. Some reformers thought this true not only
for men but also for women.

However, this respect for manual labor among black reformers did not
halt the evolution of class distinctions within the black community. Some
still believed that blacks could best demonstrate racial equality by adopting
middle-class ways. Thus, it probably was not coincidental that the men applying for cartmen's licenses were so overqualified for the job. Middle-class
blacks were still seen as best able to demonstrate the equality of all blacks.
These new secular reforms still contained more than a hint of perfectionism.

Further, middle-class blacks continued to debate vigorously which types of manual labor were useful to the struggle for black equality. Black middle-class reformers continued to wrestle with the meaningfulness of various occupations. But when some middle-class reformers defined domestic service or waitering as menial or degrading, other blacks, both reformers and workers, defended these occupations, claiming dignity for all labor and pride in their own work.

In this changed context, black reformers revived or continued older projects. Some black reformers continued to encourage traditional methods of reform among blacks, such as moral and classical education. Blacks also revived the national black conventions, as well as the manual labor school project. But the linkages between precariously middle-class blacks and working-class blacks, as well as the rise of a new secular leadership, led some black reformers to seek ways outside of traditional reform efforts to make contact with and improve the status of working-class blacks. Through the American League of Colored Laborers (a national organization based in New York) and during the New York waiters' strike in 1855, as well as in newspapers and other forums, middle-class black leaders attempted both to reform black workers and to address issues of importance to them. The failure of these efforts reveals the growing class separation, despite the ties of race, between black workers and black reformers.

■ ■ ■

The election of a white woman, Abby Kelley, to the Business Committee of the American Anti-Slavery Society at its 1840 annual meeting in New York precipitated the society's split into Garrisonian and Tappanite camps. Following Kelley's election, over three hundred delegates, led by Lewis Tappan, marched out of the convention to form the American and Foreign Anti-Slavery Society. Male and female abolitionists in New York City had always been more conservative than Garrison and his supporters on the issue of women's right to greater public roles, but Garrison and the Tappans, as well as their followers, had engaged in particularly acrimonious debate about the general direction of the society for at least three years prior to this event.

In 1837, Garrison had begun to embrace the perfectionist ideals of John Humphrey Noyes. Noyes was the most radical of a group of reformers who believed that men and women could become morally perfect and free from sin on earth. To preserve their own sinless state, men and women should withdraw from institutions that continued to sin. Noyes himself went far beyond claiming the possibility of human moral perfection. He believed that he himself was God's principal messenger on earth. By the mid-1840s,

Noyes had also begun to advocate "complex marriage." At the utopian Oneida community he founded in upstate New York in 1848, Noyes sought to perfect the human race by engineering sexual relationships among the most intelligent men and women in the community. He believed that in the perfect human community there would be no need for marriage or monogamy. The Oneida community became known by its critics as a center of "free love." [5]

Garrison did not embrace all of Noyes's radical notions. However, he did adapt the basic idea of human perfectibility and freedom from sin into his vision of antislavery activism after meeting with Noyes in 1837. He began to argue that churches and governments stood in the way of human perfectibility. Abolitionists should renounce voting, office-holding, and religious affiliations, all of which forced individuals to compromise their antislavery principles. Additionally, Garrison supported Angelina and Sarah Grimké in their public lectures on antislavery. The sisters had migrated north from South Carolina and were among the first white women to speak before "promiscuous" audiences of men and women. Their actions deeply disturbed many in the North, who saw them as overturning women's traditional roles in society. In 1837, the divisions among supporters of antislavery became apparent when two groups of conservative antislavery clergymen denounced Garrison's views on women and religious organizations. When Garrison asked Lewis Tappan to marshal the support of the AASS's Executive Committee on his behalf, Tappan evaded the request. He and the committee (which was dominated by New Yorkers, including Arthur Tappan, John Rankin, Samuel Cornish, and Theodore Wright) had already begun to discuss ways to decrease the association in the public mind between antislavery and Garrison's radical ideas about women's rights, religion, and government. The Tappans believed that the antislavery society should focus solely on eradicating slavery. By encouraging women to speak in public and debating other controversial issues, abolitionists risked alienating potential supporters. Samuel Cornish agreed, stating, "Shall such men as the noble Garrison . . . leave their appropriate work, to quarrel about such things of minor importance? . . . [T]he Abolitionists of New England . . . seem to have lost the peaceful spirit of abolition, and forgotten the poor down-trodden slave." The issues of social, political, and economic equality for blacks also contributed to the split between Garrison and the New Yorkers; the riots of 1834 exacerbated the New York City abolitionists' tendencies toward limited, less controversial goals for the antislavery movement.[6]

Between 1839 and 1840, Lewis Tappan began investigating ways to form a new organization that would work solely to eradicate slavery and leave behind issues such as women's rights. The election of Abby Kelley provided the catalyst he needed. When Tappan walked out of the meeting, he took with him over three hundred fellow members, two hundred of whom joined him that afternoon to form the American and Foreign Anti-Slavery Society. (Arthur Tappan had already resigned his presidency of the AASS by letter.) Black abolitionists chose sides in the debate for a variety of reasons, as did whites. Black New Yorkers Christopher Rush, Theodore Wright, and Henry Highland Garnet walked out of the meeting with Lewis Tappan, but Garnet had supported women's rights to greater participation in the convention the previous year. These men worried more about Garrison's increasingly negative stance on government than his stance on women's participation. Garrison was proposing the disavowal of citizenship rights that blacks had not even fully attained. But other blacks chose to remain with the society, or support both the new and the old societies. New Yorker Charles B. Ray did not leave the convention that day, and loyalty to Garrison led a number of New York blacks to try to remain a part of the American Anti-Slavery Society as well as participate in the Tappans' new society.

Samuel Cornish was not present at the AASS meeting, but he did join the American and Foreign Anti-Slavery Society. He may have agreed with the Tappans' denunciation of the election of Abby Kelley to the board. Cornish had also been dismayed by the American Anti-Slavery Society's decision to dismiss the agents assigned to address the problems of free blacks, and Garrison's increasingly vocal stances against organized religion and government worried him. Cornish became a member of the Executive Committee of the American and Foreign Anti-Slavery Society, but as with other New York blacks, he tried to support both organizations. In an editorial that appeared in the *Colored American* soon after the schism, Cornish stated, "[W]e do not see sufficient reasons, why WE should leave the American Anti-Slavery Society; we are satisfied with the principles of its constitution . . . and there were not sufficient reasons, in our opinion, for division. We, therefore, remain a member of the AMERICAN ANTI-SLAVERY SOCIETY." As Charles B. Ray stated, "[O]ur friends having multiplied . . . as a necessary consequence our good feeling is scattered upon all, instead of being concentrated upon one, as when Mr. Garrison stood alone."[7]

But no matter which group blacks chose to join during the schism, it quickly became clear that white concern for eliminating racial prejudice and improving the condition of free blacks would fall into the chasm separating the two groups. Ray stayed at the American Anti-Slavery Society meeting following the departure of the Tappans, and he attempted to nominate a black woman, Hester Lane, for an empty position on the Executive

Committee. Lane, an ex-slave from Maryland, was a New York business-woman who, according to travel writer E. S. Abdy, had "discover[ed] a new mode of coloring walls." She owned her own shop as well as her own home. Her greater fame in New York City stemmed from her generosity in purchasing the freedom of eleven men, women, and children enslaved in Maryland. The society had already elected three white women (Lucretia Mott of Philadelphia and Lydia Maria Child and Maria Weston Chapman of Boston) and one black man (New York restaurateur Thomas Van Rensellaer) to the committee, but the organization refused to add Hester Lane. Ray commented, "Mrs. Hester Lane is well known in this city [New York] as a woman of good character and sense, and has been a slave, but 'principle' could not carry her color!"[8]

Even more troubling to many blacks was Garrison's lack of interest in helping blacks achieve the vote. Beginning in 1837 and continuing until the Civil War, New York City blacks took the lead in a petition campaign to the state legislature "to give the right of voting to ALL the male citizens of the State on the same terms, without distinction of color." The state legislature voted down the first series of petitions for equal suffrage in March 1837, so New York City blacks met in August to "authorize agents of the *Colored American*," Charles B. Ray and Philip Bell, to travel throughout the state to gather even more signatures from blacks to deliver to the next state legislative session in January 1839. A group of New York City's "colored young men" also established a Standing Corresponding Committee of ten to fifteen members to oversee cooperation among blacks in New York State and draw up the petitions to the legislature. The first members of the committee, chaired by Timothy Seaman, included Henry Highland Garnet, Peter Paul Simons, Charles Reason, John Jay Zuille, Edward V. Clark, George Downing, and Samuel Cornish. The Corresponding Committee established Ward Committees, which canvassed New York City wards gathering black men's signatures on the petitions. By 1839, the committee had expanded into the New York Association for the Political Elevation and Improvement of the People of Color, with a broader membership base. The public meetings of both the Standing Corresponding Committee and the New York Political Association brought together diverse members of New York City's black community and became the impetus for the establishment of the black state convention movement, as well as the resuscitation of the national black conventions in the 1840s.[9]

Achievement of the vote was central to many New York City blacks' strategies for ending slavery and bringing about racial equality. But by the 1840s, Garrison was encouraging abolitionists to abandon the political arena in favor of working solely through moral suasion. He argued that the U.S. Constitution was a proslavery document: it upheld slavery through its three-fifths clause, which included three-fifths of the southern slave population as part of the South's total population for purposes of congressional representation; and through the fugitive slave clause, which ordered states to return fugitive servants to their owners. Because the Constitution upheld slavery, Garrison argued, both it and the federal government were corrupt. Abolitionists should refuse to participate in activities that supported the proslavery Constitution—chiefly, voting and office holding—in order to prevent themselves from compromising their own antislavery principles. In 1844, Garrison and the American Anti-Slavery Society advocated disunion of the antislavery North from the slaveholding South.[10]

In contrast, the Tappans and the American and Foreign Anti-Slavery Society embraced political activism and thus were more supportive of the political goals of blacks. In 1840 the Tappans, Gerrit Smith, and others established the Liberty Party, the first antislavery political party, and ran the first antislavery ticket, with James Birney as its presidential candidate. The Tappans, and particularly Gerrit Smith, worked with blacks to obtain equal suffrage in New York State. Smith was the son a wealthy landowner in upstate New York. In the 1830s he, as the Tappans before him, turned from supporting the American Colonization Society to embracing the abolitionist cause. By the mid-1840s, Smith had inherited nearly a million acres of land from his father. In 1846, Smith began donating lots of land in Franklin and Essex counties to black heads-of-household from New York City. Smith hoped the land would provide blacks with greater economic independence and enable black men to meet the 250-dollar property requirement for voting.[11] Unfortunately, Smith's land grant program, though noble, failed. The land itself was better suited for harvesting timber than farming, and few grantees had the experience necessary to survive in the rural environs.

The American and Foreign Anti-Slavery Society did little else to address the material needs of free blacks in New York City or the problems of white racism any more effectively than had the AASS. Like the AASS, the American and Foreign Anti-Slavery Society made the improvement of the condition of free blacks an explicit part of its constitution: "It is our desire to secure for our colored brethren, both bond and free, the enjoyment of all their rights, as men and members of society." The constitution stated that the organization should find "some suitable person or persons of color" to establish "Intelligence Offices" for those "colored youth who may desire a place in business" and should support the establishment of schools, and moral reform and literary societies among free blacks. But the organization provided no money for these projects. In practice, the Tappans and others continued to advocate moral reform as the central way for northern free blacks to achieve equality.

The founding of the American Missionary Association (AMA) in 1846 further reinforced the choice of white abolitionists like the Tappans to focus on the moral reform of free blacks rather than blacks' economic problems or social and political equality. The AMA grew out of several organizations focused on converting non-Christians overseas. In response to the *Amistad* trial, in which the U.S. Supreme Court granted freedom to illegally captured Africans aboard a Spanish slave ship, black abolitionists led by Hartford, Connecticut, Congregationalist minister James W. C. Pennington formed the United Missionary Society in 1841. The society sought to involve African Americans in Christian missions to Africa. Unable to raise funds from financially strapped black churches, the United Missionary Society in 1842 merged with Lewis Tappan's *Amistad* Committee, which had raised funds for the defense of the *Amistad* captives and wished to become involved in missions to Africa. In 1846, disaffected white abolitionists left the American Board of Commissioners for Foreign Missions to form the AMA, and the United Missionary Society merged with the new organization shortly thereafter. The United Missionary Society and the AMA both had substantial black memberships. Pennington served as president of the United Missionary Society until its merger with the AMA, at which point white abolitionist William Jackson of Massachusetts was elected president of the AMA. Still, blacks continued to hold a number of AMA offices. Theodore S. Wright and Samuel Cornish served as vice presidents until their deaths in 1847 and 1858, respectively. Charles B. Ray and Pennington served on the executive board with Wright and Cornish and with their replacements, Henry Highland Garnet and Amos Freeman.[12]

The involvement of Lewis and Arthur Tappan put the AMA on a firmer footing financially. But even in this organization, with its focus on moral reform, the Tappans stinted on efforts at "home" in New York City. Although known for its work in establishing numerous schools and colleges for freedmen in the South after the Civil War, the AMA before the war focused largely on missionary work. Home missionaries handed out free Bibles, established churches, and walked the streets in search of the "unchurched," encouraging them to convert to Christianity.

Black ministers Charles B. Ray and Henry Highland Garnet were among the missionaries who worked among the black population in New York City. Ray was born in 1807 in Falmouth, Massachusetts, the son of a mail carrier. His first occupation was as a boot maker. At age twenty-three, he experienced a religious conversion and decided to become a Methodist minister. In 1832, after having attended the Wesleyan Academy in Wilbraham, Massachusetts, he was admitted to Wesleyan University in Connecticut, then a training ground for future Methodist teachers and preachers. However, the hostility that his presence aroused among white students caused him to leave the school. After applying to other schools without success, he settled in New York City around 1833. Theodore Wright, who was then minister of the First Colored Presbyterian Church, became his mentor, as well as Samuel Cornish, with whom he opened a boot-making business. He also worked as assistant editor and agent of Cornish's *Colored American* from 1837 through its demise in 1841. As agent, he traveled in New England and New York securing subscriptions for the newspaper and, when in New York State, securing signatures for petitions to the state legislature on black rights issues such as equal suffrage. He also reported on the conditions of blacks in the various communities he visited. By the time the *Colored American* folded in 1841, Ray had returned to New York City.[13]

Under the United Missionary Society and the American Missionary Association, Ray worked as City Missionary to the Destitute Colored Population. As a missionary, Ray focused on the spiritual needs of New York City's poor blacks, visiting them in their homes, tending to them when sick and dying, preaching to them, and handing out Bibles, from the 1840s until after the Civil War. Through his religious work he was able to attract enough black men and women to establish the Bethesda Congregational Church in lower Manhattan in 1845. Ray also held a weekly religious meeting at the Colored Home, a black almshouse run by the some of the same conservative Quaker women who ran the Association for the Benefit of Colored Orphans. But despite his successes and the AMA's approval of his work, in 1851 the Association voted to completely cut Ray's funding. Ray was supposed to receive six hundred dollars a year for his work as city missionary; previously the association had expected him to take most of that sum from donations he received, with the organization supplementing what he lacked. But in 1851 the organization stated its fears that other city missionaries would deluge them with requests for funding if it continued to pay Ray. Ray and his family were left to rely solely on contributions from their congregation and from individuals.[14]

Garnet's experiences with obtaining funding from the American Missionary Association were little better. Garnet was born a slave in Maryland in 1815 and came north as a fugitive with his family in 1824. After studying at the African Free Schools and the Phoenix High School for Colored Youth, he attended the Noyes Academy in New Hampshire. Driven out of the academy by an anti-integration mob, he graduated in 1839 from the Oneida Institute. In 1837, he was the first former slave to give an address before the American Anti-Slavery Society. Between 1840 and 1856 he lived in Troy, New York; Britain; and Jamaica before becoming pastor of the First Colored Presbyterian Church in New York City, now known as Prince Street Presbyterian or Shiloh Presbyterian, where he remained until 1864. While pastor of the church, Garnet also served as an AMA city missionary, receiving an annual stipend of between 200 and 300 dollars from the AMA, which supplemented the income he received from Shiloh (which ranged from 500 to 750 dollars). Garnet was more outspoken in his salary needs than Ray had been. He had made a more generous salary a condition of accepting the dual post, and in 1859 his threats to resign from the church when he thought his financial needs would not be met resulted in the continuation of his generous salary from the church and the AMA.

Garnet was unable to convince the American Missionary Association to devote more time and money to the improvement of free blacks, however. In several letters to the AMA in 1859, Garnet attempted to convince the association to support "an efficient agency established in New York for the especial purpose of improving the moral, and intellectual condition of the people of colour." He felt that, alone, he could not make much of an impact among New York's working-class blacks. Increased support from the AMA would allow him to hire additional help with his religious missionary work, as well as maintain the Anglo-African Reading Room, an informal place where young men and women might stop by to read the latest books and newspapers. Garnet would also be able to visit and support black schools and generally "promote the educational, economical and moral interests of the colored people in this city." For Garnet, as for many other blacks, his requests were well within the scope of what abolitionist organizations should do to improve the condition of northern free blacks. "The time has come, when my personal friends, and the friends of my race, must stand by me, or I must abandon this field," Garnet stated. "I think I have a right to look to you for help—not as a matter of favour, but as being within the scope of the legitimate work of the association and a most promising use of its funds." But the AMA refused his request. The association's refusals to fund Ray and Garnet resulted from its chronic shortage of funds for city missionaries. But for blacks it also reflected the continuing pattern among abolitionists to provide less funding for problems close to home than for those in the South or even overseas. And although the AMA board held a fair number of blacks, whites controlled the purse strings.[15]

White abolitionists also continued to be ambivalent as to the abilities of black workers and thus remained ineffective in assisting blacks in combating negative stereotypes about them. The Tappans came under particular attack after 1840 for their condescension toward black workers. In 1840, Lewis Tappan hired twenty-year-old Patrick Reason to do an engraving of his brother Benjamin. Reason was a graduate of the African Free Schools, and his engraving of African Free School No. 2 was the frontispiece of Charles Andrews's 1831 *History of the New-York African Free Schools*. Organizations such as the Steward's and Cook's Marine Benevolent Society had commissioned Reason to design emblems for them. Lewis Tappan admitted that the engraving of his brother demonstrated the competitive potential of black skilled laborers and would "advance" the antislavery cause "if it were known that a Negro was capable of such craftsmanship." But rather than publicize Reason's work, Tappan stated patronizingly, "[P]erhaps it will be best to wait until you have engraved two or three more before the secret is let out."[16]

At the 1852 meeting of the American and Foreign Anti-Slavery Society, black jeweler and former shoemaker Edward Clark publicly accused white abolitionists and Arthur Tappan in particular of not recognizing or promoting the abilities of blacks. "Abolitionists [do] not encourage colored men in business as they [do] white men," Clark stated. "Wherever the colored man is connected with the houses of these gentlemen it is as the lowest drudges. If a colored man enters as a porter in the store of Mr. Tappan, does he advance him afterward according to his merits?" In responding, Tappan demonstrated his own automatic association of blacks with the lowest level of labor, as well as a reluctance to train blacks. "I offered a situation in my office to a colored man," Tappan said, "and told my clerks that if they should all leave I was determined to take him; but he was not qualified. I would not ask an Irishman sawing wood in the street, and covered with sweat, to come in and sit with my family. Neither would I a colored man, though I have been accused of it."[17] Tappan's response was particularly tied to the post-1834 attitude of New York's white abolitionists. The riots of 1834, with their charges of amalgamation, had both frightened abolitionists and allowed them to take refuge in their own prejudices without question. Further, Tappan's response conflated race with class; both blacks and Irish symbolized the lowest working classes. Abolitionists like Tappan, even as they espoused beliefs in the necessity to uplift blacks, were unable to overcome their own assumptions and prejudices against blacks and, more particularly, their associations of blacks with the lowest forms of labor, and their beliefs that such work degraded those who performed it.[18]

Some white abolitionists realized and tried to work on their prejudices. But their increasing awareness of their own racial prejudice solved only part of the problem. In 1849, Lewis Tappan stated that although abolitionists were "in theory the enemies of caste, it is to be lamented that so few are its practical opponents." Samuel May of Syracuse, New York, revealed, "We are prejudiced against the blacks; and our prejudices are indurated . . . by the secret, vague consciousness of the wrong we are doing them." Angelina Grimké asked northern free blacks to "be willing to mingle with us whilst we have the prejudice, because it is only by associating with you that we shall be able to overcome it." But her request was aimed at educated, middle-class or aspiring middle-class black abolitionists, not the black working class. White abolitionists' recognition of the racial prejudice they held against those blacks whom they were trying to see as their intellectual equals did not address the class divisions that distanced white middle-class abolitionists from the problems and concerns of the vast majority of the black community.[19]

For black middle-class abolitionist-reformers of the 1840s and 1850s, the symbolic equality of sitting at the table with the white middle classes was not as important as the need to find lucrative, meaningful employment for New York City's blacks. At times, the black middle class included themselves in this search. James McCune Smith stated that, although the American and Foreign Anti-Slavery Society had expended a total of 150,000 dollars in salaries, "A colored man never got a $1,200 salary [from them] yet. The executive [committee] have either failed in their duty or they are blind to the abilities of colored men."[20] While continuing their own fight for middle-class status, these new leaders began to search for different methods of alleviating the under- and unemployment of blacks. Through a mixture of old and new programs, men such as McCune Smith, Frederick Douglass, and Tunis G. Campbell sought to place the problems and issues of the black worker at the center of both national and local campaigns for black uplift.

These men debated among themselves, with white abolitionists, and with black workers the meaning of black labor to American society, urban and rural; the shape of the black working class, present and future; and the central role of the black worker to the uplift of the black race. Their interest and concerns grew out of their own former and continuing experiences as laborers. Although by the 1840s and 1850s most held high-ranking positions in the abolitionist movement or were businessmen or other professionals, they drew on and prided themselves on their past as laborers, seeing their past as central to their present success. Whereas Cornish and other 1830s black leaders had rarely if ever referred to their laboring past or present or their struggles to become educated, these new leaders considered such trials to be central to their sense of self.

Although not a New York City resident, Frederick Douglass is the best example of this type of leader. Born a slave in Maryland in 1818, Douglass escaped at the age of twenty, traveling through Baltimore and New York before settling in New Bedford, Massachusetts, with his wife, Anna Murray. There, he came into contact with Garrisonian abolitionists, who encouraged him to go on the antislavery lecture circuit and tell his story. In 1841 Douglass delivered his first public address under the auspices of the American Anti-Slavery Society. He quickly became one of the most popular speakers on the antislavery circuit. Initially he spoke mostly of his experiences under slavery, but he soon expanded his speeches and his philosophy to include discussion of the special problems of free blacks, the equality of women, and the relationship between slave and free labor. Douglass also explored these issues in his antebellum newspaper, the *North Star*, founded in December 1847 and continued as *Frederick Douglass' Paper* until 1860. In 1847, Douglass moved to Rochester, New York, his main residence through the Civil War.[21]

Douglass's rise to power changed the ways some blacks and whites viewed the issues of racial uplift, class division, and education of blacks. He was unequaled among black or white abolitionist lecturers. His command of the language and his range of topics and issues, as well as his depth of knowledge, astounded most readers and listeners. He almost single-handedly changed the public's perception of the potential of black slaves.[22] Douglass said that before he appeared on the antislavery circuit, "a colored man was deemed a fool who confessed himself a runaway slave . . . because it was a confession of a very *low* origin!"[23] At the same time, however, his achievements showed the possibility of black perfectibility on middle-class terms and may have reinforced black and white abolitionist-reformers' belief in the superiority of such a path. There was a conflict among black reformers between the value of upholding the manual labor blacks performed and the working-class lives they lived as dignified and honorable and the undeniable economic and political power inherent in middle-class education and occupations.

Douglass, only recently out of slavery, spent the 1840s consolidating his ideas and goals. In preparing his antislavery lectures and in writing his first autobiography (published 1845), Douglass shaped the convictions and the self-image that would allow him to assume a prime role in the debate over black labor issues in the 1850s, a role that would end only after the Civil War. His combination of experiences as a fugitive slave, a common laborer,

a skilled worker, and a radical abolitionist were not unique among black abolitionist leaders. However, the ways he used those experiences to create his
persona and build his following were unparalleled among antebellum blacks.
From his earliest speeches, in which he presented himself as an unschooled
former slave, to his three autobiographies, which delineate his struggles as a
free laborer, Douglass not only informed America of the evils of slavery and
racism, but also demonstrated the potential of the black worker, even the enslaved or uneducated black worker.

Douglass was the foremost of a group of black leaders in the 1840s and
1850s who celebrated the labor blacks performed under slavery and in freedom. Henry Highland Garnet lectured the 1840 meeting of the American
Anti-Slavery Society on the centrality of slave labor to the American economy. "The people of color [are the] bone and sinew, [the] life and blood"
of the South, he proclaimed. The products blacks produced in the South en-
riched the North.[24] In his 1849 autobiography, *The Fugitive Blacksmith*,
James W. C. Pennington, pastor of New York's First Colored Presbyterian
Church, detailed the relationship between his skilled laborer status and his
identity as a slave. Under slavery, he wrote, he had "always aimed to be trust-
worthy" and felt "a high degree of mechanical pride" in his work. He "aimed
to do [his] work with dispatch and skill; [his] blacksmith's pride and taste was
the one thing that had reconciled [him] so long to remain a slave." Such depictions of slave labor, by showing the pride that blacks took in their work
even under slavery and the importance of black labor to the economy, demonstrated the respectability of all black workers.[25]

These black reformers attempted to redeem black workers in the eyes
of the nation. The descriptions of Garnet, Pennington, and others also paralleled the beliefs of white abolitionists and white workers who claimed that
slavery degraded labor. Pennington's slave master, for example, destroyed
Pennington's "mechanical pride." As Pennington recounts, while he was
shoeing a horse, his master, believing Pennington had rolled his eyes at him,
"came down upon me with his cane, and laid on over my shoulders, arms,
and legs, about a dozen severe blows, so that my limbs and flesh were sore
for several weeks." After this incident, Pennington "thought of nothing
but the family disgrace under which we were smarting, and how to get out
of it."[26]

In the northern free black community, this group of leaders brought a
new energy to efforts to improve the conditions of the black working class,
especially in New York City. Douglass had a strong impact on the discussion
of these labor issues. In the National Conventions of the Free People of Color
of the 1840s and 1850s, he debated with New Yorkers and others the nature

of black labor, the need for a black manual labor school, and other issues of importance to black workers. In the pages of his newspapers, the *North Star* and *Frederick Douglass' Paper,* he published accounts of workers' conditions in New York City, often editorializing on the types of labor blacks performed and the tactics black workers used to achieve economic parity. Douglass stimulated debate on black workers' conditions throughout the nation, but one of the debate's important focal points was New York City.

Douglass was not the only middle-class black leader concerned with the issues of black workers at this time. In New York City, James McCune Smith often opposed Douglass's views on the subject. Born in New York City in 1813 and educated at the African Free Schools, McCune Smith spent four years as a blacksmith before obtaining a medical degree at Glasgow University in Scotland in 1832, having been denied admission to American colleges. In 1837, he returned to New York City and established the first black-owned pharmacy in the country as well as a medical practice. However, his success did not remove him from the problems of the black working class in New York; rather, he went out of his way to address their needs in his medical practice and in his writings in newspapers, most notably in Frederick Douglass's papers, and as physician for the Colored Orphan Asylum from 1842. Perhaps his experiences with the self-directed working-class parents and children of the asylum caused him to become an imaginative and outspoken supporter of all types of black labor, as well as a proponent of ways for black workers to improve themselves.[27]

Douglass and McCune Smith represented two poles of black thought about labor after the 1830s. Blacks evaluated certain types of labor as positive or negative, as uplifting or damaging to the black community, according to the value that allegedly inhered in each. Increasingly through the 1840s and 1850s, black leaders and workers aligned with Douglass began to criticize, often in gendered terms, those who either voluntarily or through necessity held service jobs as domestic workers, waiters, and barbers. They considered such jobs to be degrading, and Douglass led the fight to encourage blacks to obtain skilled jobs instead. McCune Smith, on the other hand, was part of a group of blacks who defended all types of labor that blacks performed. McCune Smith and others attempted to demonstrate the potential for self-respect in any job.

The discussion over the value of particular jobs was central to black self-help efforts in the 1840s and 1850s. In 1843, New York City blacks led the movement to revive the black national conventions. The expansion of blacks into smaller towns in Philadelphia, New York, and Massachusetts, as well as into western communities such as Ohio and Illinois, somewhat diluted the

influence of delegates from New York City. Still, New Yorkers often sent the
most delegates and were chief among the conventioneers who discussed the
types of occupations to which blacks had access. At the conventions, the issue of black jobs led to discussions of the types of labor that would be most
useful and meaningful to the overall project of recreating the black community in the eyes of society. In a sense, labor replaced moral reform as the
primary method through which blacks could achieve equality in American
society. Black leaders began to identify labor as a social and political com-
modity with which status and political rights could be bought outside the
workplace. They began to rank the value of different occupations.

Most conventioneers upheld the "mechanical arts" or skilled labor as the
minimum ideal to which all urban black male workers should aspire: "We
cannot too earnestly recommend to our people the importance of the mechanic arts. . . . In almost every age of the world . . . the nearer the mechanical arts have been carried to perfection, the higher have the people risen in
wealth and intellect." Agricultural labor was held to be equal to the mechanical arts; some black abolitionist-reformers focused their energy on encouraging blacks to move out of the city, into the countryside to form farming collectives.[28]

The emphasis on skilled labor in the rhetoric of educated convention
delegates caused conflicts with some workers who attended the conventions.
At the 1848 convention, for example, activist Martin Delany said that he
"would rather receive a telegraphic despatch [sic] that his wife and two children had fallen victims to a loathsome disease, than to hear that they had become servants of any man." Delany was born to a free mother and a slave
father in Charles Town, Virginia, in 1812, but spent most of his youth and
young adulthood in Pittsburgh, Pennsylvania. Although Delany was trained
as a doctor, Delany's wife Catherine, whom he married in 1843, provided
much of the family income through her work as a seamstress, particularly
while Delany traveled western Pennsylvania, Ohio, and Michigan as coeditor of Frederick Douglass's North Star from 1847 to 1849. Throughout
his life, historian Nell Painter states, Delany was known for his support
of "elevation . . . which meant more than material success and upward mobility. [Elevation included] the acquisition of gentlemanly culture and correct speech, of upright morals, independent thought, and 'manly' religion,
(as opposed to religiosity, which he disdained as servile). Elevation meant
achievement that would earn the world's applause, such as owning a successful business or governing a prosperous nation. Delany wanted for his people
the sort of collective self-respect that he thought only education, wealth, and
recognition would secure."[29] For Delany, the large numbers of black men

and women employed as domestic servants limited the status of the race as a whole, and hampered the fight for racial equality.

· Delany's vituperative remarks against domestics also grew out of the general belief that female domestics were at special risk for sexual advances from employers. Further, domestic servitude, particularly if the domestic worker "lived in" with the family he or she worked for, could result in familial separation. Such separations were more common for black women than for white; black female domestic servants tended on average to be older than their white counterparts, and thus more likely to be married with children. Both improper sexual advances and familial separations were similar to the trials that plagued black families under slavery.

But in the 1840s, some blacks began to object to these characterizations of the only occupations available to many blacks. No domestics were present to speak up for themselves, despite the fact that the convention attendees represented a fair number of different types of workers. The vast majority of domestic servants were women, and although the conventioneers resolved in 1848 to "invite females hereafter to take part in our deliberations" because they "fully believed in the equality of the sexes," only one black woman, Mary Ann Shadd Cary, the first female newspaper editor, attended a convention before the Civil War. But despite the absence of women and of domestic servants, male and female, convention delegates in other occupations spoke on behalf of domestic work. J. D. Patterson, who may have been a minister, "argued that those who were in the editorial chair and others, not in places of servants, must not cast slurs upon those, who were in such places from necessity." John Watson of Ohio "took exception" to the underlying premise of Delany's remark, that "if we became the boot-blacks, the white mechanics would look down on us, but if we became mechanics, etc., they would respect us." Watson doubted that improvement of occupational status would decrease racism among whites. Convention president Frederick Douglass stopped this line of criticism, stating that the discussion "had taken a desultory turn," and suggested a compromise resolution: "Let us say what is necessary to be done, is honorable to do; and leave situations in which we are considered degraded, as soon as necessity ceases." Although domestic service occupations were "right in themselves," they were "degrading to us as a class." [30]

In passing this resolution about domestic service, the convention also argued that domestic work degraded black men much more than it degraded black women. That domestic service was increasingly identified with women made the position of black male domestics even more debased in the eyes of the delegates. Black reformers, as well as white workers, had promulgated these ideas since the early nineteenth century. The presence of domestic jobs "so long and universally filled by colored men" had "become a badge of degradation" for blacks. In their resolution the conventioneers largely ignored the potential problems of domestic service for black women. The conventioneers also ignored women workers in their other resolutions regarding labor. The convention passed two separate resolutions reinforcing the importance of skilled trades and business occupations to the uplift of the race. "Whatever is necessary for the elevation of one class is necessary for the elevation of another; the respectable industrial occupations, as mechanical trades, farming . . . mercantile and professional business, wealth and education, being necessary for the elevation of the whites . . . are necessary for the elevation of us." Blacks should work harder to obtain training in these higher-status occupations. But these were occupations that black men would hold, not black women. Thus, in the 1840s, despite the large numbers of black women who had to work to help support their families and the increasing debate in the larger society regarding women's roles, the all-male convention movement spent little time discussing the improvement of conditions for black women workers.[31]

Black conventioneers did not criticize domestic work only. They also took black barbers to task for "refusing to treat colored men on equality with the whites," thus encouraging "prejudice among the whites of the several States." Such behavior made barbers "base serviles, worthy only of the condemnation, censure and defamation of all lovers of liberty, equality, and right." Although barbers were also within the realm of personal service, the conventioneers did not deem the occupation itself unworthy, only barbers' actions against racial equality. Barbers at their best were independent businessmen, owning their own shops and tools. They not only cut hair, but also performed minor medical services, such as pulling teeth. Barbers potentially exemplified an alternate model of independent manhood, outside of the workshops, in which black men performed necessary personal services for the community and retained their independence. The conventioneers censured them so heavily because, theoretically at least, they could run their shops as they wished. But black barbers were in a bind. No doubt if they chose to integrate their shops, most whites would take their business to other, segregated shops. But for black barbers to operate segregated shops reinforced negative racial and class stereotypes of blacks.[32]

To achieve the goal of creating a skilled, higher-status black working class, the conventioneers resurrected the manual labor school project at the 1853 convention. The context of the discussion differed from that of the 1830s. White abolitionists largely ignored black efforts to establish the school, leaving them on their own to plan and fundraise for the project. Also, the black convention movement's delegation itself had changed. Delegates came from a broader geographical area, including New England and the growing black communities in the Midwest. Many of the delegates of the 1840s and 1850s had recently been laborers, slave and free, and they spoke from experience of the need for blacks to obtain occupational training. Finally, the manual labor school was part of a range of secular reforms that removed moral reform as the catalyst for change. These leaders instead argued that when blacks had substantial, meaningful jobs, moral reform, self-respect, and racial uplift would follow.

The Manual Labor School Committee at the 1853 convention consisted of Charles L. Reason, George B. Vashon, and Charles H. Langston. These three men represented geographically the old and new power bases in the national black community. Charles Reason was the brother of engraver Patrick Reason. Born and raised in New York City, he was educated at the New York African Free Schools and became a teacher there in 1832. In 1849, New York Central College in McGrawville, New York, appointed him professor of literature and languages, but he left after three years to work at Philadelphia's Institute for Colored Youth, a manual labor school, where he was employed at the time of the 1853 convention. Vashon grew up in Pittsburgh, Pennsylvania, where he participated in the abolition movement from a young age. The first black student to graduate from Oberlin College, which was then a manual labor school, Vashon returned to Pennsylvania in 1844 to take the state bar examination. However, bar officials refused to allow him to sit for the exam because of his race. Vashon moved to Syracuse, New York, passed the bar, and became New York State's first black lawyer in 1847. After spending a few years in Haiti, he returned to Syracuse in 1850 and became involved in the abolition movement there. Committee member Charles Langston, also an Oberlin graduate, was an Ohio farmer and surgeon-dentist.[33]

Reason, Vashon, and Langston brought their experiences with manual labor schools to their report on the convention's black manual labor school plan. The committee sought to recapture some of the idealism of the abolitionist manual labor schools, in which educators had hoped to instill equal respect for intellectual and manual work. The committee wished to establish a school that would not only provide a liberal education, which alone would make a student a "mere scholar," but also prepare students for work. Teachers in the school would need to place manual labor on an equal level of importance with liberal education. Other manual labor schools had not achieved this goal: "The department of labor has ever remained crude and unseemly—subordinate in position and outline to the other, and, therefore unable to provide that extensive field for industry, as to warrant the title assumed by them of Manual Labor Institutions." Whereas other schools had used manual labor only as a means of assisting poor students in obtaining an education, these leaders sought to use the manual labor school curriculum to "remedy . . . as far as may be [possible] the disadvantages under which we [meaning blacks] labor in acquiring a knowledge of the mechanical arts." This curriculum would include "an Agricultural Professorship . . . a professorship to superintend the practical application of mathematics and natural philosophy to surveying, mechanics, and engineering; the following branches of industry: general smithing, turning, wheelwrighting and cabinet-making; and a general work-shop in which may be combined such applications of skill in wood, iron, and other material as to produce a variety of saleable articles." The school would reinforce the importance of manual labor training by paying "competent workmen . . . precisely as other teachers were paid." By placing "workmen" instructors on the same level with intellectuals, the conventioneers upheld the equality of intellectual and manual labor, even as that belief was fading in other sectors of the society. Further, unlike the 1830s project, which focused overwhelmingly on moral education, leaders of the 1840s and 1850s focused on the practicality of providing true mechanical training and on what they perceived as the need "to induce in [blacks] habits and inclinations of industrial competition."[34]

The 1853 convention appointed a national committee to handle the details of establishing the manual labor school, such as fundraising, choosing a location, and establishing a curriculum. However, this committee was inactive for almost two years, finally convening as part of a national council meeting held in 1855 in New York City to plan the agenda for the October, 1855, national convention. Delegates from New York and Brooklyn held a majority of the votes and actively participated in the discussion of the path that the school should take. Issues dividing the delegates regarding the establishment of the school included the practicality of the manual labor school as a method of teaching mechanical skills and whether the school should be racially exclusive, both in teaching staff and in student body. New York City jeweler and former boot maker Edward Clark questioned whether "the Manual Labor School . . . could develop any degree of perfection in mechanical or agricultural education among its pupils. At Oberlin, Oneida, and elsewhere [the failure to do so] had long since become apparent." James Duffin of Geneva, New York, countered that "the failure of Oberlin . . . was not caused by an attempt to blend mechanics with classics; it was the permission of such members as could afford to work or not as they took choice, the admission of a sort of *lily*-fingered aristocracy, which degraded the labor whence income should be derived, and drove the poorer and more substantial students hence." Middle-class white students had been unable or unwilling to accept the full implications of the manual labor system: respect for manual labor as equal to intellectual work. Apparently, only those forced to work out of necessity, and perhaps blacks, had elected courses in the manual labor portion of the curriculum. But at a black manual labor school, those attending the school would be more appreciative of the equality of the two types of work, perhaps because so many of them would have themselvs performed or would in future be limited to this kind of labor. James McCune Smith marshaled further support for the school by stating that "nearly every gentleman who advocated this industrial school had been or was a mechanic, and those who opposed it had never been engaged in any mechanical avocation."[35]

Some black delegates felt that working-class blacks had not done enough to improve themselves. George T. Downing, wealthy son of restaurateur Thomas Downing, stated that "there are more opportunities for colored youths than colored youths to accept them." Advocating a strict self-help philosophy despite his own comfortable and inherited position, he stated, "I need to bring up a dark picture of our own shortcomings. . . . Your boys do not apply for situations." He claimed that "we are a set of paupers, relying upon charity and any menial occupation that may be thrown in our way; the fault is entirely with ourselves. We must educate ourselves from birth up before we root out this servile spirit of dependence."[36] But opinions like Downing's were few. Most conventioneers agreed that the racism of white workers and employers kept the majority of free blacks in low-paying, low-status occupations, rather than blacks' own shortcomings.

The project was put to a vote and passed by two. But at the 1855 national convention a few months later, conventioneers concluded that the plan was impracticable. Blacks had been unable to raise the funds necessary for the school, despite appeals to Harriet Beecher Stowe and other white abolitionists and organizations. Further, the conventioneers were overwhelmed by the seeming difficulty in providing training for different types of skilled labor for large numbers of students in an institutionalized setting. Estimating that it took "from three to five years, working ten hours per day" to effectively train someone in a skilled labor occupation, combining academics with manual training was practically impossible. Not until after the Civil War, with the vast resources of the American Missionary Association, would institutionalized vocational education succeed in schools such as the Hampton Institute and Tuskeegee. The conventioneers instead voted to establish a "Mechanical Bureau," through which those interested in obtaining skilled training or jobs might be matched with those wishing to train and hire blacks.[37]

Locally, black abolitionist-reformers continued their attempts to reshape the lives of New York's black workers. Some black abolitionists were able to unite their belief in moral uplift and abolition with practical programs to improve the conditions of black workers. In 1839, the abolitionist and former sailor William Powell opened the Colored Sailors' Home at the corner of John and Gold Streets in lower Manhattan. Powell was born the free son of a slave father in 1807 in upstate New York. After an elementary education, he apprenticed as a sailor. In the 1830s, he married and settled in New Bedford, Massachusetts, where he opened his first boarding house for sailors. While in Massachusetts, he was an active participant in the American Anti-Slavery Society and the New England Anti-Slavery Society, as well as in efforts to obtain equal rights for blacks in Massachusetts.[38]

In 1839, Powell moved with his wife and children to New York City, where he operated the Colored Sailors' Home under the auspices of the predominantly white American Seamen's Friend Society. Powell provided food, clothing, and shelter for black sailors in port, and an employment agency for sailors wishing to return to sea. In the boarding house, "the banner of Reform float[ed] conspicuous." Powell established the home as an alternative to the rowdy conditions of other sailors' boarding houses. No alcohol was allowed; the house held a library and reading room; and "at meal time, and every occasion of interview, conversations [were] introduced on the various questions incidental to the elevation of man."[39] Potentially, then, the home provided an opportunity to shape men into the worker-scholar ideal upheld by black reformers from Samuel Cornish to Frederick Douglass. As such, the Colored Sailors' Home received black reformers' full support.

Powell also used the Sailors' Home to host abolitionist meetings and to hide fugitive slaves. He may have drawn on his sailor-residents to aid in the protection of fugitives. In the "Atlantic community of color," black sailors acted as messengers, giving information on free black communities to slaves in the South and the Caribbean. Thus, many of the sailors who came to Powell's boarding house were probably already politicized regarding the abolitionist struggle and may have been more than willing to assist Powell in his abolitionist endeavors.[40]

When Powell left New York in 1851, in the wake of the Fugitive Slave Law, to spend the next ten years in Europe, Albro Lyons Sr. took over the management of the Colored Sailors' Home and continued its abolitionist tradition. He and his wife, Mary, and their family lived in the home and carried

on Powell's practice of providing aid to fugitive slaves. Their daughter, Mar-
itcha, estimated that between 1851 and Powell's return as manager of the
home in 1862, Albro and Mary Lyons provided aid to about a thousand
refugees from slavery, "thanks to mother's devotion and discretion": "Father's connection with the underground railroad brought many strange faces
to our house, for it was semi-public and persons could go in and out without
attracting special attention. Under mother's vigilant eye, refugees were kept
long enough to be fed and to have disguises changed and be met by those
prepared to speed them on in the journey toward the North Star. Father used
to say humorously that this part of his business was 'keeping a cake and
apple stand.'"[41]

The Colored Sailors' Home was almost unique as a successful institution
formed by black abolitionist-reformers to aid black workers. No doubt its
success was based on the fact that it received support from the financially
stable American Seamen's Friend Society. Most black abolitionist-reformers
were forced to take other paths in uplifting New York's blacks, paths that required little or no funding. In the 1850s, abolitionist-reformers attempted to
use the organizational forms of workers, such as unions and leagues, as
a way to infiltrate and shape the evolving black working class. In June of
1850, Douglass and other black reformers formed the American League
of Colored Laborers, an organization designed to improve the condition of
black workers. Participants included William Powell of the Colored Sailors'
Home; physician James McCune Smith; jeweler Edward Clark; minister and
boot maker Charles Ray; wealthy restaurateur George Downing; and educator Charles Reason. The Reverend Samuel Ringgold Ward was elected president, and Lewis Woodson of Philadelphia and Frederick Douglass, vice presidents. Of the twenty Executive Committee members, twelve were New
Yorkers, the majority of whom had worked closely with the black working
class for at least a decade. The group united reformers who held varying
views regarding ways to assist black workers, but does not seem to have attracted any workers. Although a fair was planned for 1852, the league seems
not to have survived past this first organizational meeting.

Despite the American League's short life, its stated objectives demonstrate the changes among black reformers between the 1830s and the 1850s.
Beginning with the observation that "one very great evil now suffered by
the free colored people of the United States, is the want of money," the
league organizers recommended "the attainment of Learning and Riches."
Both would "procur[e] for us much personal comfort, and inspir[e] us with
respect for ourselves, and for each other, and . . . [gain] for us the respect
of men generally." The emphasis on "personal comfort" and "riches" was a

departure from the frugal ways of white abolitionists. White middle-class abolitionists as early as the 1830s had sometimes criticized their black colleagues for what they saw as unseemly displays of wealth. On visiting Samuel Cornish's comfortable home in 1837, Sarah Grimké and Theodore Dwight Weld wrote that it was "like the abode of sanctimonious pride and pharisaical aristocracy." White abolitionists failed to understand that middle-class blacks may have needed material displays of bourgeois comfort to counter the claims of less sympathetic whites that blacks were uncultured. Further, this wealth was not only for individual use. Wealthy blacks could set aside money in communal funds that would aid less-fortunate blacks in their communities. Larger homes could hide fugitive slaves or allow wealthier blacks to house poorer relatives or friends, as Cornish had housed Charles Ray's wife in the 1830s.[42]

The discussion of skilled jobs and the meaning of wealth to the black community continued in the pages of *Frederick Douglass' Paper* in the early 1850s. In 1852, James McCune Smith began publishing a series of articles entitled "Heads of the Colored People." In these articles, he described the lives of skilled and unskilled black workers he met on the streets of New York: newspaper vendors, bootblacks, washerwomen, whitewashers—the very people and occupations that the national conventions criticized. In these vignettes, he gave these common laborers a dignity that other middle-class black reformers and white workers sought to deny them. Many of those McCune Smith interviewed had escaped slavery and supported families in New York on their meager salaries. "Wiser than dandy opinion," they were proud of their work, which did not degrade them as Douglass and others charged. Rather, their occupations gave them the ability to educate their children and in a few cases to purchase small homes in the city. In describing a bootblack, McCune Smith criticized the emphasis on wealth that had overtaken some blacks, focusing on character instead: "As a class, boot-polishers are thrifty, energetic, progressive. Free muscles, steadily exercised, produce free thought, energy, progress. . . . [Boot blacking] is *the* calling which has produced the best average colored men, and has made men of *character*, not of *wealth*."[43] In his writings, McCune Smith attempted to bring dignity to all types of manual labor and warned against the confusion of individual wealth with character.

Reformers like Douglass, however, found McCune Smith's elevation and glorification of certain forms of manual labor dangerous to the cause of black equality. After publishing a year-long series of McCune Smith's articles, Frederick Douglass began his critiques of them. In "Learn Trades or Starve," Douglass criticized the basic premises of McCune Smith's articles. Citing the increased immigration into the United States, and into New York in particular, he observed that "[e]mployments and callings, formerly monopolized by us, are so no longer. . . . White men are becoming house-servants, cooks and stewards on vessels—at hotels.—They are becoming porters, stevedores, woodsawyers, hod-carriers, brick-makers, white-washers, and barbers, so that the blacks can scarcely find the means of subsistence—a few years ago, and a *white* barber would have been a curiosity—now their poles stand on every street. Formerly blacks were almost the exclusive coachmen in wealthy families; this is so no longer; white men are now employed, and for aught we see, they fill their servile station with an obsequiousness as profound as that of the blacks."[44] Competition with whites and particularly with Irish immigrants was an important factor in the difficulties that blacks faced in the 1850s.

Douglass was, however, only partially concerned with black workers' competition with whites, which would occur in any occupation that blacks undertook and would increase if blacks attempted to hold skilled jobs. It was the inherent meanings of the jobs in which blacks were employed, and their value in terms of social and political power, that worried him most. Two weeks after appealing to blacks' material interests in "Learn Trades or Starve," Douglass attacked what he saw as the moral, social, and political consequences of blacks holding "menial" occupations. In "Make your Sons Mechanics and Farmers—not Waiters Porters and Barbers," he argued that menial occupations as service workers to the wealthy led "those engaged in them, [to] improvidence, wastefulness, [and] a fondness for dress and display." Service workers were misled by the luxurious ways of the wealthy into thinking that fine clothing and appearances mattered more than frugality and simplicity. Black workers "expend our all in trying to imitate the customs and to follow the fashions and follies of the rich, with whom our vocations bring us into contact."[45] Thus, in an argument similar to working-class republican thought about the wealthy, Douglass linked the choices that domestic workers made in terms of frugality and fashion to their contact with the wealthy, whom the white working class often deemed corrupt. The selfishness of the wealthy made them unstable community members; and blacks who followed the lead of the wealthy were less focused than they should be on community uplift. Such pronouncements seemingly contradicted the earlier call for wealth of the American League of Colored Laborers. But the American League's interest in black wealth was for the uplift of the community, not just for individual gain.

Black workers divided over Douglass's series. Uriah Boston, a barber, defended his occupation, but Peter Pringle was more critical of the occupations of most blacks. Pringle had been "a waiter, hostler, and boot-black," and he believed that it was blacks' own fault that "the mass of us are menials," not the fault of "slavery or prejudice." Blacks' character as a race was "soft, light, effeminate," and most black men "choose rather to follow menial occupations than to contend with negro-hating apprentices and journeymen in shops, or to contend with the negro-hating indisposition to give work to a black mechanic." By not directly challenging the prejudice of white workers, black men (and thus the black race) would lose their manliness: "A few generations hence we shall . . . be unfit to contend for the positions of men, or feel the awkwardness of our false unmanly position."[46]

Douglass, Pringle, and other critics of blacks who held these occupations were indifferent to, hostile to, or unaware of the ways blacks in so-called menial occupations asserted both their rights as workers and racial equality. In the 1850s, as Douglass, McCune Smith, and others debated the meaning of labor, one group of black workers in "menial" positions, black waiters, asserted their rights as workers and as blacks. In March of 1853, white and black waiters joined together to form the Waiters' Protective Union Society (WPUS). Five hundred men, black and white, met in the Grand Street Hall. Hotels, saloons, and restaurants employed many, but some also worked for families. The waiters sought wages of eighteen dollars a month. Most white waiters were earning between ten and fourteen dollars a month. Black waiters, however, had previously demanded, and received, sixteen dollars a month. According to the white organizer William Hamilton, black waiters commanded higher wages because of their pride in and commitment to their work. "The main reason why white men work for ten, twelve and fourteen dollars a month, is that they are generally driven, by a combination of unfortunate circumstances, to become waiters, and are . . . ashamed of being so, and are consequently indifferent."[47]

Black waiters placed themselves at the center of this movement for better wages. One waiter, identified only as Mr. Hickman, asserted that "the colored men are the pioneers of the movement, and would not work for less than eighteen dollars a month, only they dreaded that the numerous body of white men would have taken less if [blacks] left [their jobs over wages]."[48] By the first week of April, several hotels had agreed to the new wages. Despite this success, however, the interracial coalition began to crumble. To encourage their fellow white waiters to continue the strike, the Astor Place waiters called on fears of black competition and black superiority: "The poor African that's stole from his native land, sold a slave, he buys his freedom, has got more than we white men, and sons of freemen . . . so come one, come all, get your shoulder to the wheel; the colored men are at your back, and never stop till you roll eighteen dollars to the top." [49]

The response of black middle-class reformers to this interracial strike was ambivalent at best. They perhaps saw it as doomed to fail both on the level of interracial cooperation and as an effort to raise wages. William J. Wilson, who had been involved with the American League of Colored Laborers, wrote in the *North Star* (under the pseudonym Ethiop) that black waiters were striking for wages "in imitation . . . of their paler brothers." Wilson doubted "if they have discovered the great disparity existing between" blacks and whites—differences that meant that black strikers would be less likely to achieve their objectives than white strikers. Wilson ended, "If the movement does not make many of them breadless ere next winter ends, I shall be most happy." [50]

Probably many middle-class black reformers agreed with Wilson's negative assessment of the strike's potential for success. But black reformers were also threatened by the class-based division that the strike could spawn, and its repercussions not only in the waiters' industry, but also in the black community. Interested in creating a unified community, middle-class blacks wanted laborers and employers to work together. They saw the strike as a threat to their project of racial unity.

Such concerns may have been what spurred black abolitionist and headwaiter Tunis G. Campbell to form a rival, race-based organization, the First United Association of Colored Waiters, during the strike. Campbell was born in 1812 in Middlebrook, New Jersey, the youngest son of a blacksmith. After completing his education at a school in Babylon, Long Island, in 1830, Campbell returned home to his parents, who had moved to New Brunswick. There, in 1832, he founded an anticolonization society and began preaching for the Methodist Church. He lectured on antislavery and, in the interracial working-class New York City district of the Five Points, he preached on moral reform as, according to his own account, "the first moral reformer and temperance lecturer" there. He also participated in the black national convention movement. [51]

However, Campbell's work as a reformer was only part of his identity. For most of his life Campbell worked in hotels. Between 1832 and 1842, he worked as a hotel steward in New York City. For three years, until 1845, he served as headwaiter at New York's Howard Hotel. From 1848 until about 1853, he worked in Boston at the Adams House. While in Boston he published his first book, *Hotel Keepers, Head Waiters, and Housekeepers' Guide*, which seems to be the first guide on the supervision and management of hotels published in the United States.[52] The 1848 *Guide* was a detailed account of Campbell's innovations in the field of hotel management, particularly the management of the dining area. Hotels in the United States were organized on what was known as the American Plan. Rather than having a restaurant that was open at all hours, at which hotel guests might dine at their leisure, hotels served meals to all guests at set times. As hotels grew larger, cooks and waiters could be responsible for serving several hundred guests at one sitting. Campbell's book describes his own innovations to the drill system by which waiters organized the dining room. Waiters served meals in rhythm, in perfect step with each other. Headwaiters used bells, music, or voice commands to put the waiters through their paces. Thus, waiting table was a combination of skill and obedience.[53] Although he did not invent this drill system, Campbell carried it to new heights of efficiency.

Campbell remained at the Adams House in Boston until the 1850s. The precise date of or reasons for his return to New York are unknown, but by 1853 he was a headwaiter at New York City's National Hotel. Just over two weeks after the interracial Waiters' Protective Union Society had formed, and barely a week after the owner of the National Hotel, George Seely, had agreed to the union's demands to raise waiters' wages to eighteen dollars a month, Campbell formed the First United Association of Colored Waiters. The number of waiters who attended the organizational meeting is unknown. The group's motives were clearly designed to forestall any divisions between hotel owners and workers, as well as to improve the status of black waiters for the good of the black community. Headwaiters such as Campbell occupied a middle position between waiters and employers, akin to that of master craftsmen in skilled mechanical trades. Headwaiters or master craftsmen were in supervisory positions and had a better chance of becoming owners and reaping the rewards of the new capitalism. But they needed the cooperation of those under them, and they often encouraged workers to cooperate with owners, rather than strike for higher wages or better working conditions. In forming the Association of Colored Waiters, Campbell hoped to create harmony between employers and employees. The association pledged to discourage waiters from strikes and other methods of maximizing their income, such as changing jobs, and to encourage waiters' loyalty to their employers. Thanking those employers who had agreed to the wage increases, the association suggested that waiters should show their appreciation by staying in the city during the summer season, rather than going to "the Springs and watering places," in upstate New York unless they were so poor that they "owe[d] it as a duty to [their] families and to [them]selves to seek employment where it is most to our advantage." Waiters who were members of the association could leave the city only for wages of at least twenty dollars a month.[54]

The association's expressed goal was to produce "an identity of interest between the employer and the employed." By remaining in the city, the waiters would show "interest in the business in which they are engaged; and . . . establish a mutual feeling of confidence and good will between the employer and the employed." Further, the association was willing to trust the employers "to arrange such a scale of prices as will be satisfactory to us— the colored waiters of the city of New York." The association ordered head-waiters, not waiters, to "secure for all men under [them] sixteen dollars per month"; any headwaiter who would not stand up for this minimum "shall be considered incapable of filling the place to which [they] aspire[d], and all [waiters] shall be at liberty to leave him." Finally, the association denied any connection with a massive waiters' strike planned for April 15 by the Waiters' Protective Union Society.[55]

As with other reform-led organizations aimed at black workers, the Association of Colored Waiters undervalued the labor that waiters performed. Although membership in the organization would be granted only to those waiters of "gentlemanly deportment" who possessed "a practical knowledge of the professional," the association accepted the "generally degraded position that waiters, as a class, hold in the scale of society." Black waiters should not take pride in their labor. Only through "moral and intellectual improvement" would they, and the race, be elevated.[56]

Black waiters who supported the interracial Waiters' Protective Union quickly dissociated themselves from the new organization. "Arouse Waiters, Traitors in the Camp" ran the headline of their brief ad in the New York Herald. At a Protective Union meeting, they pledged loyalty to the decisions of the body of the Waiters' Protective Union, thus asserting their separate class identity.[57]

The conflict between Campbell's group and the black waiters who supported the strike continued the rift between middle-class and aspiring middle-class blacks and black workers. Although workers and middle-class leaders had always split informally over life choices in urban areas, the overwhelming concerns of southern slavery and racial prejudice caused many blacks to join together across class lines to address issues of race. But the 1850s marked the beginning of a transition in which black workers not only expressed views that were at odds with those of middle-class leaders, but created organizations that mobilized for their own interests.

As black and white abolitionist-reformers discussed the problems of working-class blacks in the 1840s and 1850s in ever-increasing detail, they often alluded to but never fully described the lives of the poorest blacks in New York City, the community at the Five Points. However, other writers and reformers in the city eagerly stepped into the vacuum and delineated a lurid geography of interracial sexuality and crime.

CHAPTER EIGHT

"Rulers of the Five Points":
Blacks, Irish Immigrants, and Amalgamation

As New York's abolitionists debated ways to improve the conditions of working-class blacks in the 1840s and 1850s, other groups in the city created a new discourse of poverty, criminality, race, and sexuality that focused on the relationship between the working-class black and Irish communities in the Five Points district of New York City. Proslavery, anti-equality New York journalists and conservative religious reformers depicted interracial sex and socializing, or amalgamation, between working-class blacks and Irish as a major threat to New York's racial and social order. Perhaps fearing a repeat of the 1834 riots, black and white abolitionists largely avoided these discussions. White abolitionists continued their focus on southern slavery as the major race problem in the United States. Black abolitionists of the 1840s and 1850s were embarrassed by the links between blacks, prostitution, and crime in discussions of amalgamation and avoided public discussions of the Five Points.

For other, white New Yorkers, the discourse of amalgamation in the 1840s and 1850s continued the anxiety over sexuality and race that had triggered the 1834 riots and would be a factor in the 1863 Draft Riots.[1] New York State never outlawed interracial marriage, but throughout the antebellum period various groups of white New Yorkers depicted amalgamation as threatening to New York City's social structure. In the 1830s, proslavery and anti-equality whites led the charge against interracial socializing and sex. After New York's middle-class abolitionists rejected interracial marriage in the wake of the 1834 riots, a new group of journalists and reformers largely depicted amalgamation in New York City as a problem of the lower classes. Unlike the accusations of amalgamation aimed at abolitionists in the 1830s, the discussions of interracial sex in the 1840s were rooted in fact—some Irish and other whites did cohabitate and intermarry with their black neighbors. In the 1840s, the explosion in the number of Irish immigrants and their settlement in the Five Points area, which had been home to free blacks since the early decades of emancipation, led journalists and reformers to link amalgamation to crime, poverty, and the alleged decline of the city.

Unlike the rioters of 1834, who feared a power shift in favor of blacks, the critics of amalgamation in the 1840s and 1850s apparently did not believe that interracial sex and socializing between working-class blacks and Irish would give political or social power to either of these powerless groups. Rather, these relationships signaled the immorality and dangerousness of the city. Journalists and travel writers, building on the work of Charles Dickens's *American Notes for General Circulation*, focused on the Five Points area as a center of amalgamation and crime. By 1850, these writers' descriptions of the Five Points had influenced reformers who, alarmed with the increasing poverty and (as they viewed it) moral decline of the city, used some of the same characterizations to justify their own programs. In eyewitness accounts of interracial dance halls, sexual relationships, and children born out of wedlock, some reformers stated that amalgamation reinforced the degeneracy of the Irish. For a few reformers, amalgamation with the Irish threatened blacks' attempts to achieve moral equality. Although not the only factor, the critique of amalgamation by journalists and moral reformers may have led to the breakdown in Irish-black relations by the time of the Civil War.

■ ■ ■

After the 1834 riots and the retreat of black and white middle-class abolitionists from charges of fostering intermarriage, newspaper editors, travel writers, and finally reformers linked interracial sex to New York's working classes. Social and sexual relationships between New York's black and white workers had in fact existed since slavery. During moments of crisis, such as the 1741 slave plot or the 1818 Rose Butler arson trial, reformers, judges, slave owners, and others concerned about the potential disruption to the social order held up interracial relationships for public scrutiny. But the word "amalgamation," with its increasingly negative connotations, was used in association with the working classes only after the 1834 riots.

Immediately after the 1834 riots, the penny press began describing incidents of working-class amalgamation in New York City. The *New York Transcript* regularly published accounts of and conflicts over interracial socializing and sex taken from police reports and court cases. These ranged from accounts of prostitution to conflicts between interracial couples to altercations over dancing between blacks and whites. Such accounts reveal the continuation of interracial sexual encounters even after the violence of July 1834. In November of that year, for example, "the indefatigable inspector of the Sixth Ward, M'Grath," arrested fourteen women, black and white, for prostitution. The women allegedly spent their time together "enticing sailors into their haunt" in the Five Points, "making them drunk, and robbing them." In March 1835, as part of a night of escapades, white workers Samuel Dunn and Dan Turner supposedly began their evening by "blackguarding some black beauties whom chance placed in their path." John Curry, a white sailor accused of "striking a female with his fist," defended himself by saying that women, "black or white, red or brown, I love 'em all; and with they'd all only get one mouth, and I had the kissing on't." A New York City court convicted two white women of "assaulting a black man and trying to kiss him."[2]

These and other descriptions of "amalgamators" were often more concerned with the actions of whites than of blacks and sought to demonstrate the moral weakness of whites who socialized with or married blacks. In such stories, blacks were often more morally upright than their partners. Charles Albraith, for example, "a dapper little tailor from Philadelphia . . . became enamoured of a *black* woman," Mary Brown, the owner of an oyster cellar. Soon after their engagement, Albraith became so drunk, so "riotous and noisy," that Mary became angry. He responded by striking her, and so she broke off the engagement and had him arrested. The court withheld a conviction of assault on the condition that Albraith return to Philadelphia. In this instance, Albraith's descent into amalgamation proved his damaged masculinity: he wanted to marry a black woman, he drank excessively, and he assaulted a woman. Mary's actions, including her decision to break off the engagement, displayed her moral uprightness and helped restore racial order to this small segment of New York City.[3]

The dangers to single white women of interracial sexual contacts was the theme of a complicated account reprinted in the *New York Transcript* in September 1835. Elias Kent met chambermaid Mary Ann Markey in Albany, New York. The white couple soon moved to New York City and married. Within two weeks of the wedding, the new bride discovered that her husband was an "infernal scoundrel." "A *coloured girl* called at the house of her father" and stated that Kent had been married to her for over three years, that she had had two children for him, and that she had come to claim her husband. Mary Ann's father "was so enraged to think that she had married such a fellow upon six weeks acquaintance, that he turned her out of doors."[4]

This story provided a racial twist to reformers' fears about young, single, working-class women in the 1830s, who were developing urban lives independent of their families beginning in the early part of that decade. Mary Ann had been a chambermaid in Albany, on her own and far from the guidance of her father, when she met Elias.[5]

In the stories of Charles Albraith and Mary Ann Markey, the writers italicized the adjectives "black" or "colored" as if to note that they were surprised at such contact (and that their readers would be, too). After the riots of 1834, many whites increasingly expected, or sought to ensure, that whites would reject black-white socializing. Some working-class blacks and whites continued to embrace a fluid set of race relations. But journalists were quick to play up instances in which whites upheld the color line. In October 1834, a black boatman, Michael Cracken, walked past a house where recent German immigrants were holding a party. When Cracken joined in, "the Germans very naturally and very properly ejected him." Cracken then fetched a number of his friends "to retaliate for the insult which he conceived had been put upon him." He and his friends threw brickbats at the house until the watchman came and dispersed the "rioters," arrested three of them, and ordered them to pay a 500-dollar bail or go to jail.[6]

Such newspaper accounts demonstrated that not all working-class blacks, immigrants, and native-born whites agreed so easily to the separation of the races. But from the 1840s through the Civil War, middle-class journalists and reformers linked amalgamation, first between blacks and native-born whites and then between blacks and Irish, to their allegations of the increasing poverty and crime of New York City. The Sixth Ward in lower Manhattan, and particularly the Five Points region of that ward, became the focus of accounts of black-white interracial sex. The Five Points (fig. 21), named for the intersection of five streets, was the geographic center of the first free black settlements in the city during the emancipation years. By the mid-1830s the Sixth Ward had the largest concentration of blacks in New York. During that same time, it became one of the leading centers of prostitution in the city, containing 31 percent of the city's brothels.[7]

After the mid-1840s, the Sixth Ward also became known as the "Irish ward" because of the large numbers of Irish immigrants who made the Five Points area their home. The Irish increasingly "whitened" residential and social spaces previously designated as good enough only for blacks. Largely poor and confined to low-wage, unskilled jobs, the Irish competed with blacks for positions as waiters, domestics, and laborers. By the 1840s and 1850s, the Irish were winning the battle. But this success came at a price.

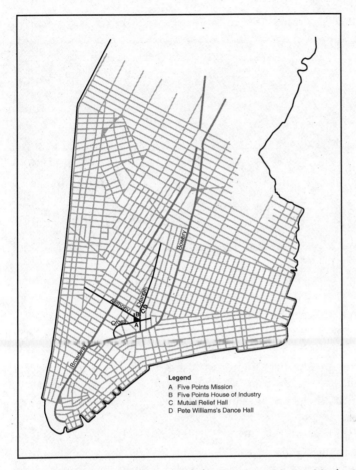

Fig. 21 Map of the Five Points area, including Five Points Mission. Map by Sarah Zingarelli

Occupying the jobs formerly the domain of blacks, jobs to which associations of servility and dependence still clung, the Irish experienced a prejudice akin to that blacks had endured for so long. Indeed, some called the Irish "white niggers," and blacks, "smoked Irish."[8] Thus, Irish and blacks uneasily shared geographic, social, economic, and cultural space in New York City in the 1840s and 1850s.

Although the Five Points comprised only five city blocks, it became for white middle-class New Yorkers the center of what they saw as a maelstrom of prostitution, interracial sex, murder, and theft that threatened to engulf the city through an influx of lower-class Irish and blacks. The proximity of

Fig. 22 This drawing, allegedly of the Five Points in 1827, was published in *Valentine's Manual* in 1885. Neg. no. 35910. © Collection of the New-York Historical Society.

the Five Points to the center of the city and to Broadway fueled white middle-class anxiety. These areas experienced middle-class flight as wealthier New Yorkers moved farther north in the city. The writers who documented this process of white middle-class flight and black-Irish immigration reflected the concerns of New Yorkers over the changing ethnic and geographic nature of poverty and also helped to shape their attitudes to those changes (figs. 22 and 23).

The changing nature of the Broadway area and the Five Points had been outlined in the police and court sections of the *New York Transcript* and other penny newspapers in the 1830s. Charles Dickens's *American Notes for General Circulation* (1842) fixed a geographic specificity to concerns about the connection between amalgamation and poverty in New York City and shaped the ways white middle-class New York writers and reformers would view the Five Points and interracial working-class contacts down to the Civil War.

Unlike the earlier *New York Transcript* descriptions, Dickens's descriptions were not taken from police reports or court transcripts, but from his own explorations of the Five Points. His account focused on the poverty of the district, a poverty peopled by African Americans. Dickens detailed his visits to the homes of some of the poor who lived in the Five Points, a practice that would become formulaic for travel writers and reformers after 1840. At his initial "descent" into the neighborhood, accompanied by two police

Fig. 23 A drawing of the Five Points in 1859, published in *Valentine's Manual* in 1860. Neg. no. 74639. © Collection of the New-York Historical Society.

officers, Dickens described the blacks he met there in animalistic terms: "Many . . . pigs live here. Do they ever wonder why their masters walk upright in lieu of going on all-fours? and why they talk instead of grunting?"[9] At the same time, Dickens elevated the district as a central site of New York black cultural activity, which he admired. With his trip to "Almack's," a black-owned dance hall, Dickens catapulted the owner and black dancing to international fame. Dickens was clearly awestruck by the skill of the dancers there: "Single shuffle, double shuffle, cut and cross-cut: snapping his fingers, rolling his eyes, turning in his knees, presenting the backs of his legs in front, spinning about on his toes and heels like nothing. . . . And in what walk of life, or dance of life, does man ever get such stimulating applause as thunders about him, when, having danced his partner off her feet . . . he finishes by leaping glouriously [*sic*] on the bar-counter . . . with the chuckle of a million of counterfeit Jim Crows, in one inimitable sound!" Similar to the minstrel performers of the period, Dickens combined disgust and admiration in his depictions of black life and culture. Indeed, Dickens viewed the dancing through the caricatures of minstrelsy itself: "rolling his eyes," "chuckle of . . . Jim Crows."[10]

American Notes was immensely popular. Dickens's American tour, on which he based the book, had itself been widely publicized. The book sold fifty thousand copies in three days, and newspapers across the country reprinted excerpts from it. *American Notes* inspired outrage, admiration, and most important, imitation among the new investigative journalists in American cities. In this genre of sensational journalism, writers were both observers and participants; they provided their voyeuristic middle-class readers with intimate glimpses into the parts of the city that they were warning them away from. Beginning in the early 1840s, their stories were serialized in penny newspapers and magazines and then republished in cheap paperback books. Dickens's work was particularly important in sparking among journalists a new discussion of race relations in the American city, beginning with New York.[11]

In other places in the United States, critics saw Dickens's writings as too critical of American customs. New York writers, however, saw the work as too *positive* in its depiction of the Five Points. Dickens described no prostitution or danger to himself, no fighting or riots, no interracial dancing or living arrangements. The free-wheeling sexuality for which the Points had been and would continue to be made famous was largely absent from his account, and only the presence of several "mulatto" women at Almack's Place hinted at the interracial sex that the *New York Transcript* had already located in the district. In response, white middle-class journalists such as Nathaniel Parker Willis and George Foster and reformers such as Louis M. Pease and Samuel Halliday capitalized on the popularity of *American Notes* and explicitly challenged what they saw as a romanticized depiction of life in the Five Points. Using *American Notes* as a starting point, travel writers and reformers through the Civil War reconstructed the neighborhood in their descriptions, focusing on poverty and interracial sex and in the process creating a geography of vice in Manhattan's Five Points area.

Within a year of the publication of *American Notes*, Willis had retraced Dickens's steps, with New York newspapers publishing his accounts. Having at first glance seen "well-dressed and well-mannered people" at Almack's, on second look he noticed "a few 'young men about town,' mixed up with the blacks; and altogether it was a picture of 'amalgamation,' such as I had never before seen," and which Dickens's "superficial eye" had turned into "the merriest quarter of New York." Willis established the connection between amalgamation and crime when one of his companions discovered that his pocket had been picked.[12]

Willis's account reflected his view of the changing geography of poverty and race in New York. Before venturing to "Dickens' Hole" (as Almack's had come to be known), he "had had an idea that this celebrated spot was on the eastern limit of the city, at the end of one of the omnibus-routes." But to his surprise, poor blacks and interracial vice had shifted from their location in the 1820s, on the docks at the edge of the city, to "not more than three minutes' walk from Broadway, and in full view from one of the fashionable corners." Willis's account of the Five Points ended with a cry for the reclamation of the Points and the areas around it from blacks: "We should like to know, among other things, why the broadest, most accessible, most convenient street in New York, the noble avenue of WEST BROADWAY, is entirely given up to negroes?" Thus, Willis ultimately laid the blame for amalgamation and the degradation of the city at the feet of blacks alone, ignoring white consumers and participants. In an early move against flight to more suburban locales, he stated, "The *rage* is to move up town," and called for the white middle class to stay and hold out against encroaching black poverty.[13]

In 1850, George Foster, one of the most popular writers in this genre, published *New York by Gas-light*, which sold two hundred thousand copies.[14] Foster cast blacks as owners of the major establishments, responsible economically and culturally for the character of the Five Points. In doing so, he erased the role of the whites who were landlords of the buildings containing brothels and dance halls. Foster acknowledged the achievement of some black men in being able to "scrape together a good deal of money" through such activities. But Foster believed that black men used this economic power to gain "white wives or white mistresses," to "associate upon at least equal terms with the men and women of the parish," and to be "regarded as desirable companions and lovers by the 'girls.'" According to Foster, such attempts to achieve racial equality were in vain, for black men's humanity was irredeemable: "They are savage, sullen, reckless dogs, and are continually promoting some 'muss' or other, which not unfrequently leads to absolute riot."[15]

Foster and other writers reserved special scorn for the most successful of the black dance-hall owners, Peter Williams (no relation to the minister Peter Williams), the owner of Almack's Place. New York writers acknowledged that "Pete Williams, Esq." had "made an immense amount of money from the profits of his dance-house." Citing a cultural rather than sexual amalgamation, one writer described Williams thus: "in complexion and features . . . [he was] thoroughly African, [but] in his business tact and intuitive knowledge of men and things, he was decidedly Yankee." But Foster undercut any praise for Williams's business acumen by claiming Williams "regularly [gambles the money] away at the sweat-cloth or the roulette-table as fast as it comes in."[16]

Thus, for many white journalists in the 1840s and 1850s, blacks were "the rulers of the Five Points," as white South Carolina travel writer William Bobo dubbed them in his critical view of New York City.[17] These writers blamed amalgamation on blacks, largely ignoring the fact that most blacks in the Five Points rented from whites, and that their dance halls and brothels catered to native-born, middle-class whites as well as to working-class whites and blacks. As historians Elizabeth Blackmar and Timothy Gilfoyle have documented, white landlords and entrepreneurially minded black New Yorkers together formed this district of dance halls, bars, gambling houses, and prostitution. White landlords who owned property in the Five Points and were unable to rent to "respectable" tenants did not hesitate to lease their property to businesses outside the compass of moral reform. Black workers and would-be entrepreneurs, unable to find legitimate jobs or open legitimate businesses, moved into the jobs and businesses such activities provided. Peter Williams was only the most famous of these black entrepreneurs in the Five Points. Black women also owned brothels throughout the district. These brothels addressed specific clientele: some catered only to black men, while others employed black and white women, or provided black prostitutes for poor to upper-class white men.[18]

Many of these black men and women made substantial money as entrepreneurs in the Five Points. According to the 1850 census, Peter Williams lived with his wife and daughter in the Sixth Ward and held five thousand dollars in property. But money and property did not translate into middle-class status for these men and women. Although whites who owned the property blacks leased often held political power and sometimes parlayed their earnings into more respectable establishments, black entrepreneurs did not have this opportunity for a number of reasons. The most significant obstacle was racism, but black entrepreneurs were also too close to their businesses. White landlords were one step removed from the places of vice they rented out; theoretically, they could plead ignorance as to what occurred there. But those such as Peter Williams and the female brothel owners were on site nightly in their places of business, associating with customers and identifying with employees.[19]

Among blacks, even more than among whites, the definitions of middle class were tightly bound up with moral respectability. Black leaders' calls for increased entrepreneurship among blacks did not include the opening of brothels, bars, and dance halls. Black reformers at times considered self-employed barbers as damaging to black reputations and racial uplift: the job was too menial and reinforced whites' ideas of black inferiority and servitude. The topic of black ownership of brothels, bars, and dance halls was so far beyond the pale of respectability that blacks in the 1840s did not discuss these activities publicly, for to discuss the details of the Five Points would have been to confirm the worst characterizations of free blacks made by proslavery whites, southerners, colonizationists and other critics. William Bobo, for example, did not miss the opportunity to expose the evils of the Five Points and thus impugn the efforts of abolitionists. After making the obligatory trip to Peter Williams's dance hall and pronouncing blacks "the rulers of the Five Points," Bobo stated that "there are more cases of crime presented at [the courts], in the city of New-York alone, than all the South put together. In fact, there is more poverty, prostitution, wretchedness, drunkenness, and all the attending vices, in this city, than the whole South." Such rampant criminality and immorality made hypocrites of abolitionists. "When the Abolitionists have cleared their own skirts, let them then hold up their hands in holy horror at the slave-holder, and the enormity of his sins." [20] Accounts like Bobo's confirmed black and white abolitionists' worst fears of the damage black immorality could wreak on their efforts to free southern slaves and demonstrate racial equality. There are no accounts of interactions between Peter Williams and New York City's black abolitionists, but Williams, like porter-activist Peter Paul Simons, presented a challenge to black reformers' efforts to establish morally perfect, middeclass definitions of black workers and entrepreneurs. Williams, however, was even more threatening to their project than was Simons. Thus, although black abolitionists such as Henry Highland Garnet and Charles Ray worked daily in the Five Points community under the auspices of the American Missionary Association, they remained silent on the topics raised by the travel writers, even in their reports to the association. Detailed descriptions and discussion of the Five Points were left to white travel writers and nonabolitionist reformers.

Dickens's, Willis's, Foster's and other writers' depictions of the Five Points had perhaps their greatest impact on New York City's nonabolitionist reformers. These writers spurred reformers to action and helped to shape the ways they evaluated the Five Points district and the people who lived there. From 1848 through the Civil War, the missionaries of the Five Points printed accounts of those who lived at the Points and of their own missionary efforts in reform journals, annual reports, and published memoirs.

In 1848, the Ladies' Home Missionary Society of the Methodist Episcopal Church turned to the Five Points as a place to begin a new city mission. As historian Carroll Smith-Rosenberg has shown, the Five Points "was for them a most grievous example of the evil afflicting American society."[21] By 1850, they had involved a group of wealthy men to act as their board of trustees and had founded the Five Points Mission. They hired Louis M. Pease as their first missionary and established the Five Points Mission at the corner of Little Water and Cross Streets in the heart of the slum (see fig. 21). Within a year, Pease had expanded the mission's work in its chapel and day school to include job training, housing, and employment. Pease granted assistance on the condition that all who wished to obtain training and jobs live at the mission. The response from Five Points residents was positive enough that, in February 1851, Pease rented an adjoining building. Pease also moved to the district with his wife and children, into a house next door to the Methodist chapel. But the women who had founded the mission objected to Pease's materialist bent. By 1852, Pease had split off from the more religiously oriented women, and in 1854 he separately incorporated the Five Points House of Industry. Through the Civil War, Pease and his successors, Benjamin Barlow and Samuel Halliday, ran one of the largest and most well known missions in New York City, while the female missionaries continued their more religiously oriented work.[22]

In their separate endeavors, both Pease and the Ladies' Home Missionary Society established themselves as a new type of observer-participant in the life of the Five Points. They utilized the sensationalist tactics Dickens had introduced in *American Notes,* but set themselves above the population as reformers rather than mere critics. Although most historians see their efforts as focused on the white immigrants of the Five Points area, their accounts demonstrate their belief in the centrality of the black presence to the slum conditions that prevailed in the area. The Ladies' Home Missionary Society's 1854 anniversary publication, for example, cites the black presence as having disturbed an earlier, healthier Five Points consisting of ponds, creeks, and meadows. This bucolic scene ended with "the first records of human history, [which] in this place are stained with blood"—a reference to the slave conspiracy of 1741, following which the British burned thirteen blacks at the stake and hung twenty more in chains on an island in the neighborhood's Fresh Water Pond. This account ignored the fact that independent black landowners had lived in this area under Dutch rule, and that the area's leather tanners had destroyed the Fresh Water Pond by dumping their refuse there. Further, although the majority of the residents of the Five Points were white immigrants by the mid-1850s, the women quoted verbatim Dickens's description of blacks in the Five Points, "the details [of which] make the *tout ensemble* of horrors."[23] Thus, by 1854, reformers and writers linked not only the immorality of the present, but the sordid prehistory of the Five Points to images of degraded, immoral blacks.

But the Five Points Mission and the House of Industry were also influenced by the romantic racialism of the moderate abolitionists, particularly that of Harriet Beecher Stowe's *Uncle Tom's Cabin*.[24] In his *Monthly Record of the Five Points House of Industry*, which began publication in 1857, Louis Pease portrayed images of black degradation and romanticization side by side. The *Monthly Record* reveals the complex ways reformers unaffiliated with either the abolitionist or antislavery movement assimilated the images that antislavery blacks and whites had been developing since the end of slavery and the rise of radical abolition in New York City.

An early issue of the *Monthly Record* introduced its readers to Topsy, a four-year-old black girl. The writers of the *Monthly Record* gave most of the inhabitants of the Five Points pseudonyms, but only Topsy was so clearly identified with a specific popular character, in this case the black child from Stowe's *Uncle Tom's Cabin*. Topsy was a recurring character in the magazine, "her eyes as black as her face, and her face as black as ebony." Topsy's mother, "though compelled by poverty" to live "in a dark and fearful place, in Cow-bay . . . with none but thieves and abandoned women around her . . . is almost always happy." A washerwoman, she was most happy, according to the reformers, when her simple need "to pay the rent of her little room and supply her with the most common necessities of life" had been met by earnings gained through her own labor.[25]

Topsy's mother did not appear again in the *Monthly Record*, but Topsy was a faithful participant in the activities of the mission, attending the school and other programs it sponsored. According to the reformers' accounts, she "sometimes act[ed] as a voluntary agent" for the mission. On one occasion, at a temperance meeting held for the children of the Five Points, "Little Topsy came from her seat, took the hand of a stalwart negro, marched up to the speaker's desk and said: 'I have brought my uncle to sign the pledge.' It was administered, [and] Topsy's eyes sparkled with delight."[26]

The emphasis on Topsy's reform rather than her mother's may have been due to the Five Points Mission's increased emphasis on children. From 1857 through 1863, children accounted for the vast majority of the mission's beneficiaries. According to Smith-Rosenberg, the mission turned its attention to children in an attempt to wield greater religious influence upon the largely Irish Catholic population of the Five Points.[27] No doubt the Five Points Mission reformers felt, as had reformers before them, that children were more malleable than adults, and thus more energy should be focused upon them. By removing children of any creed or race from the influence of immoral parents, the missionaries felt that the population could be saved.

In the case of one child, Lizzie, the emphasis was not only religious, but cultural and racial reform. Topsy brought Lizzie to the mission. "A little girl about [Topsy's] own age," Lizzie had "bright eyes, fair complexion, and . . . wavy hair, shading a face of innocence and beauty." Topsy stated, "I have brought a new scholar. . . . She and her mother live with a black man next door to me, and she was hungry, so I told her to come to school and get her dinner." The description's focus on Lizzie's fair complexion and wavy hair, as well as her mother's relationship with a black man, implied that Lizzie might be a mulatto. Lizzie began to attend school, and within two weeks her mother allowed her to move into the mission. "To this proposition we [the reformers] gave joyful consent. Perhaps we might yet rescue her from her prospectively sad fate." No doubt this rescue would involve the erasure of her connection with the interracial mixing of her previous living arrangement. Despite the fact that she might have been part black, her youthfulness and light skin presented a unique opportunity. The conflation of reform with elevation to middle-class standards often included the removal of "black" traits and history, particularly when reformers identified blackness only with poverty or with the negative effects of racism.[28]

Although many reformers saw blacks as central to the problems of the Five Points, the increase in Irish immigration following the Great Famine of the 1840s led some to point to Irish and native-born whites as partly to blame. By the late 1840s, the increased presence of immigrant Irish in the Five Points area led some reformers to question who were the real "rulers of the Five Points"—blacks or Irish? The Five Points reformers ultimately gave the Irish equal blame for the slum conditions of the area. Separation of the races, and particularly of blacks from Irish, was crucial to the uplift of the Five Points, for "where the blacks were found by themselves, we generally encountered tidiness, and some sincere attempt at industry and honest self-support." As one reformer noted, "the negroes of the Five Points are fifty per cent in advance of the Irish as to sobriety and decency." [29]

Concern about the "Irish problem" in New York City reached the state capitol at Albany, where in 1857 the state legislature established a "Special Committee on Tenement Houses in New-York and Brooklyn." This committee visited the Five Points district and found "the Irish . . . predominant, as occupants" of "hundreds of dilapidated, dirty and densely populated old structures." In a rare attack on German as well as Irish immigrants, the committee noted that "in some of the better class of houses built for the tenantry, negroes have been preferred as occupants to Irish or German poor; the incentive of possessing comparatively decent quarters appearing to inspire the colored residents with more desire for personal cleanliness and regard for property than is impressed upon the whites of their own condition."[30]

The increasing numbers of Irish immigrants in New York City raised the issue of racial status. Although in Europe the Irish had been considered a different, inferior race from the English, in the United States, with the presence of black slaves as the ultimate symbol of dependence and degradation, the position of the Irish was up for grabs. Did the Irish have the potential to become "white"? Should native-born whites embrace them and reshape them into "whites," thus lifting them above blacks? Or were blacks in fact morally, and thus racially, superior to the Irish? Although some called the Irish "white niggers," others used the words "white" and "Irish" almost interchangeably in their descriptions of these immigrants.[31]

For reformers, however, the worst fate of the city was not in the presence of one or the other group, but in the mixture of blacks and Irish. This fate was clearly spelled out in an 1861 visit to the Points conducted by missionary Benjamin Barlow and a policeman for the benefit of readers of the *Independent* newspaper. In a garret, adjacent to an apartment where only recently police had found "a millionaire's beautiful daughter . . . lying on the bare floor with a drunken negro," Barlow and the policeman supposedly came across "old Sambo over his brazier of coals." In a corner of the room, from under "a long pile of rags . . . an Irish woman lift[ed] her tangled mop of a head. . . . 'Look here, gentlemen, look at this little codfish'; and with this she lift[ed] out from beneath the rags a diminutive mulatto child of a few weeks old, to the great delight of Sambo, who reveal[ed] all his ivory." According to the reformers, the fate of such a child would be to have "rum its first medicine, theft its first lesson, a prison its first house, and the Potter's Field its final resting-place."[32] This composite picture of familial ruin incorporated the well-worn specters of alcoholism, crime, and proverty, ineluctably combined through amalgamation.

Barlow's account also points to another element of the missionaries' depiction of amalgamation. According to the missionaries, there were few instances of white men consorting with black women. "In nearly every garret we entered," one report stated, "the same practical amalgamation was in fashion; but in each case a black Othello had won a fair Desdemona—not one white man was found with a colored wife." Whether this was perception or reality remains unclear. The apparently casual nature of the relationships depicted appears to have prevented their documentation in the census records of the 1840s and 1850s, which might have provided a clue to the actual number of interracial households.[33]

Reformers' visits "under the crust" of New York marked the beginning of a new intimacy between middle-class and working-class New Yorkers. During and after the Civil War, middle-class men and women continued to live in the Points and other slums not simply as voyeurs, but as resident activists. The missionaries' interactions in the day-to-day lives of the Five Points' residents may have influenced the attitudes of working-class whites and immigrants, who began to achieve political and social equality by distinguishing themselves from their black neighbors. By the eve of the Civil War, reformers had identified amalgamation as one of the main evils of the poor of New York City. Poor blacks and whites continued to socialize, cooperate, and marry throughout the antebellum period, but around them journalists and reformers depicted these cross-race interactions as distasteful, and damaging to the New York community. Fears of amalgamation became part of the constellation of forces that made the city, once viewed as a haven, increasingly dangerous for blacks, and particularly black workers, on the eve of the Civil War.

CHAPTER NINE

The Failures of the City

In 1859, Thomas DeVoe, the historian of New York City's markets, spoke with an elderly black woman who was selling "roots and herbs" in Essex Market. She was "one of the last of the 'Long Island Negroes,'" for whom New York City in the eras of slavery and emancipation had been the center of a vibrant community life. DeVoe asked, "How many of the old colored persons (once slaves) are there now left, who yet come here?" She answered, "[T]here was only about *four* who occasionally came—*the rest are all dead.*" For DeVoe, the death of these former slaves was not simply due to the passing of time and generations, but indicated a deeper malaise in New York City's black community—a malaise resulting from the limits on black freedom in the city. DeVoe lamented the condition of many free blacks as "poor, squalid, dirty, half-dressed, ill-fed and bred, and some no doubt with a strong inclination to be thievish." DeVoe ignored the many institutions blacks had built and blacks' political activism. But he rightly blamed the impoverished conditions of many blacks on the inadequacies of simple freedom in the face of racism: "I felt that when Government made them free, Government should have removed some of the obstacles which interfered with the intellectual progress and the domestic comfort of the newly liberated African race—that they might have appeared not only here [at the markets] on a Sunday morning, but any day and anywhere, and be a useful and respectable body of people."[1]

During the Civil War era, an escalation of attacks on free blacks both locally and nationally increased pressure on New York City's African Americans. Competition with Irish immigrants and other working-class whites forced many blacks out of the menial jobs they had dominated for much of the antebellum period. At the same time, white workers were increasingly violent toward blacks in the 1850s. Politically, the New York State legislature refused to grant blacks voting rights, despite numerous petitions from blacks and white abolitionists throughout the state.

Perhaps most damaging were the actions of the federal government in the 1840s and 1850s. In 1842, in *Prigg v. Pennsylvania*, the Supreme Court revoked the rights of fugitives to trial by jury, a right black New Yorkers had won only two years before. In 1850, the Fugitive Slave Law put all blacks at a much higher risk of being enslaved than at any time in the antebellum period. And in 1857, the Supreme Court's Dred Scott decision explicitly stated that blacks, free or slave, were not citizens of the United States under the Constitution.

Some New York City blacks responded to these myriad threats to their freedom by leaving the city. The city experienced a drastic drop in the black population as men, women, and children fled to rural areas, away from the confines of the city, where slave catchers and angry white workers increasingly roamed the streets in pursuit of vulnerable black residents. Black and white abolitionists encouraged this flight. White abolitionist Gerrit Smith, working with Charles B. Ray and James McCune Smith, offered New York City blacks free farm land in upstate New York. Other blacks fled west, some as far as California. For a few, particularly after the Dred Scott decision, the United States itself was too dangerous. Some fled to Canada. Henry Highland Garnet and Alexander Crummell encouraged blacks to emigrate to the West Indies and Africa. But most blacks refused to leave the United States. Blacks' struggles seemed to be rewarded by the outbreak of Civil War in 1861. Defining the war as one fought on behalf of freedom for slaves as much as preservation of the Union, New York City blacks prepared to fight alongside whites. But the war exposed and accelerated the tensions between blacks and whites in the city. Before New York's blacks could fight on behalf of southern slaves, they had to fight for their own lives in the most violent and traumatic riots of nineteenth-century New York City, the 1863 Draft Riots.

■ ■ ■

Between 1840 and the Civil War, the white majority continued to exclude blacks from skilled positions, so that by 1850, only 5.44 percent of black men held artisanal jobs. Irish, German, and British immigrants, as well as native-born whites, dominated the skilled trades. More devastating to the economic viability of the African American community, Irish immigrants displaced New York City's blacks as domestics, waiters, and laborers, occupa-tions blacks had dominated during the antebellum period.[2]

Tensions also grew between black and white workers on the docks of New York in the mid-1850s. Throughout the antebellum period, whites had in-creasingly excluded blacks from the docks. When white workers struck for higher wages in January 1855, some blacks acted as strikebreakers, eagerly taking the $1.50 per day the white longshoremen spurned. Blacks were not the only strikebreakers; according to newspaper reports, "hundreds of poor men are desirous of labour at the present price." But blacks as a group gained the hostility of white workers, who viewed them as having the "sympathy of the employers, the public, and the law" on their side. An Irish man at-tacked a black man leaving the docks one evening, striking him in the head. The black man fired a gun and escaped, but within minutes, "several hun-dred longshoremen . . . gathered upon the wharf," prepared to harass other strikebreakers. Ultimately, strikebreaking did not increase the number of jobs available to blacks. Once the strikes ended, white workers and employ-ers again excluded blacks from longshore work (fig. 24).[3]

Poverty was detrimental to the health of New York City's blacks, as abo-litionists and colonizationists alike noted. Black abolitionist and missionary Charles B. Ray said of black life in the 1840s, "Scarcely ever have I known, in the absence of an epidemic, so many sick among the colored people, espe-cially the young, as now." John Griscom, a member of the American Colo-nization Society and a former physician to the City Dispensary and New York Hospital, stated in a talk on the "sanitary condition of the laboring pop-ulation," that "there is an immense amount of sickness, physical disability, and premature mortality, among the poorer classes." Illnesses hit blacks par-ticularly hard because of their living conditions. The damp, airless cellar res-idences that blacks had occupied since slavery exacerbated the illnesses to which all poor people were subject: tuberculosis, pneumonia, and typhus, among other diseases.[4]

According to the Association for the Improvement of the Condition of the Poor (AICP), such health problems led to pauperism and crime. Their so-lution was to encourage "capitalists" to take more responsibility for the ten-ements they owned. "By providing the laboring classes with better tene-ments, improved ventilation, and healthy and cleanly [sic] arrangements in respect to yards, sinks and sewerage, they will certainly suffer less from sick-ness and premature mortality, and a vast amount of pauperism, crime, and wretchedness [will] be prevented."[5] To set an example, the association built a "model dwelling." Blacks, whom the association viewed as the segment of

Fig. 24 Throughout the antebellum period, whites increasingly excluded blacks, such as this stevedore, from the docks. When white workers struck for higher wages in January 1855, some blacks acted as strikebreakers. Neg. no. 51254. © Collection of the New-York Historical Society.

THE COLORED STEVEDORE.—A REMINISCENCE.

the working class most in need of aid, were the sole occupants of the building when it opened in 1854 under the auspices of the AICP's subcommittee, the Workingmen's Home Association. By 1857, the building contained almost four hundred blacks in eighty-seven light, spacious apartments equipped with private bathrooms and gaslights, rarities among working-class residences. The building also contained an auditorium designed to be used for lectures, concerts, and other gatherings. A committee of the New York State Assembly pronounced it "the best arranged building" they had visited. Through 1865, the building was one of the best dwellings for the poor in New York City.[6]

But the building stood alone as a housing reform effort in pre–Civil War New York City. Further, as the AICP was constructing its model tenement, the city was dismantling one of the few areas of persistent black land ownership. In 1853, the city condemned Seneca Village to make way for Central Park. Although the city paid landowners for their property, "more was at stake than money"—the residents of Seneca Village had established a community. For black men, landownership was still the key to full political participation, and the money they received for their land was not enough to buy property elsewhere in New York City. By 1857, the residents of Seneca

Village had scattered, and the city had razed the community's churches, schools, and homes.[7]

In other parts of the city, the segregation of blacks and whites increased. By 1852, 86 percent of New York City's approximately 13,800 blacks lived below Fourteenth Street; almost half of these residents lived in a fifty-block area that included parts of the third, fifth, and eighth wards. Seventy-five percent of New York's streets held no black residents at all.[8] Some blacks blamed this segregation on the new immigrants. In 1855, "Ethiop" wrote in *Frederick Douglass' Paper* that immigrant "Dutch" (probably German) businessmen now occupied the "palaces" near Broadway, making of them grocery stores and bars. These new residents replaced the older "New York aristocratic *ilk*" of "the Auchincloses, the Edgars, the Newbolds, the Whites, the Todds" with "rude Dutchdom." But the immigrants also replaced the black residents whom Nathaniel Parker Willis and others had railed against barely ten years before. As Ethiop walked through the neighborhood, "they stared at me" as a "wonderful curiosity," for "so few blacks pass this way." Additionally, these immigrants, for all their alleged rudeness, had stepped onto the path of upward mobility in ways that blacks could not hope to emulate. "The Dutch beer-seller[s] of to-day . . . are the clerks of twenty years since; the clerks of to-day will be the Gotham princes of twenty years hence." As they improved their economic standing, European immigrants joined native-born whites in excluding New York City's blacks from business opportunities and from many residential neighborhoods.[9]

The economic crisis New York City's blacks experienced in the 1840s and 1850s was matched by a series of political crises. Despite repeated petitions to the state legislature in the two decades before the Civil War, African Americans and their white allies could not convince New York's governing whites that blacks were worthy of equal political citizenship. Blacks' largest setback in the struggle for suffrage came during the New York State Constitutional Convention of 1846. As the convention began to set its agenda, blacks and white abolitionists pressured the delegates to include the question of black suffrage. Supporters of black suffrage had worked for over a decade to remove suffrage restrictions on blacks. By 1841, the Judiciary Committee of the New York State Assembly was convinced that there was "public sentiment in all quarters" in support of an equal suffrage amendment for blacks. Not all legislators, particularly not Democrats, agreed with the committee's assessment. But the rise of the Liberty Party and especially its success in the 1844 presidential election in providing the swing vote that defeated Henry Clay, the candidate of both Whigs and Democrats, led legislators to seriously consider the possibility that abolitionists could mobilize voters on behalf of black suffrage.[10]

The 1846 constitutional convention debates over equal suffrage revealed nevertheless that little had changed in conceptions of black political equality in the twenty-five years since the previous convention restricted black suffrage. The state lacked broad support for black equality, and the discussion of black suffrage by the convention delegates (elected by district, separately from the legislature) paralleled that of 1821 in focusing on blacks' alleged inferiority and comparing their status to that of women and children. John Leslie Russell of St. Lawrence County affirmed the right of the convention to enforce distinctions among electors and to exclude those the general population believed unworthy of the privilege of voting. "The republican form of government," he stated "is . . . the best for any people who have the capabilities necessary to maintain it." But not all should have a hand in governing: "the sovereign power should be lodged in a portion—not, the whole number of individuals, whose social rights are protected by it." Women, blacks, and men under the age of twenty-one "cannot have any voice." John Kennedy of New York City cited prison statistics to show that blacks' "aggregate moral character" should keep them from voting. New York City's courts convicted blacks of crimes at three and a half times the rate of whites; and the state prisons held thirteen and a half times as many blacks as whites, vastly out of proportion to their percentages in the population. According to Kennedy, "there was nothing to sustain the slightest suspicion that injustice had been done" in prosecuting the cases of black criminal defendants. The disparity between black and white crime statistics reflected the "distinctions and divisions that nature designed to exist" between blacks and whites. Government should not "overthrow or ignore these differences" by legislating equal suffrage. John Hunt, also of New York City, supported colonization. He believed that blacks had "gained much in their intercourse with civilized men. They were no longer idolators—no longer naked savages." They should now take this knowledge with them "to the home of their race"—Africa—"where they could hold the position of superiors and teachers. . . . Such was the path [Hunt] would point out to them—the destiny he would aid them to accomplish."[11]

The 1846 debate also added new concerns that reflected themes common in the politics of the time: manifest destiny, fears of southern emancipation, and the role of immigrants. Delegate Russell argued that whites in particular had the right to decide who was worthy of full citizenship. Ignoring the labor of slaves in the South as well as free blacks in the North and Native Americans throughout the country, Russell based whites' superiority on their alleged taming of the country's natural resources, echoing many whites' beliefs in the themes of manifest destiny—that whites were destined, because of their racial and cultural superiority, to rule North America. "The white race, who have here subdued nature's savage wilderness to the use of civilized man, and to his civil power, have . . . the right to declare and fix the governing body, and to admit new members of it, on such conditions only, as they may deem safe and wise, for the good of all." Other classes whom government "necessarily denied" full political participation included "the white foreigner, of our own race and kindred," who could not vote until he had served a residency of five years in the state and sworn an oath of allegiance to the new country. If New York State offered equal voting rights to black men, racially inferior blacks would deluge the state: "the next ten years will bring thousands of them among us." "The people of St. Lawrence county" had no wish to share with black "co-partners" the "civil power of governing." These black men were "fresh from an inferior race of men, for ages debased by the chains of servitude." "The proposition that the intellectual power of the white race is vastly superior to that of the black, is a "fixed fact," Russell stated, "not the mere conclusion of prejudice." [12]

Finally, Russell raised the specter of amalgamation. He "hoped, that there was no class of men, in this body . . . who advocated negro suffrage for the intended object of degrading our white laboring classes, to the same servile condition of that class in other countries." Citing "Mexican and South American republics," Russell argued that racial mixture diluted not only the superior European intellect, but also "the savage['s] . . . own native excellence." "If Providence had intended such unions for good," Russell concluded, "the results now exhibited would have been far different." [13]

Delegates defending black equal suffrage spoke of the racism that had limited blacks' opportunities and of the potential for black advancement in the United States. Federal Dana of Madison County stated that "it was not surprising" that blacks were convicted of crimes in such high numbers; rather, "the wonder was that all the colored people were not degraded so low by the treatment they met with." Isaac Burr of Delaware County doubted that white poll inspectors could always tell who were black men and who were not. "If a full-blooded African should approach the poll . . . he would readily be known as a man of color, and his vote would be rejected. But suppose the next man who offered his vote should be a free native born black citizen, whose father was a white man and his mother a black woman . . . was he not entitled to vote? . . . Suppose [a fair-skinned black person] should offer his vote . . . how should the inspectors determine the question?" For Burr, such difficulties pointed to the limited utility of racial characteristics (which he defined as purely physical) as a determinant of the equality of blacks and whites. He doubted that "a distinct race . . . of Africans" existed in New York State and looked to a future without blacks: "There were individuals of pure African blood, but their number was constantly diminishing, and the process of amalgamation which was going on, in a few generations would whiten them out of existence." For Burr, this process demonstrated a form of black equality: the ability, through amalgamation, to remove any negative racial characteristics blacks might possess.[14]

The constitutional convention held four separate votes on the issue of black suffrage, but in the end retained the existing limitations. Blacks still had to own 250 dollars in property in order to vote in New York State. Only with the passage of the Fifteenth Amendment in 1869 would New York's blacks, along with the southern freedmen, gain equal suffrage.[15]

New York City's African Americans struggled to extend other rights through the courts, and sometimes won. But later rulings often limited or negated these important victories in the 1840s and 1850s. For years, black New Yorkers had fought for equal access to streetcars. Although the cars were "public" transportation, the private companies who operated the cars ruled that blacks could only ride on cars designated for them specifically. These regulations had led to skirmishes between blacks and white streetcar drivers and conductors from the 1830s. In 1854, following the violent ejection of Elizabeth Jennings and Sarah Adams from a Third Avenue Railway Company streetcar, black New Yorkers organized the Legal Rights Association to address this issue. Elizabeth Jennings, the daughter of New York black abolitionist Thomas Jennings, was an elementary school teacher and the organist for Charles B. Ray's First Colored American Congregational Church. One Sunday, she and Sarah Adams, late for church, boarded a streetcar. But the conductor told them to disembark and wait for a car with the sign "Colored People Allowed in This Car." Jennings began arguing with the conductor, explaining that she was late. Finally, the conductor allowed her to board, but stated that "if the passengers raise any objections you shall go out . . . or I'll put you out." Jennings, infuriated, stated, "I [am] a respectable person, born and raised in New-York. . . . [I do] not know where [you were] born. . . .[You are] a good for nothing impudent fellow for insulting decent persons while on their way to church." The conductor replied, "I was born in Ireland," "dragged" Sarah Adams off the car, and then, with the assistance of the driver, "took hold" of Jennings and "pulled and dragged [her] flat down on the bottom of the platform, so that [her] feet hung one way and [her] head the other, nearly on the ground." Jennings brought suit against the Third

Avenue Railway Company in the New York State Supreme Court and won. The judge in the case instructed the jury that the cars "were common carriers, and as such bound to carry all respectable persons; that colored persons, if sober, well-behaved, and free from disease, had the same rights as others; and could neither be excluded by any rules of the Company, nor by force or violence." The jury ordered the company to pay Jennings 225 dollars—less than half of the 500 dollars in damages she had requested. The judge increased the award by 10 percent and added to it Jennings's court costs.[16]

But this ruling did little to discourage other streetcar companies from segregating black passengers. In 1855, Reverend J. W. C. Pennington preached a sermon at Shiloh Presbyterian Church encouraging his parishioners to take full advantage of the ruling. But only a few weeks later a conductor ejected Pennington from a streetcar. He waited two years for his case, in which he claimed one thousand dollars in damages, to come to trial, only to have the jury rule in favor of the railway company after Judge John Slosson advised them that the company had the right to make whatever "reasonable rules" it wished. Not until 1860 did some railway companies begin to voluntarily admit blacks on streetcars equally with whites. But the fact that these actions were voluntary, rather than enforced by the courts or the legislature, meant that railway companies were under no obligation to continue these actions; indeed, the Sixth Avenue Railway Company, the company that Pennington sued, refused to integrate its cars.[17]

Most troubling to blacks were the series of court rulings and laws that limited the hard-won rights of accused fugitive slaves. As we have seen, in 1840, following a three-year petition campaign by black and white abolitionists, the New York State legislature passed a law that guaranteed the right of accused fugitives to jury trials. This law eliminated the power of individual proslavery judges and magistrates such as Richard Riker to rule on the free status of blacks. Additionally, accused fugitives would have the assistance of state defense attorneys, thus eliminating the need for fugitives to find and pay for private counsel. But only two years later, the United States Supreme Court ruled in *Prigg v. Pennsylvania* that individual states did not have the right to mandate jury trials in fugitive slave cases. To do so would negate the fugitive slave clause of the constitution, which required states to deliver fugitives from labor to their employers or owners. Although Massachusetts and Pennsylvania tried to work around the ruling, in New York the rise to power of the Democratic Party led the state government to retreat on the issue of protecting fugitive slaves. In 1843, Democratic state legislators, with the support of Governor William Bourck, introduced a bill to repeal the 1840 law. Although unable to pass the bill in the 1840s, the 1842 Prigg decision and the increasing power of the Democrats in state and city government had a chilling effect overall. With no clear directive from the legislature, state judges divided on whether their courts had the power to grant jury trials to fugitives.[18]

Ultimately, the United States Congress resolved the ambiguities stemming from the Prigg decision with the Fugitive Slave Law of 1850. The law established an efficient structure to facilitate the return of fugitive slaves southward, and specifically defined the responsibilities of citizens and local governments to return fugitives to their owners. The law increased the number of officials authorized to hear the claims of masters seeking runaway slaves. It also rewarded officials who judged that a black person was a runaway slave: such officials received a payment of ten dollars; an official who decided that a person was free received only five dollars. The law also removed the rights of fugitives to trial by jury and the right of accused blacks to testify on their own behalf, enacting the 1842 Supreme Court decision in *Prigg v. Pennsylvania.* Finally, the law empowered commissioners attempting to recapture a slave to summon the aid of bystanders and commanded "all good citizens . . . to aid and assist in the prompt and efficient execution of this law, whenever their services may be required." Those found guilty of obstructing the actions of the commissioners and their agents were fined one thousand dollars and given a six-month prison term.[19]

Blacks and their white abolitionist supporters moved into action against the Fugitive Slave Law. Through the beginning of the Civil War, they openly advocated resistance to the law, through force if necessary. Alongside the revitalized New York State Committee of Vigilance, New York City blacks formed a Committee of Thirteen, whose members included John J. Zuille, member and historian of the New York African Society for Mutual Relief; Philip Bell; James McCune Smith; and George Downing, among others. As had the New York Committee of Vigilance before it, the Committee of Thirteen organized mass meetings and raised funds to provide legal services to blacks accused of being fugitives. However, there was little the committee could do to guarantee the freedom of New York's blacks.

In contrast, New York City merchants mobilized in support of the law, which was only one element of the Compromise of 1850, an omnibus package of laws designed by Senator Henry Clay of Kentucky to prevent the southern states from seceding. The Compromise grew out of congressional debates over whether new territories in the west should allow slavery. Supporters of slavery argued for the right to take their slave property into new territories. Anti-slavery advocates argued that the expansion of slavery into the new lands would increase the power of the "slavocracy" in Congress and that competition from slave labor would limit the ability of white settlers in the west to achieve economic success. The Fugitive Slave Law was designed to appease southerners; for northerners, the slave trade (but not slavery) was abolished in the nation's capital. In addition, California was admitted as a free state, and the territories of New Mexico and Utah would decide through popular sovereignty whether to be free or slave.[20]

Although New York's merchants opposed the expansion of slavery, they feared southern secession more. In 1850 one hundred New York merchants formed the Union Safety Committee. Their goal was to create public support throughout the state on behalf of the 1850 Compromise, and in particular to create support for the Fugitive Slave Law. The committee sent letters to clergy, asking them to set aside a Sunday to preach acquiescence to the law, and raised thousands of dollars to support the publication of pro-Compromise pamphlets. In 1851, the Union Safety Committee put forward a state-wide Union slate of candidates for the state legislature elections, and all but one of its candidates won. The Union Safety Committee's support also contributed to the election of Franklin Pierce to the presidency the following year.[21]

A further insult to New York City's, and the nation's, blacks in the antebellum period was the 1857 U.S. Supreme Court ruling in *Dred Scott v. Sandford*. In 1846, Dred Scott and his wife Harriet filed suit in Missouri courts against Irene Emerson for their freedom. The Scotts' previous master and Irene's late husband, John Emerson, had held Dred, Harriet, and their two daughters in free territory for several years in the 1830s before returning with his wife and the Scott family to Missouri in 1838. Upon Emerson's death in 1843, Irene Emerson inherited his estate, with her brother John Sanford as executor. The Scotts argued that because they had lived in free territory with John Emerson, Irene Emerson no longer had the right to continue to own them. By the time the case reached the Supreme Court in 1857, Sanford (misspelled "Sandford" in the court documents) had been named the chief defendant in the Scotts' suit for freedom.[22]

The enslaved family's arguments for freedom raised a crucial and unresolved debate: Did the laws of one state nullify the laws of another? Did New York State have the license to remove the rights of a slave master over his property once that master took up residence in the state? Abolitionists argued yes. State governments, though, tried to maintain their good relations with economically important southern slaveholders by hedging the issue, providing short terms of residency during which southerners in free states retained ownership of the slaves they brought with them. Until 1841, a slave owner could reside in New York with his slaves for nine months without fear of government reprisal. But in 1841, the New York State legislature passed a law that any slaves brought by their slave owners to New York were automatically freed. Abolitionists rejoiced, but southerners seethed.[23]

The Supreme Court's decision in the Dred Scott case, authored by Chief Justice Roger Taney, gave southerners the victory. Slaves did not become free merely because their masters brought them to states or territories which had abolished or forbidden slavery. Slave owners' property rights in humans held across state lines. But Taney went further in his ruling. Born in Maryland to wealthy slave owners, Taney had long supported slavery and despised free blacks. As attorney general in Maryland in 1827, he had declared that "the African race in the United States even when free, are everywhere a degraded class. . . . The privileges they are allowed to enjoy, are accorded to them as a matter of kindness and benevolence rather than right. . . . They are not looked upon as citizens by the contracting parties who formed the [United States] Constitution." Thirty years later in the Dred Scott decision, Taney took the opportunity to make his beliefs about blacks the law of the land. At the time of the writing of the Constitution, he stated, blacks "had no rights a white man was bound to respect," and thus the Founding Fathers had never admitted blacks into citizenship. Dred Scott was not a citizen, and therefore had no right to even bring his case to trial. Nor did any other blacks have the right to bring their cases to court. The previous body of government mandates restricting the rights of fugitive slaves had implied that slaves were not citizens. But the Supreme Court's ruling revoked the citizenship of all blacks. [24]

African Americans were furious. In 1858, the Suffrage Convention of the Colored Citizens of New York State condemned the decision. Playing on Taney's wording, the conventioneers declared that the decision was a "foul and infamous lie, which neither black men nor white men are bound to respect. It is a bold, impudent and atrocious attempt to extend and perpetuate the blasting curse of human bondage." The convention declared the decision itself unconstitutional, "in striking contrast with the sacred guarantees for liberty with which the Constitution abounds." The Supreme Court's support of slavery through the decision endangered not only "the colored citizens of the Republic," but "the natural rights of all who form a part of the nation." Blacks and whites should "trample, in self-defence, the dicta of Judge Taney beneath their feet, as of no binding authority." [25]

But such resolutions did little good. Many New York City blacks between 1840 and 1860 felt that between economic pressures and political disfranchisement, they were fighting a losing battle for survival, much less equality. In these years of distress and discouragement, blacks began to leave New York City; for the first time since the Revolution, the black population there declined. Between 1840 and 1850, it fell by over 2,500, from 16,358 to 13,815. Five years after the passage of the Fugitive Slave Law in 1850, the black population had declined by another 15 percent, to approximately 11,740. The population rebounded slightly in 1860, to 12,472. But for a number of blacks, migration out of the city was the best option. Some blacks fled only as far as Brooklyn, where the black population during the same period grew from just under 1,800 to just over 2,400. Brooklyn was not as heavily involved with the slave trade as New York, and thus it was perhaps less likely that southerners seeking fugitives would search the community there. Other blacks moved to rural areas in upstate New York or the West during these years. A few believed that it was time again for blacks to consider migrating out of the country, to Europe, Africa, and Haiti.[26]

Black and white abolitionist-reformers organized a number of different schemes designed to draw blacks out of the city. Black reformers had encouraged blacks to leave the city since shortly after emancipation. Throughout the early 1830s Samuel Cornish had tried to convince blacks to return to the rural areas from which they had fled. On the eve of New York's emancipation, he feared for the ex-slaves who moved into the city and advised them to "turn their attention to agriculture, for most of them are acquainted with that business, they will be likely to succeed, and become useful citizens."[27] At the National Conventions of the Free People of Color of the 1830s and 1840s, black reformers continued to encourage blacks in cities to move to farms. At the 1843 national convention, the Committee on Agriculture stated that the only real wealth lay in the possession of land: "The soil alone possesses a real value—all other things have only a relative value: their value is to be computed from the amount of land they will purchase."[28] The black conventioneers saw land ownership and farming as a road to equality. A farmer is "upon the same level with his neighbors—their occupation is one, their hopes and interests are one; his neighbors see him now, not as in other situations they may have done as a servant; but an independent man; . . . they are not above him nor he above them; . . . and it is only by placing men in the same position in society, that all casts [sic] are lost sight of; all cast in his case, were he previously of a proscribed class, will fade away and be forgotten."[29] Thus, farming would erase the "badges of servitude" that blacks had acquired under slavery and that would continue to plague them if they remained in degraded occupations as free men.

In 1846, white abolitionist Gerrit Smith provided the land to implement black reformers' agrarian ideals. Smith had inherited from his father nearly

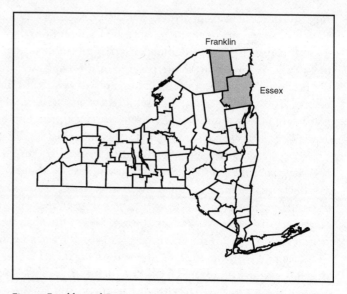

Fig. 25 Franklin and Essex Counties in New York State. Map by Sarah
Zingarelli.

one million acres of land, scattered in forty-three of the fifty-five counties in
New York State, although the bulk of the land was in the Adirondack region.
Smith had long wished to give away the land to the poor, but had not done
so previously because of the nearly 600,000 dollars in mortgages and taxes
he owed on the land. In August of 1846, with over three-fourths of the debt
paid off, Smith sent a letter to New York City black abolitionists Theodore S.
Wright, Charles B. Ray, and James McCune Smith to advise them of his plan
to donate land to black city-dwellers and to ask their help in its implementa-
tion. Over a three-year period, Gerrit Smith planned to make out three
thousand deeds of land, in lots of forty to sixty acres each, in Franklin and
Essex counties, in the Adirondacks (fig. 25). Smith designated the land for
poor blacks, whom he saw as "the poorest of the poor, and the most deeply
wronged class of our citizens." Smith, who called himself "an agrarian," saw
himself as providing black families with an alternative to city life. Wright,
Ray, and McCune Smith were to choose by lottery from among male heads
of household aged between twenty-one and sixty. Gerrit Smith, a temperance advocate, stated that "no drunkard" was allowed to apply for the land.
Out of the 1,985 names to be chosen in the first round of the lottery, 861
were to be chosen from New York City. Smith saw the land as a way to increase the number of black voters in the state, a consideration that "had no

little effect" in leading him to give his land to blacks. The increase in black voters, however small, could possibly aid in the success of the Liberty Party, in which he was also heavily involved during the years of the land project, 1846 through 1849.[30]

Smith's ideas about the land echoed some of the pronouncements of black reformers. He believed that the equal distribution of land would give free blacks economic equality, which would lead to social and political equality with their neighbors, whether black or white. Land and labor together would prove blacks' worth: "there is no life like that of the farmer, for overcoming the mere prejudice against color," Smith stated. "The owners of adjacent farms are *neighbours*. The condition, the position, the very accidents of their lives, compel them to be such."[31] Smith envisioned farming communities in which "mutual assistance, mutual and equal dependence, [and] mutual sympathy" would lead to cooperation among black and white laborers in pursuit of the common dream of economic independence.[32]

Gerrit Smith's land offered some blacks a way to achieve the goals of equality and stability. In 1848, sailor William Smith wrote to the managers of the Colored Orphan Asylum requesting they release his children Jane and Thomas to him. The children had been residents of the asylum since 1841. Smith's job as a sailor had enabled him to pay full board for his children, unlike many of the other parents. He even owned a piece of land in upper Manhattan in the area known as Harlaem. But the death of his wife and his life as a sailor had prevented him from giving his children a home of their own. When Gerrit Smith began offering plots of land to black men and their families, William Smith decided that this was his chance to provide his motherless children a permanent home. He moved to Franklin County to try his hand at farming.[33]

William Smith may have succeeded at farming, for he had previously lived in rural Upper Canada. Others were skeptical of the land offer. Anna Shotwell, founder of the Colored Orphan Asylum, wrote to Gerrit Smith for information about the land, hoping to enter into an agreement with Smith to give land to orphans upon completion of their indentures. But after several letters to Smith, Shotwell decided that the program was too risky because of the taxes that Smith still owed on the land, which the new owners had to pay. Of those who took the risk of settling on the land, few were able to take full advantage of it. Some were swindled out of their land by men posing as guides, who took them to the wrong lot and charged a fee for the "service." Others offered land recipients cash for their lots at far less than its worth. More simply, however, many of those who wished to farm the land

did not possess the skills to do so, or were unlucky. In such cases, families
were forced to return to the city. Shoemaker James Henderson, his wife,
Susan, and their six children attempted to make a living on Essex County
land they had received from Gerrit Smith. When James froze to death in the
forest in 1851, his widow and their six children returned to the city, where
she placed them in the Colored Orphan Asylum; she was not able to retrieve
them until six years later. Some tenants were also unfamiliar with the responsibilities of land ownership, particularly the payment of property taxes.
In 1853, a newspaper reported that hundreds of parcels of land given away
by Gerrit Smith had been advertised to be sold for taxes. Finally, the land in
Franklin and Essex Counties was of poor soil and unproductive for farming.
Although the land contained valuable timber, individual families would have
had difficulty harvesting the wood and taking it to market. Gerrit Smith's
idealism outstripped the practicalities of rural life. His project had mixed results at best.[34]

As Smith's land grant program failed, other blacks, most notably Henry
Highland Garnet and Alexander Crummell, revived emigration schemes to
independent black states in the West Indies and Africa. From 1854 to 1856,
Garnet was a missionary in Jamaica, a position that had grown out of his involvement in the Free Produce movement. Upon his return to New York
City in 1856, Garnet advocated emigration to the West Indies and Africa as
an extension of that movement: if blacks in those countries produced alter-
natives to slave-produced goods, they would contribute to the downfall of
the slave system, as well as provide income for themselves. To promote interest in emigration, Garnet founded the African Civilization Society in
1858.[35] Garnet's boyhood friend Alexander Crummell, after spending the
1840s as an active participant in the antislavery movement, moved to Liberia
as a missionary in 1853 and spent the next twenty years there before returning to the United States.[36] As had been true earlier in the century when
blacks ostracized John Russwurm for his support of Liberia, many blacks in
the 1850s viewed these emigrationists as threatening. A runaway slave who
signed himself "Carolina," aware that the population of New York City was
decreasing, spoke out strongly against "colored men" who encouraged colonization.[37] At public meetings on the issue through the early 1850s, blacks
again organized against colonization. But this time, they repudiated black
colonizationists as often as white.

The outbreak of the Civil War in 1861 temporarily halted the exodus out of
New York City as blacks, along with their antislavery supporters, saw in the

war an opportunity to attain their greatest hope—the freedom of southern slaves. Defining the war as one for freedom also gave New York City blacks reason to believe that the United States would soon grant them full citizenship status. Hoping to participate in the northern army, some black New Yorkers formed a military club and drilled until stopped by the police. From the earliest days of the war, blacks offered their services to the northern army, but the army rejected them until July 1862, when a bill written by Senator Preston King of New York passed Congress and was signed into law by President Lincoln. The law allowed the use of blacks in the "constructing of entrenchments, or performing camp service, or any war service for which they may be found competent." As during the Revolutionary War and the War of 1812, whites yet again restricted blacks to service occupations in the army, refusing to arm them until desperate for manpower.[38]

In September of 1862, President Abraham Lincoln announced the Emancipation Proclamation, which would take effect January 1, 1863, and free slaves in those states or regions still in rebellion against the Union. If any southern state returned to the Union between September and January, whites in that state theoretically would not lose ownership of their slaves. Despite its limits, free blacks, slaves, and abolitionists across the country hailed it as one of the most important actions on behalf of freedom in the nation's history. The Emancipation Proclamation brought formal recognition that the war was being fought, at least in part, on behalf of black freedom and equality.[39]

The enactment of the Emancipation Proclamation in January 1863 capped two years of increasing support for emancipation in New York City. Although Republicans attempted to keep abolitionists from taking a leading role in New York's antislavery politics during the early years of the war, by 1862 abolitionist speakers drew huge audiences, black and white, in the city.[40] Increasing support for the abolitionists and for emancipation led to anxiety among New York's white proslavery supporters of the Democratic Party, particularly the Irish. From the time of Lincoln's election in 1860, the Democratic Party had warned New York's Irish and German residents to prepare for the emancipation of slaves and the resultant labor competition when southern blacks would supposedly flee north. To these New Yorkers, the Emancipation Proclamation was confirmation of their worst fears. In March 1863, fuel was added to the fire in the form of a stricter federal draft law. All male citizens between twenty and thirty-five and all unmarried men between thirty-five and forty-five years of age were subject to military duty. The federal government entered all eligible men into a lottery. Those who could afford to hire a substitute or pay the government three hundred dollars might avoid enlistment. Blacks, who were not considered citizens, were exempt from the draft.[41]

In the month preceding the July 1863 lottery, in a pattern similar to the 1834 anti-abolition riots, antiwar newspaper editors published inflammatory attacks on the draft law aimed at inciting the white working class. They criticized the federal government's intrusion into local affairs on behalf of the "nigger war." Democratic Party leaders raised the specter of a New York deluged with southern blacks in the aftermath of the Emancipation Proclamation. White workers compared their value unfavorably to that of southern slaves, stating that "[we] are sold for $300 [the price of exemption from war service] whilst they pay $1000 for negroes." In the midst of war-time economic distress, they believed that their political leverage and economic status was rapidly declining as blacks appeared to be gaining power.[42] On Saturday, July 11, 1863, the first lottery of the conscription law was held. For twenty-four hours the city remained quiet. On Monday, July 13, 1863, between 6 and 7 A.M., the five days of mayhem and bloodshed that would be known as the Civil War Draft Riots began.[43]

The rioters' targets initially included only military and governmental buildings, symbols of the unfairness of the draft. Mobs attacked only those individuals who interfered with their actions. But by afternoon of the first day, some of the rioters had turned to attacks on black people, and on things symbolic of black political, economic, and social power (fig. 26).[44] Rioters attacked a black fruit vendor and a nine-year-old boy at the corner of Broadway and Chambers Street before moving to the Colored Orphan Asylum on Fifth Avenue between Forty-third and Forty-fourth Streets. By the spring of 1863, the managers had built a home large enough to house over two hundred children. Financially stable and well-stocked with food, clothing, and other provisions, the four-story orphanage was an imposing symbol of white charity toward blacks and black upward mobility. At 4 P.M. on July 13, "the children numbering 233, were quietly seated in their school rooms, playing in the nursery, or reclining on a sick bed in the Hospital when an infuriated mob, consisting of several thousand men, women and children, armed with clubs, brick bats etc. advanced upon the Institution." The crowd took as much of the bedding, clothing, food, and other transportable articles as they could and set fire to the building (fig. 27). John Decker, chief engineer of the fire department, was on hand, but firefighters were unable to save the building. The destruction took twenty minutes.[45]

In the meantime, the superintendent and matron of the asylum assembled the children and led them out to Forty-fourth Street. Miraculously,

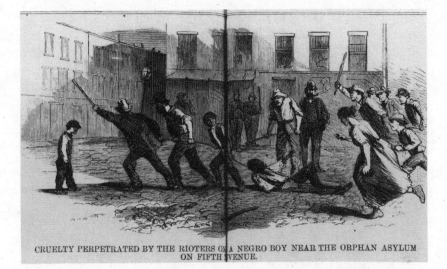

CRUELTY PERPETRATED BY THE RIOTERS ON A NEGRO BOY NEAR THE ORPHAN ASYLUM ON FIFTH AVENUE.

Fig. 26 One of the many scenes from the riot that appeared in New York City newspapers. From *New York Illustrated News*, August 8, 1863, 232–233 (detail). Neg. no. 43200. © Collection of the New-York Historical Society.

the mob refrained from assaulting the children. But when an Irish observer of the scene called out, "If there is a man among you, with a heart within him come and help these poor children," the mob "laid hold of him, and appeared ready to tear him to pieces." The children made their way to the Thirty-fifth Street Police Station, where they remained for three days and nights before moving to the almshouse on Blackwell's Island—ironically, the very place from which the orphanage's founders had hoped to keep black children when they built the asylum almost thirty years earlier.[46]

The Irish man who castigated the mob for not helping the black children was not the only white person punished by rioters for seeming overly sympathetic to blacks. Throughout the week of riots, mobs harassed and sometimes killed blacks and their supporters and destroyed their property. Rioters burned the home of Abby Hopper Gibbons, prison reformer and daughter of abolitionist Isaac Hopper. They also attacked white "amalgamationists," such as Ann Derrickson and Ann Martin, two women who were married to black men; and Mary Burke, a white prostitute who catered to black men. Near the docks, tensions that had been brewing since the mid-1850s between white longshoremen and black workers boiled over. As recently as March of 1863, white employers had hired blacks as longshoremen, with whom Irish men refused to work. An Irish mob then attacked two

The Fire of 1863—from an old etching.

THE MOST DRAMATIC INCIDENT
IN THE HISTORY OF THE
COLORED ORPHAN
ASYLUM

IN the draft riots of July, 1863, a
maddened mob of men and women
stormed the Asylum on Fifth Avenue.
Almost by a miracle the 233 children
were saved, but the buildings were
utterly destroyed.

*Tablet at the left perpetuates the memories of the heroic firemen who
risked their lives in an attempt to save the buildings and of the brave
child who dared the flames to rescue the Asylum Bible.*

Fig. 27 This drawing of the Colored Orphan Asylum in flames was reprinted in the
orphanage's anniversary booklet, over seventy years after the destruction. Neg. no. 74634.
© Collection of the New-York Historical Society.

Fig. 28 Rioters tortured black men, women, and children. Neg. no. 40828. © Collection of the New-York Historical Society.

hundred blacks who were working on the docks, while other rioters went into the streets in search of "all the negro porters, cartmen and laborers . . . they could find." They were routed by the police. But in July 1863, white longshoremen took advantage of the chaos of the Draft Riots to attempt to remove all evidence of a black and interracial social life from the area near the docks. White dockworkers attacked and destroyed brothels, dance halls, boarding houses, and tenements that catered to blacks; mobs stripped the clothing off the white owners of these businesses.[47]

Black men and black women were attacked, but the rioters singled out the men for special violence (figs. 28 and 29). On the waterfront, they hanged William Jones and then burned his body. White dock workers also beat and nearly drowned Charles Jackson, and they beat Jeremiah Robinson to death and threw his body in the river. Rioters also made a sport of mutilating black men's bodies, sometimes sexually. A group of white men and boys mortally attacked black sailor William Williams—jumping on his chest, plunging a knife into him, smashing his body with stones—while

BRUTAL MURDER OF A NEGRO MAN IN CLARKSON STREET BY THE RIOTERS, WHO STRIPPED OFF HIS CLOTHES AND HUNG HIM TO A TREE, AFTERWARDS BURNING THE BODY, ON MONDAY, JULY 13.

Fig. 29 Rioters subjected black men to the most brutal violence: torture, hanging, and burning (detail). Neg. no. 48125. © Collection of the New-York Historical Society.

a crowd of men, women, and children watched. None intervened, and when the mob was done with Williams, they cheered, pledging "vengeance on every nigger in New York." A white laborer, George Glass, rousted black coachman Abraham Franklin from his apartment and dragged him through the streets. A crowd gathered and hanged Franklin from a lamppost as they cheered for Jefferson Davis, the Confederate president. After the mob pulled Franklin's body from the lamppost, a sixteen-year-old Irish man, Patrick Butler, dragged the body through the streets by its genitals. Black men who tried to defend themselves fared no better. The crowds were pitiless. After James Costello shot at and fled from a white attacker, six white men beat, stomped, kicked, and stoned him before hanging him from a lamppost.[48]

With these actions white workers enacted their desires to eradicate the working-class black male presence from the city. The Longshoreman's Association, a white labor union, patrolled the piers during the riots, insisting that "the colored people must and shall be driven to other parts of industry." But "other parts of industry," such as cartmen and hack drivers, not to mention skilled artisans, also sought to exclude black workers. The riots gave all these workers license to physically remove blacks not only from worksites, but also from neighborhoods and leisure spaces. The rioters' actions also indicate the degree to which the sensational journalists and reformers of the 1840s and 1850s had achieved their goals of convincing whites, and particularly the Irish, that interracial socializing and marriage were evil and degrading practices. The riots unequivocally divided white workers from blacks. The act of rioting may itself have released guilt and shame over former interracial pleasures. Finally, and most simply, white workers asserted their superiority over blacks through the riots. The Civil War and the rise of the Republican Party and Lincoln to power indicated to New York's largely Democratic white workers a reversal of power in the nation; black labor competition indicated a reversal of fortunes in New York City itself. White workers sought to remedy their upside-down world through mob violence.[49]

Ironically, the most well known center of black and interracial social life, the Five Points, was relatively quiet during the riots. Mobs neither attacked the brothels there nor killed black people within its borders. There were also instances of interracial cooperation. When a mob threatened black drugstore owner Philip White in his store at the corner of Gold and Frankfurt Streets, his Irish neighbors drove the mob away, for he had often extended them credit. And when rioters invaded Hart's Alley and became trapped at its dead end, the black and white residents of the alley together leaned out of their windows and poured hot starch on them, driving them from the neighborhood.[50] But such incidents were few compared to the widespread hatred of blacks expressed during and after the riots.

In all, rioters lynched eleven black men over the five days of mayhem.[51] The riots forced hundreds of blacks out of the city. As historian Iver Bernstein states, "For months after the riots the public life of the city became a more noticeably white domain." During the riots, landlords drove blacks from their residences, fearing the destruction of their property. After the riots, when the Colored Orphan Asylum attempted to rebuild on the site of its old building, neighboring property owners asked them to leave. The orphanage relocated to 51st Street for four years before moving into a new residence at 143rd Street between Amsterdam and Broadway, in the midst of what would become New York's predominantly black neighborhood in the twentieth century, Harlem. But in 1867, the area was barely settled and far removed from the center of New York City.[52] Black families also fled the city altogether. Albro Lyons, keeper of the Colored Sailors' Home, was able to protect the boardinghouse on the first day of the riots, but soon fled to the neighborhood police station to seek an escort from the city for his wife and family. An officer accompanied the Lyons family to the Sailors' Home, where they gathered up what belongings they could carry before boarding the Roosevelt Street ferry, which took them to Williamsburg in Brooklyn. "From the moment they put foot on the boat, that was the last time they ever resided in New York City, leaving it forever." Other blacks fled to New Jersey and beyond. By 1865, the black population had plummeted to just under ten thousand, its lowest since 1820.[53]

Those blacks who remained in the city found a somewhat chastened elite eager to help New York's black residents recover in the aftermath of the riots. The seven-month-old Union League Club (which had as one of its main tenets black uplift) and the Committee of Merchants for the Relief of Colored People spearheaded relief efforts to blacks, providing forty thousand dollars to almost twenty-five hundred riot victims and finding new jobs and homes for blacks. Just under a year later, Republican elites and New York City blacks publicly celebrated their renewed alliance. In December of 1863, the secretary of war gave the Union League Club permission to raise a black regiment. The Union League Club decided to march the regiment of over one thousand black men through the streets of New York to the Hudson River, where the ship that would take them south waited. On March 5, 1864, before a crowd of one hundred thousand black and white New Yorkers, the black regiment processed, making "a fine appearance in their blue uniform, white gloves and white leggings." They were preceded by the police superintendent, one hundred policemen, the Union League Club itself, "colored friends of the recruits," and a band (fig. 30). In a powerful display, the parade publicly linked blacks with the leaders of the new order being ushered in by the Civil War.[54]

But the event could not completely erase the racial concerns that had been part of the Draft Riots, if indeed its organizers sought to. One account said of the soldiers, "a majority of them are black; indeed there are but few mulattoes among them," an attempt to downplay the obvious fears of racial mixing that white workers displayed before and during the riots, fears which many white elites may have shared. Observers also used the event to contrast the loyalty of blacks to the Union and their good behavior with the recent rioting as well as the general culture of white workers: "The 20th is emphatically an African regiment, and to its credit be it spoken, not one of its members disobeyed orders, no one broke ranks to greet enthusiastic friends, no one used intoxicating drinks to excess, no one manifested the least incli-

Fig. 30 This drawing captures the joy and pride of many black New Yorkers as the Twentieth U.S. Colored Infantry received its colors. Neg. no. 52715. © Collection of the New-York Historical Society.

nation to leave the service, and their marching was very creditable."[55] The New York elite presented the black troops as symbols of the new orderly working class they desired: sober, solemn, obedient, and dedicated to the Union cause.[56] But such simple symbolism obscured the complex divisions of status, class, outlook and aspiration that had been part of New York's free black community from its inception.

As the Union Army marched south, it brought with it black and white abolitionists (many affiliated with the American Missionary Association, others independent of organized efforts) who sought to reform southern blacks during and after the war. These largely middle-class activists carried ideas of racial uplift first promulgated in the northeast, from creating manual labor schools to moral reform to enhancing wage labor. They encountered newly free blacks eager for educational and economic betterment, but just as certainly shaping their own definitions of independence and equality. During the Civil War and Reconstruction years, black and white people from urban and rural areas in the north and south were challenged to create new opportunities for the freed people. But New York City had never unified to overcome the problems of racism and fully embrace black freedom; neither would the nation.[57]

Over two and a half centuries New York's African and African American inhabitants forged new lives in a city that was seldom entirely hospitable but which offered the prospect of survival and collective existence. From the earliest days of Dutch colonialism to the extraordinary violence of the Civil War Draft Riots, black New Yorkers fought for the right to live, work, and gather together. They struggled for their own safety and freedom even as they attempted to define the very meaning of African American and American identity.

The history of these years followed no pre-ordained pattern. Rather, black and white New Yorkers' participation in these events speaks to a never-ending process of change and conflict, of contestation for power and influence over the resources and life of the city. Black men, women, and children comprised an integral part of New York City's economic, political, social, and cultural life. Black New Yorkers built the city, sustained its daily existence, and gave their lives—willingly or not—for its continued prosperity. Subject to physical, cultural, and spiritual violence, black New Yorkers manifested an audacious capacity to survive, to resist repression, and to sustain a diverse community.

As I was completing the revisions of this manuscript, two hijacked jetliners flew into the World Trade Center. Again the southern tip of Manhattan became an emblem of the extreme violence possible when entangled racial, cultural, and economic relationships render extreme inequality—in this case, on an international scale.

In the wake of the terrorism of September 11, 2001, Americans continue to struggle with the desire for a quick fix to problems that have evolved over centuries. The experiences of men and women of African descent in New York City demonstrate as effectively as any the slow pace of historical change. The various coalitions that worked toward greater racial equality in pre–Civil War New York City provide an example of vision and commitment—and then revision and recommitment—and ultimately, a model of endurance, which we forget at our peril.

A few weeks after the World Trade Center's destruction, a colleague informed me that one of the casualties was the African Burial Ground Project office. Initially crestfallen at the second loss of so much valuable historical material, I remembered that history is only lost when we choose to forget. As lower Manhattan is rebuilt, it is up to those who remain to insist that neither the events of 2001, nor those of four hundred years past, are paved over.

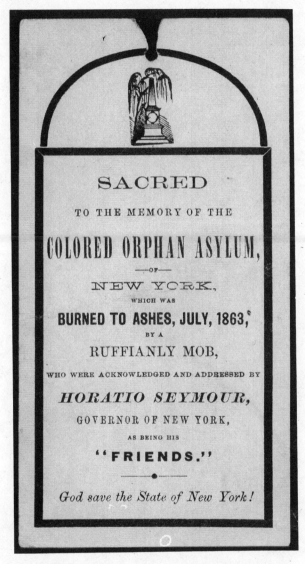

Fig. 31 Card memorializing the Colored Orphan Asylum.
Neg. no. 74636. © Collection of the New-York Historical Society.

INTRODUCTION

1. There is an extensive newspaper discussion of the events surrounding the discovery of the cemetery and subsequent debates about it: "Dig Unearths Early Black Burial Ground," *New York Times*, October 9, 1991; "Black Cemetery Hints at Colonial Past of New York," *New York Times*, October 11, 1991; "Retrieving Old New York," *Washington Post*, December 25, 1991; "Unfree, Unknown," *New York Times*, December 26, 1991; "Black Cemetery Yields Wealth of History," *New York Times*, August 9, 1992; and "Grave Injustice," *San Diego Union-Tribune*, September 15, 1999. See also Hansen and McGowan, *Breaking Ground*; La Roche and Blakey, "Seizing Intellectual Power," 84–106; and La Roche, "Beads from the African Burial Ground," 3–30. On the heart-shaped symbol as a *sankofa*, see "Grave Injustice"; and "Bones of Forebears," *Washington Post*, August 3, 1995; as an *akoma*, see Hansen and McGowan, *Breaking Ground*, 55–56.

2. On the disruption of the burial sites and academic and community involvement, see La Roche and Blakey, "Seizing Intellectual Power"; "Mistake Disturbs Graves at Black Burial Ground," *New York Times*, February 21, 1992; "Dinkins Seeks to Halt Work at Site of Black Cemetery," *New York Times*, July 21, 1992; "Unlikely Hero for Cemetery," *New York Times*, August 9, 1992; "Bad Blood at the Burial Ground," *New York Times*, September 12, 1992; "Activists Wage Campaign to Save Burial Ground," *Los Angeles Times*, September 12, 1992; "Black Cemetery in NYC New Key to Colonial Times," *USA Today*, September 15, 1992; "Con Edison Crew Unearths Bones Near Early Black Graveyard," *New York Times*, February 14, 1993; "African Burial Ground Made Historic Site," *New York Times*, February 26, 1993; and "A Black Cemetery Takes Its Place in History," *New York Times*, February 28, 1993. Melish describes the ways the history of slavery was covered over and forgotten in New England in *Disowning Slavery*.

3. See Roediger, *Wages of Whiteness*; and Lott, *Love and Theft*, for explications of the importance of blacks to white working-class identity. Scholars are beginning to

fill the puzzling lacunae concerning early black life in New York City. Important books and dissertations on blacks in New York City include Graham Hodges, *Root and Branch;* White, *Somewhat More Independent;* Thomas Davis, *Rumor of Revolt;* McManus, *Negro Slavery in New York;* Johnson, *Black Manhattan;* Ottley and Weatherby, *The Negro in New York;* George Walker, *The Afro-American in New York City;* Freeman, *The Free Negro in New York City;* Kruger, "Born to Run"; Foote, "Black Life"; Gellman, "Inescapable Discourse"; Alexander, "'Onward Forever'"; and Dabel, "From Her Own Labor."

4. Recent works focusing on the interaction between race and class include Roediger, *Wages of Whiteness;* Saxton, *Rise and Fall of the White Republic;* and Lott, *Love and Theft.* These works, however, examine whites' definitions of class and race in the nineteenth century.

5. See Gutman, "Work, Culture, and Society in Industrializing America, 1815–1919," in *Work, Culture, and Society,* 3–78.

6. In his seminal essay, Gutman states that "bound workers [and] nonwhite free laborers, mostly blacks and Asian immigrants and their descendants . . . were affected by the tensions" that he describes as central to working-class formation in the United States, "a fact that emphasizes the central place they deserve in any comprehensive study of American work habits and changing American working-class behavior." Ibid., 12–13. Despite his own extensive research in the history of slavery, Gutman omitted these workers from his analysis in "Work, Culture, and Society in Industrializing America, 1815–1919." Unfortunately, many subsequent labor historians, excepting those historians specifically committed to excavating the history of racial minorities in the United States, have followed his practice rather than his theory. For an assessment of Gutman's research on black workers, race, and class in the twentieth century, see Hill, "Myth-Making as Labor History" and the associated roundtable responses, 132–200, 361–595.

7. Wilentz, *Chants Democratic;* and Stansell, *City of Women.* Wilentz and Stansell are not alone in their omissions. The literature on New York's working class is voluminous, and in it very little attention is paid to black workers. Works which begin to address these issues in New York are White, *Somewhat More Independent,* and Roediger, *Wages of Whiteness.*

8. See, for example, Wesley, *Negro Labor;* Woodson and Greene, *The Negro Wage Earner;* Spero and Harris, *The Black Worker;* W. E. B. Du Bois, *The Negro Artisan;* and W.E.B. Du Bois, *Black Reconstruction.*

9. Litwack, *North of Slavery;* Horton and Horton, *Black Bostonians;* Nash, *Forging Freedom;* Winch, *Philadelphia's Black Elite.* An important synthesis of this literature is Horton and Horton, *In Hope of Liberty.* Foner's *Organized Labor and the Black Worker, 1619–1981* keeps class concerns present but, because Foner's focus is on formal labor organizations, spends little time on antebellum black workers. But see his collection of primary documents on antebellum black labor: Philip Foner and Ronald Lewis, *The Black Worker to 1869.*

10. In contrast, historians of the post–Civil War black experience have begun a rich discussion of the interplay between racial identity, racism, and class and gender identities. See, for example, Earl Lewis, *Race, Class, and Power;* Trotter, *Black Milwaukee;* Hunter, *To 'Joy My Freedom;* Arnesen, *Workers on the Waterfront in New*

Orleans; and Kelley, *Hammer and Hoe;* Gaines, *Uplifting the Race;* Shaw, *What a Woman Ought to Be and to Do.*

11. See Roediger, "'Neither a Servant nor a Master Am I': Keywords in the Languages of White Labor Republicanism," in Roediger, *Wages of Whiteness,* 43–64.

12. Figures are from Curry, *Free Black in Urban America,* appendix A, table A-7, p. 250; and Ernst, *Immigrant Life in New York City,* table 17, pp. 198–199.

CHAPTER ONE

1. On comparisons between New York and southern slavery, see Berlin, *Many Thousands Gone,* 50–51. For explicit arguments on the reliance of southern colonists on slave labor and on African knowledge, see Morgan, "Idle Indian and Lazy Englishman," in *American Slavery, American Freedom;* and Peter Wood, "Black Labor— White Race" and "Black Pioneers," in *Black Majority.* See also Berlin, *Many Thousands Gone,* passim. For the reliance of New England on the slave trade, see David Richardson, "Slavery, Trade, and Economic Growth," 237–264.

2. On class divisions in colonial America, see Innes, *Labor in a New Land;* and Schultz, "A Class Society?" 203–221. On class, race, and slavery, see Berlin, "Making Slavery, Making Race," in *Many Thousands Gone,* 1–14 (quotation on page 5); and Fields, "Slavery, Race, and Ideology," 95–118.

3. Graham Hodges has recentered the history of blacks in colonial New Amsterdam and New York with his work *Root and Branch.* On Jan Rodrigues, see pages 6–7. See also Burrows and Wallace, *Gotham,* 19.

4. McManus, *Negro Slavery in New York,* 3–4; Rink, *Holland on the Hudson,* 79–81.

5. It remains unclear what Minuit purchased from whom. For traditional accounts of the purchase of Manhattan that emphasize that Manhattan was the "best buy in the world," bought from Native Americans for a "trifle" of sixty guilders, or in "beads and trinkets," see Van Der Zee and Van Der Zee, *Sweet and Alien Land,* 1–2; and Rink, *Holland on the Hudson,* 86–87. For a discussion of the ways the mythical aspects of the purchase have developed, see Burrows and Wallace, *Gotham,* xi–xvi, 23–24.

6. Rink, *Holland on the Hudson,* 155; quotation in Graham Hodges, *Root and Branch,* 31–32; Burrows and Wallace, *Gotham,* 31.

7. Rink, *Holland on the Hudson,* 69–138; Goodfriend, *Before the Melting Pot,* 13; Burrows and Wallace, *Gotham,* 30.

8. Rink, *Holland on the Hudson,* 85–86; Goodfriend, "Burghers and Blacks," 129–130; Van der Zee and Van der Zee, *Sweet and Alien Land,* 13; Foote, "Black Life," 9–10.

9. Goodfriend, "Burghers and Blacks," 127–129; Foote, "Black Life," 6–8.

10. McManus, *Negro Slavery in New York,* 5–8. On the importance of New Amsterdam as a slave port, see Graham Hodges, *Root and Branch,* 29; and Burrows and Wallace, *Gotham,* 48–49. On the changing nature of New Amsterdam's population, see Burrows and Wallace, *Gotham,* 48–55. The description of *Witte Paert* is from Rink, *Holland on the Hudson,* 163; and Burrows and Wallace, *Gotham,* 49.

11. On the growth of laws regulating slavery in the colonial period, see A. Leon Higginbotham, *In the Matter of Color,* esp. 19–20; and Jordan, *White over Black,* 44–98. On class, race, and slavery, see Berlin, *Many Thousands Gone,* 5; Fields, "Slavery, Race and Ideology," 95–118. Details of the legal rights of New Netherland's slaves are from Christoph, "Freedmen of New Amsterdam," 157; Graham Hodges, *Root and Branch,* 10–12.

12. On indentured servants' relationships with slaves in Virginia, see Morgan, *American Slavery, American Freedom,* 327–328, 330–333; A. Leon Higginbotham, *In the Matter of Color,* 26–30; in South Carolina, see Peter Wood, *Black Majority,* 53–55.

13. McManus, *Negro Slavery in New York,* 10. On the limited opportunities available to free workers, see Burrows and Wallace, *Gotham,* 31. On the 1628 agreement, see Foote, "Black Life," 9. On the 1657 agreement and Stuyvesant quote, see Goodfriend, "Burghers and Blacks," 131.

14. On Christian debates in Europe and Africa over enslaving Christians and converts, see David Brion Davis, *Problem of Slavery in Western Culture.* On debates among British Christians in America later in the seventeenth century, and the "vague but persistent notion that no Christian might lawfully hold another Christian as a slave," see Jordan, *White over Black,* 181–187.

15. The best discussion of the conflict within the Dutch Reformed Church over enslaving converts is Graham Hodges, *Root and Branch,* 18–25, Selyns quoted on 23. See also DeJong, "Dutch Reformed Church and Negro Slavery," 423–436, esp. 424–426, 428–430; Christoph, "Freedmen of New Amsterdam," 160; and Goodfriend, "Black Families," 149.

16. McManus, *Negro Slavery in New York,* 18–19.

17. Berlin, *Many Thousands Gone,* 17–28. Law and Mann argue that Berlin exaggerates the extent of creolization that occurred in the seventeenth century in West Africa. For their critique, see Law and Mann, "West Africa in the Atlantic Community," esp. 308–310. The experiences of these eleven slaves, however, appear to fit the description of Atlantic Creoles Berlin puts forward.

18. For the names of the first eleven slaves, see Christoph, "Freedmen of New Amsterdam," 158; and Foote, "Black Life," 12. For Europeans' assumptions about Angolan and Congolese slaves, see Gomez, *Exchanging Our Country Marks,* 136–137. For the complex relationship between European and African Christianity, see John Thornton, *Africa and Africans,* 235–271.

19. Foote, "Black Life," 5–6; Graham Hodges, *Root and Branch,* 7–9. On Portuguese-Dutch relations, see Goodfriend, "Burghers and Blacks," 134; and Berlin, *Many Thousands Gone,* 19. The slave trade from Angola and Congo was controlled by the Portuguese from 1482 until 1637, when it was captured by the Dutch. The Dutch captured Brazil in the 1630s, but the Portuguese regained the colony in 1654. The Dutch gained the island of Curaçao from the Spanish in the 1650s.

20. Christoph states that de Reus was a form of de Reux, the name of the owner of Manuel de Reus, in "Freedmen of New Amsterdam," 167n. On the other names, see Christoph, "Freedmen of New Amsterdam," 158; Foote, "Black Life," 12. On Jan from Fort Orange, see Sullivan, *Punishment of Crime,* 71, 271–272n.

21. Berlin, *Many Thousands Gone*, 17–28, 50; John Thornton, *Africa and Africans*, 253–271; Graham Hodges, *Root and Branch*, 8–9.

22. McManus, *Negro Slavery in New York*, 17; Christianson, "Criminal Punishment in New Netherland," 87; Sullivan, *Punishment of Crime*, 71, 271–272n.

23. See Berlin, *Many Thousands Gone*, 51–52; Graham Hodges, *Root and Branch*, 10.

24. Graham Hodges, *Root and Branch*, 9–12; Christoph, "Freedmen of New Amsterdam," 157.

25. Foote, "Black Life," 6; Christianson, "Criminal Punishment in New Netherland," 87. The sex ratio is from Kruger, "Born to Run," 43; The Stuyvesant quote is from Goodfriend, "Black Families," 148.

26. Stuyvesant quoted in Goodfriend, "Black Families," 149; numbers of slave marriages and baptisms, 149, 151.

27. Foote, "Black Life," 6; Christianson, "Criminal Punishment in New Netherland," 87; Goodfriend, "Black Families," 148–149; Swan, "The Other Fort Amsterdam," 27; Graham Hodges, *Root and Branch*, 29–31; Berlin, *Many Thousands Gone*, 51.

28. Goodfriend, "Black Families," 152.

29. For the 1649 incident, see DeJong, "Dutch Reformed Church and Negro Slavery," 430–431. On fears that conversion would result in freedom and on ending baptism, see Graham Hodges, *Root and Branch*, 22–23; Christoph, "Freedmen of New Amsterdam," 160, Goodfriend, "Black Families," 152, and DeJong, "Dutch Reformed Church and Negro Slavery," 430–431.

30. On the opportunism of Atlantic Creoles in New Netherland, see Berlin, *Many Thousands Gone*, 49–52; on rights of slaves in Angola, see Graham Hodges, *Root and Branch*, 10.

31. For details of half-freedom, see McManus, *Negro Slavery in New York*, 13–15; Christoph, "Freedmen of New Amsterdam," 158–159; Thomas Davis, "Slavery in Colonial New York City," 54–56; Berlin, *Many Thousands Gone*, 52–53; Foote, "Black Life," 12–13; Goodfriend, *Before the Melting Pot*, 116; and Graham Hodges, *Root and Branch*, 12–13. The quotations are from Kruger, "Born to Run," 48; and Christoph, "Freedmen of New Amsterdam," 158, respectively.

32. McManus, *Negro Slavery in New York*, 13–14; Berlin, *Many Thousands Gone*, 52; Foote, "Black Life," 13.

33. The quotation is from Christoph, "Freedmen of New Amsterdam," 159, 165; and Graham Hodges, *Root and Branch*, 13–15. On later incarnations of this area, see [Stokes], "New York City Slums," Notes 1:3; and [The Five Points Mission], *The Old Brewery*, 16.

34. Kruger, "Born to Run," 48.

35. Christoph, "Freedmen of New Amsterdam," 167–168n.

36. Goodfriend, "Black Families," 151–152; petition of Emmanuel Pietersen quoted on 152. See also Kruger, "Born to Run," 50–51, for details of this case and two others involving orphaned slave children.

37. Goodfriend, "Black Families," 152.

38. For details of the British turnover, see Kammen, *Colonial New York,* 71–72. On full emancipation, see Foote, "Black Life," 13–14; McManus, *Negro Slavery in New York,* 13–15; Thomas Davis, "Slavery in Colonial New York City," 55–56; and Goodfriend, *Before the Melting Pot,* 116.

39. McManus, *Negro Slavery in New York,* 23, 34–35.

40. Kammen, *Colonial New York,* 179; McManus, *Negro Slavery in New York,* 41–43.

41. On the creation of slave laws in Virginia and other colonies, see A. Leon Higginbotham, *In the Matter of Color,* 32–40 and passim; and Berlin, *Many Thousands Gone,* 9 and passim. On the racial ideologies of the British, see Jordan, *White over Black,* esp. 3–43, 91–98, 179–265.

42. Foote, "Black Life," 128–131; Thomas Davis, "Slavery in Colonial New York City," 72–80; Graham Hodges, *Root and Branch,* 36–38. On parallel trends in other colonies, see A. Leon Higginbotham, *In the Matter of Color.*

43. Foote, "Black Life," 28–29, 25–26.

44. McManus, *Negro Slavery in New York,* 25–27. On Adolph Philipse and the responsibilities of tenants, see Kammen, *Colonial New York,* 174, 301–302.

45. For slave populations, see Berlin, *Many Thousands Gone,* table 1, pp. 369–370.

46. Foote has illuminated the vagaries of the slave trade in early eighteenth-century New York; see "Black Life," 30–46. See also McManus, *Negro Slavery in New York,* 25–29, 197.

47. Berlin, *Many Thousands Gone,* table 1, pp. 369–370; Foote, "Black Life," 54–58.

48. Berlin, *Many Thousands Gone,* 54, 183.

49. Kruger, "Born to Run," 79–82; Foote, "Black Life," 31–32, 58; Graham Hodges, *Root and Branch,* 38.

50. Kruger, "Born to Run," 78–79; Foote, "Black Life," 32–37; Graham Hodges, *Root and Branch,* 38–40.

51. McManus, *Negro Slavery in New York,* 87–89; Foote, "Black Life," 214–215.

52. Foote, "Black Life," 91–117; Graham Hodges, *Root and Branch,* 40–41.

53. McManus, *Negro Slavery in New York,* 47; Goodfriend, *Before the Melting Pot,* 118–121; White, *Somewhat More Independent,* 10–13; 36–37. On women's work in artisan households, see Boydston, *Home and Work,* 14–15, 37–38. For listings of the various skilled jobs held by whites between 1694 and 1706, see Thomas Davis, "Slavery in Colonial New York City," 64–66. For slaves' work on farms, see Graham Hodges, *Root and Branch,* 82–83.

54. Foote, "Black Life," 97–98; Graham Hodges, *Root and Branch,* 41–42, 83, 107–110.

55. Details of the porters' petition and the quotation are from McManus, *Negro Slavery in New York,* 48.

56. Details of the coopers' petition and the quotation are from McManus, *Negro Slavery in New York,* 48–49; Graham Hodges, *Root and Branch,* 108. On cartmen, see Hodges, *Root and Branch,* 43.

57. Samuel McKee, *Labor in Colonial New York*, 90–95; quotations on 91n, 94; Goodfriend, *Beyond the Melting Pot*, 55, 118, 134–135.

58. On the distribution of slaves in New York City, Foote, "Black Life," 77–86; quotations from slave masters in McManus, *Negro Slavery in New York*, 45. Eighteenth-century southern slave owners were more encouraging of slave families than Manhattan's masters, but less so than their nineteenth-century counterparts. Manhattan slave owners' attitudes were similar to those of slave masters throughout the northeast during the eighteenth century. See Berlin, *Many Thousands Gone*, 128–33, 185–86.

59. McKee, *Labor in Colonial New York*, 142–144; McManus, *Negro Slavery in New York*, 80–83; Thomas Davis, "Slavery in Colonial New York City," 84–88.

60. Roediger, *Wages of Whiteness*, esp. 19–40.

61. For the increased reliance on slave labor at the expense of European servants in North America, see Berlin, *Many Thousands Gone*, 82, 109, 110, 113–114, 181–182, 184; and Morgan, "Towards Slavery," in *American Slavery, American Freedom*, esp. pp. 299–300. The exception that proves the rule in the southern colonies is Georgia, which limited slave importations almost until the Revolutionary War in favor of European immigrants.

62. On 1712 laws, see Graham Hodges, *Root and Branch*, 67–68.

63. Graham Hodges's account of the relationship among the SPG, slaves, and slave masters is the fullest to date. See *Root and Branch*, 53–63; on female students, 85.

64. On Neau and the reluctance of slave masters to convert their slaves, see Foote, "Black Life," 170–172, 179–186; on whites' lack of religiosity, 162–164.

65. Graham Hodges has done the best work on the roles of the various churches in New York City among blacks; see *Root and Branch*, 53–63, 84–88. For numbers of slaves baptized, see Foote, "Black Life," 179–187.

66. Graham Hodges, *Root and Branch*, 53–63; Foote, "Black Life," 179–187.

67. Foote, "Black Life," 45.

68. Kruger, "Born to Run," 87–88; Foote, "Black Life," 188, 191–194.

69. On African names in use in New York, see Kruger, "Born to Run," 88–89. On "Sambo," see Peter Wood, *Black Majority*, 185; on "Quaco," 182.

70. See Thomas Davis, "Slavery in Colonial New York City," esp. 56, 149–151.

71. Ibid., 82, 161; McManus, *Negro Slavery in New York*, passim.

72. McKee, *Labor in Colonial New York*, 143–144.

73. The most complete accounts of the 1712 rebellion are Kenneth Scott, "Insurrection," 43–74; Foote, "Black Life," 198–226; and Thomas Davis, "Slavery in Colonial New York City," 99–114. For details of the burning of the outhouse and of the arming of slaves, see Kenneth Scott, "Insurrection," 47.

74. Foote, "Black Life," 198–199, 220–221.

75. Kenneth Scott, "Insurrection," 57–59; Foote, "Black Life," 200. Scott states that only eighteen were executed, although a primary source he quotes puts the number at twenty-one; Foote states that nineteen were executed. See Kenneth Scott, 57; and Foote, 200.

76. Foote, "Black Life," 201–214; Graham Hodges, *Root and Branch*, 64–65.

77. Foote, "Black Life," 202, 207–208; Graham Hodges, *Root and Branch*, 64–66.

78. Foote, "Black Life," 214–215.

79. The quotation is from Kruger, "Born to Run," 81–82. Peter the Doctor is named as a defendant in Kenneth Scott, "Insurrection," 65; and as a conjurer in Foote, "Black Life," 188; see also Graham Hodges, *Root and Branch*, 65. Peter the Doctor was charged with being an accessory to murder but was ultimately acquitted.

80. Thomas Davis, "Slavery in Colonial New York City," 109–110.

81. Kenneth Scott, "Insurrection," 71–72; Davis, "Slavery in New York City," 113; McManus, *Negro Slavery in New York*, 43.

82. Foote, "Black Life," 231; Thomas Davis, "Slavery in Colonial New York City," 112–113; David Cohen, *The Ramapo Mountain People*, 31–34; Foote, "Crossroads or Settlement?" 123.

83. Graham Hodges, *Root and Branch*, 67–68; Foote, "Black Life," 230–231.

84. See McManus, Negro *Slavery in New York*, 61–64; and Thomas Davis, "Slavery in Colonial New York City," 149–170, on the distance between the legal and actual status of some slaves.

85. On slaves bargaining for rights during sales, see White, *Somewhat More Independent*, 106–111. On Esther Burr, see Graham Hodges, *Root and Branch*, 111; on the lack of manumissions, 70–72. On New York City masters parceling out privileges, see Thomas Davis, "Slavery in Colonial New York City," 174. On the possibilities and limitations of resistance practices that may reinforce systems of oppression, see James Scott, *Weapons of the Weak*; Kelley, *Race Rebels*; and Genovese, *Roll Jordan Roll*.

86. The literature on Pinkster is rich and controversial. On the ecstatic religious nature of pre–Revolutionary War Pinkster, see Graham Hodges, *Root and Branch*, 87–88. On late-eighteenth and early-nineteenth-century Pinkster, see White, "Pinkster: Afro-Dutch Syncretism," 68–75; Williams-Myers, "Pinkster Carnival," 7–17; Stuckey, *Slave Culture*, 80–83, 141–145, 227; Stuckey, "The Skies of Consciousness: African Dance at Pinkster in New York, 1750–1840," in *Going Through the Storm*, 53–80; and Reidy, "'Negro Election Day' and Black Community Life," 102–117.

87. For slaves' use of holiday celebrations, see Foote, "Black Life," 232–233; quotation on 233. On the lax control of slaves by masters, see Thomas Davis, "Slavery in Colonial New York City," 149–150.

88. Foote, "Black Life," 235.

89. On African precedents to markets, see Graham Hodges, *Root and Branch*, 14–15, 96. On particular markets under British rule, see Foote, "Black Life," 236–239. On whites' attitudes toward theft by slaves, see Thomas Davis, "Slavery in Colonial New York City," 149–150, 161.

90. On the Geneva Club and the Smith Fly Boys, see Foote, "Black Life," 239–241; see also Thomas Davis, "Slavery in Colonial New York City," 149–150, 161; and Graham Hodges, *Root and Branch*, 96–97.

91. On connections among these workers, see Linebaugh and Rediker, *Many-Headed Hydra*, 181–182; Thomas Davis, "Slavery in Colonial New York City," 85; and Foote, "Black Life," 229–231.

92. Since the time of the conspiracy there have been debates as to whether a conspiracy actually existed. Doubtless slaves and some whites talked of burning the city and taking it over for their own benefit; and some slaves burned the city's main fort, Fort George, and several other buildings over the course of three weeks. The primary source on which all accounts of the plot are based is Horsmanden, *Detection of the Conspiracy*. The standard and most thorough secondary account of the plot is Thomas Davis, *Rumor of Revolt*. In "The Outcasts of the Nations of the Earth," in *Many-Headed Hydra*, Linebaugh and Rediker link the plot to events in the Atlantic World and emphasize the class and cultural connections among the participants. See Foote, "Black Life," 274–340, for an account that focuses on the ways whites shaped the meaning of the arson attacks into a wide-ranging international plot. Other accounts include Graham Hodges, *Root and Branch*, 88–99; and McManus, *Negro Slavery in New York*, 124–139.

93. Thomas Davis, *Rumor of Revolt*, 17, 18–21, 35.

94. Ibid., 4–8, 12–21, 29–31; on the Hughsons, Thomas Davis, *Rumor of Revolt*, 102–104; Linebaugh and Rediker, *Many-Headed Hydra*, 182–183.

95. Thomas Davis, *Rumor of Revolt*, 4–8, 12–21, 29–31; on Irish soldiers, Thomas Davis, *Rumor of Revolt*, 23.

96. On Quaco, see Thomas Davis, *Rumor of Revolt*, 89–91, 96–97. During the trial, others gave Quaco this motive; Quaco only confessed to burning the fort in the hope of saving himself from being burned at the stake, to no avail. On African practices in the rebellion, see Linebaugh and Rediker, *Many-Headed Hydra*, 184–186.

97. On Spanish Negroes, see Thomas Davis, *Rumor of Revolt*, 131–137, 225; and Linebaugh and Rediker, *Many-Headed Hydra*, 188–190; quote on 188.

98. Thomas Davis, *Rumor of Revolt*, 44, 31–32.

99. Ibid., 225, 252.

100. Ibid., 37.

101. For slaves as status symbols, see McManus, *Negro Slavery in New York*, 46–47. For slaves as status symbols in the late eighteenth century, see White, *Somewhat More Independent*, 44.

102. Thomas Davis, *Rumor of Revolt*, 261; McManus, *Negro Slavery in New York*, 140.

103. Thomas Davis, *Rumor of Revolt*, 252; Thomas Davis, "Slavery in Colonial New York City," 184–187.

104. Foote, "Black Life," 31, 57–58; Graham Hodges, *Root and Branch*, 103–105; Berlin, *Many Thousands Gone*, 182–183.

105. Graham Hodges, *Root and Branch*, 100–102, 115–119.

106. The best discussion of the influence of the Great Awakening and other changes in religion after 1741 is Graham Hodges, *Root and Branch*, 119–128.

CHAPTER TWO

1. On Quakers, see Soderlund, *Quakers and Slavery*. On the language of slavery during the American Revolution, see Bailyn, *Ideological Origins of the American Revolution*, 232–246; and Gellman, "Inescapable Discourse," 50–54. Major works

on black opportunities for freedom during the war include Quarles, *Negro in the American Revolution;* Graham Hodges, "Black Revolt in New York City," 65–86; and Berlin, "The Revolution in Black Life," 349–382.

2. The literature on republicanism is voluminous. For useful overviews, see Shall-hope, "Toward a Republican Synthesis," 334–56; Shallhope, "Republicanism and Early American Historiography," 49–80. On revolutionary republicanism, see Gordon Wood, *Creation of the American Republic.* On working-class republicanism, see Wilentz, *Chants Democratic.* On the interaction between republicanism and antislavery, see David Brion Davis, *Slavery in the Age of Revolution.*

3. Soderlund, *Quakers and Slavery,* 17–18, 29–32, 43–46; Zilversmit, *The First Emancipation,* 55–56, 71–77. The Philadelphia Meeting did not punish members for retaining slaves already owned.

4. Zilversmit, *The First Emancipation,* 80–83.

5. Nash, *Forging Freedom,* 28–29, 180, 191.

6. On Methodism and antislavery, see Graham Hodges, *Root and Branch,* 125–126; and Graham Hodges, ed., *Black Itinerants,* 3–9.

7. On the Dutch Reformed Church, see Graham Hodges, *Root and Branch,* 122–123.

8. Ibid., 119–122.

9. Graham Hodges has done the best job of uncovering the religiosity of New York–area blacks. See *Root and Branch,* 122–124; and *Black Itinerants,* 5–6.

10. *The New York Gazette; or, The Weekly Post-Boy,* July 26, 1756, and *The New York Gazette and the Weekly Mercury,* June 30, 1777, reprinted in Graham Hodges and Alan Edward Brown, eds., *Runaway Slave Advertisements,* 60, 202.

11. Graham Hodges, *Root and Branch,* 131–133.

12. David Brion Davis, *Problem of Slavery in Western Culture,* 402–410, 433–435.

13. On the language of slavery during the American Revolution, see Bailyn, *Ideological Origins of the American Revolution,* 232–246; and Gellman, "Inescapable Discourse," 50–54. On its limits, see David Brion Davis, *Slavery in the Age of Revolution,* 257; and White, *Somewhat More Independent,* 62–63. "Political enslavement" is from Gellman, "Inescapable Discourse," 54; Jay quotations are from Gellman, "Inescapable Discourse," 53–54; and White, *Somewhat More Independent,* 56, respectively.

14. Zilversmit, *The First Emancipation,* 139–140.

15. The fullest account of the effects of Lord Dunmore's proclamation in the South is Frey, *Water from the Rock.* See also Quarles, *Negro in the American Revolution,* 19–31. On Dunmore's and Clinton's proclamations and their effects on New York, see James W. St. G. Walker, *The Black Loyalists,* 1–3; quotation on 2; Graham Hodges, "Black Revolt in New York City," 68, 79; and McManus, *Negro Slavery in New York,* 154–155.

16. Quarles, *Negro in the American Revolution,* 9–18, 51–67.

17. Ibid., 111–114, 119, 146–152; Horton and Horton, *In Hope of Liberty,* 58–62. On the black companies, see Graham Hodges, "Black Revolt in New York City," 77.

18. Quarles, *Negro in the American Revolution*, 83–93, 152–156.

19. Ibid., 111–114, 119, 146–152; Horton and Horton, *In Hope of Liberty*, 58–62.

20. Quarles, *Negro in the American Revolution*, 97–105, 134–157, with quotation appearing on 98. Graham Hodges, "Black Revolt in New York City," 77–79.

21. Graham Hodges has constructed the most complete account of the lives of blacks during the occupation of New York City; see Hodges, "Black Revolt in New York City," 79–80; and Hodges, *Root and Branch*, 144–161. See also Quarles, "The Revolutionary War," 283–301; and Berlin, *Many Thousands Gone*, 230–231. For details of the participation of New York's blacks in the Revolutionary War on the American side, see Quarles, *Negro in the American Revolution*, 70, 98; on their use by the British, 134–135; and on their evacuation with the British, 167–172.

22. On the evacuation, see Quarles, *Negro in the American Revolution*, 158–181; Graham Hodges, "Black Revolt in New York City," 85–86; and Horton and Horton, *In Hope of Liberty*, 62–63. On conditions in Nova Scotia and Sierra Leone, see James W. St. G. Walker, *The Black Loyalists*.

23. Zilversmit, *The First Emancipation*, 112–116, 119–137, 146–147.

24. Graham Hodges, *Root and Branch*, 162–63.

25. The most complete account of the Manumission Society's history is Moseley, "History of the New-York Manumission Society." Details of the first meeting are found on page 21. See also Minutes of January 25, 1785, in Minutes of the Manumission Society of New-York, vol. 1, 1785–1797, Papers of the New York Manumission Society MS.

26. It is unclear whether Prior was a Manumission Society member. An attempt in 1784 to introduce such a bill and begin a discussion about emancipation failed.

27. New York State Legislature, Assembly, *Journal of the Assembly 1785*, 14.

28. Ibid., 55–56.

29. Ibid., 55–57.

30. Ibid., 62–63.

31. Ibid., 77.

32. For details of New York's suffrage laws, see Chilton Williamson, *American Suffrage*, 107–108. For election of the legislature, see Countryman, *A People in Revolution*, 161. For rural representatives and emancipation, see Zilversmit, *The First Emancipation*, 148–150; Gellman, "Inescapable Discourse," 148–155; Countryman, *A People in Revolution*, 248–249.

33. New York State Legislature, Senate, *Journal of the Senate, 1785*, 39, 42; New York State Legislature, Assembly, *Journal of the Assembly 1785*, 76–77, 86.

34. Duties of the Council of Revision appear in article 3 of the 1777 Constitution of the State of New-York, in Carter and Stone, eds., *Convention of 1821*, 13.

35. New York State Legislature, Assembly, *Journal of the Assembly 1785*, 119.

36. Ibid.

37. Ibid., 120.

38. Ibid.

39. The figures on leadership and the quotation are from David Brion Davis, *Slavery in the Age of Revolution*, 239–242. See also White, *Somewhat More Independent*, 83–84; and Moseley, "History of the New-York Manumission Society," 1–2, 20–45.

40. On federalism generally, see Elkins and McKitrick, *The Age of Federalism*. On federalists, slavery, and race, see David Brion Davis, *Slavery in the Age of Revolution*, 46, 241–242, 265–266; Finkelman, "Problem of Slavery in the Age of Federalism," in Ben-Atar and Oberg, *Federalists Reconsidered*, 135–56.

41. David Brion Davis points out the paradox of successful economic development based on slavery in Adam Smith's theories in *Slavery in the Age of Revolution*, 351–353. On Manumission Society attitudes toward slavery, see White, *Somewhat More Independent*, 81–82.

42. Zilversmit, The *First Emancipation*, 208; Hodges, *Root and Branch*, 168–169.

43. My discussion here draws on White, "Impious Prayers," in *Somewhat More Independent*, esp. 59–63; and David Brion Davis, *Slavery in the Age of Revolution*, 257–258, 304.

44. White, *Somewhat More Independent*, 62–63.

45. David Brion Davis, *Slavery in the Age of Revolution*, 44–49. I use "man" and "mankind" here as they would have been used in the eighteenth century.

46. Ibid., 257.

47. White, *Somewhat More Independent*, 59–61; 64–65.

48. Report of the School Committee to the New York Manumission Society, November 20, 1788, in Minutes of the Manumission Society of New York, vol. 1, 1785–1797, Papers of the New York Manumission Society, MS.

49. Moseley, "History of the New-York Manumission Society," 181–182.

50. Report of the School Committee to the New York Manumission Society, November 15, 1787, and November 20, 1788, in Minutes of the New-York Manumission Society, vol. 1, 1785–1797. Papers of the New York Manumission Society, MS; Moseley, "History of the New-York Manumission Society," 176, 234–235.

51. Society quoted in Moseley, "History of the New-York Manumission Society," 177.

52. Report of the Board of Trustees ~~of the African~~ of the ~~Free~~ School [*sic*], [January?] 17th, 1797; and School Committee Report to the New York Manumission Society, November 20, 1788, both in Minutes of the New York Manumission Society, vol. 1, 1785–1797.

53. Rury argues that the school's "essential purpose . . . throughout its initial twenty-five years" was the moral education of blacks; see Rury, "Philanthropy, Self Help, and Social Control," 236.

54. Report of the Committee for Preventing Irregular Conduct in Free Negroes, February 21, 1788, in Minutes of the Manumission Society of New-York, vol. 1, 1785–1797, Papers of the New York Manumission Society, MS.

55. My information on Teasman is taken from Swan's illuminating article, "John Teasman," 331–356.

56. On the hiring of Teasman and the purchase of the Cliff St. property, see Report of the Board of Trustees ~~of the African~~ of the ~~Free~~ School [sic], [January?] 17th, 1797, in Papers of the New York Manumission Society, 1785–1797, New-York Historical Society. For his early life and success at the school, see Swan, "John Teasman," 337, 338–339.

57. Ransom, *America's First Negro Poet*, 13–14; Moss, *Slavery on Long Island*, 182.

58. On Hammon's waged work and book purchases, see Moss, *Slavery on Long Island*, 182; and Ransom, *America's First Negro Poet*, 14. On his publications, see Ransom, *America's First Negro Poet*, 11–12.

59. Ransom, *America's First Negro Poet*, 109.

60. Hammon, "An Address," reprinted in Ransom, *America's First Negro Poet*, 108.

61. Ibid., 110, 113.

62. The quotation is from ibid., 112. On Hammon's refusal of freedom, see Moss, *Slavery on Long Island*, 182.

63. Hammon, "An Address," in Ransom, *America's First Negro Poet*, 112–113.

64. Ibid., 117.

65. There is a growing literature on this period of rebellion. See Curtin, *Rise and Fall*, 144–169; and Blackburn, *Overthrow of Colonial Slavery*. For the best recent study on the ways slaves were affected by the revolutionary ideology of the United States, see Egerton, *Gabriel's Rebellion*. On the range of uprisings during the early national period, particularly the Louisiana uprising, see Wright, *African-Americans in the Early Republic*, 85–100; and Harding, *There is a River*, 44–64.

66. New York Manumission Society, Minutes of the Standing Committee of the New York Manumission Society, April 24, 1792, and March 18, 1800 (annual report for 1799), Papers of the New York Manumission Society, MS.

67. White has done the most thorough research on New York–area runaways during the 1790s. See White, *Somewhat More Independent*, 114–144. Descriptions of the runaways are from the *New York Daily Advertiser*, January 1, February 1, and June 13, 1799.

68. White, *Somewhat More Independent*, 145–146.

69. See ibid., 95–106. For the importance of Pinkster to rural blacks seeking to build community, see Stuckey, "The Skies Of Consciousness: African Dance at Pinkster in New York, 1750–1840," in *Going Through the Storm*, 56–57.

70. For the mixture of influences in the Pinkster festival, see White, "Pinkster: Afro-Dutch Syncretization," 68–75; and White, *Somewhat More Independent*, 96–105. Stuckey has analyzed most fully the meaning of African culture and particularly dance in this festival in "The Skies of Consciousness: African Dance at Pinkster in New York, 1750–1840," in *Going through the Storm*, esp. 53–54, 59–60, 67–70.

71. DeVoe, *The Market Book*, 322, 344–345. See also Stuckey, "The Skies of Consciousness: African Dance at Pinkster in New York, 1750–1840," in *Going through the Storm*, 69–71; and White, "'It was a proud day,'" 13–50.

72. J. C. Dongan to Jay, February 27, 1792, cited in Zilversmit, *The First Emancipation*, 165–166.

73. Ibid., 161, 165–166.

74. White, *Somewhat More Independent*, 64–65.

75. For details of the 1799 emancipation law, see Zilversmit, *The First Emancipation*, 181–184.

76. On indentures as a form of relief for the poor, see Schneider, *The History of Public Welfare*, 179–181. On the decline of the apprenticeship system, see Wilentz, *Chants Democratic*, 24–35. On the effect of the separation of workshops from residences on the labor slaves and servants performed, see White, *Somewhat More Independent*, 43.

CHAPTER THREE

1. White, *Somewhat More Independent*, 106–111, 151–152. After 1799, census workers defined both indentured blacks and completely free blacks as free.

2. White, *Somewhat More Independent*, 106–111, 151–152; Curry, *Free Black in Urban America*, 250. For the influx of Haitian slaveholders and slaves, see White, *Somewhat More Independent*, 31–32, 122, 155–156; and Gilje, *Road to Mobocracy*, 147. Bolster describes an "Atlantic community of Color," in which slave sailors were messengers, bringing news of foreign places to enslaved blacks in the Americas. This knowledge may account for the movement of Caribbean blacks to New York; see Bolster, "African-American Seamen," 90–91. Birth data are from Records of Admissions, Municipal Almshouse, MS, New York City Municipal Archives, for years 1827, 1830, and 1840.

3. See White, *Somewhat More Independent*, table 4, p. 26. The uneven sex ratios among the black population throughout New York City's history may have facilitated or encouraged same-sex erotic relationships among black people there, as historians have documented for other single-sex environments (schools, prisons, and the military) where normative heterosexuality may have been difficult to achieve, or where men and women may have been freer to follow their same-sex desires. In general, I found little evidence of the private emotional and sexual lives of African Americans in pre-Civil War New York City. For a tantalizing glimpse of what may await historians more skilled in this area, see Griffin, ed., *Beloved Sisters and Loving Friends*, and Hansen, "'No Kisses Is Like Youres.'" Both works detail the erotic correspondence between Rebecca Primus and Addie Brown, two black women who lived in the Northeast during the pre-Civil War era.

4. On the movement of blacks into the Fifth and Sixth Wards, see White, *Somewhat More Independent*, 172–179, and maps 5, 6, and 7 on pp. 172, 174, and 176, respectively. On the Fresh Water Pond, also known as the Collect Pond, see Asbury, *The Gangs of New York*, 4–5.

5. Historians Elizabeth Blackmar and Roy Rosenzweig have done a remarkable job of reconstructing the history of the unique community of Seneca Village. My discussion is based on their pioneering research; see Blackmar and Rosenzweig, *Park and the People*, 64–73. A similar all-black community that also existed in the New York City area during this time was Weeksville, founded in 1838 in Brooklyn; see

Blackmar and Rosenzweig, *Park and the People*, 65, 547n; and Wilder, *A Covenant with Color*, 113–114.

6. Blackmar and Rosenzweig, *Park and the People*, 67. Seneca Village was razed in 1857 to make way for Central Park.

7. My discussion here draws on Scherzer, *Unbounded Community*, 13; White, *Somewhat More Independent*, 171–179; and Curry, *Free Black in Urban America*, 54–57, 78–80.

8. For black housing conditions and "vertical segregation," see White, *Somewhat More Independent*, 171–179, esp. 178. Details on cellars are from Griscom, *The Sanitary Condition of the Laboring Population of New York*, 8–15.

9. On blacks and the John Street Methodist Church, see White, *Somewhat More Independent*, 173–175.

10. Bolster, *Black Jacks*, 182–189; Scherzer, *Unbounded Community*, 112–119.

11. New York City Municipal Almshouse, Records of Admissions, for years 1827, 1830, and 1840, New York City Municipal Archives.

12. White, *Somewhat More Independent*, 7–8, 10–12. Numerically, merchants held the largest number of slaves, 449, compared to 426 held by artisans. But 225 artisan households held slaves, compared with 178 merchant households and 179 retail households (which held 295 slaves). Neither free blacks nor slaves were distinguished by sex in census records until 1820. Ibid., xxvii.

13. White, "'We Dwell in Safety,'" 453–455. Although absolute numbers of blacks in artisan jobs increased in 1810, the percentage of blacks in artisan jobs dropped due to the rapidly growing free black population.

14. On chimney sweeps, see Gilje and Rock, "'Sweep O! Sweep O!,'" 507–519.

15. On Downing and Cato, see Dayton, *Knickerbocker Life*, 128–133, 322–325; and Graham Hodges, *Root and Branch*, 232. On Downing, see Curry, *Free Black in Urban America*, 24. On pleasure gardens, see Dayton, *Knickerbocker Life*, 159–161; and McAllister, "African Grove/African Theatre," 150–153.

16. The most recent and complete account of Brown's pleasure garden and subsequent theater is McAllister, "African Grove/African Theatre."

17. Ibid., 1, 149.

18. For details of performances, see McAllister, "African Grove/African Theatre," passim; on naming, see 7, 219.

19. See White, *Somewhat More Independent*, 37, 43.

20. For the changing meaning of slaveholding in New York City, see White, *Somewhat More Independent*, 37, 43, 44–46, 54; on numbers of female slaves, 12; quotation on 43. For a comparison of attitudes toward mothers and wives and domestic wage workers, see Blackmar, *Manhattan for Rent*, 116–120. Some exceptions to this general decline in the use of black labor included the continued use of black labor, slave and free, in maritime occupations and the continued use of slave labor by butchers and bakers through the early years of the 1800s. For the role of slaves in seafaring work, see Bolster, "African-American Seamen," 82–83, 422ff. For continued use of slave labor by butchers and bakers, see White, *Somewhat More Independent*, 36–37.

21. For lives of black maritime workers, see Bolster, *Black Jacks*. For examples of female maritime workers, see John W. Kennedy Admission Record, Association for the Benefit of Colored Orphans, Admissions of Children, October 1849 to December, 1860, Papers of the Association for the Benefit of Colored Orphans, MS; and *Seventeenth Annual Report of the Colored Orphan Asylum* (1853), Papers of the Association for the Benefit of Colored Orphans, MS, 8. (Subsequent references to the Association for the Benefit of Colored Orphans, the organization and related source materials, shall appear as ABCO.)

22. Henry Bradshaw Fearon, *Sketches of America. A narrative of a journey of five thousand miles through the Eastern and Western states of America; contained in eight reports addressed to the thirty-nine English families by whom the author was deputed, in June 1817, to ascertain whether any, and what part of the United States would be suitable for their residence. With remarks on Mr. Birbeck's "Notes" and "Letters."* (London: Longman, Hurst, Rees, Orme, and Brown, 1819), 5–61, 86–87. This work appears in [Stokes], "New York City Slums," Notes, 1:317–318.

23. On the conditions of child chimney sweeps, see Phillips, *American Chimney Sweeps;* Strange, *The Climbing Boys;* and Pensylvania Society for the Promotion of Public Economy, *Report of the Committee on Domestic Economy*. See also Gilje and Rock, "'Sweep O! Sweep O!'" 507–519.

24. De Voe, *The Market Book*, 345.

25. Blackmar, *Manhattan for Rent*, 116–120.

26. ABCO, Books of Indentures of ABCO, Package 1, "Birthdates 1829–1853; Admissions 1837–1856 (with some going as late as 1866)" (hereafter cited as ABCO Admission Book 1), Papers of ABCO, MS, passim. The servants of John Pintard are cited in Blackmar, *Manhattan for Rent*, 116–120.

27. Stansell, *City of Women*, 13–14. For a comparison with black women's work in the late nineteenth-century South, see Hunter, *To 'Joy My Freedom;* and Woodson, "Negro Washerwoman," 269–277.

28. On the lives of black sailors, see Bolster, *Black Jacks*, 158–189; and "Black Seamen in the Northern States," 1173–1199. William Smith and his children are mentioned in parental agreements, ABCO Admission Book 1, January 27, 1841, and July 29, 1845; admission record for Thomas Smith, ibid., January 27, 1841; and ABCO Minute Book 2, April 14, 1848, entry. Papers of the ABCO, MS.

29. On numbers of black children who boarded, see Scherzer, *Unbounded Community*, 117. On the rules of the Colored Orphan Asylum regarding parental visits, see ABCO, Minute Book 1, May 11, 1838 entry, Papers of the ABCO, MS.

30. C. Peter Ripley et al., *Black Abolitionist Papers*, 3:188n; Ottley and Weatherby, *The Negro in New York*, 63; White, *Somewhat More Independent*, 160.

31. Graham Hodges, *Root and Branch*, 180–185; Curry, *Free Black in Urban America*, 189; Walls, *The African Methodist Episcopal Zion Church*, 51–58, 68–69; George Hodges, *Early Negro Church Life*, 8–13

32. George Hodges, *Early Negro Church Life*, 16; C. Peter Ripley et. al., *Black Abolitionist Papers*, 3:224–225n; Curry, *Free Black in Urban America*, 189; Freeman, *The Free Negro in New York City*, 208, 288.

33. Bradley, *A.M.E. Zion Church*, 50–54, 71–79.

34. Bradley, *A.M.E. Zion Church,* 71–72, 78, 80–81, 104; George Hodges, *Early Negro Church Life,* 8–13; Walls, *The African Methodist Episcopal Zion Church,* 68–71, 124.

35. Swift, *Black Prophets of Justice,* 22–23; Alexander, *Presbyter of New York,* '44–45, 66–67; George Hodges, *Early Negro Church Life,* 19–20.

36. Harry Williamson, "Folks in Old New York," TS, 9.

37. Blackmar and Rosenzweig, *Park and the People,* 63–73.

38. George Walker, *The Afro-American in New York City,* 63. The information on Philadelphia is from Sterling, ed., *We Are Your Sisters,* 105. Craig Wilder alerted me to the connection between the mutual aid societies and black churches. See his article "Rise and Influence of the New York African Society for Mutual Relief," 7–17.

39. On sex-segregated societies in Africa and their continuation in the Americas, see Gomez, *Exchanging Our Country Marks,* 94–101. For more general discussion of African cultural retention in the Northeast, see Piersen, *Black Yankees.*

40. New York African Society for Mutual Relief, *Constitution of the New-York African Society,* 7. New York African Clarkson Association, *African Clarkson Association.* On ministers in the African Society for Mutual Relief, see Graham Hodges, *Root and Branch,* 187–188.

41. *Anti-Slavery Record,* April 1836.

42. Gilje and Rock have constructed a list of black chimney sweeps in "Sweep O! Sweep O!" 534–538. I compared this list with that of the antebellum membership of the New York African Society for Mutual Relief, in Zuille, *Historical Sketch of the New York African Society,* 27–33. Although Gilje and Rock's list may not represent all black chimney sweeps, it does represent those who were active on behalf of the profession and so were in some sense civic minded. Thus, it is all the more significant that they did not join, or perhaps were excluded from, the African Society.

43. Zuille, *Historical Sketch of the New York African Society,* 15, 16; Curry, *Free Black in Urban America,* 198; Wilder, "Rise and Influence of the New York African Society for Mutual Relief," 9.

44. My arguments about the changes in celebrations among New York's blacks during the emancipation era are indebted to White, "'It Was a Proud Day,'" 13–50. On parades and other popular celebrations generally, see Waldstreicher, *In the Midst of Perpetual Fetes;* and Newman, *Parades and the Politics of the Streets.*

45. On the political meanings of parades and celebrations in the early republic, and blacks' transformation of those meanings, see Waldstreicher, *In the Midst of Perpetual Fetes,* esp. 323–325.

46. Swan, "John Teasman," 343–344.

47. "From Our New York Correspondent," *Frederick Douglass' Paper,* February 16, 1855. The correspondent was abolitionist James McCune Smith; his role in the New York black community will be discussed in subsequent chapters.

48. The description of the Wilberforce Society parade is from White, "'It Was a Proud Day,'" 44.

49. For the transformation of women's roles in blacks' public celebrations, see White, "'It Was a Proud Day,'" 48.

50. Waldstreicher, *In the Midst of Perpetual Fetes,* 328.

51. The program of the 1808 celebration and Williams's speech are reprinted in Porter, ed., *Early Negro Writing,* 343–354.

52. On black political support for the Democratic-Republicans, see Swan, "John Teasman," 351–352; and Waldstreicher, *In the Midst of Perpetual Fetes,* 332.

53. Hamilton, "Mutual Interest," in Foner and Branham, *Lift Every Voice,* 81.

54. "An Oration on the Abolition of the Slave Trade; delivered in the African Church, in the City of New York, January 2, 1809. By Henry Sipkins, A descendant of Africa," reprinted in Porter, *Early Negro Writing,* 371.

55. Hamilton, "Mutual Interest," in Foner and Branham, *Lift Every Voice,* 85.

56. Sidney, "An Oration Commemorative of the Abolition of the Slave Trade in the United States," in Porter, *Early Negro Writing,* 356–357, 362–363. For Hamilton's and Sipkins's expressions of gratitude to white benefactors, see Foner and Branham, *Lift Every Voice,* 84; and Porter, *Early Negro Writing,* 370.

57. Sidney, "Oration," in Porter, *Early Negro Writing,* 359–360.

58. Ibid., 360–361.

59. White, *Somewhat More Independent,* 144–145; Gilje, *Road to Mobocracy,* 147–153.

60. For chimney sweeps, see Samuel Wood, *Cries of New-York,* 45. On tubmen, see Gilje and Rock, *Keepers of the Revolution,* 218–221.

61. On black leisure activities during the emancipation era, see White, *Somewhat More Independent,* 179–182. See also Stansell, "Women in the Neighborhood," in *City of Women,* for a discussion of similar issues for white working-class women during the same period.

62. White, *Somewhat More Independent,* 179, 207–209.

63. The information about Quaker women's participation in New York City education is from William Wood, *Friends of the City,* 28–31, 33. The annual reports for the Female Union Society show that in the majority of the adult schools, the population was at least 50 percent, if not overwhelmingly, black; see *First Report of the New-York Female Union Society for the Promotion of Sabbath Schools: Read at their Annual Meeting, April 1, 1817,* and subsequent reports through 1820. See also Boylan, *Sunday School,* 22–29; and Smith-Rosenberg, *Religion and the Rise of the American City,* 26–27, 54–55.

64. *New-York Evening Post,* August 20, 1814, 3; also cited in White, *Somewhat More Independent,* 150–151, 207.

65. Swan, "John Teasman," 352–354; "Patriotism of the Africans," *New-York Evening Post,* August 22, 1814, 2.

66. On the enlistment of black men in the army in 1814, see Joseph Wilson, *Black Phalanx,* 82–84. On black naval participation in the war, see Fabel, "Self-Help in Dartmoor," esp. 165, 169.

67. Lincoln, *Messages from the Governors,* 2:881–882.

68. Zilversmit, *The First Emancipation,* 213–214.

69. Carleton Mabee, with Susan Mabee Newhouse, *Sojourner Truth: Slave,*

Prophet, Legend, 14; Painter, *Sojourner Truth: A Life, A Symbol,* 19–37, 60, 66–68, 100–102, 298n. Isabella lived with her son Peter in New York in the 1830s. Her husband Thomas died soon after emancipation. Sojourner Truth lived with her three daughters for a time in Massachusetts in the 1840s.

CHAPTER FOUR

1. On the July 5 parade and blacks' exclusion from July 4 celebrations, see Swan, "John Teasman," 343–344; and Waldstreicher, *In the Midst of Perpetual Fetes,* 328–329. On the Tammany Society, see Wilentz, *Chants Democratic,* 70, 73, 88.

2. On Revolutionary republicanism, see Wood, *Creation of the American Republic;* and Bailyn, *Ideological Origins of the American Revolution.* On working-class republicanism, see Wilentz, *Chants Democratic,* esp. 14–15, 23, 61–103. See also Bloch, "Gendered Meanings of Virtue," 37–58.

3. On republican motherhood, see Kerber, *Women of the Republic,* 11–12, 283–286; and Bloch, "Gendered Meanings of Virtue," 46–47. On women in republican ideology and class distinctions, see Stansell, *City of Women,* 19–30.

4. On women and reform, see Stansell, *City of Women,* 30–37. On domestic servants in white households, see White, *Somewhat More Independent,* 43–45; and Stansell, *City of Women,* 13. On the conflation of free blacks and slaves, see White, *Somewhat More Independent,* 47; for a similar conflation of free blacks and slaves in New England, see Melish, *Disowning Slavery,* 95–118. On slavery, servants, and republicanism, see Roediger, *Wages of Whiteness,* 43–64, esp. 47–50.

5. On the devaluation of domestic labor, see Boydston, *Home and Work,* 35–74.

6. On the changes in skilled labor during this time, see Wilentz, *Chants Democratic,* 24–60; and Sellers, *Market Revolution,* 21–27. On the embargo and debt imprisonment, see Sellers, *Market Revolution,* 25.

7. Bolster, *Black Jacks,* 69–75; Roediger, *Wages of Whiteness,* 45.

8. On the sailors' strike, see Gilje, *Road to Mobocracy,* 181. On the waiters' strike, see Philip Foner and Ronald Lewis, *The Black Worker to 1869,* 191–195. On white workers' exclusion of blacks, see Roediger, *Wages of Whiteness,* 43–60, esp. 44–46. Implicitly, Sean Wilentz places unskilled jobs, in which the vast majority of black workers and at least half of all other workers participated, outside of his schema of working-class development and consciousness. He focuses on a class of skilled artisans and tradesmen who, by his own accounting, make up for only two-fifths to one-half of all employed males in New York City (Wilentz, *Chants Democratic,* 27n). These figures also exclude working-class women who held jobs outside of the workshops; see Stansell, *City of Women.* For a work which gives attention to nonartisan workers in New York, see Stott, *Workers in the Metropolis.*

9. *American Minerva,* August 22, 1793.

10. Samuel Wood, *Cries of New-York,* 15–16.

11. Samuel Wood, *Cries of New-York,* 15–16; Swan, "John Teasman," 338, 342–343.

12. Samuel Wood, *Cries of New-York,* 45–46.

13. Wilentz, *Chants Democratic,* 66–77; Hamilton quoted on 67.

14. Dixon Ryan Fox, "The Negro Vote," 256–257. Van Ness and Wordworth, Laws of the State of New-York, 253–254, with quotation on 253.

15. Swan, "John Teasman," 338, 342–343, 349–350.

16. On black leisure activities and their links to crime during the emancipation era, see White, *Somewhat More Independent,* 179–182. See also Stansell, "Women in the Neighborhood," in *City of Women,* for a discussion of similar issues for white working-class women during the same period; and Gutman's classic essay "Work, Culture, and Society in Industrializing America, 1815–1919," *Work, Culture and Society,* esp. 13–31, for a discussion of the tensions between employers and free white laborers over leisure activities and drinking in the period before 1843.

17. On colonial crime pamphlets, see Slotkin, "Narratives of Negro Crime," 3–31. For a more general overview of eighteenth- and nineteenth-century crime narratives, see Daniel Cohen, *Pillars of Salt,* ix and passim; and Halttunen, *Murder Most Foul.*

18. See, for example, the story in the *New-York City Hall Recorder,* vol. 1, no. 8, August 1816, page 130, in which two Irish men are convicted of assault and battery. The court observed in this case that "until a short time past, their crimes were almost unheard of in this country. And that it was a just subject of felicitation, and reflected much honor on our countrymen, that the commission of such heinous offenses was confined principally to foreigners." Similar remarks were made in this journal about British counterfeiters.

19. To my knowledge, none of these crime narratives was written by blacks.

20. [Sampson], *Trial of James Johnson,* 3. See Shane White's deep and convincing analysis of this court case and its importance to understanding early-nineteenth-century New York City black culture, "The Death of James Johnson," 753–795.

21. Sampson, *Trial of James Johnson,* 12–13, 15.

22. Ibid., 17.

23. Ibid., 19–20.

24. White, "The Death of James Johnson," 779.

25. Sean Wilentz identifies Broad as "much-persecuted," probably for his religious activities, in *Chants Democratic,* 81. His Baptist congregation at 51 Rose Street, which he acquired in 1810, was the scene of a riot in 1817, in which a hundred persons took over the church and destroyed hymnals and other items. In addition, "a black boy, ascending and seating himself in the pulpit, completed a scene of mockery and derision to the vile and worthless." Perhaps the boy knew of Broad's abuse of his slaves. For a description of the riot, see *New-York City-Hall Recorder,* vol. 2, no. 2, (February 1817) 25.

26. *Trial of Amos Broad,* 6–10, 14.

27. Ibid., 6–10, 14.

28. Ibid., 31. Hannah was not part of the indictments in this case, and it is unclear whether she was a slave or an indentured servant.

29. Ibid., 24–25.

30. Ibid., 30.

31. Lincoln, *Messages from the Governors*, 2:692–694.

32. Lincoln, *Messages from the Governors*, 2:692–694

33. *Trial of Captain James Dunn*, 5–6.

34. Ibid., 1, 5–6, 14. On judgments in rape cases at this time, see Stansell, *City of Women*, 23–30. Graham Hodges makes a different argument about this "comical" case—that the Pattersons were engaged in a confidence game with Dunn—hence the low fine; see Graham Hodges, *Root and Branch*, 210–211.

35. "Law Intelligence Extraordinary, Sessions Court" in *New York Commercial Advertiser*, June 17, 1808, 2. Also in *Trial of Doctor William Little*, 4–6.

36. *Trial of Doctor William Little*, 7, 8; "Law Intelligence Extraordinary, Sessions Court" in *New York Commercial Advertiser*, June 17, 1808, 2.

37. On the economic effects of the 1807 Embargo Act, see Sellers, *Market Revolution*, 21–23.

38. *Trial of Doctor William Little*, 9.

39. Ibid., 11, 14.

40. See Kerber, *No Constitutional Right*, 3–46, for a discussion of women's lack of property rights after marriage.

41. *Trial of Doctor William Little*, 11–14.

42. According to Leonard Curry's calculations, between 1810 and 1820, the city's free black population gained 2,231 people, while the slave population declined by 1,168. The entire black population, slave and free, increased by 1,063. Curry, *Free Black in Urban America*, tables A-1, A-4, A-7, pp. 244–245, 247, 250.

43. The quotation is from Noah, "Africans," *National Advocate*, August 3, 1821, 2, reprinted in McAllister, "African Grove/African Theatre," 153–154.

44. Stanford, *Case and Conduct of Rose Butler*, 3.

45. Ibid.; DeVoe, *The Market Book*, 480–481; Dorothy Ripley, *An Account of Rose Butler*; *New-York Evening Post*, June 11 and July 10, 1819.

46. De Voe, *The Market Book*, 481.

47. Smith-Rosenberg, *Religion and the Rise of the American City*, 52–53; Mohl, *Poverty in New York*, 193–195; Stanford, Diary, 1816–1831, MS, New-York Historical Society.

48. Stanford, *Case and Conduct of Rose Butler*, 9.

49. Stansell, *City of Women*, 68–74.

50. Stansell cites the Butler case as illustrative of the lives of domestic servants, but does not explicate its racial content; see Stansell, *City of Women*, 86.

51. Thomas Davis, "Slavery in Colonial New York City," 149–174; McManus, *Negro Slavery in New York*, 82–83, 85–87. See also White, *Somewhat More Independent*, 179–184.

52. Stanford, *Case and Conduct of Rose Butler*, 11.

53. Dorothy Ripley, *An Account of Rose Butler*, 4. As Louis Masur states in his study of capital punishment, during those years "the goals of reformation and

perfection seemed palpable, almost inevitable." This was certainly true for Ripley. See Masur, *Rites of Execution,* esp. 30–81.

54. Johnny Edwards quoted in DeVoe, *The Market Book,* 480; for Edwards's evangelicalism and association with Dorothy Ripley in an 1810 religious revival, see Wilentz, *Chants Democratic,* 81–82. For Edwards's antislavery views, see *Trial of John Edwards,* 5–7.

55. *New-York Evening Post,* June 11, 1819; and *Columbian Spectator,* July 9 and July 19, 1819, both quoted in DeVoe, *The Market Book,* 480–481. Black ministers appear to have supported the execution of a black man in a similar case in Philadelphia.

56. Chilton Williamson, *American Suffrage,* 107–108, 196; Nash, "Emancipation Experience," table 7, p. 2.

57. Carter and Stone, eds., *Convention of 1821,* 195–196.

58. Ibid., 189–190.

59. Ibid., 195–196, 189–190, 185–186.

60. Ibid., 180–183.

61. On Root, see Zilversmit, *The First Emancipation,* 181.

62. Carter and Stone, eds., *Convention of 1821,* 183–185.

63. Ibid., 186–188.

64. Williamson, *American Suffrage,* 202–206.

65. Carter and Stone, eds., *Convention of 1821,* 364.

66. Numbers of eligible voters are from Freeman, *The Free Negro in New York City,* 92–93.

67. Blackmar and Rosenzweig, *Park and the People,* 67.

68. For the economic basis of middle-class development, see Blumin, *Emergence of the Middle Class.* For the growth of a middle-class morality, see, among others, Ryan, *Cradle of the Middle Class;* and Sellers, *Market Revolution,* chapters 8 and 10.

69. Membership requirements in New York African Society for Mutual Relief, *Constitution,* 3; quotation about widowhood, 7. For the Mutual Relief Society's influence on other organizations, see Wilder, "Rise and Influence," especially 7–8, 10, 12, 15–16. The society's historian, John Jay Zuille, called the society the "parent of other societies" in the New York area; Zuille, *Historical Sketch,* 15.

70. Quotation is in Zuille, *Historical Sketch,* 21–22; membership rolls, 22, | 27–35.

71. "Abolition of Slavery," *Freedom's Journal,* April 20, 1827.

72. Ibid., for "deem[ed] it proper"; Frederick Douglass, "What to the Slave is the Fourth of July?: An Address Delivered in Rochester, New York, on 5 July 1852," in Blassingame, *Frederick Douglass Papers,* ser. 1, vol. 2, (1847–1854–): 359–388.

73. "Meeting of the People of Colour," *Freedom's Journal,* April 27, 1827.

74. The differences between middle-class and working-class uses of public space are explored in Stansell, *City of Women,* 193–216; and Ryan, *Women in Public,* passim.

75. "Abolition of Slavery in the State of New-York," in *Freedom's Journal,* May 4, 1827.

76. Ibid.

77. "For the Freedom's Journal," *Freedom's Journal*, June 29, 1827.

78. "The following editorial . . . ," *Freedom's Journal*, June 29, 1827.

79. "Abolition of Slavery," *Freedom's Journal*, July 6, 1827.

80. White, "'It Was a Proud Day,'" 39.

81. See *Minutes of the Fourth Annual Convention, For the Improvement of the Free People of Colour, in the United States, Held by Adjournments, in the Asbury Church, New-York, From the 2d to the 12th of June inclusive, 1834*, 14, 15–16, in Bell, ed., *Proceedings of the National Negro Conventions*.

82. "The Brooklyn Celebration," *Freedom's Journal*, July 18, 1828.

83. "From the L. I. Star," *Freedom's Journal*, August 1, 1828.

84. Rael, "Besieged by Freedom's Army," in *Black Identity and Black Protest*, 54–81.

85. "City Free Schools," *Freedom's Journal*, January 11, 1828.

86. Information on the African Dorcas Association is from "Worthy of Notice," *Freedom's Journal*, January 25, 1828; "Notice," *Freedom's Journal*, February 1, 1828; "African Dorcas Association," *Freedom's Journal*, February 15, 1828; "For the Freedom's Journal. Female Dorcas Association," *Freedom's Journal*, September 26, 1828; "Dorcas Association," *Freedom's Journal*, November 21, 1828; "Our Dorcas Society," *Freedom's Journal*, January 9, 1829; and "Dorcas Association," *Freedom's Journal*, February 7, 1829.

87. *An Address to the Parents and Guardians of the Children belonging to the New-York African Free School, by the Trustees of the Institution*, 17; New-York African Free School, Regulations for the African Free School, MS, in Volume 1, Records of the New-York African Free Schools: Regulations, By-Laws, and Reports, 1817–1832.

88. New York City Common Council, *Minutes of the Common Council*, 7:4.

89. Pennsylvania Society for the Promotion of Public Economy, *Report of the Committee on Domestic Economy*, passim.

90. New York City Common Council, *Appointment of the Superintendent*, 7–14. See also Gilje and Rock, eds., *Keepers of the Revolution*, 221–224.

91. Sweeps' petition reprinted in Gilje and Rock, *Keepers of the Revolution*, 223; Common Council response in December 16, 1816, *Minutes of the Common Council*, 8:724.

92. See "Old Scenes Revisited," *Monthly Record of the Five Points House of Industry*, vol. 3, no. 6 (October 1859) 128–131.

93. Rury, "Philanthropy, Self Help, and Social Control," 233, 235, 237.

94. New York Manumission Society, *Address to the Parents and Guardians*, 4.

95. Ibid., 4–7, 9–12.

96. Ibid., 9, 21. Italics in original.

97. Ibid., 20–21.

98. Ibid., 22. See also David Brion Davis, *Slavery in the Age of Revolution*, 241–242, 305–306.

Chapter Five

1. The history of the Colored Orphan Asylum illuminates a little-studied aspect of Northern antebellum reform: the relationship between race and class in the sphere of women's benevolence. Recent studies of women's roles in antebellum reform have carefully delineated the relationship between class and gender ideologies in the benevolent institutions women established. However, as Evelyn Brooks Higginbotham has noted of women's history generally, such studies have often left race and blacks by the sidelines as white women's historians "continue to analyze their own experience in ever more sophisticated forms"; see Evelyn Higginbotham, "Metalanguage of Race," 251–252. This is true not only of the literature on women's reform, but the literature on reform generally. For general accounts of antebellum reform, see Smith-Rosenberg, *Religion and the Rise of the American City;* Boyer, *Urban Masses;* and Katz, *Shadow of the Poorhouse.* Works on women's reform in the antebellum era include Ginzberg, *Women and the Work of Benevolence;* the essays in McCarthy, ed., *Lady Bountiful Revisited;* and Stansell, *City of Women.* Exceptions include Lebsock's *Free Women of Petersburg,* which discusses issues of race and reform in a southern context. In the postbellum period, works that have opened the door to studying the influence of race on reform include Pascoe, *Relations of Rescue;* and Frankel and Dye, eds., *Reform in the Progressive Era.* The exceptions for antebellum New York City include Cray "White Welfare and Black Strategies"; Rury, "Philanthropy, Self-Help, and Social Control"; and Carleton Mabee, "Charity in Travail."

2. My discussion of the power of black working-class agency on reformers' goals and perceptions is influenced by the work of Linda Gordon; see Gordon, "Family Violence, Feminism, and Social Control," 141–156; and Gordon, *Heroes of Their Own Lives.* For an alternative viewpoint to Gordon's work, see the exchange between Linda Gordon and Joan Scott in the book review section of the summer 1990 issue of *Signs,* pages 848–860.

3. Moseley, "History of the New-York Manumission Society," 217; Charles Andrews, *History of the New-York African Free Schools,* passim.

4. The information on McCune Smith, Henry Highland Garnet, and Alexander Crummell is from C. Peter Ripley et al., *Black Abolitionist Papers,* 3:349–351n; 336–337n; and 471–472n. Additional information on Garnet can be found in Swift, *Black Prophets of Justice,* 113–172; and on Crummell, in Moses, *Alexander Crummell,* 11–33.

5. Swift, *Black Prophets of Justice,* 115. On Samuel Ringgold Ward, see C. Peter Ripley et al., *Black Abolitionist Papers,* 4:41n. On Patrick and Charles Reason, see C. Peter Ripley et al., *Black Abolitionist Papers,* 4:193–194n. On Ira Aldridge, see Ottley and Weatherby, *The Negro in New York,* 73.

6. Charles Andrews, *History of the New-York African Free Schools,* 121–122.

7. Ibid., 122–123.

8. "From the New York Tract Magazine," *African Repository and Colonial Journal,* vol. 1, no. 3 (May 1825), 91–92.

9. For an overview of the ideas behind the colonization movement, see Fredrickson, *Black Image in the White Mind,* 6–21.

10. American Convention for Promoting the Abolition of Slavery and Improving the Condition of the African Race, *Minutes of the Proceedings of the Fifteenth American Convention for Promoting the Abolition of Slavery. . .* (Philadelphia: Merritt, 1817), 30–31; *Minutes of the Seventeenth Session of the American Convention. . .* (Philadelphia: Atkinson and Alexander, 1821), 43–45; *Minutes of an Adjourned Session of the American Convention for Promoting the Abolition of Slavery. . .* (Baltimore: Benjamin Lundy, 1826), 5–7, 48–49; and *Minutes of the American Convention for Promoting the Abolition of Slavery and Improving the Condition of the African Race. Convened at the City of Washington, December 8, A.D. 1829* (Philadelphia: Thomas P. Town, 1829), 29–30, 34–35, 51. All can be found in the multivolume source *Minutes, Constitutions, Addresses, Memorials, Resolutions, Reports, Committees, and Antislavery Tracts, 1794–1829* by the American Convention for Promoting the Abolition of Slavery.

11. Charles Andrews, *History of the New-York African Free Schools*, 117–119; Quarles, *Black Abolitionists*, 12; Moseley, "History of the New-York Manumission Society," 211–212; Russwurm quoted in Quarles, *Black Abolitionists*, 7.

12. Garrison, *Thoughts on African Colonization*, part 2, pp. 13–14. Italics in original.

13. Quarles, *Black Abolitionists*, 12–13; Foner and Lewis, *The Black Worker to 1869*, 134–135.

14. Swift, *Black Prophets of Justice*, 40–41; Moseley, "History of the New-York Manumission Society," 213–218.

15. Harry Williamson, "Folks in Old New York," TS, 6. This was also a time when corporal punishment as a way to inculcate morals was falling into disrepute among educators; see Glenn, "School Discipline," 395–408.

16. Carleton Mabee, *Black Education*, 22–23.

17. C. Peter Ripley et al., *Black Abolitionist Papers*, 3:471n 4.

18. Harry Williamson, "Folks in Old New York," TS, 6; Moseley, "History of the New-York Manumission Society," 190–191, 217–218.

19. On the influence of the leadership struggle on the trustees' decision, see Moseley, "History of the New-York Manumission Society," 189n; on the finances of the school, see 220–229, 244–246; and on the transfer of the schools, see 244–246.

20. Moseley, "History of the New-York Manumission Society," 244–246.

21. Ibid.

22. ABCO, *From Cherry Street to Green Pastures: A History of the Colored Orphan Asylum at Riverdale-On-Hudson. 1836–1936 — anniversary publication*, 3, in Papers of the ABCO (hereafter cited as *From Cherry Street.*)

23. In 1829, American Quakers split into two branches, Hicksite and Orthodox. Hicksite Quakers tended to join radical abolitionist groups. Manumission Society members and their descendants tended to be Orthodox Quakers, who were more conservative. For a detailed discussion of the theological and political implications of the split, see Ingle, *Quakers in Conflict*.

24. Information about Murray's and Shotwell's families can be found in Cox, *Quakerism in the City*, 64, 119–122.

25. Information about Quaker women's participation in New York City education is from William Wood, *Friends of the City*, 28–31, 33. See also Smith-Rosenberg, *Religion and the Rise of the American City*, 26–27, 54–55. Ginzberg too notes the importance of family ties to the success of women's benevolent work; see Ginzberg, *Women and the Work of Benevolence*, 38–39, 44.

26. On women's movement into the public sphere, see Boylan, "Women and Politics," esp. 364–366; Ginzberg, *Women and the Work of Benevolence*, esp. chapter 2; and McCarthy, "Parallel Power Structures: Women and the Voluntary Sphere," in *Lady Bountiful Revisited*, esp. 1–6.

27. Schneider, *The History of Public Welfare*, 1:339–41.

28. Schneider, *The History of Public Welfare*, 1:187–191; ABCO, *From Cherry Street*, 6–7. Other orphanages at this time did not receive funds from municipal sources either.

29. ABCO, *From Cherry Street*, 6.

30. ABCO Minute Book 1, June 9, 1837, entry.

31. The anniversary pamphlet *From Cherry Street* states that eleven children were taken from the almshouse, but the asylum records state that only five were removed; see p.8. The almshouse commissioners refused to supply any funding for the children Shotwell and Murray took in. Stating that they had recently arranged for the education of the black children in the almshouse, they were "willing to part with them to those who will provide altogether for their wants," and particularly to the association, which was "founded in Christian principles." But they were not willing to "contract for partial support of this class of inmates"; see ABCO, Minute Book 1, July 11, 1837, entry, Papers of ABCO.

The disease and death rates of the children taken from the almshouse were so high that the managers began to fear that the illnesses would be communicated to the other children in the asylum. After April 1838, almshouse children were required to undergo a medical examination before acceptance by the orphanage. By October 1839, the managers had begun to use the almshouse as a place for their own undesirables. Despite the fact that there was still no education available for those in the "Colored department," the women stated that "an evident improvement appears manifest in the bodily comfort of the inmates" there. They sent an "unsuitable inmate," four-year-old Jeremiah King, to the institution because diseases of the head and eyes made it difficult to care for him at the asylum. The managers' policy toward such inmates changed again after the building of a larger asylum in 1843, which contained a separate hospital and infirmary, allowed them to care for sick orphans on the grounds; see ABCO Minute Book 1, April 13 and July 13, 1838, and October 11, 1839, entries.

32. The radical abolitionists and the 1834 riots will be discussed more fully in chapter 6.

33. ABCO Minute Book 1, January 13, 1837, entry; "First Annual Report" (1837), ABCO Minute Book 1, December 12, 1837, entry and March 17 and April 7, 1837, entries. For the racism the women encountered in trying to find a location for the orphanage, and details of the purchase, see ABCO, *From Cherry Street*, 7. For the number of children taken from the almshouse, see ABCO Minute Book 2

(1847–1857), July 19, 1847, entry. All found in Papers of ABCO, MS, New-York Historical Society.

34. ABCO, *Sixth Annual Report* (1842), 3–4, 7; ABCO, *Seventh Annual Report* (1843), 3–6; both in ABCO, *Annual Reports of the Colored Orphan Asylum, 1837–1870*. ABCO Minute Book 2, July 19 and October 19, 1847, entries; both found in Papers of ABCO.

35. Ginzberg, *Work of Benevolence*, 65–66.

36. ABCO Minute Book 1, December 8, 1837, entry; "First Annual Report" (1837), ABCO Minute Book 1, December 12, 1837, entry, MS. On exclusion of black charitable organizations from municipal funds, see Boylan, "Women and Politics," 372.

37. Hankins, *Women of New York*, 54–57.

38. On women's moral authority, see Boylan, "Women and Politics," 373–377. The quotation is from ABCO, *Fifth Annual Report* (1841), 6, in ABCO, *Annual Reports of the Colored Orphan Asylum, 1837–1870*. Elizabeth Pleck sees the early national and antebellum period as a time of "revitalized belief in family privacy" in which women made "the home a refuge" that "seal[ed] off domestic activities from community surveillance." But the example of the ABCO shows that many middle-class women moved beyond the confines of the home. Further, they displayed little reluctance in invading the homes of working-class blacks and surveying their domestic activities. Pleck, *Domestic Tyranny*, 37–48.

39. In *Women and the Work of Benevolence*, Lori Ginzberg notes that the legislators who wrote charity corporate charters in Boston "took care to protect the corporation from its members' legal dependence" on their husbands by making husbands liable to be sued if the wife embezzled money from the corporation on his behalf; see p. 51. In the case of the Colored Orphan Asylum, however, the husbands' property was also protected from the activities of their wives, indicating perhaps a greater belief among New York legislators in the independence of women than among Boston legislators: "The husband of any married woman who is or may be a member of the said corporation shall not be liable to the said corporation for any loss occasioned by the neglect or misfeasance of his wife, but if he shall have received any money from his wife belonging to the said corporation, or the same shall have been applied to his use, he shall be accountable therefor"; see ABCO, "Act to Incorporate the Association for the Benefit of Colored Orphans in the City of New York," in ABCO, *First Annual Report of the Association for the Benefit of Colored Orphans*, 12, in ABCO, *Annual Reports of the Colored Orphan Asylum, 1837–1870*.

40. ABCO, "Rules and Regulations Adopted by the Board of Managers for the Government of the Asylum for Colored Orphans, under the Careful Supervision of the Executive Committee," in *First Annual Report* (1837), 17; mention of superintendent in ABCO Minute Book 2, October 10, 1856, entry. Because of the missing minute books for the years 1841–1847, it is impossible to know when the male superintendent was hired. His name may have been Mr. Davis; two letters from former asylum members addressed to a Mr. Davis appear in the 1861 and 1862 annual reports; see ABCO, *Twenty-Fifth Annual Report* (1861), appendix; and ABCO, *Twenty-Sixth Annual Report* (1862), appendix, both in ABCO, *Annual Reports of the Colored Orphan Asylum, 1837–1870*. Although the staff women were single, they did not come

alone. The first matron, Mrs. Morse, had several children who lived with her at the orphanage. The second matron, Rachel Johnson, was responsible for her aged father, who was allowed to live in the small cottage at the back of the orphanage. The hiring of women with children or other dependents was not necessarily a pattern, but the managers did not seem to shy away from allowing their employees to bring their kin to work with them. The managers also hired husband and wife teams, such as shoemaker Henry Chester and his unnamed wife; see ABCO Minute Book 1, February 10, May 12, and July 14, 1837, entries. For benevolent middle-class women's reluctance to discuss their salaries, see Ginzberg, *Women and the Work of Benevolence*, 55–59.

41. "Dear parentless children," in "Colored Orphan Asylum," *Colored American*, October 28, 1837; "The Turpin Legacy," *Colored American*, December 30, 1837.

42. "The Turpin Legacy," *Colored American*, December 30, 1837.

43. "Another Legacy to Educate Colored Youth," *Colored American*, March 3, 1838.

44. See, for example, "Colored Orphan Asylum: Physician's Report," *Colored American*, January 26, 1839. On the scientific and medical debates about African American physiology in the antebellum period, see Fredrickson, *Black Image in the White Mind*, chap. 3.

45. "Colored Orphan's Asylum: Physician's Report," *Colored American*, January 26, 1839.

46. ABCO Minute Book 1, July 13, 1838, entry.

47. Ibid., February 8, 1839, entry.

48. ABCO Minute Book 2, June 8, 1855, entry. No more is written of Dongo in this minute book. The minute book for the years 1857–1860 is missing.

49. Admission records 1837–1860, in ABCO, Admission Book 1; admission record for Sarah Williams, ibid., June 9, 1837; admission record for Jacob Becket Lee, ibid., October 10, 1837.

50. Case records for Jeremiah and Adaline Rawle and Wiley Rawle, ABCO Admission Book 1, November 20, 1837; "First Annual Report" (1837), ABCO Minute Book 1, December 12, 1837, entry.

51. ABCO Minute Book 1, December 8, 1837, entry.

52. For the Oviedo children, see ABCO Admission Book, October 1849–December 1860 (hereafter cited as ABCO Admission Book 2) February 1857 ; and ABCO Admission Book 1 February 23, 1857, entry.

53. ABCO Minute book 1, December 12, 1836, and March 17 and July 14, 1837, entries.

54. Case records for 1838, 1840, 1850, and 1860, ABCO Admission Book 1. Note that for these years, even if the number of orphans of uncertain parentage were added to the number of orphans (total 66), they would still account for fewer children than half-orphans and non-orphans (119). Occasionally parents would be taken away by work and a child would be thought to be an orphan. Some parents returned to claim their children as much as four years later.

55. Pascoe's work *Relations of Rescue*, 73–111, informs my discussion here.

ABCO, *Second Annual Report* (1838), 3, in ABCO, *Annual Reports of the Colored Orphan Asylum, 1837–1870.* The focus on chimney sweeps follows the earlier campaign by the New York Manumission Society to regulate the use of black children as sweeps. "Second Annual Report" (1838), ABCO Minute Book 1, December 10, 1838, entry, MS.

56. Case records for 1837, 1840, 1850, and 1860, ABCO Admission Book 1.

57. "By-Laws," ABCO Minute Book 1, March 17, 1837, entry. The parental agreement is from ABCO Admission Book 1 (inside cover of ledger). I saw only one case in which the managers recorded that a child who was born out of wedlock had been admitted.

58. Single parent agreement of Rachel Johnson, signed July 30, 1844, and single parent agreement of William A. Smith, ABCO Admission Book 1, July 28, 1845.

59. New bylaws in ABCO Minute Book 1, May 11, 1838, entry. Case record for Eliza Giles, ABCO Admission Book 1, August 8, 1842. Eliza's brothers John and Henry were also in the asylum, but were not taken away by their mother; see case record for John and Henry Giles, ABCO Admission Book 1, June 6, 1839.

60. ABCO Minute Book 1, March 8 and April 12, 1839, entries; case record for Jeremiah and Adaline Rawle, ABCO, Admission Book 1, November 10, 1837. For a discussion of personalism and its role in women's benevolent organizations, see Lebsock, *Free Women of Petersburg,* chap. 7; and McCarthy, "Parallel Power Structures: Women and the Voluntary Sphere," *Lady Bountiful Revisited,* 4.

61. Single parent agreement of Rosanna Peterson, ABCO Admission Book 1, September 1, 1843; Admission record for Frederica Matilda Isaacs in ABCO Admission Book 1, April 16, 1840.

62. Stansell, *City of Women,* 209–214.

63. "Rules and Regulations," in ABCO, *First Annual Report* (1837), 17.

64. "Rules and Regulations," in ABCO, *First Annual Report* (1837), 17; case record for Sidney Johnson, ABCO Admission Book 1, July 25, 1837; ABCO Minute Book 1, January 12, 1838, entry.

65. ABCO Minute Book 1, March 3, 1838, November 9, 1838, and July 13, 1838, entries.

66. On David Shutt's indenture, see ABCO Minute Book 2, October 6, 1852, entry. The managers used the words "indenture" and "apprentice" interchangeably in the minutes, but the agreements were, legally, indentures. For eighteenth-century indenturing practices, see Schneider, *The History of Public Welfare,* 1:76, 111, 179ff; Cray, *Paupers and Poor Relief,* 43, 71, 81–82, 89; and Mohl, *Poverty in New York,* 55, 71. The Association for the Benefit of Colored Orphans continued to indenture children into the late nineteenth century. The managers' emphasis on getting children out of the city precedes the work of Charles Loring Brace's Children's Aid Society, the largest and best-known organization for "placing out" children. Unlike Brace's work, which focused overwhelmingly on boys, the women appear to have placed out boys and girls in almost equal numbers. On Brace, see Langsam, *Children West;* and Holt, *Orphan Trains.*

67. "By-Laws," *First Annual Report* (1837), 15; ABCO, *Eighteenth Annual Report* (1854), 7; both in ABCO, *Annual Reports of the Colored Orphan Asylum, 1837–1870.*

68. ABCO, *Tenth Annual Report* (1846), appendix; *Fifteenth Annual Report* (1851), 10; ABCO, *Eighteenth Annual Report* (1854), 7; all appearing in ABCO, *Annual Reports of the Colored Orphan Asylum, 1837–1870.* See also ABCO Minute Book 2, June 11, 1852, entry. ABCO Minute Book 2, December 10, 1851, entry. Because of the scattered nature of references to skilled jobs, a numerical tally would be meaningless. For examples of the girls asked to remain at the orphanage, see ABCO Minute Book 1, April 12, 1839, entry; and ABCO, *Eighteenth Annual Report* (1854), 7.

In contrast to the association's recordkeeping, the Juvenile Home kept detailed records of the occupations to which their children were indentured. Between 1824 and 1834, 733 boys were indentured. Of these, 302 were sent "To Farmers." The remaining 431 were placed in occupations ranging from whale fishery to butchers to cloth manufacturers, for a range of forty-two occupations. The 201 girls from the Juvenile Home were placed in only three occupations: 197 in "Housewifery"; 3 to milliners; and 1 to a tailor; see "To What Trades and Callings the Children have been Indentured, the First Ten Years of the Establishment of the Institution, That is from 7th January 1824 to the 1st of Jan'y, 1834," MS.

69. The information on indentures is taken from case records in ABCO Admission Book 1 and Book of Indentures—Accounting of the Association, 1860–1886.

70. Case record for Mary Wales, ABCO Admission Book 1, October 29, 1841; case record for James Hitchcock, ibid., April 10, 1839.

71. The information on indentures is from ABCO Admission Book 1 and Book of Indentures—Accounting of the Association, 1860–1886.

72. Case record for Mary Jackson, ABCO Admission Book 1, March 5, 1847; ABCO, *Tenth Annual Report* (1846), appendix.

73. Case record for William King, ABCO Admission Book 1, December 24, 1847; case record for Benjamin Charles Bowen, ibid., February 10, 1846.

74. Case record for Moses Brooks, ibid., October 9, 1837. ABCO Minute Book 1, July 12, 1839, entry; case record for Elizabeth Dennis, ABCO Admission Book 1, April 10, 1838; case records for Abijiah Norton and George Norton, ibid., August 6, 1860.

75. "Second Annual Report" (1838), in ABCO Minute Book 1, December 10, 1838, entry.

76. *Twenty-fifth Annual Report* (1861), appendix; and ABCO, *Twenty-Sixth Annual Report* (1862), appendix, both in ABCO, *Annual Reports of the Colored Orphan Asylum, 1837–1870.*

Chapter Six

1. The quotation is from article 3 of "Constitution of the American Anti-Slavery Society," in *Second Annual Report of the American Anti-Slavery Society* (1835), 74. On blacks' influence on radical abolitionists, see Quarles, *Black Abolitionists,* 3–36; and Goodman, *Of One Blood,* 36–53. On religious influences, see Walters,

Antislavery Appeal, 37–53; Wyatt-Brown, *Lewis Tappan,* 1–14, 23–36, 41–55, 81–83; and John Thomas, *The Liberator: William Lloyd Garrison,* 62–67, 69–73.

2. See Quarles, *Black Abolitionists,* especially chapter 1, for accounts of black mass support of the abolitionist movement.

3. On abolitionist activism, see Kraditor, *Means and Ends,* 3–38; and Walters, *Antislavery Appeal,* 12–20.

4. For the growth of a middle-class morality, see, among others, Ryan, *Cradle of the Middle Class;* and Sellers, *Market Revolution,* chaps. 8 and 10.

5. Aptheker, *One Continual Cry,* esp. 29–37, 45–53; Pease and Pease, *They Who Would Be Free,* 20–23. Hinks's *To Awaken My Afflicted Brethren* is the most complete discussion of Walker's *Appeal,* its meaning, and its impact on antislavery activism. Hinks argues for a close alliance between Walker and other middle-class reformers during this time, with which I agree and will discuss later in this chapter; see Hinks, idem, 34, 91–115. The quotation is from David Walker, *David Walker's Appeal to the Coloured Citizens of the World, but in particular, and very expressly, to those of The United States of America,* ed. Sean Wilentz, 28.

6. *Constitution of the American Society of Free Persons of Colour, For Improving Their Condition in the United States; for Purchasing Lands; and for the Establishment of a Settlement in Upper Canada. Also the Proceeding of the Convention, with their Address to the Free Persons of Colour in the United States,* reprinted in Bell, *Proceedings of the National Negro Conventions.* For an overview of the history of the National Convention Movement, see Bell, *Negro Convention Movement.* On tensions between New Yorkers and Philadelphians, see Winch, *Philadelphia's Black Elite,* 91–92; and Bell, *Negro Convention Movement,* 15.

7. *Minutes and Proceedings of the First Annual Convention of the People of Colour, Held by Adjournments in the City of Philadelphia, From the Sixth to the Eleventh of June, Inclusive, 1831,* in Bell, *Proceedings of the National Negro Conventions.*

8. Quarles, *Black Abolitionists,* 18–21; Garrison, *Thoughts on African Colonization.*

9. Wyatt-Brown, *Lewis Tappan,* 84–87, 92, 102–103.

10. Kraditor has most successfully outlined the strengths and weaknesses of the range of opinions in organized antislavery of the 1830s and 1840s in *Means and Ends.* See also Friedman, *Gregarious Saints.*

11. *Minutes and Proceedings of the First Annual Convention of the People of Colour, Held by Adjournments in the City of Philadelphia, From the Sixth to the Eleventh of June, Inclusive, 1831,* 6–7, 14, in Bell, *Proceedings of the National Negro Convention.*

12. Anderson, "Manual Labor School Movement," 369–386. On abolitionists' particular attachment to manual labor schools, see Goodman, "The Manual Labor Movement and the Origins of Abolitionism," esp. 360–364.

13. Anderson, "Manual Labor School Movement," 383.

14. Goodman, "The Manual Labor Movement and the Origins of Abolitionism," 364.

15. *Minutes . . . of the First Annual Convention of the People of Colour* (1831), 14, in Bell, *Proceedings of the National Negro Conventions.*

16. *Minutes and Proceedings of the Third Annual Convention, for the Improvement of the Free People of Colour in these United States, Held by Adjournments in the City of Philadelphia, from the 3rd to the 13th of June inclusive, 1833,* 33, in Bell, *Proceedings of the National Negro Conventions.*

17. On Maria Stewart in Boston, see Marilyn Richardson, *Maria Stewart,* 3–27; quotation is from Stewart's speech, 70; and *Colored American,* July 10, 1841. My thanks to Anne Boylan for information about Maria Stewart's activities in New York City.

18. "Notice," *Freedom's Journal,* February 1, 1828; advisory board, quoted in "African Dorcas Association," *Freedom's Journal,* February 15, 1822, and "New York African Free School," *Freedom's Journal,* March 7, 1828; "Female Dorcas Society," written by "A Member," *Freedom's Journal,* September 26, 1828; "Notice," written by "Margt Francis Pres.," *Freedom's Journal,* March 14, 1829. On middle-class women's work and family roles, see Stansell, *City of Women,* 41, 146, 158–160; and Ryan, *Cradle of the Middle Class,* 198–210.

19. "Third Anniversary of the Ladies Literary Society of the City of New York," *Colored American,* September 23, 1837; "On the Death of Mrs. Ray," *Colored American,* March 4, 1837. On literary societies forming a bridge between domestic and public spheres for women, see McHenry, "'Dreaded Eloquence,'" 49–53.

20. For middle-class women's work and family roles, see Stansell, *City of Women,* 41, 146, 158–60; and Ryan, *Cradle of the Middle Class,* 198–210. For women's waged work, see Stansell, *City of Women,* 71–72, 105–106, 108, 110–113, 157.

21. On similar issues between white working-class families and middle-class reformers, see Stansell, *City of Women,* especially 193–216.

22. Winch, *Philadelphia's Black Elite,* 135–142; C. Peter Ripley et al., *Black Abolitionist Papers,* 3:80–81n; Chilton Williamson, *American Suffrage,* 93–96, 111.

23. On the manual labor school committee, see *First Annual Convention of the People of Colour,* 6–7; in Bell, *Proceedings of the National Negro Conventions.* The information on Downing and Bell is from George Walker, *The Afro-American in New York City,* 37. The account of Boston Crummell is from Moses, *Alexander Crummell,* 11–16. I have been unable to find any information on Peter Vogelsang.

24. *First Annual Report of the Society for the Encouragement of Faithful Domestic Servants in New-York,* 3, 5, 11, 15.

25. Wyatt-Brown, *Lewis Tappan,* 88.

26. Wyatt-Brown, *Lewis Tappan,* 87–89. On New Haven as particularly pious, see *First Annual Convention of the Free People of Colour,* 6, in Bell, *Proceedings of the National Negro Conventions.* On the New England Anti-Slavery Society, see Pease and Pease, *They Who Would Be Free,* 136–138.

27. *Minutes of the Fourth Annual Convention, for the Improvement of the Free People of Colour, in the United States, Held by Adjournments in the Asbury Church, New-York, From the 2d to the 12th of June inclusive, 1834,* 31–32 in Bell, *Proceedings of the National Negro Conventions;* Bell, *Survey of the Negro Convention Move-*

ment, 34–37; "Moral Reform Convention," *Colored American,* August 26, 1837; "Cranberry Moral Reform Society," *Colored American,* January 12, 1839. There were some Philadelphians who opposed the American Moral Reform Society's goals.

28. The quotations are from a letter Frederick Hinton wrote to Samuel Cornish, published in *Colored American,* September 2, 1837. Hinton was a Philadelphian; see Winch, *Philadelphia's Black Elite,* 114.

29. On the American Moral Reform Society and disagreements between Philadelphians and New Yorkers, see Winch, *Philadelphia's Black Elite,* 109–112, 114, 117–118. Gerrit Smith in upstate New York and a group of Quakers in Philadelphia built small manual labor schools for blacks in the 1830s.

30. C. Peter Ripley et al., *Black Abolitionist Papers,* 3:187–188n.

31. Swift, *Black Prophets of Justice,* 59–60; Mabee, *Black Education,* 57–59.

32. "On the Death of Mrs. Ray," *Colored American,* March 4, 1837; "Phoenixonian Literary Society," *Colored American,* July 8, 1837; "Third Anniversary of the Ladies Literary Society of the City of New York," *Colored American,* September 23, 1837; "Phoenixonian Society," *Colored American,* July 13, 1839; "Union Lyceum," *Colored American,* November 23, 1839; "Public Lectures of the New York Phoenixonian Literary Society," *Colored American,* February 6, 1841. Boylan, "Henrietta Green Regulus Ray," in Hine, et al., eds., *Black Women in America,* 2:966; Porter, "Educational Activities," 555–576.

33. Quotations are in "Education," *Colored American,* September 30, 1837.

34. Article 3, "Constitution of the American Anti-Slavery Society," in *Second Annual Report of the American Anti-Slavery Society, with the Speeches Delivered at the Anniversary Meeting, Held in the City of New-York, on the 12th of May, 1835, and the Minutes of the Meetings of the Society for Business,* 74.

35. "American Colonization Society. For the Freedom's Journal. Conclusion," *Freedom's Journal,* November 23, 1827.

36. For the methods and success of the abolitionists, see Levine, *Half Slave and Half Free,* 154–155; Walters, *Antislavery Appeal,* 19–33, 47–49, 106–108; Quarles, *Black Abolitionists,* 23–30; Goodman, *Of One Blood,* 122–136.

37. Reese, *Humbugs of New York,* 143. For the tensions caused by the increasing power of abolitionists and the decreasing power of the colonizationists, see Richards, *"Gentlemen of Property and Standing,"* 24–25, 30–31, 48–49, 168.

38. Foner, *Business and Slavery,* esp. 1–14; DeBow quotation, 4; figures on New York profit on southern cotton and on New York merchandise sold south, 7; Albion, *New York Port,* 14, 95–121.

39. Smith-Rosenberg, *Religion and the Rise of the American City,* 98–101; Tappan, *Life of Arthur Tappan,* 113, 116; Gilfoyle, *City of Eros,* 43–46.

40. Gilfoyle, *City of Eros,* 42–46; Wyatt-Brown, *Lewis Tappan,* 68–70. The quotation is from Barnabas Bates, "An Address Delivered at a General Meeting of the Citizens of the City of New-York," in Wyatt-Brown, *Lewis Tappan,* 68. Bogardus is not identified as a brothel landlord in Gilfoyle's *City of Eros.* Smith-Rosenberg, *Religion and the Rise of the American City,* 100–101; Tappan, *Life of Arthur Tappan,* 113, 116.

41. Gilfoyle, *City of Eros*, 17–22, 29; Smith-Rosenberg, *Religion and the Rise of the American City*, 98–100.

42. On definitions and uses of "amalgamation," see *Oxford English Dictionary;* Richard H. Thornton, *An American Glossary*, 1:13. and Craigie and Hulbert, *A Dictionary of American English on Historical Principles*, 37. "Amalgamation" also referred to the mixing of metals. Pascoe's, "Miscegenation Law, Court Cases, and Ideologies of 'Race' in Twentieth-Century America," 44–69, although about post–Civil War miscegenation, is useful in delineating the various levels of interracial relationships encapsulated in the word "miscegenation." A similar process occurred with "amalgamation" in the antebellum era.

43. On interracial socializing, see Mabee, *Nonviolent Abolitionists*, 103–111. According to Mabee, a few black abolitionist men did marry white women, but only after the 1834 riots, and not in New York City.

44. "Meeting of the Vigilance Committee," *Emancipator*, December 15, 1836. The best treatment of the radicalism of the abolitionists on race is Goodman, *Of One Blood*, especially 11–64, 233–260.

45. On working-class resentment of the Tappans, see Wilentz, *Chants Democratic*, 263–266.

46. Child, *Class of Americans*, 196.

47. *First Annual Report of the American Anti-Slavery Society; with the Speeches Delivered at the Anniversary Meeting, Held in Chatham-Street Chapel, in the city of New-York, on the sixth day of May, 1834 . . .* , 8–9. Thome's descriptions of the houses of blacks as open to anyone throughout the night parallel descriptions of the poor in urban areas in the North, whose home lives often spilled out into the streets. See also Ronald Walters, "The Erotic South," 177–201.

48. "Major Noah's 'Negroes,'" *Freedom's Journal*, August 24, 1827, and "For the Freedom [*sic*] Journal, *Freedom's Journal*, August 17, 1827. The pseudonymous Mordecai is not to be confused with the anti-abolitionist Mordecai Noah mentioned above. The *Freedom's Journal* writer may have taken the name Mordecai as a counterpoint to Noah's tendency to criticize blacks in mainstream New York newspapers.

49. Quoted in Tappan, *Life of Arthur Tappan*, 171–72.

50. "Dr. Cox's Letter on Abolition," *New York Journal of Commerce*, April 30, 1834.

51. "The Fanatics," *Morning Courier and New-York Enquirer*, June 23, 1834. The debate over amalgamation and colonization may have been further exacerbated by the fact that free blacks also held their convention in New York in June of that year, although the convention was not discussed in New York City's white newspapers.

52. Primary accounts of the riots can be found in Tappan, *Life of Arthur Tappan*, and in New York newspapers. Secondary source accounts include Linda Kerber, "Abolitionists and Amalgamators," 28–39, reprinted in Kusmer, ed., *Antebellum America*, 376–387; Richards, *"Gentlemen of Property and Standing"*; Gilje, *Road to Mobocracy*, 162–170; Wilentz, *Chants Democratic*, 264–266; Anbinder, *Five Points*, 7–13.

53. Tappan, *Life of Arthur Tappan*, 203–204.

54. Richards, *"Gentlemen of Property and Standing,"* 150–153; Wilentz, *Chants Democratic,* 264–266. For economic beliefs of the abolitionists, see Walters, *Antislavery Appeal,* 111–128.

55. Gilfoyle, *Road to Mobocracy,* 166; "The Riots," *Mercantile Advertiser and New York Advocate,* July 14, 1834, p. 2; Tappan, *Life of Arthur Tappan,* 215–216.

56. Tappan, *Life of Arthur Tappan,* 215–216.

57. "An Appeal of the American Anti-Slavery Society to the People of the City of New-York," *Emancipator,* August 19, 1834, 1; "To the Hon. Cornelius W. Lawrence, Mayor of the City of New York," *New York Commercial Advertiser,* July 18, 1834, 3; "For the Freedom's Journal," *Freedom's Journal,* June 29, 1827.

58. The Massachusetts law was not repealed until 1841. See Fredrickson, *Black Image in the White Mind,* 122–123, for the attitudes of abolitionists toward amalgamation.

59. Child is quoted in Fredrickson, *Black Image in the White Mind,* 37; on white workers, see Roediger, *Wages of Whiteness,* passim; "could be used . . . " in Fredrickson, *Black Image in the White Mind,* 37.

60. See, for example, "Address of Rev. Peter Williams," *New York Commercial Advertiser,* July 15, 1834, 2; and the American Colonization Society's *African Repository and Colonial Journal,* August 1834.

61. "Address of Rev. Peter Williams," in *New York Commercial Advertiser,* July 15, 1834, 2; "Mission School," *Rights of All,* August 7, 1829.

62. Kraditor, *Means and Ends,* 103, 30–31; Smith quoted in *Third Annual Report of the American Anti-Slavery Society; with the Speeches Delivered at the Anniversary Meeting, Held in the City of New-York, on the 10th May, 1836, and the Minutes of the Meetings of the Society for Business* (1836), 16–17.

63. *Third Annual Report of the American Anti-Slavery Society* (1836), 27; "More Practical Measures," *Colored American,* October 27, 1838; Swift, *Black Prophets of Justice,* 92–93.

64. "Steward's and Cook's Marine Benevolent Society," *Colored American,* May 2, 1840.

65. C. Peter Ripley and the staff of the Black Abolitionist Papers have recovered the speeches and life of this lesser-known black abolitionist. My interpretation of his role rests on their ground-breaking research. See C. Peter Ripley et al., *Black Abolitionist Papers,* 3:292–293n., for a summary of Simons's life.

66. "Wicked Conspiracy," *Colored American,* December 30, 1837.

67. "Nov. 24, 1837. Most Dear and Valuable Sir," *Colored American,* December 30, 1837; "For the Colored American." *Colored American,* January 13, 1838.

68. "Mission School," *Rights of All,* August 7, 1829.

69. Horton, "Freedom's Yoke: Gender Conventions among Free Blacks," in *Free People of Color,* 102–103; "Parallel of the Sexes," *Colored American,* September 14, 1839, quoted in Horton, *Free People of Color,* 102–103. During the 1840 schism among abolitionists concerning the role of women, Samuel Cornish left the American Anti-Slavery Society in part because of the increased role which was being given to

women, as represented by Abby Kelley. See C. Peter Ripley et al., *Black Abolitionist Papers*, 3:95–96n.

70. "An Oration, Delivered 23rd of April, 1839, by Peter Paul Simons," *Colored American*, June 1, 1839.

71. Ibid.

72. "Mr. Peter Paul Simons' Oration," *Colored American*, June 8, 1839.

73. In 1841, abolitionist William Seward was elected governor and repealed the nine-months clause of the 1810 emancipation law, effectively claiming that all slaves who traveled in New York State became free upon touching New York soil. See Finkelman, *Imperfect Union*, 18, 71–72, 75–76.

74. "Land of Liberty," *Freedom's Journal*, December 5, 1828.

75. "The New York Committee of Vigilance: Secretary's Monthly Report, no. 2," *Emancipator*, November 2, 1837.

76. The information about the provisions of the 1793 Fugitive Slave Law is from Finkelman, "Kidnapping of John Davis," 419–420.

77. "The case of Hannah Conyers in "Child Lost," *Emancipator*, December, 1835; the case of Dorcas Brown in "Another Slave Case," *Emancipator*, October 13, 1836; and the case of James Emerson in "Meeting of the Vigilance Committee," *Emancipator*, December 1, 1836. For dangers to black seamen, see Bolster, "African-American Seamen," 278 and passim.

78. Douglass, *My Bondage and My Freedom*, ed. William L. Andrews, 206.

79. Jacobs, *Incidents in the Life of a Slave Girl, Written by Herself*, ed. Jean Fagan Yellin, 164–170, 223–225.

80. Ibid., 191–192.

81. "Scenes in the City Prison of New-York," *Anti-Slavery Record*, vol. 1, no. 6, June 1835, 63; C. Peter Ripley et al., *Black Abolitionist Papers*, 3:175–176n and 179n; Pease and Pease, *They Who Would Be Free*, 209–210.

82. Information on the New York Committee of Vigilance in C. Peter Ripley et al., *Black Abolitionist Papers*, 3:37, 179n, and 175–176n; and Pease and Pease, *They Who Would Be Free*, 208–212.

83. See C. Peter Ripley et al., *Black Abolitionist Papers*, 3: 175–176n and 179n.

84. "Meeting of the Vigilance Committee," *Emancipator*, December. 1, 1836.

85. On Ruggles's life, see Porter, "David Ruggles," 23–49.

86. Douglass, *My Bondage and My Freedom*, 208.

87. "David Ruggles and the Daily Papers," *Emancipator*, August 30, 1838.

88. Ibid.

89. "City Recorder—Kidnapping and the Free People of Color in New-York," *Emancipator*, October 6, 1836.

90. Cornish in *Colored American*, April 15, 1837, quoted in Pease and Pease, *They Who Would Be Free*, 209–210.

91. "The New York Committee of Vigilance, Secretary's Monthly Report, no. 2," *Emancipator*, November 23, 1837.

92. Kraditor, *Means and Ends*, 6, 82–83, 111n.

93. On tensions between Ruggles and Cornish, see Pease and Pease, *They Who Would Be Free*, 210–211. See also "Libel Suit," in *Colored American*, November 3, 1838, and October 20, 1838; "Friends, do not forget us," *Colored American*, November 10, 1838; "Agent of the Vigilance Committee," *Colored American*, January 26, 1839; and February 23, 1839, *Colored American*. On Ruggles's life, see Porter, "David Ruggles," 23–50. "From the Mirror of Liberty. The Libel Suit," "David Ruggles," "Office 36 Lispenard Street," article beginning "By the above . . . ," all in *Colored American*, February 23, 1839.

94. On Seward, see Finkelman, "Protection of Black Rights," 211–234; and Carol Wilson, *Freedom at Risk*, 73–75, 111.

CHAPTER SEVEN

1. "New York City Corporation, *vs.* Mr. Henry Graves and His Handcart," *Colored American*, May 9, 1840.

2. For accounts of William Hewlett and Anthony Provost, see Graham Hodges, *New York City Cartmen*, 158–159.

3. On the masculine ideology and racism of cartmen, see ibid., esp. 158–160.

4. Quarles, *Black Abolitionists*, chapter 3, esp. p. 47.

5. On John Humphrey Noyes, see Klaw, *Without Sin*, 15–16, 24–26, 30–31, 38–42, 57, 65–76.

6. Wyatt-Brown, *Lewis Tappan*, 185–190; Kraditor, *Means and Ends*, 29–30, 54, 55, 58, 62, 90, 91, 103, 106, 206, 208; AASS executive committee members in *Fourth Annual Report of the American Anti-Slavery Society* (1837), 28. Cornish, "Eastern Controversy," *Colored American*, October 7, 1837.

7. Quarles, *Black Abolitionists*, 44–47; Charles B. Ray quotation, 45–46. Swift, *Black Prophets of Justice*, 108–111, particularly 110 and 110n on black abolitionists and women's rights. Cornish, "Our Future Course," *Colored American*, May 23, 1840.

8. Swift, *Black Prophets of Justice*, 110. On Hester Lane, see Quarles, *Black Abolitionists*, 61; and E. S. Abdy, *Journal of a Residence*, 2:31–34. My thanks to Anne Boylan for directing me to the latter.

9. Swift, *Black Prophets of Justice*, 105–109; "Right of Suffrage," *Colored American*, March 4, 1837; "Reception of Our Petition," *Colored American*, March 11, 1837; "Important Meeting," *Colored American*, September 2, 1837; "Right of Suffrage," *Colored American*, December 30, 1837; "Public Meeting," *Colored American*, June 16, 1838; "[Constitution of the New York Political Association]," *Colored American*, June 23, 1838.

10. Kraditor, *Means and Ends*, 178–234, esp. 185–186, 196–197, 208–210; Swift, *Black Prophets of Justice*, 108–109.

11. Gerrit Smith's land grants will be discussed in greater detail in chapter 8. On Gerrit Smith's life, see Harlow, *Gerrit Smith: Philanthropist and Reformer;* and Frothingham, *Gerrit Smith: A Biography*.

12. "Resolutions of the American and Foreign Anti-Slavery Society," *Colored American*, June 27, 1840. For an overview of the efforts of the American Missionary Association, see DeBoer, "Afro-Americans in the Origin and Work of the American

Missionary Association"; and DeBoer, *Be Jubilant My Feet.* On numbers of blacks in leadership positions in the AMA, see DeBoer, *Be Jubilant My Feet,* 85–87.

13. Swift, *Black Prophets of Justice,* 78–90.

14. Ibid., 155–161. Report of Charles B. Ray to the Executive Committee of the American Missionary Association, AD, February 1848, American Missionary Association Archives (Box/Document 78809–78810), Amistad Research Center, Tulane University, New Orleans.

15. Biographical information on Garnet from C. Peter Ripley et al., *Black Abolitionist Papers,* 3:336–337n; and Swift, *Black Prophets of Justice,* 3, 113–172. On financial conflicts, see Swift, *Black Prophets of Justice,* 289–291. For Garnet's requests to the AMA for additional aid for missionary work, see Henry Highland Garnet to Simeon S. Jocelyn, ALS, September 14, 1859, American Missionary Association Archives (Box/Document 84310); and Letter from Henry Highland Garnet to Simeon S. Jocelyn, ALS, November 27, 1859, American Missionary Association Archives (Box/Document 84410).

16. Lewis Tappan is quoted in Quarles, *Black Abolitionists,* 50. Reason's other engraving can be found in "Steward and Cook's Marine Benevolent Society," *Colored American,* May 2, 1840.

17. "From the National Anti-Slavery Standard: Eighteenth Anniversary of the American Anti-Slavery Society . . . The Colonization of the Colored Race—Attack of the Black Upon the White Abolitionists—Escape of a Fugitive Slave," *Frederick Douglass' Paper,* May 27, 1852. Although this was a meeting of the "American and Foreign Anti-Slavery Society," they used the title "American Anti-Slavery Society" to highlight their legitimacy in the antislavery struggle.

18. For cultural connections between the work performed by blacks and Irish, see Roediger, "Irish-American Workers and White Racial Formation in the Antebellum United States," in *Wages of Whiteness,* esp. 133–134, 144–150.

19. The quotations are from Friedman, *Gregarious Saints,* 173–174.

20. "From the National Anti-Slavery Standard: Eighteenth Anniversary of the American Anti-Slavery Society . . . Attack of the Black Upon the White Abolitionists . . . " *Frederick Douglass' Paper,* May 27, 1852.

21. Details of Douglass's life from McFeely, *Frederick Douglass.* See also Blassingame, *The Frederick Douglass Papers. Series One: Speeches, Debates, and Interviews,* vols. 1–5, for the most complete selection of Douglass' important writings.

22. On Douglass's powerful oratory style and his influence, see Blassingame, "Introduction," *Frederick Douglass Papers,* series 1, vol. 1, esp. xxii–xxxv. On the influence of this generation of black antislavery lecturers more generally, see William Andrews, *To Tell a Free Story,* 99; and Gara, "The Professional Fugitive."

23. Quoted in William Andrews, *To Tell a Free Story,* 99.

24. "Speech of Henry Highland Garnet, Delivered at the Seventh Anniversary of the American Anti-Slavery Society," *Colored American,* May 30, 1840.

25. Pennington, *The Fugitive Blacksmith,* 212.

26. Pennington, *The Fugitive Blacksmith,* 212. On white abolitionists' views of the degradation blacks suffered under slavery, see Fredrickson, *Black Image in the*

White Mind, 34–36. On their beliefs in the degradation of labor under slavery, see Goodman, "The Manual Labor Movement and the Origins of Abolitionism," 362. On white workers' negative views of slave and free black labor, see Roediger, *Wages of Whiteness,* 65–92, 119–120.

27. C. Peter Ripley et. al., *Black Abolitionist Papers,* 3:350–51n.

28. *Minutes of the National Convention of Colored Citizens: Held at Buffalo, on the 15th, 16th, 17th, 18th and 19th of August 1843. For the Purpose of Considering their Moral and Political Condition as American Citizens,* 27, in Bell, *Proceedings of the National Negro Conventions.*

29. For Delany's quotation, see *Report of the Proceedings of the Colored National Convention Held at Cleveland, Ohio, on Wednesday, September 6, 1848,* 5, in Bell, *Proceedings of the National Negro Conventions.* For Delany's life, see Painter, "Martin R. Delany: Elitism and Black Nationalism," in Litwack and Meier, eds., *Black Leaders of the Nineteenth Century,* 149–171; quotation on 152. For Delany's work with Frederick Douglass, see Robert S. Levine, *Martin Delany, Frederick Douglass, and the Politics of Representative Identity,* 18–22.

30. *Report of the Proceedings of the Colored National Convention Held at Cleveland, Ohio, on Wednesday, September 6, 1848,* 5–6, 13, 19, in Bell, *Proceedings of the National Negro Conventions.* According to an informal survey taken at the 1848 convention, delegates included "Printers, Carpenters, Blacksmiths, Shoemakers, Engineer, Dentist, Gunsmiths, Editors, Tailors, Merchants, Wheelwrights, Painters, Farmers, Physicians, Plasterers, Masons, Students, Clergymen, Barbers and Hairdressers, Laborers, Coopers, Livery Stable Keepers, Bath House Keepers, Grocery Keepers." *Report of the Proceedings of the Colored National Convention . . . 1848,* 12. Singular and plural forms are reproduced as written in the source. On Mary Ann Shadd Cary, see Rhodes, *Mary Ann Shadd Cary: The Black Press and Protest;* and Carolyn Calloway-Thomas, "Mary Ann Shadd Cary," Hine et al., *Black Women in America: An Historical Encyclopedia,* 1:224–226.

31. The quotations are from *Report of the Proceedings of the Colored National Convention . . . 1848,* 5–6, 13, 19, in Bell, *Proceedings of the National Negro Conventions.*

32. Ibid., 17.

33. The information on Reason is from C. Peter Ripley et al., *Black Abolitionist Papers,* 4:193–194n; on Vashon, 3:321–322n; on Langston, 4:282n.

34. "Report of the Committee on the Manual Labor School," in *Proceedings of the Colored National Convention, Held in Rochester, July 6th, 7th, and 8th, 1853,* 31–32, in Bell, *Proceedings of the National Negro Conventions;* "Proceedings of the National Council of the Colored People, in New York, New York, on 8, 9, 10 May 1855," in Blassingame, *The Frederick Douglass Papers,* series 1, 3:65.

35. "Proceedings of the National Council of the Colored People, in New York, New York, on 8, 9, 10 May 1855," in Blassingame, *The Frederick Douglass Papers,* series 1, 3:64, 67, 71.

36. Ibid., 75.

37. *Proceedings of the Colored National Convention, Held in Franklin Hall, Sixth*

Street, Below Arch, Philadelphia, October 16th, 17th and 18th, 1855, 10–12, in Bell, *Proceedings of the National Negro Conventions*.

38. Ripley et al., *Black Abolitionist Papers*, 3:302–303n; Foner, "William P. Powell," 88–111.

39. "Gleanings by the Wayside," *North Star*, February 11, 1848.

40. Bolster, "African-American Seamen," 90–91 and passim.

41. Marticha Lyons' story is reprinted in Sterling, *We Are Your Sisters*, 220–221.

42. "American League of Colored Laborers," *North Star*, June 13, 1850; Grimké and Weld are quoted in Pease and Pease, *They Who Would Be Free*, 14.

43. "Heads of the Colored People—No. 2," *Frederick Douglass' Paper*, April 15, 1852.

44. "Learn Trades or Starve," *Frederick Douglass' Paper*, March 4, 1853.

45. "Make Your Sons Mechanics and Farmers," *Frederick Douglass' Paper*, March 18, 1853.

46. "The Way it is Exactly," *Frederick Douglass' Paper*, April 22, 1853.

47. "Meeting of the Hotel and Saloon Waiters—Formation of a Protective Union," *New York Herald*, March 31, 1853, reprinted in Foner and Lewis, *The Black Worker to 1869*, 191–192. The white waiter William Hamilton should not be confused with the black abolitionist William Hamilton, who died in 1836.

48. Ibid.

49. Advertisements of the Waiters Union in *New York Herald*, April 5, 1853, reprinted in Foner and Lewis, *The Black Worker to 1869*, 192–193.

50. "From Our Brooklyn Correspondent," *Frederick Douglass' Paper*, April 1, 1853.

51. Tunis Campbell's life is described in Tunis Campbell, *Sufferings of the Rev. T. G. Campbell and his Family, in Georgia*, 5–6; King, Introduction, *Never Let People Be Kept Waiting*, xxiii–xxv; and Duncan, *Freedom's Shore*, 12–16.

52. King, Introduction, *Never Let People Be Kept Waiting*, xxi–xxii.

53. For descriptions of nineteenth-century waiting, see ibid., xii–xiii.

54. "First United Association of Colored Waiters," *New York Herald*, April 13, 1853, reprinted in Foner and Lewis, *The Black Worker to 1869*, 193–194. On the position of master craftsmen, see Wilentz, *Chants Democratic*, 285–286.

55. "First United Association of Colored Waiters,"*New York Herald*, April 13, 1853, reprinted in Foner and Lewis, *The Black Worker to 1869*, 193–194.

56. Ibid.

57. "Arouse Waiters," *New York Herald*, April 14, 1853; "Meeting of the Waiters' Protective Union," in *New York Herald*, April 16, 1853, both reprinted in Foner and Lewis, *The Black Worker to 1869*, 194–196.

CHAPTER EIGHT

1. The accounts of interracial sexuality with which historians are most familiar are those of the nineteenth-century South after the Civil War in which black men were depicted as rapists. Increasingly, historians are also uncovering the extent of the

rape of black women by slave masters in the antebellum era. For a summary of the literature on interracial sex in the South, see D'Emilio and Freedman, *Intimate Matters*, 93–108; Painter, "Of *Lily*, Linda Brent, and Freud," 241–259; and Clinton, "Caught in the Web." See also Joel Williamson, *Miscegenation and Mulattoes;* McLaurin, *Celia, A Slave;* and Hine, "Rape and the Inner Lives of Black Women," 292–297. George Fredrickson and Winthrop Jordan examine both northern and southern thought about interracial sex; see Fredrickson, *Black Image in the White Mind*, esp. 117–124; and Jordan, *White over Black*, esp. 469–475, 542–569. See also Fowler, *Northern Attitudes towards Interracial Marriage.*

There is a growing number of new works on interracial sex that move beyond these paradigms. For a work that examines consensual sex in the antebellum South, see Hodes, *White Women, Black Men*. For works that move beyond the South and black-white sex, see the essays in Hodes, ed., *Sex, Love, Race* and Pascoe, "Miscegenation Law, Court Cases, and Ideologies of 'Race' in Twentieth-Century America," 44–69.

2. "A Large Haul," *New York Transcript*, November 13, 1834; "Police Office," *New York Transcript*, March 11, 15, 27, 1835. Although blackguarding has many definitions, here it probably means making remarks of a sexual or seductive nature.

3. "Practical Amalgamation," *New York Transcript*, July 24, 1835; "Special Sessions—Yesterday," *New York Transcript*, July 25, 1835.

4. "Police Office: Othello Travestie," *New York Transcript*, September 8, 1835.

5. See Stansell, *City of Women*, 89–91.

6. "Police Office," *New York Transcript*, October 16, 1834.

7. Ernst, *Immigrant Life in New York City*, 41; Gilfoyle, *City of Eros*, 34.

8. See David Roediger's excellent analysis of the cultural relationship between blacks and Irish in *Wages of Whiteness*, 133–63. See also Ignatiev, *How the Irish Became White*, esp. 76, 87, 140–44; and Graham Hodges, "'Desirable Companions and Lovers,'" 122–144.

9. Dickens, *American Notes*, 272.

10. Dickens, *American Notes*, 272. On minstrelsy, see Lott, *Love and Theft*.

11. Lackey, "Eighteenth-Century Aesthetic Theory," 34; Blumin, "Introduction" *New York by Gas-Light and Other Urban Sketches by George C. Foster*, 17–19. See also Siegel, *Image of the American City*, for a detailed overview of this literature. Most literary scholars and historians have overlooked Dickens's *American Notes* as an inspiration for some of the new literature about the city written by Americans in the 1840s. Many focus on the larger European tradition of travel writing, or even Dickens's descriptions of London in *Sketches by Boz* (1836), as the source of American writers' new mode of describing the city. Others focus on the French writer Eugene Sue, whose *Les Mystères de Paris* was the inspiration for numerous works on American cities whose titles began *The Mysteries and Miseries of . . . .* See, for example, Brand, *The Spectator and the City*, 41–78; and Blumin, "Introduction," *New York by Gas-Light*, 24–27. But Sue's work appeared in the United States in 1843, a year after Dickens's *American Notes* was published. Works that point to Sue as the source of American travel writing also avoid the topic of race, which was a central part of Dickens's work, as well as the works of the writers who followed him.

12. Nathaniel Parker Willis, *The Complete Works of Nathaniel Parker Willis*, source verbatim in [Stokes], "New York City Slums Notes," 2:670.

13. Ibid., 668, 672.

14. Foster, *New York By Gaslight and Other Urban Sketches*, 38.

15. Foster, *New York by Gas Light*, 124.

16. Foster, *New York by Gas Light*, 145–146; "Dance Houses of the Five Points," *Monthly Record of the Five Points House of Industry* 1 (October 1857), 149.

17. Bobo, *Glimpses of New-York City*, 95–97.

18. Blackmar, *Manhattan for Rent*, 169–175; Gilfoyle, *City of Eros*, 119–142. Gilfoyle has compiled the most complete descriptions to date of the economy of the Five Points and other areas, and the roles black men and women played. On black-owned brothels and their predilections, see Gilfoyle, *City of Eros*, 41.

19. For white landlords' respectable businesses and ties to the political estab-lishment, see Gilfoyle, *City of Eros*, 119–142, especially the example of Amos Eno, 124.

20. Bobo, *Glimpses of New-York City*, 95–97.

21. Smith-Rosenberg, *Religion and the Rise of the American City*, 226.

22. The account of the Five Points Mission is from Smith-Rosenberg, "Five Points House of Industry," in *Religion and the Rise of the American City*; and Asbury, *The Gangs of New York*, 16–19.

23. [Five Points Mission], *The Old Brewery*, 15–16.

24. For a discussion of romantic racialism, see Fredrickson, "Uncle Tom and the Anglo-Saxons: Romantic Racialism in the North," in *Black Image in the White Mind*.

25. "A Sabbath with the Children at the Five Points House of Industry," *Monthly Record of the Five Points House of Industry* 1 (May, 1857), 19–24.

26. "Lizzie—The Changes of Early Life," *Monthly Record of the Five Points House of Industry* 1 (December 1857), 212–213; and "Band of Hope Meetings," *Monthly Record of the Five Points House of Industry* 1 (February 1858), 255–257.

27. Smith-Rosenberg, *Religion and the Rise of the American City*, 234–237.

28. "Lizzie—The Changes of Early Life," *Monthly Record of the Five Points House of Industry* 1 (December 1857), 212–213.

29. "(From the Independent) A Peep into Cut-Throat Alley. By Rev. Theodore L. Cuyler," in *Monthly Record of the Five Points House of Industry* 4 (1861), 266.

30. *Documents of the Assembly of the State of New-York. Eighteenth Session.—1857*, in Stokes, "New York City Slums" 784–85.

31. Roediger, *Wages of Whiteness*, 133–63; Ignatiev, *How the Irish Became White*, esp. 76, 87, 140–44; and Graham Hodges, "'Desirable Companions and Lovers.'"

32. "(From the Independent) A Peep into Cut-Throat Alley. By Rev. Theo-dore L. Cuyler," *Monthly Record of the Five Points House of Industry* 4 (April 1861), 265–266.

33. "(From the Independent) A Peep into Cut-Throat Alley. By Rev. Theodore L. Cuyler," *Monthly Record of the Five Points House of Industry* 4 (April 1861), 266, 267. See also Graham Hodges, "'Desirable Companions and Lovers.'"

CHAPTER NINE

1. DeVoe, The *Market Book,* 369–370.

2. The 1850 census was the first to enumerate occupations.

3. *Frederick Douglass' Paper,* February 2, 1855; "Alleged Rioting of Stevedores," *New York Tribune,* January 18, 1855, reprinted in Foner and Lewis, *The Black Worker to 1869,* 178–179.

4. Report of Charles B. Ray to the Executive Committee of the American Missionary Association, ALS, February 1848 (Document / Box #78809–78810), American Missionary Archives, Amistad Research Center; Griscom, *The Sanitary Condition of the Laboring Population of New York,* 2 and passim.

5. Association for the Improvement of the Condition of the Poor, *First Report of a Committee on the Sanitary Condition,* 4.

6. Information on the AICP model tenement in Freeman, *The Free Negro in New York City,* 168–170.

7. Blackmar and Rosenzweig, *Park and the People,* 88–89; quote on 89.

8. Curry, *Free Black in Urban America,* 60, 73, 68–69, 79.

9. "From Our Brooklyn Correspondent," *Frederick Douglass' Paper,* February 16, 1855.

10. Field, *The Politics of Race in New York,* 44–46.

11. Bishop and Attree, *Report of the Debates and Proceedings 1846,* 1018; Croswell and Sutton, *Revision of the Constitution,* 783–784, 786.

12. Bishop and Attree, *Report of the Debates and Proceedings 1846,* 1019.

13. Ibid.

14. Dana in Croswell and Sutton, *Revision of the Constitution,* 785; Burr in Bishop and Attree, *Report of the Debates and Proceedings 1846,* 1014–1015. Such beliefs about the blending of the races assumed that negative traits whites possessed would also disappear.

15. Field, *The Politics of Race in New York,* 53, 181–183.

16. John Hewitt, "Search for Elizabeth Jennings," 390–397; Jennings's account of the incident, quoted on 390–392; quotes from the jury instructions, 396.

17. John Hewitt, "Search for Elizabeth Jennings," 406–407.

18. Morris, *Free Men All,* 79–84, 94–106, 119–123.

19. Details of the Fugitive Slave Law of 1850 in Morris, *Free Men All,* 145–146.

20. For the Compromise of 1850, see David Potter, *The Impending Crisis,* 63–144.

21. Freeman, *The Free Negro in New York City,* 32, 61–65; Stanley Campbell, *The Slave Catchers,* 110–115, 199–207; Foner, *Business and Slavery,* 15–87.

22. The standard work on the Dred Scott case is Fehrenbacher, *Dred Scott.* See also Finkelman, *Dred Scott v. Sandford.* It is unclear why Sanford was involved in the

case at all. See Fehrenbacher, 272–275. On residency in free states and its impact on the status of slaves, Fehrenbacher, 50–61.

23. Fehrenbacher, *Dred Scott*, 50–61; Finkelman, "Protection of Black Rights," 211–234.

24. Finkelman, *Dred Scott v. Sandford*, 55–56, 57–64, 69, 76–77; Fehrenbacher, *Dred Scott*, 70, 340–364.

25. Foner and Walker, *Proceedings of the Black State Conventions*, 1:99–100.

26. Figures from Curry, *Free Black in Urban America*, table A-7, p. 250; Swift, *Black Prophets of Justice*, 260; and Ernst, *Immigrant Life in New York City*, 198–199.

27. *Freedom's Journal*, May 4, 1827.

28. "Report of Committee upon Agriculture," in *Minutes of the National Convention of Colored Citizens . . . 1843*, 31, in Bell, *Proceedings of the National Negro Convention*.

29. Ibid., 32.

30. Harlow, *Gerrit Smith: Philanthropist and Reformer*, 26–28, 241–243; Gerrit Smith, *An Address to the Three Thousand Colored Citizens of New-York*, 5. In 1847, Smith also began donating land in Madison County to poor whites.

31. Ibid., 10.

32. Ibid., 10–11.

33. ABCO, Indenture Agreement of William Smith, July 29, 1845, and Admission Record of Thomas Smith, January 27, 1841, in Admission Book 1; and ABCO, Minute Book 2, entry for April 14, 1848.

34. "Gerrit Smith's Land," *North Star*, February 25, 1848; ABCO, case record of James G. Henderson, AMs, October 26, 1852, in Admission Book 1; Harlow, *Gerrit Smith: Philanthropist and Reformer*, 26, 243–244, 251–252.

35. Swift, *Black Prophets of Justice*, 251–257; Moses, *Golden Age of Black Nationalism*, 18, 38.

36. C. Peter Ripley et al., *Black Abolitionist Papers*, 3:471–472n.

37. "A Glance at New York—Colonization," *Frederick Douglass' Paper*, November 13, 1851.

38. Ottley and Weatherby, *Negro in New York*, 110, 112–113.

39. Franklin, *Emancipation Proclamation*; Berlin et. al., *Slaves No More*, 49–53.

40. McPherson, *The Struggle For Equality*, 77–90.

41. Bernstein, *New York City Draft Riots*, 8–9.

42. Ottley and Weatherby, *The Negro in New York*, 114–116; Bernstein, *New York City Draft Riots*, 8–11.

43. The Draft Riots and their full political significance have been described in great detail by historians, most recently in the panoramic 1990 study by Bernstein, *New York City Draft Riots*. See also Cook, *Armies of the Streets*; and Headley, "Draft Riots of 1863," in *Pen and Pencil Sketches of the Great Riots*.

44. See Bernstein, *New York City Draft Riots*, 22.

45. ABCO, "Annual Report of the ABCO," December 1863, in Minute Book 3 (1863–1874), Papers of the ABCO.

46. Ibid.

47. Bernstein, *New York City Draft Riots*, 25–28; Child, *Isaac T. Hopper: A True Life*, v–vii; *New-York Evening Post*, March 13, 1863, reprinted in Foner and Lewis, *The Black Worker to 1869*, 286–287.

48. Descriptions of rioters and victims from Bernstein, *New York City Draft Riots*, 27–29.

49. Bernstein, *New York City Draft Riots*, 27–33 and passim. See Roediger, *Wages of Whiteness*, 150–156, for a discussion of blacks as representative of pre-industrial guilty pleasures to the Irish; see also Lott, *Love and Theft*, passim.

50. Harry Williamson, "Folks in Old New York and Brooklyn," TS, 2–5.

51. The total number of riot-related deaths was just over one hundred. The majority of dead were white men and boys killed by federal troops attempting to quell the disorder; see Bernstein, *New York City Draft Riots*, 5.

52. Bernstein, *New York City Draft Riots*, 48; ABCO, *Twenty-Eighth Annual Report of the Colored Orphan Asylum* (1864), 6; *Twenty-Ninth Annual Report of the Colored Orphan Asylum* (1865), 3, both in ABCO, *Annual Reports of the Colored Orphan Asylum, 1837–1870*; and ABCO, *From Cherry Street*, 19–24.

53. Lyons Family in Harry Williamson, "Folks in Old New York and Brooklyn," TS, 5; Wilder, *A Covenant with Color*, 99–100; Bernstein, *New York City Draft Riots*, 66, 267.

54. O'Rielly, *First Organization of Colored Troops*, 19. Bernstein, *New York City Draft Riots*, 56–58.

55. O'Rielly, *First Organization of Colored Troops*, 19.

56. Bernstein, *New York City Draft Riots*, 56–57, 66–68.

57. The literature on the interaction between northern reformers and southern blacks and whites during the Civil War and Reconstruction era is voluminous. Central to understanding this period is Eric Foner, *Reconstruction*. Other important works that evaluate the ways southern blacks envisioned freedom differently from northerners include Rose, *Rehearsal for Reconstruction*; Jones, *Soldiers of Light and Love*; Saville, *The Work of Reconstruction*; Litwack, *Been in the Storm So Long*; and Painter, *Exodusters*.

PRIMARY SOURCES

Manuscript Collections

American Missionary Association. Archives of the American Missionary Association. MS. Amistad Research Center, Tulane University, New Orleans.

American Seamen's Friend Society Records. Colored Sailors' Home Reports, (New York), 1855–66. MS. G. W. Blunt White Library, Mystic Seaport, Conn.

Association for the Benefit of Colored Orphans. Papers of the Association for the Benefit of Colored Orphans. MS. Manuscript Collection. New-York Historical Society, New York.

New-York African Free School. Records of the New-York African Free Schools: Regulations, By-Laws, and Reports, 1817–1832. MS. Manuscript Collection. New-York Historical Society, New York.

New York City Municipal Almshouse. Records of Admissions for the years 1827, 1830, and 1840. MS. New York City Municipal Archives, New York.

New York Juvenile Home. "To What Trades and Callings the Children have been Indentured, the First Ten Years of the Establishment of the Institution, That is from 7th January 1824 to the 1st of Jan'y, 1834." MS. Manuscript Collection, New-York Historical Society, New York.

New York Manumission Society. Papers of the New York Manumission Society, 1785–1849. MS. Manuscript Collection. New-York Historical Society, New York.

Stanford, John. Diary, 1816–1831. MS. Manuscript Collection. New-York Historical Society, New York.

[Stokes, I. N. Phelps]. "New York City Slums. Notes taken for I. N. Phelps Stokes in preparation of the book, *The Iconography of Manhattan Island* (New York: Robert H. Dodd, 1915–1928)." TS. 12 vols. Rare Book and Manuscript Room, New York Public Library, New York.

Williamson, Harry A. "Folks in Old New York and Brooklyn." 1953. TS. Library,
    New-York Historical Society, New York.

Periodicals

African Repository and Colonial Journal, 1825–50

American Minerva, 1796

Anti-Slavery Record, 1835–37

Anti-Slavery Reporter, 1833

Colored American, 1837–41

Emancipator, 1833–40

Frederick Douglass' Paper, 1851–55

Freedom's Journal, 1827–29

Mercantile Advertiser and New York Advocate, 1834

Mirror of Liberty, 1838–40

Monthly Record of the Five Points House of Industry, 1857–63

Morning Courier and New-York Enquirer, 1834

New-York City Hall Recorder, 1816–19

New York Commercial Advertiser, 1808, 1834

New York Daily Advertiser, 1785, 1799, 1807

New York Enquirer, 1826–29

New York Evening Post, 1817–21

New York Journal and State Gazette, 1784–85

New York Journal of Commerce, 1834

New York Judicial Repository, 1818

New York Packet, 1784–86

New York Transcript, 1834–35

North Star, 1847–51

Rights of All, 1829

Government Documents

Bishop, William G., and William H. Attree. *Report of the Debates and Proceedings of
    the Convention for the Revision of the Constitution of the State of New-York,
    1846*. Albany, N.Y.: Office of the *Evening Atlas*, 1846.

Carter, Nathaniel, and William Stone, eds. *Reports of the Proceedings and Debates of
    the Convention of 1821, Assembled for the Purpose of Amending the Constitu-
    tion of the State of New-York: Containing all the Official Documents Relating to
    the Subject, and Other Valuable Matter*. Albany, N.Y.: Hosford, 1821.

Croswell, S., and R. Sutton. *Debates and Proceedings in the New-York State Conven-
    tion, for the Revision of the Constitution*. Albany, N.Y.: Office of the *Albany Ar-
    gus*, 1846.

Lincoln, Charles Z., ed. *Messages from the Governors, comprising Executive Communications to the Legislature and Other Papers Relating to Legislation from the Organization of the First Colonial Assembly in 1683 to and Including the Year 1906*. Vol. 2. Albany, N.Y.: J. B. Lyon, 1909.

New York City Common Council. *Minutes of the Common Council of the City of New York*. Vols. 1–19. Edited by E. B. O'Callaghan. New York: City of New York, 1917.

———. Report of the Committee on the Appointment of the Superintendent of Sweeps. In Common Council, December 22, 1817. New York: Thomas P. Low, 1817.

New York State. *Laws of the State of New-York, Comprising the Constitution, and the Acts of the Legislature, since the Revolution, from the first to the Twentieth Session, Inclusive.* 3 vols. New York: Thomas Greenleaf, 1798.

———. *Laws of the State of New-York, passed at the Twenty-second session, second meeting, of the legislature, begun and held at the city of Albany, January second, 1799.* Albany, N.Y.: Loring Andrews, 1799.

———. *Public Laws of the State of New-York, Passed at the Thirty-Second Session of the Legislature, Begun and Held at the City of Albany, The First Day of November, 1808.* Albany, N.Y.: H. C. Southwick, 1809.

New York State Legislature, Assembly. *Journal of the Assembly of the State of New-York, At their second Meeting of the Eighth Session, begun and holden in the City of New York, on Friday the Twenty-Seventh Day of January, 1785.* New York: printed by S. Loudon, printer to the state, 1785.

———. *Journal of the Assembly of the State of New-York, at their Twenty-Second Session, Second Meeting, Began and Held at the city of Albany, the second day of January, 1799.* Albany, N.Y.: Loring Andrews, [1799].

———. Senate. *Journal of the Senate of the State of New-York, At their second Meeting of the Eighth Session, begun and holden in the City of New-York, on Monday the Twenty-fourth Day of January, 1785.* New York: printed by S. Loudon, printer to the state, 1785.

———. *Journal of the Senate of the State of New-York; At Their Twenty-Second Session, Second Meeting, Began and Held at the City of Albany, the second day of January, 1799.* Albany, N.Y.: Loring Andrews, [1799].

Van Ness, William, and John Woodworth. *Laws of the State of New-York, Revised and Passed at the Thirty-Sixth Session of the Legislature, With Marginal Notes and References.* Albany, N.Y.: H. C. Southwick, 1813.

Published Trials

The Commissioners of the Alms-House vs. Alexander Whistelo, a Black Man; Being a Remarkable Case of Bastardy, Tried and Adjudged by the Mayor, Recorder, and Several Aldermen of the City of New York. New York: David Longworth, 1808. Reprinted in *Free Blacks, Slaves, and Slaveowners in Civil and Criminal Courts: The Pamphlet Literature,* edited by Paul Finkelman, 123–78. Ser. 6, vol. 1. New York: Garland, 1988.

[Edwards, John]. *Account of the Trial of John Edwards, of the City of New York, Who was prosecuted for "Collecting, or promoting an assembly of persons, under the pretence of public worship in a public street, on Sunday, June 16, 1822." With a short account of his life, and address to the Mayor and Corporation, and advice to the Police Magistrates, &c. Written by John Edwards, Except the trial which was taken down in short hand*. New York: printed for the author, 1822.

A Faithful Report of the Trial of Doctor William Little, on an Indictment for an Assault and Battery, Committed upon the Body of His Lawful Wife, Mrs. Jane Little, a Black Lady. New York: printed for the purchasers, 1808. Reprinted in *Free Blacks, Slaves, and Slaveowners in Civil and Criminal Courts: The Pamphlet Literature*, edited by Paul Finkelman, 101–123. Ser. 6, vol. 1. New York: Garland, 1988.

Horsmanden, Daniel. *Journal of the Proceedings in the Detection of the Conspiracy formed by Some White People in Conjunction with Negro and Other Slaves for Burning the City of New-York in America and Murdering the Inhabitants*. New York: James Parker, 1744.

Ripley, Dorothy. *An Account of Rose Butler, Aged Nineteen Years, Whose Execution I Attended in the Potter's Field, On the 9th of 7th Mo. for Setting Fire to Her Mistress' Dwelling House*. New York: John C. Totten, 1819.

[Sampson, William.] *Murders. Report of the Trial of James Johnson, a Black Man, for the Murder of Lewis Robinson, a Black Man, on the 23rd of October last. Also, the Trial of John Sinclair, A German. Aged Seventy-seven years, for the Murder of David Hill, on the Eighth Day of April last. Had before his Honour, Chief Justice Kent, the Hon. Jacob Radcliff, Mayor, and the Hon, Josiah Ogden Hoffman, Recorder of the city of New-York, on Wednesday, the 19th, and Thursday, the 20th December, 1810. Published from the Short Hand Notes of William Sampson, Esquire, Counsellor at Law, Ec*. New York: Southwick and Pelsue, 1811.

Stanford, John. *An Authentic Statement of the Case and Conduct of Rose Butler, Who was Tried, Convicted, and Executed for the Crime of Arson. Reviewed and Approved by the Rev. John Stanford, M.A., Chaplain to the Public Institutions*. New York: Broderick and Ritter, 1819.

The Trial of Amos Broad and his Wife, on three several Indictments for Assaulting and Beating Betty, a Slave, and her little Female Child Sarah, Aged Three Years, Had at the Court of Special Sessions of the Peace, held in and for the City and County of New-York, at the City-Hall of the said City, on Tuesday, the 28th day of February, 1809. New York: Henry C. Southwick, 1809.

Trial of Captain James Dunn, for an assault, with an Intent to Seduce Sylvia Patterson, a Black Woman, the Wife of James Patterson; Held at Martling's Long Room, Before Referees, Appointed by consent of parties, Dec. 15th, 1808. New York: printed for the reporter, 1809.

Other Printed Sources

Abdy, E. S. *Journal of a Residence and Tour in the United States of North America, from April, 1833, to October, 1834*. 3 vols. London: John Murray, 1835.

American Anti-Slavery Society. *Annual Reports of the American Anti-Slavery Society, 1834–1840*. New York: William S. Dorr. Reprint, New York: Kraus, 1972.

American Convention for Promoting the Abolition of Slavery and Improving the Condition of the African Race. *Minutes, Constitutions, Addresses, Memorials, Resolutions, Reports, Committees, and Antislavery Tracts, 1794–1829*. 3 vols. Reprint, New York: Bergman, 1969.

Andrews, Charles C. *The History of the New-York African Free Schools, From Their Establishment in 1787, to the Present Time; Embracing a Period of More than Forty Years: Also a Brief Account of the Successful Labors of the New-York Manumission Society*. New York: Mahlon Day, 1830. Reprint, New York: Negro Universities Press, 1969.

Association for the Benefit of Colored Orphans. *Annual Reports of the Colored Orphan Asylum, 1837–1870*. Reprint, New York: Trow and Smith Manufacturing, 1870.

Association for the Improvement of the Condition of the Poor. *First Report of a Committee on the Sanitary Condition of the Laboring Classes in the City of New York, with Remedial Suggestions*. New York: John F. Trow, 1853.

Bell, Howard H., ed. *Minutes of the Proceedings of the National Negro Conventions, 1830–1864*. New York: Arno Press, 1969.

Blassingame, John, ed. *Series One: Speeches, Debates, and Interviews*. Vols. 1–5 of *The Frederick Douglass Papers*. New Haven, Conn.: Yale University Press, 1979–.

Bobo, William M. *Glimpses of New-York City, by a South Carolinian (who had nothing else to do)*. Charleston: J. J. McCarter, 1852.

Brace, Charles Loring. *The Dangerous Classes of New York, and Twenty Years' Work Among Them*. New York: Wynkoop and Hallenbeck, 1872.

Campbell, Tunis G. *Sufferings of the Rev. T. G. Campbell and his Family, in Georgia*. Washington: Enterprise Publishing Co., 1877.

Chambers, William. *Things as They Are in America*. 1854. Reprint, New York: Negro Universities Press, 1968.

Child, Lydia Maria. *An Appeal in Favor of that Class of Americans Called Africans*. 1836. Reprint, Salem, N.H.: Ayer, 1994.

———. *Isaac T. Hopper: A True Life*. New York: Dodd, Mead, 1881.

———. *Letters from New York*. New York: Charles S. Francis and Co., 1843.

De Voe, Thomas F. *The Market Book: A History of the Public Markets of the City of New York*. 1862. Reprint, New York: Augustus M. Kelley, 1970.

Dickens, Charles. *Pictures from Italy and American Notes for General Circulation*. 1842. Reprint, London: Chapman and Hall, n.d.

Douglass, Frederick. *My Bondage and My Freedom*. 1855. Reprint, edited by William L. Andrews, Urbana: University of Illinois Press, 1987.

[Five Points Mission]. *The Old Brewery and the New Mission House at the Five Points. By the Ladies of the Mission*. New York: Stringer and Townsend, 1854.

Foner, Philip S., ed. *The Democratic-Republican Societies, 1790–1800: A Documentary Sourcebook of Constitutions, Declarations, Addresses, Resolutions, and Toasts.* Westport, Conn.: Greewood Press, 1976.

Foner, Philip, and Robert Branham, eds. *Lift Every Voice: African American Oratory, 1787–1900.* Tuscaloosa: University of Alabama Press, 1998.

Foner, Philip, and George Walker, eds. *Proceedings of the Black State Conventions, 1840–1865.* 2 vols. Philadelphia: Temple University Press, 1979.

Foner, Philip, and Ronald Lewis, eds. *The Black Worker to 1869.* Vol. 1, *The Black Worker: A Documentary History from Colonial Times to the Present.* Philadelphia: Temple University Press, 1978.

Foster, George. *New York By Gas-Light, With Here and There a Streak of Sunshine.* 1850. Reprinted in *New York by Gas-Light and Other Urban Sketches by George C. Foster,* edited by Stuart M. Blumin. Berkeley: University of California Press, 1990.

Garrison, William Lloyd. *Thoughts on African Colonization; or An Impartial Exhibition of the Doctrines, Principles, and Purposes of the American Colonization Society. Together with the Resolutions, Addresses, and Remonstrances of the Free People of Color.* Boston: Garrison and Knapp, 1832.

Gilbert, Olive. *Narrative of Sojourner Truth.* 1878. Reprint, edited by Margaret Creel, New York: Vintage, 1993.

Griffiths, Julia ed. *Autographs for Freedom.* Vol. 1, Boston: Jewett, 1853. Vol. 2, Auburn: Alden, Beardsley and Co., 1854.

Griscom, John, M.D. *The Sanitary Condition of the Laboring Population of New York. With Suggestions for its Improvement. A Discourse (with Additions) Delivered on the 30th December, 1844, at the Repository of the American Institute.* New York: Harper and Brothers, 1845. Reprint, New York: Arno, 1970.

Halliday, Samuel Byram. *Lost and Found; or, Life Among the Poor.* New York: Blakeman and Mason, 1859.

Hamilton, William. "Mutual Interst, Mutual Benefit, Mutual Relief." In *Lift Every Voice: African American Oratory, 1787–1900,* edited by Philip Foner and Robert Branham, 80–86. Tuscaloosa, University of Alabama Press, 1998.

Hammon, Jupiter. *An Address to the Negroes in the State of New York.* 1787. Reprinted in Stanley Austin Ransom Jr., ed. *America's First Negro Poet: The Complete Works of Jupiter Hammon of Long Island.* Port Washington, N.Y.: Kennikat, 1983.

Hankins, Marie. *Women of New York.* New York: Marie Louise Hankins, 1861.

Jacobs, Harriet. *Incidents in the Life of a Slave Girl, Written by Herself.* 1861. Reprint, edited by Jean Fagan Yellin, Cambridge, Mass.: Harvard University Press, 1987.

King, Doris E., ed. *Never Let People Be Kept Waiting: A Textbook on Hotel Management. A Reprint of Tunis G. Campbell's Hotel Keepers, Head Waiters, and Housekeepers' Guide.* Boston, 1848. Reprint, Raleigh, N.C.: Graphic, 1973.

Mott, Abigail. *Biographical Sketches and Interesting Anecdotes of Persons of Color. To which is added a Selection of Pieces in Poetry.* New York: Mahlon Day, 1838.

New-York African Clarkson Association. *Constitution of the New-York African Clarkson Association.* New York: printed by E. Conrad, 1825.

New-York African Society for Mutual Relief. *Constitution of the New-York African Society for Mutual Relief, Passed June 6, 1808.* New York: printed for the society, 1808.

New York Committee of Vigilance. *The First Annual Report of the New York Committee of Vigilance, For the Year 1837, Together With Important Facts Relative to Their Proceedings.* New York: n.p., [1837]. Reprint, Philadelphia: Rhistoric, [1969].

New-York Female Union Society for the Promotion of Sabbath Schools. *Annual Reports.* New York: J. Seymour, 1817–1820.

New York Manumission Society. *An Address to the Parents and Guardians of the Children belonging to the New-York African Free School, by the Trustees of the Institution.* New York: Samuel Wood and Sons, 1818.

New York State Colonization Society. *Proceedings, of the Formation of the New-York State Colonization Society; Together with an Address to the Public, from the Managers Thereof.* Albany, N.Y.: Websters and Skinners, 1829.

———. *Proceedings of the New-York State Colonization Society, on its First Anniversary; Together with an Address to the Public, from the Managers Thereof.* Albany, N.Y.: Websters and Skinners, 1830.

———. *Proceedings of the New-York State Colonization Society, on its Second Anniversary; Together with an Address to the Public, from the Managers Thereof.* Albany, N.Y.: Websters and Skinners, 1831.

O'Rielly, Henry. *First Organization of Colored Troops in the State of New York, to aid in Suppressing the Slaveholders' Rebellion. Statements concerning the Origin, Difficulties, and Success of the Movement: Including Official Documents, Military Testimonials, Proceedings of the "Union League Club," Etc.* New York: Baker and Godwin, 1864.

Pennington, James W. C. *The Fugitive Blacksmith.* 1849. Reprinted in *Great Slave Narratives,* edited by Arna Bontemps. Boston: Beacon, 1969.

Pennsylvania Society for the Promotion of Public Economy. *Report of the Committee on Domestic Economy, to the Pennsylvania Society, For the Promotion of Public Economy, Read at its Meeting, on November 10, 1817.* Philadelphia: printed for the society by S. Merritt, 1817.

Porter, Dorothy, ed. *Early Negro Writing, 1760–1837.* Boston: Beacon, 1971. Reprint, Baltimore, Md.: Black Classic, 1995.

Ransom, Stanley Austin Jr., ed. *America's First Negro Poet: The Complete Works of Jupiter Hammon of Long Island.* Port Washington, N.Y.: Kennikat, 1983.

Reese, David Meredith. *Humbugs of New York.* 1838. Reprint, Freeport, N.Y.: Books for Libraries, 1971.

Richardson, Marilyn, ed. *Maria Stewart, America's First Black Woman Political Writer: Essays and Speeches.* Bloomington: Indiana University Press, 1987.

Smith, Gerrit. *An Address to the Three Thousand Colored Citizens of New-York, Who Are the Owners of 120,000 Acres of Land in the State of New-York, Given*

to Them by Gerrit Smith, Esq. of Peterboro, September 1, 1846. New York: n.p.,
  1846.

Society for the Encouragement of Faithful Domestic Servants. *First Annual Report of
  the Society for the Encouragement of Faithful Domestic Servants in New-York*.
  New York: D. Fanshaw, 1826.

Tappan, Lewis. *The Life of Arthur Tappan*. New York: Hurd and Houghton, 1870.

Thompson, George A. Jr. *A Documentary History of the African Theatre*. Evanston,
  Ill.: Northwestern University Press, 1998.

Thompson, Mary W. *Sketches of the History, Character, and Dying Testimony of
  Beneficiaries of the Colored Home, in the City of New-York*. New York: John F.
  Trow, 1851.

Walker, David. *David Walker's Appeal to the Coloured Citizens of the World, but in
  particular, and very expressly, to those of The United States of America*. 1829.
  Reprint, edited by Sean Wilentz, New York: Hill and Wang, 1995.

Wood, Samuel. *The Cries of New-York*. 1808. Reprint, New York: Harbor, 1931.

Woodson, Carter G., ed. *The Mind of the Negro as Reflected in Letters Written During the Crisis, 1800–1860*. Washington, D.C.: Association for the Study of Negro
  Life and History, 1926.

Zuille, John Jay. *Historical Sketch of the New York African Society for Mutual Relief*.
  New York: John Jay Zuille, 1892.

SECONDARY SOURCES

Albion, Robert G. *The Rise of the New York Port, 1815–1860*. New York: Charles
  Scribner's Sons, 1939.

Alexander, Leslie. "'Onward Forever'": Black Activism and Community Development in New York City, 1784–1860." Ph.D. diss., Cornell University, 2001.

Alexander, S. D. *The Presbyter of New York, 1738–1888*. New York: Anson D. F. Ran-
  dolph, 1888.

Anbinder, Tyler. *Five Points: The Nineteenth-Century New York City Neighborhood
  that Invented Tap Dance, Stole Elections, and Became the World's Most Notori-
  ous Slum*. New York: Free Press, 2001.

Anderson, Lewis Flint. "The Manual Labor School Movement." *Educational Review*
  46 (November 1913): 369–386.

Andrews, William L. *To Tell a Free Story: The First Century of Afro-American Autobiography, 1760–1865*. Urbana: University of Illinois Press, 1986.

Aptheker, Herbert. *One Continual Cry: David Walker's Appeal, Its Setting and Its
  Meaning*. New York: Humanities, 1965.

Arnesen, Eric. *Workers on the Waterfront in New Orleans: Race, Class, and Politics,
  1863–1923*. New York: Oxford University Press, 1991.

Asbury, Herbert. *The Gangs of New York: An Informal History of the Underworld*.
  New York: Knopf, 1928.

Bailyn, Bernard. *The Ideological Origins of the American Revolution*. Cambridge,
  Mass.: Harvard University Press, 1967.

Bell, Howard H. *A Survey of the Negro Convention Movement.* New York: Arno, 1969.

Bender, Thomas, ed. *The Antislavery Debate: Capitalism and Abolitionism as a Problem in Historical Interpretation.* Berkeley: University of California Press, 1992.

Berlin, Ira. *Many Thousands Gone: The First Two Centuries of Slavery in North America.* Cambridge, Mass.: Belknap Press of Harvard University, 1998.

———. "The Revolution in Black Life." In *The American Revolution: Explorations in the History of American Radicalism,* edited by Alfred Young, 349–382. DeKalb: Northern Illinois University Press, 1976.

———. "The Structure of the Free Negro Caste in the Antebellum United States." *Journal of Social History* 9 (1976): 297–318.

———. "Time, Space, and the Evolution of Afro-American Society on British Mainland North America." *American Historical Review* 85 (1980): 44–78.

Berlin, Ira, and Ronald Hoffman, eds. *Slavery and Freedom in the Age of the American Revolution.* Charlottesville: University Press of Virginia, 1983.

Berlin, Ira, Barbara J. Fields, Steven F. Miller, Joseph P. Reidy, and Leslie S. Rowland, eds. *Slaves No More: Three Essays on Emancipation and Civil War.* Cambridge: Cambridge University Press, 1992.

Bernstein, Iver. *The New York City Draft Riots: Their Significance for American Society and Politics in the Age of Civil War.* New York: Oxford University Press, 1990.

Blackburn, Robin. *The Overthrow of Colonial Slavery, 1776–1848.* London: Verso, 1988.

Blackmar, Elizabeth. *Manhattan for Rent, 1785–1850.* Ithaca, N.Y.: Cornell University Press, 1989.

Blackmar, Elizabeth, and Roy Rosenzweig. *The Park and the People: A History of Central Park.* Ithaca, N.Y.: Cornell University Press, 1992.

Bloch, Ruth. "The Gendered Meanings of Virtue in Revolutionary America." *Signs: Journal of Women in Culture and Society* 13 (1987): 37–58.

Blumin, Stuart. *The Emergence of the Middle Class: Social Experience in the American City, 1760–1900.* Cambridge: Cambridge University Press, 1989.

———. "Explaining the New Metropolis: Perception, Depiction, and Analysis in Mid-Nineteenth-Century New York City." *Journal of Urban History* 11 (November 1984): 9–38.

Blumin, Stuart M. Introduction to *New York by Gas-Light and Other Urban Sketches by George C. Foster,* edited by Stuart M. Blumin. Berkeley: University of California Press, 1990.

Bolster, William Jeffrey. "African-American Seamen: Race, Seafaring Work, and Atlantic Maritime Culture, 1750–1860." Ph.D. diss., Johns Hopkins University, 1992.

———. *Black Jacks: African-American Seamen in the Age of Sail.* Cambridge, Mass.: Harvard University Press, 1997.

———. "'To Feel Like a Man': Black Seamen in the Northern States, 1800–1860." *Journal of American History* 76 (March 1990): 1173–1199.

Boydston, Jeanne. *Home and Work: Housework, Wages, and the Ideology of Labor in the Early Republic.* New York: Oxford University Press, 1990.

Boyer, Paul. *Urban Masses and Moral Order in America, 1820–1920.* Cambridge, Mass.: Harvard University Press, 1978.

Boylan, Anne. "Henrietta Green Regulus Ray." In *Black Women in America: An Historical Encyclopedia,* edited by Darlene Clark Hine, Elsa Barkley Brown, and Rosalyn Terborg Penn, 966. Vol 2. Bloomington: Indiana University Press, 1993.

———. *Sunday School: The Formation of an American Institution, 1790–1860.* New Haven, Conn.: Yale University Press, 1988.

———. "Women and Politics in the Era before Seneca Falls," *Journal of the Early Republic* 10 (fall 1990): 363–382.

Bracey, John H., August Meier, and Elliot Rudwick, eds. *Blacks in the Abolitionist Movement.* Belmont, Ca.: Wadsworth, 1971.

Bradley, David Henry Sr. *A History of the A.M.E. Zion Church.* Nashville, Tenn.: Parthenon, 1956.

Brand, Dana. *The Spectator and the City in Nineteenth-Century American Literature.* New York: Cambridge University Press, 1991.

Burrows, Edwin, and Mike Wallace. *Gotham: A History of New York City to 1898.* New York: Oxford University Press, 1999.

Campbell, Stanley. *The Slave Catchers: Enforcement of the Fugitive Slave Law, 1850–1860.* Chapel Hill: University of North Carolina Press, 1970.

Christianson, Scott. "Criminal Punishment in New Netherlands." In *A Beautiful and Fruitful Place: Selected Rensellaerswijck Seminar Papers,* edited by Nancy Anne McClure Zeller, 83–90. [Albany, N.Y.]: New Netherland, 1991.

Christoph, Peter. "The Freedmen of New Amsterdam." In *A Beautiful and Fruitful Place: Selected Rensellaerswijck Seminar Papers,* edited by Nancy Anne McClure Zeller, 157–170. [Albany, N.Y.]: New Netherland, 1991.

Clinton, Catherine. "Caught in the Web of the Big House: Women and Slavery." In *The Web of Southern Social Relations: Women, Family, and Education,* edited by Walter J. Fraser Jr., R. Frank Saunders Jr., and Jon Wakelyn, 19–34. Athens: University of Georgia Press, 1985.

Cohen, Daniel. *Pillars of Salt, Monuments of Grace: New England Literature and the Origins of Popular Culture, 1674–1860.* New York: Oxford University Press, 1993.

Cohen, David. *The Ramapo Mountain People.* New Brunswick, N.J.: Rutgers University Press, 1974.

Cook, Adrian. *The Armies of the Streets: The New York City Draft Riots of 1863.* Lexington: University Press of Kentucky, 1974.

Countryman, Edward. *A People in Revolution: The American Revolution and Political Society in New York, 1760–1790.* Baltimore: Johns Hopkins University Press, 1981.

Cox, John. *Quakerism in the City of New York, 1657–1930.* New York: privately printed, 1930.

Craigie, William A., and James R. Hulbert. *A Dictionary of American English on His-torical Principles*. Chicago: University of Chicago Press, 1938.

Cray, Robert. *Paupers and Poor Relief in New York City and Its Rural Environs, 1700–1830*. Philadelphia: Temple University Press, 1988.

———. "White Welfare and Black Strategies: The Dynamics of Race and Poor Relief in Early New York, 1700–1825." *Slavery and Abolition* 7 (1986): 273–289.

Curry, Leonard. *The Free Black in Urban America, 1800–1850: The Shadow of the Dream*. Chicago: University of Chicago Press, 1981. Reprint, Chicago: University of Chicago Press, 1986.

Curtin, Philip. *The Rise and Fall of the Plantation Complex: Essays in Atlantic His-tory*. Cambridge: Cambridge University Press, 1990.

Dabel, Jane. "From Her Own Labor: African-American Laboring Women in New York City, 1827–1877." Ph.D. diss., University of California, Los Angeles, 2000.

Davis, David Brion. *The Problem of Slavery in the Age of Revolution, 1770–1823*. Ithaca, N.Y.: Cornell University Press, 1975. Reprint, New York: Oxford Univer-sity Press, 1999.

———. *The Problem of Slavery in Western Culture*. Ithaca, N.Y.: Cornell University Press, 1966. Reprint, New York: Oxford University Press, 1988.

Davis, Thomas. *A Rumor of Revolt: The "Great Negro Plot" in Colonial New York*. New York: Free Press, 1985.

———. "Slavery in Colonial New York City." Ph.D. diss., Columbia University, |1975.

———. "These Enemies of Their Own Household: Slaves in Eighteenth Century New York." In *A Beautiful and Fruitful Place: Selected Rensellaerswijck Seminar Papers*, edited by Nancy Anne McClure Zeller, 171–180. [Albany, N.Y.]: New Netherland, 1991.

Dayton, Abram C. *Last Days of Knickerbocker Life in New York*. New York: G. P. Put-nam's Sons, 1897.

DeBoer, Clara Merritt. *Be Jubilant My Feet: African American Abolitionists in the American Missionary Association, 1839–1861*. New York: Garland, 1994.

———. "The Role of Afro-Americans in the Origin and Work of the American Mis-sionary Association: 1839–1877." Ph.D. diss., Rutgers University, 1973.

DeJong, Gerald. "The Dutch Reformed Church and Negro Slavery in Colonial Amer-ica." *Church History* 40 (1971): 423–436.

D'Emilio, John, and Estelle B. Freedman. *Intimate Matters: A History of Sexuality in America*. New York: Harper and Row, 1988.

DuBois, Ellen, and Vicki Ruiz. *Unequal Sisters: A Multicultural Reader in U.S. Women's History*. New York: Routledge, 1990.

Du Bois, W. E. B. *Black Reconstruction in the United States, 1860–1880*. New York: Russell and Russell, 1935.

———. *The Negro Artisan*. Atlanta, Ga.: Atlanta University Press, 1902.

Dudden, Faye. *Serving Women: Household Service in Nineteenth-Century America*. Middletown, Conn.: Wesleyan University Press, 1983.

Duncan, Russell. *Freedom's Shore: Tunis Campbell and the Georgia Freedmen.* Athens: University of Georgia Press, 1986.

Egerton, Douglas. *Gabriel's Rebellion: The Virginia Slave Conspiracies of 1800 and 1802.* Chapel Hill: University of North Carolina, 1993.

Elkins, Stanley, and Eric McKitrick. *The Age of Federalism.* New York: Oxford University Press, 1993.

Ernst, Robert. *Immigrant Life in New York City, 1825–1863.* New York: King's Crown Press, 1949.

Fabel, Robin F. A. "Self-Help in Dartmoor: Black and White Prisoners in the War of 1812." *Journal of the Early Republic* 9 (summer 1989): 165–190.

Fehrenbacher, Don E. *The Dred Scott Case: Its Significance in American Law and Politics.* New York: Oxford University Press, 1978.

Field, Phyllis F. *The Politics of Race in New York: The Struggle for Black Suffrage in the Civil War Era.* Ithaca, N.Y.: Cornell University Press, 1982.

Fields, Barbara. "Ideology and Race in American History." In *Region, Race, and Reconstruction,* edited by J. Morgan Kousser and James M. McPherson, 143–177. New York: Oxford University Press, 1982.

———. "Slavery, Race, and Ideology in the United States of America." *New Left Review* 181 (1990): 95–118.

Finkelman, Paul. *Dred Scott v. Sandford: A Brief History with Documents.* Boston: Bedford, 1997.

———. *An Imperfect Union: Slavery, Federalism, and Comity.* Chapel Hill: University of North Carolina Press, 1981.

———. "The Kidnapping of John Davis and the Adoption of the Fugitive Slave Law of 1793." *Journal of Southern History* 56 (August 1990): 397–422.

———. "The Problem of Slavery in the Age of Federalism." In *Federalists Reconsidered,* edited by Doron Ben-Atar and Barbara Oberg, 135–156. Charlottesville, Va.: University Press of Virginia, 1998.

———. "The Protection of Black Rights in Seward's New York." *Civil War History* 34 (1988): 211–234.

Foner, Eric. *Reconstruction: America's Unfinished Revolution, 1863–1877.* New York: Harper and Row, 1988.

Foner, Philip. *Business and Slavery: The New York Merchants and the Irrepressible Conflict.* Chapel Hill: University of North Carolina Press, 1941.

———. *Organized Labor and the Black Worker, 1619–1981.* New York: International, 1981.

———. "William P. Powell: Militant Champion of Black Seamen." In *Essays in Afro-American History.* Philadelphia: Temple University Press, 1978.

Foote, Thelma Wills. "Black Life in Colonial Manhattan, 1664–1786." Ph.D. diss., Harvard University, 1991.

———. "Crossroads or Settlement? The Black Freedmen's Community in Historic Greenwich Village, 1644–1855." In *Greenwich Village: Culture and Counterculture,* edited by Rick Beard and Leslie Cohen Berlowitz, 120–133. New Brunswick, N.J.: Rutgers University Press, 1993.

Foster, Frances Smith. *Witnessing Slavery: The Development of Antebellum Slave Narratives*. Westport, Conn.: Greenwood, 1979.

Fowler, David. *Northern Attitudes towards Interracial Marriage: Legislative and Public Opinion in the Middle Atlantic and the States of the Old Northwest, 1780–1930*. New York: Garland, 1987.

Fox, Dixon Ryan. "The Negro Vote in Old New York." *Political Science Quarterly* 32 (1917): 252–275.

Fox, Richard Wightman, and T. J. Jackson Lears, eds. *The Power of Culture: Critical Essays in American History*. Chicago: University of Chicago Press, 1993.

Frankel, Noralee, and Nancy S. Dye, eds. *Gender, Class, Race, and Reform in the Progressive Era*. Lexington: University Press of Kentucky, 1991.

Franklin, John Hope. *The Emancipation Proclamation*. Wheeling, Ill.: Harlan Davidson, 1963.

Fredrickson, George M. *The Arrogance of Race: Historical Perspectives on Slavery, Racism, and Social Inequality*. Middletown, Conn.: Wesleyan University Press, 1988.

———. *The Black Image in the White Mind: The Debate on Afro-American Character and Destiny, 1817–1914*. New York: Harper and Row, 1971. Reprint, Middletown, Conn.: Wesleyan University Press, 1987.

Freeman, Rhoda Golden. *The Free Negro in New York City in the Era before the Civil War*. New York: Garland, 1994.

Frey, Sylvia. *Water from the Rock: Black Resistance in a Revolutionary Age*. Princeton, N.J.: Princeton University Press, 1991.

Friedman, Lawrence. *Gregarious Saints: Self and Community in American Abolitionism, 1830–1870*. Cambridge: Cambridge University Press, 1982.

Frothingham, Octavius Brooks. *Gerrit Smith: A Biography*. New York: G. P. Putnam's Sons, 1878.

Gaines, Kevin. *Uplifting the Race: Black Leadership, Politics, and Culture in the Twentieth Century*. Chapel Hill: University of North Carolina Press, 1996.

Gara, Larry. "The Professional Fugitive in the Abolition Movement." *Wisconsin Magazine of History* 48 (summer 1965): 196–204.

Gellman, David. "Inescapable Discourse: The Rhetoric of Slavery and the Politics of Abolition in Early National New York." Ph.D. diss., Northwestern University, 1997.

Genovese, Eugene. *Roll Jordan Roll: The World the Slaves Made*. New York: Pantheon, 1974. Reprint, New York: Vintage, 1976.

Gilfoyle, Timothy. *City of Eros: New York City, Prostitution, and the Commercialization of Sex, 1790–1920*. New York: W. W. Norton, 1992.

Gilje, Paul. *The Road to Mobocracy: Popular Disorder in New York City, 1763–1834*. Chapel Hill: University of North Carolina Press, 1987.

Gilje, Paul, and Howard Rock. *Keepers of the Revolution: New Yorkers at Work in the Early Republic*. Ithaca, N.Y.: Cornell University Press, 1992.

———. "'Sweep O! Sweep O!': African-American Chimney Sweeps and Citizenship in the New Nation." *William and Mary Quarterly*, 3d ser., 51 (1994): 507–519.

Ginzberg, Lori. *Women and the Work of Benevolence: Morality, Politics, and Class in the Nineteenth-Century United States.* New Haven, Conn.: Yale University Press, 1990.

Glenn, Myra. "School Discipline and Punishment in Antebellum America." *Journal of the Early Republic* 1 (1981): 395–408.

Glickstein, Jonathan. *Concepts of Free Labor in Antebellum America.* New Haven, Conn.: Yale University Press, 1991.

Gomez, Michael. *Exchanging Our Country Marks: The Transformation of African Identities in the Colonial and Antebellum South.* Chapel Hill: University of North Carolina Press, 1998.

Goodfriend, Joyce. *Before the Melting Pot: Society and Culture in Colonial New York City, 1664–1730.* Princeton, N.J.: Princeton University Press, 1992.

———. "Black Families in New Netherlands." In *A Beautiful and Fruitful Place: Selected Rensellaerswijck Seminar Papers,* edited by Nancy Anne McClure Zeller, 147–55. [Albany, N.Y.]: New Netherland, 1991.

———. "Burghers and Blacks: The Evolution of a Slave Society at New Amsterdam." *New York History* 59 (1978): 125–144.

Goodman, Paul. "The Manual Labor Movement and the Origins of Abolitionism." *Journal of the Early Republic* 13 (fall 1993): 355–388.

———. *Of One Blood: Abolitionism and the Origins of Racial Equality.* Berkeley: University of California Press, 1998.

Gordon, Linda. "Family Violence, Feminism, and Social Control." In *Unequal Sisters: A Multicultural Reader in U.S. Women's History,* edited by Ellen DuBois and Vicki Ruiz, 141–56. New York: Routledge, 1990.

———. *Heroes of Their Own Lives: The Politics and History of Family Violence.* New York: Viking, 1988.

Griffin, Farah Jasmine, ed. *Beloved Sisters and Loving Friends: Letters from Rebecca Primus of Royal Oak, Maryland, and Addie Brown of Hartford, Connecticut, 1854–1868.* New York: Knopf, 1999.

Gronowicz, Anthony. *Race and Class Politics in New York City before the Civil War.* Boston: Northeastern University Press, 1998.

Gutman, Herbert. *Power and Culture: Essays on the American Working Class.* Edited by Ira Berlin. New York: Pantheon Books, 1987.

———. *Work, Culture, and Society in Industrializing America.* New York: Knopf, 1977.

Halttunen, Karen. *Murder Most Foul: The Killer and the American Gothic Imagination.* Cambridge, Mass.: Harvard University Press, 1998.

Hansen, Joyce, and Gary McGowan. *Breaking Ground, Breaking Silence.* New York: Henry Holt, 1997.

Hansen, Karen. "'No *Kisses* is Like Youres': An Erotic Friendship between Two African-American Women during the Mid-nineteenth Century." *Gender and History* 7 (August 1995): 153–182.

Harding, Vincent. *There Is a River: The Black Struggle for Freedom in America.* New York: Harcourt Brace, 1981. Reprint, New York: Harcourt Brace, 1992.

Harlow, Ralph. *Gerrit Smith: Philanthropist and Reformer.* New York: Henry Holt, 1939.

Headley, J. T. *Pen and Pencil Sketches of the Great Riots.* New York: E. B. Treat, 1882.

Hewitt, John H. "The Search for Elizabeth Jennings, Heroine of a Sunday Afternoon in New York City." *New York History* 62 (1990): 387–415.

Hewitt, Nancy. *Women's Activism and Social Change: Rochester, New York, 1822–1872.* Ithaca, N.Y.: Cornell University Press, 1984.

Higginbotham, A. Leon Jr. *In the Matter of Color: Race and the American Legal Process — The Colonial Period.* New York: Oxford University Press, 1978.

Higginbotham, Evelyn Brooks. "African-American Women's History and the Metalanguage of Race." *Signs: Journal of Women in Culture and Society* 17 (1992): 251–274.

Hill, Herbert, et al. "Myth-Making as Labor History: Herbert Gutman and the United Mine Workers of America" and roundtable responses. *International Journal of Politics, Culture, and Society* 2 (1988): 132–200, 361–595.

Hine, Darlene Clark. "Rape and the Inner Lives of Black Women in the Middle West." In *Unequal Sisters: A Multicultural Reader in U.S. Women's History,* edited by Ellen DuBois and Vicki Ruiz, 292–297. New York: Routledge, 1990.

Hine, Darlene Clark, Elsa Barkley Brown, and Rosalyn Terborg Penn, eds. *Black Women in America: An Historical Encyclopedia.* 2 vols. Bloomington: Indiana University Press, 1993–94.

Hinks, Peter. *To Awaken My Afflicted Brethren: David Walker and the Problem of Antebellum Slave Resistance.* University Park: Pennsylvania State University Press, 1997.

Hodes, Martha, ed. *Sex, Love, Race: Crossing Boundaries in North American History.* New York: New York University Press, 1999.

———. *White Women, Black Men: Illicit Sex in the Nineteenth-Century South.* New Haven, Conn.: Yale University Press, 1997.

Hodges, George W. *Early Negro Church Life in New York.* New York: by the author, 1945.

Hodges, Graham Russell. *Black Itinerants of the Gospel: The Narratives of John Jea and George White.* Madison, Wis.: Madison House, 1993.

———. "Black Revolt in New York City and the Neutral Zone, 1775–1783." In *Slavery, Freedom, and Culture among Early American Workers.* Armonk, N.Y.: M. E. Sharpe, 1998.

———. "'Desirable Companions and Lovers': Irish and African Americans in the Sixth Ward of New York City, 1830–1870." In *Slavery, Freedom, and Culture among Early American Workers.* Armonk, N.Y.: M. E. Sharpe, 1998.

———. *New York City Cartmen, 1667–1850.* New York: New York University Press, 1986.

———. *Root and Branch: African Americans in New York and East Jersey, 1613–1863.* Chapel Hill: University of North Carolina Press, 1999.

Hodges, Graham Russell, and Alan Edward Brown, eds. *"Pretends to Be Free": Runaway Slave Advertisements from Colonial and Revolutionary New York and New Jersey.* New York: Garland, 1994.

Holt, Marilyn Irvin. *The Orphan Trains: Placing Out in America.* Lincoln: University of Nebraska Press, 1992.

Horton, James. *Free People of Color: Inside the African American Community.* Washington, D.C.: Smithsonian Institution Press, 1993.

Horton, James, and Lois Horton. *Black Bostonians: Family Life and Community Struggle in the Antebellum North.* New York: Holmes and Meier, 1979.

———. *In Hope of Liberty: Culture, Community, and Protest among Northern Free Blacks, 1700–1860.* New York: Oxford University Press, 1997.

Hunt, Lynn, ed. *The New Cultural History.* Berkeley: University of California Press, 1989.

Hunter, Tera. "Household Workers in the Making: Afro-American Women in Atlanta and the New South, 1861–1920." Ph.D. diss., Yale University, 1991.

———. *To 'Joy My Freedom: Black Women's Lives and Labors after the Civil War.* Cambridge, Mass.: Harvard University Press, 1997.

Ignatiev, Noel. *How the Irish Became White.* New York: Routledge, 1995.

Ingle, H. Larry. *Quakers in Conflict: The Hicksite Reformation.* Knoxville: University of Tennessee, 1986.

Innes, Stephen. *Labor in a New Land: Economy and Society in Seventeenth-Century Springfield.* Princeton, N.J.: Princeton University Press, 1983.

Jentz, John B. "Artisans, Evangelicals, and the City: A Social History of Abolition and Labor Reform in Jacksonian New York." Ph.D. diss., City University of New York, 1977.

Johnson, James Weldon. *Black Manhattan.* 1930. Reprint, New York: Da Capo, 1991.

Jones, Jacqueline. *Soldiers of Light and Love: Northern Teachers and Georgia Blacks, 1865–1873.* Chapel Hill: University of North Carolina Press, 1980.

Jordan, Winthrop. *White over Black: American Attitudes toward the Negro, 1550–1812.* Chapel Hill: University of North Carolina Press, 1968. Reprint, New York: W. W. Norton, 1977.

Kammen, Michael. *Colonial New York: A History.* New York: Oxford University Press, 1975.

Katz, Michael. *In the Shadow of the Poorhouse.* New York: Basic, 1986.

Kelley, Robin. *Hammer and Hoe: Alabama Communists during the Great Depression.* Chapel Hill: University of North Carolina Press, 1990.

———. *Race Rebels: Culture, Politics, and the Black Working Class.* New York: Free Press, 1994.

Kerber, Linda. "Abolitionists and Amalgamators: The New York City Race Riots of 1834." *New York History* 48 (1967): 28–39.

———. *No Constitutional Right to Be Ladies: Women and the Obligations of Citizenship.* New York: Hill and Wang, 1998.

———. *Women of the Republic: Intellect and Ideology in Revolutionary America.* Chapel Hill: University of North Carolina Press, 1980. Reprint, New York: W. W. Norton, 1986.

Kettner, James. *The Development of American Citizenship.* Chapel Hill: University of North Carolina Press, 1978.

Kinney, James. *Amalgamation! Race, Sex, and Rhetoric in the Nineteenth-Century Novel.* Westport, Conn.: Greenwood, 1985.

Klaw, Spencer. *Without Sin: The Life and Death of the Oneida Community.* New York: Penguin, 1993.

Kraditor, Aileen. *Means and Ends in American Abolition: Garrison and His Critics on Strategy and Tactics, 1834–1850.* New York: Pantheon, 1969. Reprint, Chicago: Ivan R. Dee, 1989.

Kruger, Vivienne. "Born to Run: The Slave Family in Early New York, 1626–1827." Ph.D. diss., Columbia University, 1985.

Kusmer, Kenneth, ed. *Antebellum America.* Vol. 2, *Black Communities and Urban Development in America, 1720–1990.* New York: Garland, 1991.

Lackey, Kris. "Eighteenth-Century Aesthetic Theory and the Nineteenth-Century Traveler in Trans-Allegheny America: F. Trollope, Dickens, Irving, and Parkman." *American Studies* 32 (spring 1991): 33–48.

Langsam, Miriam Z. *Children West: A History of the Placing-Out System of the New York Children's Aid Society, 1853–1890.* Madison: State Historical Society of Wisconsin, 1964.

La Roche, Cheryl. "Beads from the African Burial Ground, New York City: A Preliminary Assessment." *Beads: Journal of the Society of Bead Researchers* 6 (1994): 3–30.

La Roche, Cheryl J., and Michael Blakey. "Seizing Intellectual Power: The Dialogue at the New York African Burial Ground." *Historical Archaeology* 31 (1997): 84–106.

Law, Robin, and Kristin Mann. "West Africa in the Atlantic Community: The Case of the Slave Coast." *William and Mary Quarterly,* 3d ser., 56 (April 1999): 307–334.

Lebsock, Suzanne. *Free Women of Petersburg: Status and Culture in a Southern Town, 1784–1860.* New York: W. W. Norton, 1985.

Levine, Bruce. *Half Slave and Half Free: The Roots of Civil War.* New York: Hill and Wang, 1992.

Levine, Robert S. *Martin Delany, Frederick Douglass, and the Politics of Representative Identity.* Chapel Hill: University of North Carolina Press, 1997.

Lewis, Earl. *In Their Own Interests: Race, Class, and Power in Twentieth-Century Norfolk, Virginia.* Berkeley: University of California Press, 1991.

Linebaugh, Peter, and Marcus Rediker. *The Many-Headed Hydra: Sailors, Slaves, Commoners, and the Hidden History of the Revolutionary Atlantic.* Boston: Beacon Press, 2000.

Litwack, Leon. *North of Slavery: The Negro in the Free States, 1790–1860*. Chicago: University of Chicago Press, 1961. Reprint, Chicago: University of Chicago Press, Phoenix Books, 1965.

Lott, Eric. *Love and Theft: Blackface Minstrelsy and the American Working Class*. New York: Oxford University Press, 1993.

Mabee, Carleton. *Black Education in New York State from Colonial to Modern Times*. Syracuse, N.Y.: Syracuse University Press, 1979.

———. *Black Freedom: The Nonviolent Abolitionists from 1830 through the Civil War*. London: Macmillan, 1970.

———. "Charity in Travail: Two Orphan Asylums for Blacks." *New York History* 55 (1974): 55–77.

Mabee, Carleton, with Susan Mabee Newhouse. *Sojourner Truth: Slave, Prophet, Legend*. New York: New York University Press, 1993.

Masur, Louis. *Rites of Execution: Capital Punishment and the Transformation of American Culture, 1776–1865*. New York: Oxford University Press, 1989.

McAllister, Marvin. "'White People Do Not Know How to Behave at Entertainments Designated for Ladies and Gentlemen of Colour': A History of New York's African Grove/African Theatre." Ph.D. diss., Northwestern University, 1997.

McCarthy, Kathleen, ed. *Lady Bountiful Revisited: Women, Philanthropy, and Power*. New Brunswick, N.J.: Rutgers University Press, 1990.

McDougall, Marion Gleason. *Fugitive Slaves, 1619–1865*. 1891. Reprint, New York: Bergman, 1967.

McFeely, William. *Frederick Douglass*. New York: W. W. Norton, 1991.

McHenry, Elizabeth. "'Dreaded Eloquence': The Origins and Rise of African American Literary Societies and Libraries." *Harvard Library Bulletin* 6 (1995): 32–56.

McKee, Samuel. *Labor in Colonial New York, 1664–1776*. New York: Columbia University Press, 1935.

McLaurin, Melton. *Celia, A Slave*. Athens: University of Georgia Press, 1991.

McManus, Edgar J. *Black Bondage in the North*. Syracuse, N.Y.: Syracuse University Press, 1973.

———. *A History of Negro Slavery in New York*. Syracuse, N.Y.: Syracuse University Press, 1966. Reprint, Syracuse, N.Y.: Syracuse University Press, 1970.

McPherson, James. *The Struggle for Equality: Abolitionists and the Negro in the Civil War and Reconstruction*. Princeton, N.J.: Princeton University Press, 1964. Reprint, Princeton, N.J.: Princeton University Press, 1967.

Melish, Joanne Pope. *Disowning Slavery: Gradual Emancipation and "Race" in New England, 1780–1860*. Ithaca, N.Y.: Cornell University Press, 1998.

Mintz, Steven, and Susan Kellogg. *Domestic Revolutions: A Social History of American Family Life*. New York: Free Press, 1988.

Mohl, Raymond. *Poverty in New York, 1783–1825*. New York: Oxford University Press, 1971.

Morgan, Edmund. *American Slavery, American Freedom: The Ordeal of Colonial Virginia*. New York: W. W. Norton, 1975.

Morris, Thomas. *Free Men All: The Personal Liberty Laws of the North, 1780–1861.* Baltimore: Johns Hopkins University Press, 1974.

Moseley, Thomas. "A History of the New-York Manumission Society, 1785–1849." Ph.D. diss., New York University, 1963.

Moses, Wilson J. *Alexander Crummell: A Study of Civilization and Discontent.* New York: Oxford University Press, 1989.

———. *The Golden Age of Black Nationalism, 1850–1925.* New York: Oxford University Press, 1978.

Moss, Richard Shannon. *Slavery on Long Island: A Study in Local Institutional and Early African-American Communal Life.* New York: Garland Publishing, 1993.

Nash, Gary. "Forging Freedom: The Emancipation Experience in the Northern Seaport Cities, 1775–1820." In *Slavery and Freeedom in the Age of the American Revolution,* edited by Ira Berlin and Ronald Hoffman, 3–48. Charlottesville: University Press of Virginia, 1983.

———. *Forging Freedom: The Formation of Philadelphia's Black Community, 1720–1840.* Cambridge, Mass.: Harvard University Press, 1988. Reprint, Cambridge, Mass.: Harvard University Press, 1991.

Newman, Simon. *Parades and the Politics of the Streets: Festive Culture in the Early American Republic.* Philadelphia: University of Pennsylvania Press, 1997.

O'Neale, Sondra, *Jupiter Hammon and the Biblical Beginnings of African-American Literature.* Metuchen, N.J.: American Theological Library Association and Scarecrow Press, 1993.

Ottley, Roi, and William Weatherby. *The Negro in New York: An Informal Social History.* New York: New York Public Library, 1967.

Painter, Nell Irvin. *Exodusters: Black Migration to Kansas after Reconstruction.* New York: Knopf, 1976.

———. "Of *Lily,* Linda Brent, and Freud: A Non-Exceptionalist Approach to Race, Class, and Gender in the Slave South." *Georgia Historical Quarterly* 86 (summer 1992): 241–259.

———. "Martin R. Delany: Elitism and Black Nationalism," in *Black Leaders of the Nineteenth Century,* edited by Leon Litwack and August Meier, 149–171. Urbana: University of Illinois Press, 1988. Reprint, Urbana: University of Illinois Press, Illini Books, 1991.

———. *Sojourner Truth: A Life, A Symbol.* New York: W. W. Norton, 1996.

Papke, David Ray. *Framing the Criminal: Crime, Cultural Work, and the Loss of Critical Perspective, 1830–1900.* Hamden, Conn.: Archon, 1987.

Pascoe, Peggy. "Miscegenation Law, Court Cases, and Ideologies of 'Race' in Twentieth-Century America." *Journal of American History* 83 (1996): 44–69.

———. *Relations of Rescue: The Search for Female Moral Authority in the American West, 1874–1939.* New York: Oxford University Press, 1990.

Pease, Jane, and William Pease. *They Who Would Be Free: Blacks' Search for Freedom, 1830–1861.* New York: Atheneum, 1974.

Pernicone, Carol Groneman. "The 'Bloody Ould Sixth': A Social Analysis of a New York City Working-Class Community in the Mid-nineteenth Century." Ph.D. diss., University of Rochester, 1973.

Phillips, George Lewis. *American Chimney Sweeps: An Historical Account of a Once Important Trade*. Trenton, N.J.: Past Times, 1957.

Pickett, Robert S. *House of Refuge: Origins of Juvenile Reform in New York State, 1815–1857*. New York: Syracuse University Press, 1969.

Piersen, William. *Black Yankees: The Development of Afro-American Subculture in Eighteenth-Century New England*. Amherst: University of Massachusetts Press, 1988.

Pleck, Elizabeth. *Domestic Tyranny: The Making of Social Policy against Family Violence from Colonial Times to the Present*. New York: Oxford University Press, 1987.

Porter, Dorothy. "David Ruggles, An Apostle of Human Rights." *Journal of Negro History* 18 (January 1943): 23–49.

———. "The Organized Educational Activities of Negro Literary Societies, 1828–1846." *Journal of Negro Education* 5 (1936): 555–576.

Potter, David. *The Impending Crisis, 1848–1861*. Compiled and edited by Don Fehrenbacher. New York: Harper Torchbooks, 1976.

Quarles, Benjamin. *Black Abolitionists*. New York: Oxford University Press, 1969. Reprint, New York: Da Capo, 1991.

———. *The Negro in the American Revolution*. Chapel Hill: University of North Carolina Press, 1961.

———. "The Revolutionary War as a Black Declaration of Independence." In *Slavery and Freedom in the Age of the American Revolution*, edited by Ira Berlin and Ronald Hoffman, 283–301. Charlottesville: University Press of Virginia, 1983.

Rael, Patrick. "Besieged by Freedom's Army: Antislavery Celebrations and Black Activism in the Antebellum North." In *Black Identity and Black Protest in the Antebellum North*. Chapel Hill: University of North Carolina Press, 2002.

Reidy, Joseph. "'Negro Election Day' and Black Community Life in New England, 1750–1860." *Marxist Perspectives* 1 (1978): 102–117.

Reynolds, David S. *Beneath the American Renaissance: The Subversive Imagination in the Age of Emerson and Melville*. New York: Knopf, 1988.

Rhodes, Jane. *Mary Ann Shadd Cary: The Black Press and Protest in the Nineteenth Century*. Bloomington: Indiana University Press, 1998.

Richards, Leonard. *"Gentlemen of Property and Standing": Anti-Abolition Mobs in Jacksonian America*. New York: Oxford University Press, 1970.

Richardson, David. "Slavery, Trade, and Economic Growth in Eighteenth-Century New England." In *Slavery and the Rise of the Atlantic System*, edited by Barbara Solow, 237–64. Cambridge, U.K.: Cambridge University Press, 1991.

Rink, Oliver. *Holland on the Hudson: An Economic and Social History of Dutch New York*. Ithaca, N.Y.: Cornell University Press, 1986.

Ripley, C. Peter, et al., eds. *The Black Abolitionist Papers*. Vols. 3 and 4. Chapel Hill: University of North Carolina Press, 1991.

Roediger, David. *The Wages of Whiteness: Race and the Making of the American Working Class*. London: Verso, 1991.

Rose, Willie Lee. *Rehearsal for Reconstruction: The Port Royal Experiment*. Indianapolis: Bobbs-Merrill, 1964.

Rury, John L. "The New York African Free School, 1827–1836: Conflict over Community Control of Black Education." *Phylon* 44 (September 1983): 187–197.

———. "Philanthropy, Self Help, and Social Control: The New York Manumission Society and Free Blacks, 1785–1810." *Phylon* 46 (September 1985): 231–241.

Ryan, Mary. *Cradle of the Middle Class: The Family in Oneida County, New York, 1790–1865*. Cambridge: Cambridge University Press, 1981.

———. *Women in Public: Between Banners and Ballots, 1825–1880*. Baltimore: Johns Hopkins University Press, 1990.

Saville, Julie. *The Work of Reconstruction: From Slave to Wage Laborer in South Carolina, 1860–1870*. New York: Cambridge University Press, 1994.

Saxton, Alexander. *The Rise and Fall of the White Republic: Class Politics and Mass Culture in Nineteenth-Century America*. London: Verso, 1990.

Scherzer, Kenneth. *The Unbounded Community: Neighborhood Life and Social Structure in New York City, 1830–1875*. Durham, N.C.: Duke University Press, 1992.

Schneider, David M. *The History of Public Welfare in New York State, 1609–1866*. 2 vols. Chicago: University of Chicago Press, 1938. Reprint, Montclair, N.J.: Patterson Smith, 1969.

Schultz, Ronald. "A Class Society? The Nature of Inequality in Early America." In *Inequality in Early America*, edited by Carla Gardina Pestana and Sharon V. Salinger, 203–21. Hanover, N.H.: University Press of New England, 1999.

Scott, James. *Weapons of the Weak: Everyday Forms of Peasant Resistance*. New Haven, Conn.: Yale University Press, 1985.

Scott, Joan Wallach. *Gender and the Politics of History*. New York: Columbia University Press, 1988.

Scott, Kenneth. "The Slave Insurrection in New York in 1712." *New-York Historical Society Quarterly* 45 (1961): 43–74.

Sellers, Charles. *The Market Revolution: Jacksonian America, 1815–1846*. New York: Oxford University Press, 1991.

Shallhope, Robert. "Republicanism and Early American Historiography." *William and Mary Quarterly*, 3d ser., 29 (1972): 49–80.

———. "Toward a Republican Synthesis: The Emergence of an Understanding of Republicanism in American Historiography." *William and Mary Quarterly*, 3d ser., 39 (1982): 334–356.

Shaw, Stephanie. *What a Woman Ought to Be and to Do: Black Professional Women Workers during the Jim Crow Era*. Chicago: University of Chicago Press, 1996.

Sheehan, Arthur, and Elizabeth Odell Sheehan. *Pierre Toussaint, A Citizen of Old New York*. New York: P. J. Kennedy and Sons, 1955.

Siegel, Adrienne. *The Image of the American City in Popular Literature, 1820–1870.* Port Washington, N.Y.: Kennikat, 1981.

Slotkin, Richard. "Narratives of Negro Crime in New England, 1675–1800." *American Quarterly* 35 (March 1973): 3–31.

Smith-Rosenberg, Carroll. *Disorderly Conduct: Visions of Gender in Victorian America.* New York: Knopf, 1985. Reprint, New York: Oxford University Press, 1986.

———. *Religion and the Rise of the American City: The New York City Mission Movement, 1812–1870.* Ithaca, N.Y.: Cornell University Press, 1971.

Soderlund, Jean. *Quakers and Slavery: A Divided Spirit.* Princeton, N.J.: Princeton University Press, 1985.

Spero, Sterling, and Abram L. Harris. *The Black Worker: The Negro and the Labor Movement.* 1931. Reprint, New York: Atheneum, 1968.

Stansell, Christine. *City of Women: Sex and Class in New York, 1789–1860.* New York: Knopf, 1986. Reprint, Urbana: University of Illinois Press, 1987.

Sterling, Dorothy, ed. *We Are Your Sisters: Black Women in the Nineteenth Century.* New York: W. W. Norton, 1984.

Still, Bayrd. *Mirror for Gotham: New York As Seen by Contemporaries from Dutch Days to the Present.* New York: University Press, 1956.

Stott, Richard. *Workers in the Metropolis: Class, Ethnicity, and Youth in Antebellum New York City.* Ithaca, N.Y.: Cornell University Press, 1990.

Strange, K. H. *The Climbing Boys: A Study of Sweeps' Apprentices, 1773–1875.* London: Allison and Busby, 1982.

Stuckey, Sterling. *Going through the Storm: The Influence of African American Art in History.* New York: Oxford University Press, 1994.

———. *Slave Culture: Nationalist Theory and the Foundations of Black America.* New York: Oxford University Press, 1987.

Sullivan, Dennis. *The Punishment of Crime in Colonial New York: The Dutch Experience in Albany during the Seventeenth Century.* New York: Peter Lang, 1997.

Swan, Robert. "John Teasman: African-American Educator and the Emergence of Community in Early Black New York City, 1787–1815." *Journal of the Early Republic* 12 (fall 1992): 331–356.

———. "The Other Fort Amsterdam: New Light on Aspects of Slavery in New Netherland." *Afro-Americans in New York Life and History* 22 (1998): 19–42.

Swift, David. *Black Prophets of Justice: Activist Clergy before the Civil War.* Baton Rouge: Louisiana State University Press, 1989.

Thomas, John L. *The Liberator: William Lloyd Garrison.* Boston: Little, Brown, 1963.

Thornton, John. *Africa and Africans in the Making of the Atlantic World, 1400–1680.* Cambridge: Cambridge University Press, 1992.

Thornton, Richard H. *An American Glossary: Being an Attempt to Illustrate Certain Americanisms upon Historical Principles.* 2 vols. New York: Frederick Ungar, 1962.

Trotter, Joe William. *Black Milwaukee: The Making of an Industrial Working Class.* Urbana: University of Illinois Press, 1985.

Van Der Zee, Henri, and Barbara Van Der Zee. *A Sweet and Alien Land: The Story of Dutch New York.* New York: Viking, 1978.

Wagman, Morton. "Corporate Slavery in New Netherland." *Journal of Negro History* 65 (winter 1980): 34–42.

Waldstreicher, David. *In the Midst of Perpetual Fetes: The Making of American Nationalism, 1776–1820.* Chapel Hill: University of North Carolina Press, 1997.

Walker, George. *The Afro-American in New York City, 1827–1860.* New York: Garland, 1993.

Walker, James W. St. G. *The Black Loyalists: The Search for a Promised Land in Nova Scotia and Sierra Leone, 1785–1870.* New York: Africana, 1976.

Walkowitz, Judith. *City of Dreadful Delight: Narratives of Sexual Danger in Late-Victorian London.* Chicago: University of Chicago Press, 1992.

Walls, William J. *The African Methodist Episcopal Zion Church: Reality of the Black Church.* Charlotte, N.C.: A.M.E. Zion Publishing House, 1974.

Walters, Ronald G. *The Antislavery Appeal: American Abolitionism after 1830.* Baltimore: Johns Hopkins Press, 1978. Reprint, New York: W. W. Norton, 1984.

———. "The Erotic South: Civilization and Sexuality in American Abolitionism." *American Quarterly* 35 (May 1973): 177–201.

Weinbaum, Paul O. *Mobs and Demagogues: The New York Response to Collective Violence in the Early Nineteenth Century.* N.p.: UMI Research Press, 1979.

Wesley, Charles H. *Negro Labor in the United States, 1850–1925.* New York: Vanguard, 1927.

White, Shane. "The Death of James Johnson." *American Quarterly* 51 (December 1999): 753–795.

———. "'It was a proud day': African-Americans, Festivals, and Parades." *Journal of American History* 81 (June 1994): 13–50.

———. "Pinkster: Afro-Dutch Syncretism in New York City and the Hudson Valley." *Journal of American Folklore* 102 (1989): 68–75.

———. *Somewhat More Independent: The End of Slavery in New York City, 1770–1810.* Athens: University of Georgia Press, 1991.

———. "'We Dwell in Safety and Pursue Our Honest Callings': Free Blacks in New York City, 1783–1810." *Journal of American History* 75 (1988): 445–470.

Wilder, Craig. *A Covenant with Color: Race and Social Power in Brooklyn.* New York: Columbia University Press, 2000.

———. "The Rise and Influence of the New York African Society for Mutual Relief, 1808–1865." *Afro-Americans in New York Life and History* 22 (1998): 7–17.

Wilentz, Sean. *Chants Democratic: New York City and the Rise of the American Working Class, 1789–1850.* New York: Oxford University Press, 1984. Reprint, New York: Oxford University Press, 1986.

Williams-Myers, A.J. "Pinkster Carnival: Africanisms in the Hudson River Valley." *Afro-Americans in New York Life and History* 9 (1985): 7–17.

Williamson, Chilton. *American Suffrage from Property to Democracy, 1760–1860.* Princeton, N.J.: Princeton University Press, 1960.

Williamson, Joel. *New People: Miscegenation and Mulattoes in the United States.* New York: Free Press, 1980.

Wilson, Carol. *Freedom at Risk: The Kidnapping of Free Blacks in America, 1780–1865.* Lexington: University Press of Kentucky, 1994.

Wilson, Joseph T. *The Black Phalanx: A History of the Negro Soldiers of the United States in the Wars of 1775–1812, 1861–65.* Hartford, Conn.: American Publishing Company, 1890.

Winch, Julie. *Philadelphia's Black Elite: Activism, Accommodation, and the Struggle for Autonomy, 1787–1848.* Philadelphia: Temple University Press, 1988.

Wood, Gordon. *The Creation of the American Republic, 1776–1787.* Chapel Hill: University of North Carolina Press, 1969.

Wood, Peter. *Black Majority: Negroes in Colonial South Carolina from 1670 through the Stono Rebellion.* New York: Knopf, 1974. Reprint, New York: W. W. Norton, 1975.

Wood, William S. *Friends of the City of New York in the Nineteenth Century.* New York: privately printed, 1904.

Woodson, Carter G. "The Negro Washerwoman, A Vanishing Figure." *Journal of Negro History* 15 (1930): 269–277.

Woodson, Carter G., and Lorenzo Greene. *The Negro Wage Earner.* Washington, D.C.: Association for the Study of Negro Life and History, 1930. Reprint, New York: Russell and Russell, 1969.

Wright, Donald. *African-Americans in the Early Republic, 1789–1831.* Arlington Heights, Ill.: Harlan Davidson, 1993.

Wyatt-Brown, Bertram. *Lewis Tappan and the Evangelical War against Slavery.* Cleveland, Ohio: Case Western Reserve University Press, 1969.

Zelizer, Viviana. *Pricing the Priceless Child: The Changing Social Value of Children.* New York: Basic, 1985.

Zeller, Nancy Anne McClure, ed. *A Beautiful and Fruitful Place: Selected Rensellaerswijck Seminar Papers.* [Albany, N.Y.]: New Netherland, 1991.

Zilversmit, Arthur. *The First Emancipation: The Abolition of Slavery in the North.* Chicago: University of Chicago Press, 1967. Reprint, Chicago: University of Chicago Press, Phoenix Books, 1970.